THIRTY READINGS IN INTRODUCTORY SOCIOLOGY

Kenneth A. Gould
Brooklyn College of the City University of New York

Tammy L. Lewis
Brooklyn College of the City University of New York

W9-APH-423

New York   Oxford

OXFORD UNIVERSITY PRESS

To Anna and Isabel

Oxford University Press is a department of the University of Oxford. It furthers the University's objective of excellence in research, scholarship, and education by publishing worldwide.

Oxford New York
Auckland   Cape Town   Dar es Salaam   Hong Kong   Karachi
Kuala Lumpur   Madrid   Melbourne   Mexico City   Nairobi
New Delhi   Shanghai   Taipei   Toronto

With offices in
Argentina   Austria   Brazil   Chile   Czech Republic   France   Greece
Guatemala   Hungary   Italy   Japan   Poland   Portugal   Singapore
South Korea   Switzerland   Thailand   Turkey   Ukraine   Vietnam

For titles covered by Section 112 of the US Higher Education Opportunity Act, please visit www.oup.com/us/he for the latest information about pricing and alternate formats.

Published by Oxford University Press.
198 Madison Avenue, New York, New York 10016
http://www.oup.com

Library of Congress Cataloging-in-Publication Data

Thirty readings in introductory sociology / [edited by] Kenneth A. Gould, Tammy L. Lewis.
  p. cm.
  Includes bibliographical references and index.
  ISBN 978-0-19-993492-8 (alk. paper)
  1. Sociology. I. Gould, Kenneth Alan.   II. Lewis, Tammy L.
HM585.T49 2012
301—dc23   2012027579

Contents

Introduction and Acknowledgments

Both of us are tenured full professors, and we both love teaching Introduction to Sociology. We teach the course because we see it as vitally important to our department's curriculum as an entry point for prospective sociology majors. We also teach the course because we see it as vitally important to our college, as Introduction to Sociology may be the only sociology course that non-sociology majors ever take. As academics working in a public university, we believe that teaching this class is one of the most important things we do to contribute to our society. One of our goals for the course is to engage students in critical thinking about the world in which we live. We believe that inspiring critical thinking, along with "turning on" students' sociological imaginations, is a central mission of our discipline. *Thirty Readings in Introductory Sociology* introduces undergraduates to the field of sociology in an engaging manner. Like the textbook that it is designed to accompany *Ten Lessons in Sociology*, it is organized around four key questions: (1) Why sociology? (2) What unites society? (3) What divides society? (4) How do societies change?

Thirty Readings in Introductory Sociology and *Ten Lessons in Sociology* are designed to raise sociological questions, apply a sociological lens, illustrate how data are used, and present core sociological topics in an accessible way. The sociological imagination, which is introduced in the first chapter, is a core concept that ties the book together. Each section in this collection contains three excerpts: The first is a "classic" or "foundational" piece, the second is a piece based on qualitative data, and the third is based on quantitative data. We selected readings that will draw students into the discipline and show them the applicability of sociology to their everyday lives while also introducing them to some of the foundational pieces in the field and introducing them to both qualitative and quantitative approaches to research.

We consulted numerous colleagues to find out what pieces they found most effective in teaching their students. We thank them for their input and, in particular, would like to acknowledge some of our colleagues at Brooklyn College–CUNY: Carolina Bank-Muñoz, Naomi Braine, Namita Manohar, and Greg Smithsimon.

In addition to three anonymous reviewers, we would also like to thank the following reviewers who provided very helpful feedback:

Kelly A. Dagan, Illinois College
Joshua Gamson, University of San Francisco

Gail Murphy-Geiss, Colorado College
Ida Rousseau Mukenge, Morehouse College
Keiko Tanaka, University of Kentucky
Jeffrey M. Timberlake, University of Cincinnati

Our editor, Sherith Pankratz, plies us with good food, which almost always works to convince us to press forward. We thank her for her encouragement and patience. We also thank Cari Heicklen for her persistence in securing permissions for all of the excerpts. Thanks to Michael Khan for his office assistance at Brooklyn College. Finally, we needed someone fresh who could read our introductions to each chapter to be sure that they were appropriately pitched to our target audience. We thank Anna Learis, our favorite teenager, for her careful copyediting and for pointing out our "ostentatious" language.

An Instructor's Resource CD is available with this book; please contact Oxford University Press for more information.

Kenneth A. Gould
Tammy L. Lewis

PART 1

WHY SOCIOLOGY?

The Sociological Imagination

INTRODUCTION

What makes sociology different from other social sciences, such as psychology, political science, and economics? What's unique about a sociological view? Why is sociology foundational to a liberal arts education? The readings in this section address these questions and introduce you to a sociological perspective; more specifically, what sociologists call the "sociological imagination."

C. Wright Mills introduced the term "sociological imagination" in his classic book of the same title in 1959. For Mills, the sociological imagination is a perspective that takes us above our day-to-day experiences to a vantage point that shows how the "big picture" of the social structure affects individual lives. Rather than view a person as an isolated identity with personal problems (as a psychologist or economist might), Mills instructs his readers to understand an individual as part of their social context, as shaped by their group memberships (for example, their race, class, gender, and nationality), and as shaped by their historical era. This view defies deeply held beliefs in the United States, most notably the belief that each person is unique, an individual, and with a personality like no other. Instead, Mills argues that who we are is a result of our personal biography *and* of our social circumstances (our group memberships and our historical era). Mills, a unique character in his own right, does not dismiss the importance of individuality, but instead understands it as a *piece* of our human existence. We are made by our society. We, in turn, shape what our society will be. We have agency (individual choice), but it is limited by social structure (the rules, written and unwritten in our society). If we live our lives without an understanding of the relationship between the individual and society and between the society and individual, it is likely that our actions will simply follow social rules and reproduce the same society into which we were born. However, if a person possesses the sociological imagination, he or she is free to make a choice about how they want to live their lives and what changes to the social structure they would like to affect. In this way, Mills sees the sociological imagination as tremendously empowering. Once we can see what we have power over, and what has power over us, we can decide what futures we hope to shape. According to Mills, this is sociology's "promise."

In the second excerpt, a classic piece from Peter Berger's *Invitation to Sociology*, Berger clears up a few of the incorrect assumptions people have

3

about sociology. If you become a sociology major, be prepared to respond to these common questions: "What can you do with that major? Does that train you to become a social worker?" Berger's answer to the second question is "No." That is not to say that a degree in sociology cannot be a springboard for the so-called "helping professions." (If you want to become a social worker, there are degrees in social work.) The goal of sociology, however, is analytical. The goal of this social *science* is to "attempt to understand" society. What one does with that understanding is then the application of sociological knowledge. Like Mills, Berger talks about a transforming consciousness that comes about by studying sociology—seeing what we call "nested relationships." This is a spin on the sociological imagination. The idea of "nested" relationships and "nested" analysis suggests that to understand the smallest unit in a society (the individual), you must understand the groups and organizations that shape the individual, as well as the larger social structures that shape those groups and organizations. "Seeing" these larger elements of the social structure and how they affect individuals can sometimes be surprising. Berger likens this experience to "culture shock" at home. He warns that sociologists do not take conventional wisdom for granted. They analyze it, scrutinize it, and seek to uncover what's below the surface. Thus, Berger would argue that a degree in sociology will be useful for any career in which you need analytic skills. If you're interested in pursuing this more, we recommend that you talk to your professor and visit the pages on the American Sociological Association's website that are devoted to employment and what you can do with your major (see www.asanet.org). A final side note should be added about Berger. Though he writes repeatedly of "men," we believe that his language was influenced by his historical era (the piece was published in 1963). If he were writing today, having been influenced by the multiple waves of the women's movement, we think he'd be writing about "people" and "humans."

Kristin Luker does not take the world for granted. In the piece excerpted from *Dubious Conceptions: The Politics of the Teenage Pregnancy Crisis*, Luker questions the media's and policy-makers' claims about a teenage pregnancy epidemic. This reading takes us out of the conceptual realm laid out by Mills and Berger and introduces us to a real-life example of applying the sociological imagination. Luker examines birthrates (quantitative evidence) that show that despite worrisome media articles about rising teen pregnancy rates, teen births were actually declining during the 1970s and 1980s. She uses social science data rather than anecdotes and information based on biased sampling to debunk conventionally held wisdom. Most sociologists believe there is some "truth" to be found in the real world that can be at least partially known through scientific data collection procedures. Once Luker uncovers the facts about teenage births, she tries to figure out what's actually going on. Why is it that teenage pregnancy has become a "moral panic"? Why are the media and policy-makers so concerned about teenage pregnancy if it's not really a growing problem? We won't give away the whole story here, but suffice it to say that Luker uses her sociological imagination to look at large-scale social change, notably the "decline of American

economic power and middle class influence," during the period she analyzed. She believes that the anxiety over teenage pregnancy was misplaced
and that, instead, Americans were really worried about how changing social
structures were reshaping their way of life.

There are a few messages you should take away from these pieces about
the study of sociology. First, sociology is a way of thinking and a perspective about the social world that examines how social structures and history
shape individuals, and how individuals in turn can shape the future. Second, sociology questions what we "already know" and encourages us to
dig deeper to learn what is going on below the surface. Third, sociology is
an empirical science that relies on data rather than impressions, feelings,
or anecdotal information to come to conclusions about the social world.
Finally, sociological knowledge can be used to shape the future. How we
use it is up to us. Seeing how society shapes us—and how we, in turn, shape
society—enables us to make conscious decisions about how we change (or
don't change) the world around us.

READING 1

Excerpt from *The Sociological Imagination*

C. WRIGHT MILLS

Nowadays men often feel that their private lives are a series of traps.
They sense that within their everyday worlds, they cannot overcome
their troubles; and in this feeling, they are often quite correct: What ordinary men are directly aware of and what they try to do are bounded by the
private orbits in which they live; their visions and their powers are limited
to the close-up scenes of job, family, neighborhood; in other milieux, they
move vicariously and remain spectators. And the more aware they become,
however vaguely, of ambitions and of threats which transcend their immediate locales, the more trapped they seem to feel.

Underlying this sense of being trapped are seemingly impersonal changes
in the very structure of continent-wide societies. The facts of contemporary
history are also facts about the success and the failure of individual men
and women. When a society is industrialized, a peasant becomes a worker;
a feudal lord is liquidated or becomes a businessman. When classes rise or
fall, a man is employed or unemployed; when the rate of investment goes

Mills, C. Wright. 1959. "The Promise" from *The Sociological Imagination*. New York:
Oxford University Press.

up or down, a man takes new heart or goes broke. When wars happen, an insurance salesman becomes a rocket launcher; a store clerk, a radar man; a wife lives alone; a child grows up without a father. Neither the life of an individual nor the history of a society can be understood without understanding both.

Yet men do not usually define the troubles they endure in terms of historical change and institutional contradiction. The well-being they enjoy, they do not usually impute to the big ups and downs of the societies in which they live. Seldom aware of the intricate connection between the patterns of their own lives and the course of world history, ordinary men do not usually know what this connection means for the kinds of men they are becoming and for the kinds of history-making in which they might take part. They do not possess the quality of mind essential to grasp the interplay of man and society, of biography and history, of self and world. They cannot cope with their personal troubles in such ways as to control the structural transformations that usually lie behind them.

Surely it is no wonder. In what period have so many men been so totally exposed at so fast a pace to such earthquakes of change? That Americans have not known such catastrophic changes as have the men and women of other societies is due to historical facts that are now quickly becoming "merely history." The history that now affects every man is world history. Within this scene and this period, in the course of a single generation, one sixth of mankind is transformed from all that is feudal and backward into all that is modern, advanced, and fearful. Political colonies are freed; new and less visible forms of imperialism installed. Revolutions occur; men feel the intimate grip of new kinds of authority. Totalitarian societies rise, and are smashed to bits—or succeed fabulously. After two centuries of ascendancy, capitalism is shown up as only one way to make society into an industrial apparatus. After two centuries of hope, even formal democracy is restricted to a quite small portion of mankind. Everywhere in the underdeveloped world, ancient ways of life are broken up and vague expectations become urgent demands. Everywhere in the overdeveloped world, the means of authority and of violence become total in scope and bureaucratic in form. Humanity itself now lies before us, the super-nation at either pole concentrating its most coordinated and massive efforts upon the preparation of World War Three.

The very shaping of history now outpaces the ability of men to orient themselves in accordance with cherished values. And which values? Even when they do not panic, men often sense that older ways of feeling and thinking have collapsed and that newer beginnings are ambiguous to the point of moral stasis. Is it any wonder that ordinary men feel they cannot cope with the larger worlds with which they are so suddenly confronted? That they cannot understand the meaning of their epoch for their own lives? That—in defense of selfhood—they become morally insensible, trying to remain altogether private men? Is it any wonder that they come to be possessed by a sense of the trap?

It is not only information that they need—in this Age of Fact, information often dominates their attention and overwhelms their capacities to assimilate it. It is not only the skills of reason that they need—although their struggles to acquire these often exhaust their limited moral energy.

What they need, and what they feel they need, is a quality of mind that will help them to use information and to develop reason in order to achieve lucid summations of what is going on in the world and of what may be happening within themselves. It is this quality, I am going to contend, that journalists and scholars, artists and publics, scientists and editors are coming to expect of what may be called the sociological imagination.

1

The sociological imagination enables its possessor to understand the larger historical scene in terms of its meaning for the inner life and the external career of a variety of individuals. It enables him to take into account how individuals, in the welter of their daily experience, often become falsely conscious of their social positions. Within that welter, the framework of modern society is sought, and within that framework the psychologies of a variety of men and women are formulated. By such means the personal uneasiness of individuals is focused upon explicit troubles and the indifference of publics is transformed into involvement with public issues.

The first fruit of this imagination—and the first lesson of the social science that embodies it—is the idea that the individual can understand his own experience and gauge his own fate only by locating himself within his period, that he can know his own chances in life only by becoming aware of those of all individuals in his circumstances. In many ways it is a terrible lesson; in many ways a magnificent one. We do not know the limits of man's capacities for supreme effort or willing degradation, for agony or glee, for pleasurable brutality or the sweetness of reason. But in our time we have come to know that the limits of 'human nature' are frighteningly broad. We have come to know that every individual lives, from one generation to the next, in some society; that he lives out a biography, and that he lives it out within some historical sequence. By the fact of his living he contributes, however minutely, to the shaping of this society and to the course of its history, even as he is made by society and by its historical push and shove.

The sociological imagination enables us to grasp history and biography and the relations between the two within society. That is its task and its promise. To recognize this task and this promise is the mark of the classic social analyst. It is characteristic of Herbert Spencer—turgid, polysyllabic, comprehensive; of E. A. Ross—graceful, muckraking, upright; of Auguste Comte and Emile Durkheim; of the intricate and subtle Karl Mannheim. It is the quality of all that is intellectually excellent in Karl Marx; it is the clue to Thorstein Veblen's brilliant and ironic insight, to Joseph Schumpeter's many-sided constructions of reality; it is the basis of the psychological sweep of

W. E. H. Lecky no less than of the profundity and clarity of Max Weber. And it is the signal of what is best in contemporary studies of man and society.

No social study that does not come back to the problems of biography, of history and of their intersections within a society has completed its intellectual journey. Whatever the specific problems of the classic social analysts, however limited or however broad the features of social reality they have examined, those who have been imaginatively aware of the promise of their work have consistently asked three sorts of questions:

(1) What is the structure of this particular society as a whole? What are its essential components, and how are they related to one another? How does it differ from other varieties of social order? Within it, what is the meaning of any particular feature for its continuance and for its change?

(2) Where does this society stand in human history? What are the mechanics by which it is changing? What is its place within and its meaning for the development of humanity as a whole? How does any particular feature we are examining affect, and how is it affected by, the historical period in which it moves? And this period—what are its essential features? How does it differ from other periods? What are its characteristic ways of history-making?

(3) What varieties of men and women now prevail in this society and in this period? And what varieties are coming to prevail? In what ways are they selected and formed, liberated and repressed, made sensitive and blunted? What kinds of "human nature" are revealed in the conduct and character we observe in this society in this period? And what is the meaning for "human nature" of each and every feature of the society we are examining?

Whether the point of interest is a great power state or a minor literary mood, a family, a prison, a creed—these are the kinds of questions the best social analysts have asked. They are the intellectual pivots of classic studies of man in society—and they are the questions inevitably raised by any mind possessing the sociological imagination. For that imagination is the capacity to shift from one perspective to another—from the political to the psychological; from examination of a single family to comparative assessment of the national budgets of the world; from the theological school to the military establishment; from considerations of an oil industry to studies of contemporary poetry. It is the capacity to range from the most impersonal and remote transformations to the most intimate features of the human self—and to see the relations between the two. Back of its use there is always the urge to know the social and historical meaning of the individual in the society and in the period in which he has his quality and his being.

That, in brief, is why it is by means of the sociological imagination that men now hope to grasp what is going on in the world, and to understand what is happening in themselves as minute points of the intersections of biography and history within society. In large part, contemporary man's self-conscious view of himself as at least an outsider, if not a permanent stranger, rests upon an absorbed realization of social relativity and of the transformative power of history. The sociological imagination is the most fruitful form of this self-consciousness. By its use, men whose mentalities have swept only a series of limited orbits often come to feel as if suddenly awakened in a house with which they had only supposed themselves to be familiar. Correctly or incorrectly, they often come to feel that they can now provide themselves with adequate summations, cohesive assessments, comprehensive orientations. Older decisions that once appeared sound now seem to them products of a mind unaccountably dense. Their capacity for astonishment is made lively again. They acquire a new way of thinking, they experience a transvaluation of values: In a word, by their reflection and by their sensibility, they realize the cultural meaning of the social sciences.

2

Perhaps the most fruitful distinction with which the sociological imagination works is between "the personal troubles of milieu" and "the public issues of social structure." This distinction is an essential tool of the sociological imagination and a feature of all classic work in social science.

Troubles occur within the character of the individual and within the range of his immediate relations with others; they have to do with his self and with those limited areas of social life of which he is directly and personally aware. Accordingly, the statement and the resolution of troubles properly lie within the individual as a biographical entity and within the scope of his immediate milieu—the social setting that is directly open to his personal experience and to some extent his willful activity. A trouble is a private matter: Values cherished by an individual are felt by him to be threatened.

Issues have to do with matters that transcend these local environments of the individual and the range of his inner life. They have to do with the organization of many such milieux into the institutions of an historical society as a whole, with the ways in which various milieux overlap and interpenetrate to form the larger structure of social and historical life. An issue is a public matter: Some value cherished by publics is felt to be threatened. Often there is a debate about what that value really is and about what it is that really threatens it. This debate is often without focus if only because it is the very nature of an issue, unlike even widespread trouble, that it cannot very well be defined in terms of the immediate and everyday environments of ordinary men. An issue, in fact, often involves a crisis in institutional arrangements, and often too it involves what Marxists call "contradictions" or "antagonisms."

In these terms, consider unemployment. When, in a city of 100,000, only one man is unemployed, that is his personal trouble, and for its relief we properly look to the character of the man, his skills, and his immediate opportunities. But when in a nation of 50 million employees, 15 million men are unemployed, that is an issue, and we may not hope to find its solution within the range of opportunities open to any one individual. The very structure of opportunities has collapsed. Both the correct statement of the problem and the range of possible solutions require us to consider the economic and political institutions of the society, and not merely the personal situation and character of a scatter of individuals.

Consider war. The personal problem of war, when it occurs, may be how to survive it or how to die in it with honor; how to make money out of it; how to climb into the higher safety of the military apparatus; or how to contribute to the war's termination. In short, according to one's values, to find a set of milieux and within it to survive the war or make one's death in it meaningful. But the structural issues of war have to do with its causes; with what types of men it throws up into command; with its effects upon economic and political, family and religious institutions, with the unorganized irresponsibility of a world of nation-states.

Consider marriage. Inside a marriage a man and a woman may experience personal troubles, but when the divorce rate during the first four years of marriage is 250 out of every 1,000 attempts, this is an indication of a structural issue having to do with the institutions of marriage and the family and other institutions that bear upon them.

Or consider the metropolis—the horrible, beautiful, ugly, magnificent sprawl of the great city. For many upper-class people, the personal solution to "the problem of the city" is to have an apartment with private garage under it in the heart of the city, and forty miles out, a house by Henry Hill, garden by Garrett Eckbo, on a hundred acres of private land. In these two controlled environments—with a small staff at each end and a private helicopter connection—most people could solve many of the problems of personal milieux caused by the facts of the city. But all this, however splendid, does not solve the public issues that the structural fact of the city poses. What should be done with this wonderful monstrosity? Break it all up into scattered units, combining residence and work? Refurbish it as it stands? Or, after evacuation, dynamite it and build new cities according to new plans in new places? What should those plans be? And who is to decide and to accomplish whatever choice is made? These are structural issues; to confront them and to solve them requires us to consider political and economic issues that affect innumerable milieux.

Insofar as an economy is so arranged that slumps occur, the problem of unemployment becomes incapable of personal solution. Insofar as war is inherent in the nation-state system and in the uneven industrialization of the world, the ordinary individual in his restricted milieu will be powerless—with or without psychiatric aid—to solve the troubles this system or lack of system imposes upon him. Insofar as the family as an institution turns women into darling little slaves and men into their chief providers and unweaned dependents, the problem of a satisfactory marriage remains incapable of purely private solution. Insofar as the overdeveloped megalopolis and the overdeveloped automobile are built-in features of the overdeveloped society, the issues of urban living will not be solved by personal ingenuity and private wealth.

What we experience in various and specific milieux, I have noted, is often caused by structural changes. Accordingly, to understand the changes of many personal milieux we are required to look beyond them. And the number and variety of such structural changes increase as the institutions within which we live become more embracing and more intricately connected with one another. To be aware of the idea of social structure and to use it with sensibility is to be capable of tracing such linkages among a great variety of milieux. To be able to do that is to possess the sociological imagination.

3

What are the major issues for publics and the key troubles of private individuals in our time? To formulate issues and troubles, we must ask what values are cherished yet threatened, and what values are cherished and supported, by the characterizing trends of our period. In the case both of threat and of support we must ask what salient contradictions of structure may be involved.

When people cherish some set of values and do not feel any threat to them, they experience *well-being*. When they cherish values but *do* feel them to be threatened, they experience a crisis—either as a personal trouble or as a public issue. And if all their values seem involved, they feel the total threat of panic.

But suppose people are neither aware of any cherished values nor experience any threat? That is the experience of *indifference*, which, if it seems to involve all their values, becomes *apathy*. Suppose, finally, they are unaware of any cherished values, but still are very much aware of a threat? That is the experience of *uneasiness*, of anxiety, which, if it is total enough, becomes a deadly unspecified malaise.

Ours is a time of uneasiness and indifference—not yet formulated in such ways as to permit the work of reason and the play of sensibility. Instead of troubles—defined in terms of values and threats—there is often the misery of vague uneasiness; instead of explicit issues there is often merely the beat feeling that all is somehow not right. Neither the values threatened nor whatever threatens them has been stated; in short, they have not been carried to the point of decision. Much less have they been formulated as problems of social science.

In the thirties there was little doubt—except among certain deluded business circles that there was an economic issue which was also a pack of personal troubles. In these arguments about "the crisis of capitalism," the formulations of Marx and the many unacknowledged re-formulations of his work probably set the leading terms of the issue, and some men came to understand their personal troubles in these terms. The values threatened were plain to see and cherished by all; the structural contradictions that threatened them also seemed plain. Both were widely and deeply experienced. It was a political age.

But the values threatened in the era after World War Two are often neither widely acknowledged as values nor widely felt to be threatened. Much private uneasiness goes unformulated; much public malaise and many decisions of enormous structural relevance never become public issues. For those who accept such inherited values as reason and freedom, it is the uneasiness itself that is the trouble; it is the indifference itself that is the issue. And it is this condition, of uneasiness and indifference, that is the signal feature of our period.

All this is so striking that it is often interpreted by observers as a shift in the very kinds of problems that need now to be formulated. We are frequently told that the problems of our decade, or even the crises of our period, have shifted from the external realm of economics and now have to do with the quality of individual life—in fact with the question of whether there is soon going to be anything that can properly be called individual life. Not child labor but comic books, not poverty but mass leisure, are at the center of concern. Many great public issues as well as many private troubles are described in terms of "the psychiatric"—often, it seems, in a pathetic attempt to avoid the large issues and problems of modern society. Often this statement seems to rest upon a provincial narrowing of interest to the Western societies, or even to the United States—thus ignoring two-thirds of mankind; often, too, it arbitrarily divorces the individual life from the larger institutions within which that life is enacted, and which on occasion bear upon it more grievously than do the intimate environments of childhood.

Problems of leisure, for example, cannot even be stated without considering problems of work. Family troubles over comic books cannot be formulated as problems without considering the plight of the contemporary family in its new relations with the newer institutions of the social structure. Neither leisure nor its debilitating uses can be understood as problems without recognition of the extent to which malaise and indifference now form the social and personal climate of contemporary American society. In this climate, no problems of "the private life" can be stated and solved without recognition of the crisis of ambition that is part of the very career of men at work in the incorporated economy.

It is true, as psychoanalysts continually point out, that people do often have "the increasing sense of being moved by obscure forces within themselves which they are unable to define." But it is *not* true, as Ernest Jones asserted, that "man's chief enemy and danger is his own unruly nature and the dark forces pent up within him." On the contrary: "Man's chief danger" today lies in the unruly forces of contemporary society itself, with its alienating methods of production, its enveloping techniques of political domination, its international anarchy—in a word, its pervasive transformations of the very "nature" of man and the conditions and aims of his life.

It is now the social scientist's foremost political and intellectual task—for here the two coincide—to make clear the elements of contemporary uneasiness and indifference. It is the central demand made upon him by other cultural workmen—by physical scientists and artists, by the intellectual community in general. It is because of this task and these demands, I believe, that the social sciences are becoming the common denominator of our cultural period, and the sociological imagination our most needed quality of mind.

Excerpt from *Invitation to Sociology*

PETER BERGER

There are very few jokes about sociologists. This is frustrating for the sociologists, especially if they compare themselves with their more favored second cousins, the psychologists, who have pretty much taken over that sector of American humor that used to be occupied by clergymen. A psychologist, introduced as such at a party, at once finds himself the object of considerable attention and uncomfortable mirth. A sociologist in the same circumstance is likely to meet with no more of a reaction than if he had been announced as an insurance salesman. He will have to win his attention the hard way, just like everyone else. This is annoying and unfair, but it may also be instructive. The dearth of jokes about sociologists indicates, of course, that they are not as much part of the popular imagination as psychologists have become. But it probably also indicates that there is a certain ambiguity in the images that people do have of them. It may thus be a good starting point for our considerations to take a closer look at some of these images.

If one asks undergraduate students why they are taking sociology as a major, one often gets the reply, "because I like to work with people." If one then goes on to ask such students about their occupational future, as they envisage it, one often hears that they intend to go into social work. Of this more in a moment. Other answers are more vague and general, but all indicate that the student in question would rather deal with people than with things. Occupations mentioned in this connection include personnel work, human relations in industry, public relations, advertising, community planning or religious work of the unordained variety. The common assumption is that in all these lines of endeavor one might "do something for people," "help people," "do work that is useful for the community." The image of the sociologist involved here could be described as a secularized version of the liberal Protestant ministry, with the YMCA secretary perhaps furnishing the connecting link between sacred and profane benevolence. Sociology is seen as an up-to-date variation on the classic American theme of "uplift." The sociologist is understood as one professionally concerned with edifying activities on behalf of individuals and of the community at large.

One of these days a great American novel will have to be written on the savage disappointment this sort of motivation is bound to suffer in most of the occupations just mentioned. There is moving pathos in the fate of these likers of people who go into personnel work and come up for the first time against the human realities of a strike that they must fight on one side of the savagely drawn battle lines, or who go into public relations and discover just what it is that they are expected to put over in what experts in the field have called "the engineering of consent," or who go into community agencies to begin a brutal education in the politics of real estate speculation. But our concern here is not with the despoiling of innocence. It is rather with a particular image of the sociologist, an image that is inaccurate and misleading.

It is, of course, true that some Boy Scout types have become sociologists. It is also true that a benevolent interest in people could be the biographical starting point for sociological studies. But it is important to point out that a malevolent and misanthropic outlook could serve just as well. Sociological insights are valuable to anyone concerned with action in society. But this action need not be particularly humanitarian. Some American sociologists today are employed by governmental agencies seeking to plan more livable communities for the nation. Other American sociologists are employed by governmental agencies concerned with wiping communities of hostile nations off the map, if and when the necessity should arise. Whatever the moral implications of these respective activities may be, there is no reason why interesting sociological studies could not be carried on in both. Similarly, criminology, as a special field within sociology, has uncovered valuable information about processes of crime in modern society. This information is equally valuable for those seeking to fight crime as it would be for those interested in promoting it. The fact that more criminologists have been employed by the police than by gangsters can be ascribed to the ethical bias of the criminologists themselves, the public relations of the police, and perhaps the lack of scientific sophistication of the gangsters. It has nothing to do with the character of the information itself. In sum, "working with people" can mean getting them out of slums or getting them into jail, selling them propaganda or robbing them of their money (be it legally or illegally), making them produce better automobiles, or making them better bomber pilots. As an image of the sociologist, then, the phrase leaves something to be desired, even though it may serve to describe at least the initial impulse as a result of which some people turn to the study of sociology.

Some additional comments are called for in connection with a closely related image of the sociologist as a sort of theoretician for social work. This image is understandable in view of the development of sociology in America. At least one of the roots of American sociology is to be found in the worries of social workers confronted with the massive problems following in the wake of the industrial revolution—the rapid growth of cities and of slums within them, mass immigration, mass movements of people, the disruption of traditional ways of life, and the resulting disorientation of individuals caught in these processes. Much sociological research has been spurred by this sort of concern. And so it is still quite customary for undergraduate students planning to go into social work to major in sociology.

Actually, American social work has been far more influenced by psychology than by sociology in the development of its "theory." Very probably this fact is not unrelated to what was previously said about the relative status of sociology and psychology in the popular imagination. Social workers have had to fight an uphill battle for a long time to be recognized as "professionals" and to get the prestige, power, and (not least) pay that such recognition entails. Looking around for a "professional" model to emulate, they found that of the psychiatrist to be the most natural. And so contemporary social workers receive their "clients" in an office, conduct fifty-minute "clinical interviews" with them, record the interviews in quadruplicate, and discuss them with a hierarchy of "supervisors." Having adopted the outward paraphernalia of the psychiatrist, they naturally also adopted his ideology. Thus contemporary American social-work "theory" consists very largely of a somewhat bowdlerized version of psychoanalytic psychology, a sort of poor man's Freudianism that serves to legitimate the social worker's claim to help people in a "scientific" way. We are not interested here in investigating the "scientific" validity of this synthetic doctrine. Our point is that not only does it have very little to do with sociology, but it is marked, indeed, by a singular obtuseness with regard to social reality. The identification of sociology with social work in the minds of many people is somewhat a phenomenon of "cultural lag," dating from the period when as yet pre-"professional" social workers dealt with poverty rather than with libidinal frustration, and did so without the benefit of a dictaphone.

But even if American social work had not jumped on the bandwagon of popular psychologism, the image of the sociologist as the social worker's theoretical mentor would be misleading. Social work, whatever its theoretical rationalization, is a certain *practice* in society. Sociology is not a practice, but an *attempt to understand*. Certainly this understanding may have use for the practitioner. For that matter, we would contend that a more profound grasp of sociology would be of great use to the social worker and that such grasp would obviate the necessity of his descending into the mythological depths of the "subconscious" to explain matters that are typically quite conscious, much more simple, and, indeed, *social* in nature. But there is nothing inherent in the sociological enterprise of trying to understand society that necessarily leads to this practice or to any other. Sociological understanding can be recommended to social workers, but also to salesmen, nurses, evangelists and politicians—in fact, to anyone whose goals involve the manipulation of men, for whatever purpose and with whatever moral justification.

This conception of the sociological enterprise is implied in the classic statement by Max Weber, one of the most important figures in the development of the field, to the effect that sociology is "value-free." Since it will be necessary to return to this a number of times later, it may be well to explicate it a little further at this point. Certainly the statement does *not* mean that the sociologist has or should have no values. In any case, it is just about impossible for a human being to exist without any values at all, though, of course, there can be tremendous variation in the values one may hold. The sociologist will normally have many values as a citizen, a private person, a member of a religious group or as an adherent of some other association of people. But within the limits of his activities as a sociologist there is one fundamental value only—that of scientific integrity. Even there, of course, the sociologist, being human, will have to reckon with his convictions, emotions and prejudices. But it is part of his intellectual training that he tries to understand and control these as *bias* that ought to be eliminated, as far as possible, from his work. It goes without saying that this is not always easy to do, but it is not impossible. The sociologist tries to see what is there. He may have hopes or fears concerning what he may find. But he will try to see regardless of his hopes or fears. It is thus an act of pure perception, as pure as humanly limited means allow, toward which sociology strives.

An analogy may serve to clarify this a little more. In any political or military conflict it is of advantage to capture the information used by the intelligence organs of the opposing side. But this is so only because good intelligence consists of information free of bias. If a spy does his reporting in terms of the ideology and ambitions of his superiors, his reports are useless not only to the enemy, if the latter should capture them, but also to the spy's own side. It has been claimed that one of the weaknesses of the espionage apparatus of totalitarian states is that spies report not what they find but what their superiors want to hear. This, quite evidently, is bad espionage. The good spy reports what is there. Others decide what should be done as a result of his information. The sociologist is a spy in very much the same way. His job is to report as accurately as he can about a certain social terrain. Others, or he himself in a role other than that of sociologist, will have to decide what moves ought to be made in that terrain. We would stress strongly that saying this does *not* imply that the sociologist has no responsibility to ask about the goals of his employers or the use to which they will put his work. But this asking is not sociological asking. It is asking the same questions that any man ought to ask himself about his actions in society. Again, in the same way, biological knowledge can be employed to heal or to kill. This does not mean that the biologist is free of responsibility as to which use he serves. But when he asks himself about this responsibility, he is not asking a biological question.

Another image of the sociologist, related to the two already discussed, is that of social reformer. Again, this image has historical roots, not only in America but also in Europe. Auguste Comte, the early nineteenth-century French philosopher who invented the name of the discipline, thought of sociology as the doctrine of progress, a secularized successor to theology as the mistress of the sciences. The sociologist in this view plays the role of arbiter of all branches of knowledge for the welfare of men. This notion, even when stripped of its more fantastic pretensions, died especially hard in the development of French sociology. But something of this conception survives when sociologists are expected to come up with blueprints for reform on any number of social issues.

It is gratifying from certain value positions (including some of this writer's) that sociological insights have served in a number of instances to improve the lot of groups of human beings by uncovering morally shocking conditions or by clearing away collective illusions or by showing that socially desired results could be obtained in more humane fashion. One might point, for example, to some applications of sociological knowledge in the penological practice of Western countries. Or one might cite the use made of sociological studies in the Supreme Court decision of 1954 on racial segregation in the public schools. Or one could look at the applications of other sociological studies to the humane planning of urban redevelopment. Certainly the sociologist who is morally and politically sensitive will derive gratification from such instances. But, once more, it will be well to keep in mind that what is at issue here is not sociological understanding as such but certain applications of this understanding. It is not difficult to see how the same understanding could be applied with opposite intentions. Thus the sociological understanding of the dynamics of racial prejudice can be applied effectively by those promoting intragroup hatred as well as by those wanting to spread tolerance. And the sociological understanding of the nature of human solidarity can be employed in the service of both totalitarian and democratic regimes. It is sobering to realize that the same processes that generate consensus can be manipulated by a social group worker in a summer camp in the Adirondacks and by a Communist brainwasher in a prisoner camp in China. One may readily grant that the sociologist can sometimes be called upon to give advice when it comes to changing certain social conditions deemed undesirable. But the image of the sociologist as social reformer suffers from the same confusion as the image of him as social worker.

The sociologist, then, is someone concerned with understanding society in a disciplined way. The nature of this discipline is scientific. This means that what the sociologist finds and says about the social phenomena he studies occurs within a certain rather strictly defined frame of reference. One of the main characteristics of this scientific frame of reference is that operations are bound by certain rules of evidence. As a scientist, the sociologist tries to be objective, to control his personal preferences and prejudices, to perceive clearly rather than to judge normatively. This restraint, of course, does not embrace the totality of the sociologist's existence as a human being, but is limited to his operations *qua* sociologist. Nor does the sociologist claim that his frame of reference is the only one within which society can be looked at. For that matter, very few scientists in any field would claim today that one should look at the world only scientifically. The botanist looking at a daffodil has no reason to dispute the right of the poet to look at the same object in a very different manner. There are many ways of playing. The point is not that one denies other people's games but that one is clear about the rules of one's own. The game of the sociologist, then, uses scientific rules. As a result, the sociologist must be clear in his own mind as to the meaning of these rules. That is, he must concern himself with methodological questions. Methodology does not constitute his goal. The latter, let us recall once more, is the attempt to understand society. Methodology helps in reaching this goal. In order to understand society, or that segment of it that he is studying at the moment, the sociologist will use a variety of means. Among these are statistical techniques. Statistics can be very useful in answering certain sociological questions. But statistics does not constitute sociology. As a scientist, the sociologist will have to be concerned with the exact significance of the terms he is using. That is, he will have to be careful about terminology. This does not have to mean that he must invent a new language of his own, but it does mean that he cannot naively use the language of everyday discourse. Finally, the interest of the sociologist is primarily theoretical. That is, he is interested in understanding for its own sake. He may be aware of or even concerned with the practical applicability and consequences of his findings, but at that point he leaves the sociological frame of reference as such and moves into realms of values, beliefs and ideas that he shares with other men who are not sociologists.

We would say then that the sociologist is a person intensively, endlessly, shamelessly interested in the doings of men. His natural habitat is all the human gathering places of the world, wherever men come together. The sociologist may be interested in many other things. But his consuming interest remains in the world of men, their institutions, their history, their passions. And since he is interested in men, nothing that men do can be altogether tedious for him. He will naturally be interested in the events that engage men's ultimate beliefs, their moments of tragedy and grandeur and ecstasy. But he will also be fascinated by the commonplace, the everyday. He will know reverence, but this reverence will not prevent him from wanting to see and to understand. He may sometimes feel revulsion or contempt. But this also will not deter him from wanting to have his questions answered. The sociologist, in his quest for understanding, moves through the world of men without respect for the usual lines of demarcation. Nobility and degradation, power and obscurity, intelligence and folly—these are equally *interesting* to him, however unequal they may be in his personal values or tastes. Thus his questions may lead him to all possible levels of society, the best and the least known places, the most respected and the most despised. And, if he is a good sociologist, he will find himself in all these places because his own questions have so taken possession of him that he has little choice but to seek for answers.

The sociologist will occupy himself with matters that others regard as too sacred or as too distasteful for dispassionate investigation. He will find rewarding the company of priests or of prostitutes, depending not on his personal preferences but on the questions he happens to be asking at the moment. He will also concern himself with matters that others may find much too boring. He will be interested in the human interaction that goes with warfare or with great intellectual discoveries, but also in the relations between people employed in a restaurant or between a group of little girls playing with their dolls. His main focus of attention is not the ultimate significance of what men do, but the action in itself, as another example of the infinite richness of human conduct.

The fascination of sociology lies in the fact that its perspective makes us see in a new light the very world in which we have lived all our lives. This also constitutes a transformation of consciousness. Moreover, this transformation is more relevant existentially than that of many other intellectual disciplines, because it is more difficult to segregate in some special compartment of the mind.

It can be said that the first wisdom of sociology is this—things are not what they seem. This too is a deceptively simple statement. It ceases to be simple after a while. Social reality turns out to have many layers of meaning. The discovery of each new layer changes the perception of the whole.

Anthropologists use the term "culture shock" to describe the impact of a totally new culture upon a newcomer. In an extreme instance such shock will be experienced by the Western explorer who is told, halfway through dinner, that he is eating the nice old lady he had been chatting with the previous day—a shock with predictable physiological if not moral consequences. Most explorers no longer encounter cannibalism in their travels today. However, the first encounters with polygamy or with puberty rites or even with the way some nations drive their automobiles can be quite a shock to an American visitor. With the shock may go not only disapproval or disgust but a sense of excitement that things can *really* be that different from what they are at home. To some extent, at least, this is the excitement of any first travel abroad. The experience of sociological discovery could be described as "culture shock" minus geographical displacement. In other words, the sociologist travels at home—with shocking results. He is unlikely to find that he is eating a nice old lady for dinner. But the discovery, for instance, that his own church has considerable money invested in the missile industry or that a few blocks from his home there are people who engage in cultic orgies may not be drastically different in emotional impact. Yet we would not want to imply that sociological discoveries are always or even usually outrageous to moral sentiment. Not at all. What they have in common with exploration in distant lands, however, is the sudden illumination of new and unsuspected facets of human existence in society. This is the excitement and, as we shall try to show later, the humanistic justification of sociology.

People who like to avoid shocking discoveries, who prefer to believe that society is just what they were taught in Sunday School, who like the safety of the rules and the maxims of what Alfred Schuetz has called the "world-taken-for-granted" should stay away from sociology. People who feel no temptation before closed doors, who have no curiosity about human beings, who are content to admire scenery without wondering about the people who live in those houses on the other side of that river should probably also stay away from sociology. They will find it unpleasant or, at any rate, unrewarding. People who are interested in human beings only if they can change, convert, or reform them should also be warned, for they will find sociology much less useful than they hoped. And people whose interest is mainly in their own conceptual constructions will do just as well to turn to the study of little white mice. Sociology will be satisfying, in the long run, only to those who can think of nothing more entrancing than to watch men and to understand things human.

It may now be clear that we have, albeit deliberately, understated the case in the title of this chapter. To be sure, sociology is an individual pastime in the sense that it interests some men and bores others. Some like to observe human beings, others to experiment with mice. The world is big enough to hold all kinds and there is no logical priority for one interest as against another. But the word "pastime" is weak in describing what we mean. Sociology is more like a passion. The sociological perspective is more like a demon that possesses one, that drives one compellingly, again and again, to the questions that are its own. An introduction to sociology is, therefore, an invitation to a very special kind of passion. No passion is without its dangers. The sociologist who sells his wares should make sure that he clearly pronounces a *caveat emptor* quite early in the transaction.

Excerpt from *Dubious Conceptions: The Politics of the Teenage Pregnancy Crisis*

KRISTIN LUKER

By the early 1980s, Americans had come to believe that teenagers were becoming pregnant in epidemic numbers, and the issue occupied a prominent place on the national agenda. "Teenage pregnancy," along with

Luker, Kristin. 1996. "Constructing an Epidemic" from *Dubious Conceptions: The Politics of the Teenage Pregnancy Crisis*. Cambridge, MA: Harvard University Press.

crack-addicted mothers, drive-by shootings, and the failing educational system, was beginning to be used as a form of shorthand for the country's social ills.[1] Everyone now agreed that it was a serious problem, and solutions were proposed across the ideological spectrum. Conservatives (members of the New Right, in particular) wanted to give parents more control over their daughters, including the right to determine whether they should have access to sex education and contraception.[2] Liberals, doubting that a "just say no" strategy would do much to curtail sexual activity among teenagers, continued to urge that young men and women be granted the same legal access to abortion and contraception that their elders had. Scholars debated the exact costs of early pregnancy to the individuals involved and to society, foundations targeted it for funding and investigation, government at all levels instituted programs to reduce it, and the media gave it a great deal of scrutiny.[3] In the early 1970s the phrase "teenage pregnancy" was just not part of the public lexicon. By 1978, however, a dozen articles per year were being published on the topic; by the mid-1980s the number had increased to two dozen; and by 1990 there were more than two hundred, including cover stories in both *Time* and *Newsweek*.[4]

Ironically (in view of all this media attention), births to teenagers actually *declined* in the 1970s and 1980s. During the baby boom years (1946–1964), teenagers, like older women, increased their childbearing dramatically: Their birthrates almost doubled, reaching a peak in 1957. Subsequently, the rates drifted back to their earlier levels, where they have pretty much stayed since 1975.[5] The real "epidemic" occurred when Dwight Eisenhower was in the White House and poodle skirts were the height of fashion.[6] But although birthrates among teenagers were declining, other aspects of their behavior were changing in ways that many people saw as disturbing. From the vantage point of the 1970s, the relevant statistics could have been used to tell any one of a number of stories. For example, when abortion was legalized in 1973, experts began to refer to a new demographic measure, the "pregnancy rate," which combined the rate of abortion and the rate of live births. In the case of teenagers an increasing abortion rate meant that, despite a declining birthrate, the pregnancy rate was going up, and dramatically so.[7]

Since the rise in the pregnancy rate among teenagers (and among older women as well) was entirely due to the increase in abortions, it is curious that professionals and the public identified pregnancy, rather than abortion, as the problem. It is likewise curious that although the abortion rate increased for all women, most observers limited their attention to teenagers, who have always accounted for fewer than a third of the abortions performed. Teenagers *are* proportionately overrepresented in the ranks of women having abortions. But to pay attention almost exclusively to them, while neglecting the other groups that account for 70 percent of all abortions, does not make sense.

A similar misdirection characterized the issue of illegitimacy. In the 1970s, teenagers were having fewer babies overall than in previous decades, but they—like older women—were having more babies out of wedlock. Compared to other women, teenagers have relatively few babies, and a very high proportion of these are born to unmarried parents (about 30 percent in 1970, 50 percent in 1980, and 70 percent in 1995). But although most babies born to teenagers are born out of wedlock, most babies born out of wedlock are *not* born to teens. In 1975, teens accounted for just under a half of all babies born out of wedlock; in 1980 they accounted for 40 percent; and in 1990 they accounted for fewer than a third.[8] Obviously, teens should hardly be the only population of interest.

Thus, in the 1970s and early 1980s the data revealed a number of disquieting trends, and teenagers became the focus of the public's worry about these trends. More single women were having sex, more women were having abortions, more women were having babies out of wedlock, and—contrary to prevailing stereotypes—older women and white women were slowly replacing African Americans and teens as the largest groups within the population of unwed mothers. These trends bespeak a number of social changes worth looking at closely. Sex and pregnancy had been decoupled by the contraception revolution of the 1960s; pregnancy and birth had been decoupled by the legalization of abortion in the 1970s; and more and more children were growing up in "postmodern" families—that is, without their biological mother and father—in part because divorce rates were rising and in part because more children were being born out of wedlock. But these broad demographic changes, which impinged on women and men of all ages, were seen as problems that primarily concerned *teenagers*. The teenage mother—in particular, the black teenage mother—came to personify the social, economic, and sexual trends that in one way or another affected almost everyone in America.

A number of different responses might have been devised to meet the challenge of these new trends. It would have been logical, for example, to focus on the problem of abortion, since more than a million abortions were performed each year despite the fact that people presumably had access to effective contraception. Or the problem might have been defined as the increase in out-of-wedlock births, since more and more couples were starting families without being married.[9] Or policymakers could have responded to the way in which sexual activity and childbearing were, to an ever greater extent, taking place outside marriage (in 1975 about three-fourths of all abortions were performed on single women).[10] Yet American society has never framed the problem in any of these broader terms. The widest perspective was perhaps that of the antiabortion activists, who saw the problem as abortion in general. A careful reading of the specialist and nonspecialist media suggests that, with a few exceptions, professionals and the general public paid scant attention to abortion and out-of-wedlock childbearing among older women, while agreeing that abortion and illegitimate births among teenagers constituted a major social and public-health problem. Why did Americans narrow their vision to such an extent? How did professionals, Congress, and the public come to agree that there was an "epidemic" of pregnancy among teenagers and that teenagers were the main (if not the only) population worth worrying about?[11]

A STORY THAT FITS THE DATA

Advocates for young people had used Congress and the media to publicize an account of teenagers and their circumstances that seemed to make sense of the emerging demographic data and that was extremely persuasive. In essence, they claimed that teenagers, like older women, were increasingly likely to have sex and that their sexual activity was increasingly likely to take place outside marriage. Teens, however, like poor women of earlier generations, had been left out of the contraceptive revolution that had so changed the lives of other American women. They were having babies they did not want and could not support. Many of them were too inexperienced to know how to avoid conception, to appreciate the difficulties of childrearing, or to obtain an abortion (besides, abortion was expensive). And most gave birth without the support of the partner who had impregnated them. Unless they were granted access to affordable contraception and abortion, they would continue to have babies out of wedlock and would be mired in a life of poverty. Advocates noted that most babies born to teenagers were born out of wedlock, and that babies who lived with one parent were obviously less well off than those who lived with two. Moreover, black teenagers, who have always been disadvantaged in American society, had much higher rates of childbearing and illegitimacy than whites, although the reproductive behavior of white teenagers was beginning to resemble that of blacks. And in this account, teens who gave birth were much more likely to drop out of school than those who did not, so that as adults they were less well educated and hence poorer than women who postponed their childbearing.

Taken together, the data added up to a story that made sense to many people. It convinced Americans that young mothers like Michelle Brown—those who gave birth while still in high school and who were not married—were a serious social problem that brought a host of other problems in its wake. It explained why babies like David were born prematurely, why infant mortality rates in the United States were so high compared to those in other countries, why so many American students were dropping out of high school, and why AFDC [Aid to Families with Dependent Children] costs were skyrocketing. Some people even believed that if teenagers in the United States maintained their high birthrates, the nation would not be able to compete internationally in the coming century. Others argued that distressing racial inequalities in education, income, and social standing were in large part due to the marked difference in the birthrates of white and black teenagers.

Yet this story, which fed both on itself and on diffuse social anxiety, was incomplete; the data it was based on were true, but only partial. Evidence that did not fit the argument was left out, or mentioned only in passing. Largely ignored, for example, was the fact that a substantial and growing proportion of all unmarried mothers were not teenagers. And on those rare occasions when older unwed mothers were discussed, they were not seen as a cause for concern.[12] Likewise, although the substantially higher rates of out-of-wedlock childbearing among African Americans were often remarked upon, few observers pointed out that illegitimacy rates among blacks were falling or stable while rates among whites were increasing. Few noted that most of the teenagers giving birth were eighteen- and nineteen-year-olds, or that teens under fifteen had been having babies throughout much of the century.[13]

This story, as it emerged in the media and in policy circles in the 1970s and 1980s, fulfilled the public's need to identify the cause of a spreading social malaise. It led Americans to think that teenagers were the only ones being buffeted by social changes, whereas these changes were in fact pervasive; it led them to think that heedless, promiscuous teenagers were responsible for a great many disturbing social trends; and it led them to think that teenagers were doing these things unwittingly and despite themselves. When people spoke of "children having children" or of "babies having babies," their very choice of words revealed their belief that teenage mothers, because of their youth, should not be held morally responsible for their actions. "Babies" who had babies were themselves victims; they needed protection from their own ungovernable impulses.

In another sense, limiting the issue to teenagers gave it a deceptive air of universality; after all, everyone has been or will be a teenager. Yet the large-scale changes that were taking place in American life did not affect all teenagers equally. The types of behavior that led teenagers to get pregnant and become unwed mothers (engaging in premarital sex, and bearing and keeping illegitimate children) were traditionally much more common among African Americans than among whites, and more common among the poor than among the privileged.

For average Americans in the 1970s, life had undergone profound changes in just a few short years. Unmarried couples were engaging more readily in sex, and doing so much more openly. Many of them were even living together, instead of settling for furtive sex in the back seats of cars. When an unmarried woman got pregnant, she no longer made a sudden marriage or a hasty visit to a distant aunt; now she either terminated her pregnancy or openly—even proudly—had her baby. Often she chose to live as a single parent or to set up housekeeping with her partner, rather than allowing her child to be adopted by a proper, married middle-class couple. In the 1970s, people of all ages began to follow this way of life, but the inchoate fears of the public coalesced in large part exclusively around teenagers. The new patterns of sexual behavior and new family structures were simply more visible among younger people, who had not committed themselves to the older set of choices. At the same time, teenagers, especially those who had children, were defined as people who were embarking on a lifetime of poverty. The debate, in centering on teenagers in general, thus combined two contrasting features of American society: it permitted people to talk about African Americans and poor women (categories that often overlapped) without mentioning race or class; but it also reflected the fact that the sexual behavior and reproductive patterns of white teenagers were beginning to resemble those of African Americans and poor women—that is, more and more whites were postponing marriage and having babies out of wedlock.

The myriad congressional hearings, newspaper stories, and technical reports on the "epidemic" of pregnancy among teenagers could not have convinced the public to subscribe to this view if other factors in American life had not made the story plausible. The social sciences abound with theories suggesting that the public is subject to "moral panics" which are in large part irrational, but in this case people were responding to a particular account because it helped them make sense of some very real and rapidly changing conditions in their world.[14] It appeared to explain a number of dismaying social phenomena, such as spreading signs of poverty, persistent racial inequalities, illegitimacy, freer sexual mores, and new family structures.[15] It was and continues to be a resonant issue because of the profound changes that have taken place in the meanings and practices associated with sexuality and reproduction, in the relations among sex, marriage, and childbearing, and in the national and global economies. Through the story of "teenage pregnancy," these revolutionary changes acquired a logic and a human face.[16]

THE ECONOMIC TRANSFORMATION OF AMERICAN LIFE

The fact that the public accepts out-of-wedlock births among older, affluent, white women but deplores them among young, poor, minority women is intimately tied to a profound change in the lives of Americans—namely, the decline of American economic power and of middle-class affluence.

Today's young Americans are the first generation in living memory who face the prospect of doing less well economically over their lifetimes than did their parents. In recent years the gap between the well-to-do and the poor has grown: The rich are getting richer and the poor are getting poorer.

Much more significant than income disparity is the decline in real wages that took place in the 1970s and 1980s, meaning that individual income lost purchasing power as measured in constant dollars. Between the end of World War II and the first oil embargo of 1973, real wages grew rapidly; then came nearly twenty years of very slow growth or stagnation. In the first period the median annual income of a man at the peak of his earning capacity (forty-five to fifty-four) who worked full time year-round more than doubled, going from $15,529 in 1946 to $32,752 in 1976 (in constant 1987 dollars). This represented an increase of 20 to 30 percent per decade. Between 1976 and 1986, however, real wages increased much more slowly, on the order of 1 percent a year.[17] The increase in real wages after World War II meant that the middle class was expanding, not because it was receiving a larger share of national income (although, to a modest extent, it was) but because overall wages were rising so rapidly. Median income for families (as opposed to median income for men) went from $15,000 in 1947 to $29,000 in 1969, measured in constant 1987 dollars. But after 1973, as real wages declined, family income increased only marginally—to $30,600 in 1986. To put this most dramatically, in the 1950s and 1960s a young man could expect, by age thirty, to be earning 15 percent more than his father had at the same age. By 1986, in contrast, he could expect to be earning 15 percent *less*.[18]

One large group of Americans has responded to declining real wages by making its family structure more *concentrated*. These people are postponing marriage and childbearing to an ever greater extent, having fewer and fewer children, and forming a growing number of two-career marriages. This trajectory, which we might call the yuppie pattern (after the Young Urban Professionals who adopt it), is the new middle-class norm. Women in particular are investing more time in their education, are training for careers rather than jobs, and are continuing to work even after they have children. This pattern has become so prevalent among the middle class that we often forget what a major shift in behavior it represented when it first appeared. For much of U.S. history, American women married fairly young, had their children fairly early, and retired from the work force until their children were grown. But the new yuppie pattern is available only to the affluent, people who can realistically expect that the market will reward their sacrifices. For people who have fewer resources, there is another shift in the American family: these people *rearrange* the traditional family. They either never get married or start a family at all, or they have children without being married.[19]

The traditional family of the forties and fifties thus was transformed in the seventies and even more in the eighties. The "Ozzie and Harriet" family (in which the husband worked but the wife did not) gave way to two new and distinct configurations. America's "households" (to use the Census Bureau's term for groups of people living together) ceased to consist mostly of traditional families and began to comprise married working couples on the one hand or single-parent families on the other. (Eighty-seven percent of single parents are in fact single mothers.)[20] In 1970, out of all families with children, almost nine out of ten included both spouses, whereas only one in ten was a single-parent family. Furthermore, of the single-parent families, fewer than ten percent (or about 1 percent of all families with children) were families in which the parents were unmarried. In 1992, in contrast, six out of ten American families were single-parent families, and only four in ten were two-parent families. Among single-parent families in 1992, the largest group consisted of those headed by never-married mothers. Overall, today about one out of every three families with children is headed by a woman who has never been married.[21]

Consequently, just as the issue of pregnancy among teenagers was being debated in Congress and in the media, many Americans were viewing it from the vantage point of their own restructured lives. People who were affluent and well educated, who had delayed marriage in order to further their schooling, who were members of two-earner couples, and who were postponing and limiting their childbearing had little sympathy for teenage mothers (who were often conflated in the public mind with unwed mothers). The behavior of these young women seemed not only unwise and self-destructive, but unwise and self-destructive in ways that hit particularly close to home. They seemed to be having babies before they were ready, and, worse, to be doing so without a legal husband, at a time when many Americans were becoming keenly aware that it took two or more workers in a family to maintain a middle-class lifestyle. People who had scrimped and saved until they could marry and set up a household, who lived with all of the burdens of the "second shift" (the burdens incurred when wives enter the labor force but are still expected to fulfill their traditional nurturant role), and who were postponing childbearing until they could afford it were particularly unsympathetic: Teenagers who had babies seemed to be heedless, irresponsible, and heading for trouble.[22] And those in the middle, the ones whose highly paid blue- and white-collar jobs were becoming scarce and who were having difficulty passing on these middle-class jobs to their children, were no more understanding: young people who had sex and babies too soon seemed to be bringing their troubles on themselves.[23]

In short, pregnant teenagers made a convenient lightning rod for the anxieties and tensions in Americans' lives. Economic fortunes were unstable, a postindustrial economic order was evolving, sexual and reproductive patterns were mutating. Representing such teenagers as the epitome of society's ills seemed one quick way of making sense of these enormous changes. This was particularly true as poverty was becoming ever more visible and being poor appeared to be the direct result of immoral or unwise behavior. Pregnant teenagers seemed to embody the very essence of such behavior. Indeed, the phrase "teenage pregnancy" continues to be a powerful shorthand way of referring to the problem of poverty.

NOTES

1. For example, see William Bennett, *The Index of Leading Cultural Indicators: Facts and Figures on the State of American Society* (New York: Simon and Schuster, 1994).

2. Although much of the rhetoric on the Right is about "children," conservatives and even many liberals think of pregnancy among teenagers as something fundamentally affecting "girls" or young women. The issue is usually framed in such a way that half of the people involved—namely, young men—are excluded, and this selectivity is an enormous handicap in the effort to find a solution. As we will see, thinking about the problem in terms of two sexes rather than one opens up a number of new possible solutions.

3. For an overview, see U.S. House of Representatives, 99th Congress, Select Committee on Children, Youth and Families, "Teen Pregnancy: What Is Being Done? A State-by-State Look" (Washington, D.C.: Government Printing Office, 1986); Charles Stewart Mott Foundation, *A State-by-State Look at Teenage Childbearing in the United States* (Flint, Mich.: Charles Stewart Mott Foundation, 1991); Gloria Magat, ed., *Adolescent Pregnancy: Still News in 1989* (New York:

Grantmakers Concerned with Adolescent Pregnancy, Women and Foundations/ Corporate Philanthropy, 1989); Junior League, *Teenage Pregnancy: Developing Life Options* (New York: Association of Junior Leagues, 1988). For the National Urban League's program with Kappa Alpha Psi, see Cheryl Hayes, ed., *Risking the Future: Adolescent Sexuality, Pregnancy, and Childbearing* (Washington, D.C.: National Academy Press, 1987), vol. 1, p. 178.

4. Prior to the mid-1970s, pregnant teenagers were treated by the media as a subset of "school-age mothers" or of the larger set of "unwed mothers." See *Reader's Guide to Periodic Literature*, 1968–1994. A tabulation of these stories by title and content has been compiled by Kristin Luker.

5. In 1955, out of every thousand adolescent women of all races, 90 gave birth. By 1975 the rate had fallen until it was approximately equal to that of 1915: 60 per thousand. And by 1985 it had declined even further, to only 50 per thousand. Interestingly, the fertility of teenagers has always been remarkably similar to that of older women; the birthrates for both groups rise and fall in tandem. (The similarities are most marked, of course, between the rates for teens and the rates for women who are just a little older—twenty to twenty-four.) Clearly, the fertility of American women tends to respond to large, society-wide forces. See National Center for Health Statistics, *Advance Report of Final Natality Statistics* (Hyattsville, Md.: Public Health Service, various years).

6. Robert L. Heuser, *Fertility Tables for Birth Cohorts by Color: United States, 1917–1973*, DHEW Publication no. (HRA) 76–11182 (Rockville, Md.: National Center for Health Statistics, 1976): National Center for Health Statistics, *Advance Report of Final Natality Statistics, 1987* (Rockville, Md.: National Center for Health Statistics, 1989), vol. 38, no. 3. Even the post-1988 upturn in birthrates among teenagers is still within the range of historical fluctuation, although whether this will continue to be so is uncertain.

7. In 1973, among teenage women of all races, 60 out of every thousand gave birth and 21 per thousand had abortions; thus, a total of 81 out of every thousand were becoming pregnant. In 1980, in contrast, the rate of live births was 52 per thousand and the abortion rate had more than doubled, to 44 per thousand; the pregnancy rate had thus increased to 96 per thousand.

8. For an overview, see *Statistical Abstract of the United States* (Washington, D.C.: Government Printing Office, 1993), Table 101, "Births to Unmarried Women, by Race of Child and Age of Mother, 1970–1990"; U.S. Center for Health Statistics, *Vital Statistics of the United States*, various years; idem, *Monthly Vital Statistics*, various years.

9. This has led to a set of new social practices unanticipated by Emily Post. People now speak of "my baby's father" or "my baby's mother." One proud father even placed a notice in his local paper announcing that his fiancée had just given birth to their baby (I am indebted to Sheldon Messinger for this information). In the late 1980s, commentators did begin to take note of the rising rate of out-of-wedlock births in general; but even within this broader context, experts and the media still focused on teenage mothers.

10. Larry Bumpass and James A. Sweet, "Children's Experience in Single-Parent Families: Implications of Cohabitation and Marital Transition," *Family Planning Perspectives* 21 (November–December): 256–260.

11. In 1986, polls revealed that more than 84 percent of Americans considered pregnancy among teenagers a "major" problem facing the country. Harris poll for PPFA, 1985. See also Roper Report 86–3, 1986 R37XE.

12. Some people, among them demographers such as Phillips Cutwright and polemicists such as Charles Murray, argue that the proportion or ratio of out-of-wedlock births is much more important than the rate. In demographic terms, a "rate" is an event that is standardized over a specified population for a particular period of time. Thus, the birthrate is defined as the number of births (the numerator) per thousand women aged fifteen to forty-four (the denominator) in a year. But many commentators speak of the "illegitimacy rate" or the "abortion rate" when what they really have in mind is a proportion or ratio, a figure that compares two sets of *events* rather than an event to a population. What many people call the "illegitimacy rate" is really a measure that compares the number of out-of-wedlock births (the numerator) to the total number of births (the denominator). The problem here is that there can be wide fluctuations in *both* of the events being charted, and these fluctuations can lead to dramatic changes in the measure. (Populations fluctuate, too, of course, but much less sharply.) The illegitimacy *rate* (the number of out-of-wedlock births per thousand unmarried women aged fifteen to forty-four) went from 25.4 in 1970 to 43.8 in 1990, an increase of about 70 percent, while the illegitimacy *ratio* (the proportion of out-of-wedlock births to legitimate births) went from 11 percent to 28 percent of all births during that same period, an increase of more than 250 percent. The dramatically larger increase in the ratio, compared to the increase in the rate, was due to an increase in the propensity of American women to bear children out of wedlock, and, simultaneously, a declining propensity to bear children in wedlock. Among African Americans, virtually all of the increase in the illegitimacy ratio was due to declining marital fertility (the denominator), and in fact illegitimacy rates for African American women declined for most of the 1970–1990 period. As Cutright says, what the majority of a cohort is doing matters. Still, commentators tended to emphasize troubling statistics (changes in the proportion of babies born out of wedlock) over more comforting ones (such as the decreases in the incidence of pregnancy per sexually experienced woman and in the rate of out-of-wedlock births among African Americans).

13. One could make the case that this *was* the real story: the fact that birthrates among very young women had not changed much. Since the period of childhood had gradually lengthened in the course of the nineteenth and twentieth centuries, one would have expected a reduction in births to very young women. Birthrates among fourteen-year-olds for the calendar years 1925–1990 were as follows:

1925	3.9 per thousand
1930	3.8
1935	3.7
1940	3.8
1945	3.9
1950	5.8
1955	6.1
1960	6.0
1965	5.2
1970	6.6
1975	7.1
1980	6.5

1985   6.2
1990   7.8

Source for 1925–1970: Heuser, *Fertility Tables for Birth Cohorts by Color*, "Central Birth Rates for All Women during Each Year 1917–73 by Age and Live-Birth Order for Each Cohort from 1888 to 1959," p. 37, Table 4a. Source for 1975–1990: *Vital Statistics of the United States: Natality*, "Central Birth Rates by Live-Birth Order, Current Age of Mother, and Color for Women in Each Cohort," p. 1–32, Table 1–16 (1975); p. 1–42, Table 1–18 (1980); p. 1–36, Table 1–18 (1985); p. 1–45, Table 1–19 (1990).

14. The classic example is Stanley Cohen, *Folk Devils and Moral Panics* (Oxford: Basil Blackwell, 1987). For another view, one that is more in line with the position presented here, see John Kingdon, *Agendas, Alternatives, and Public Policies* (Boston: Little, Brown, 1984).

15. This does not imply that stories told by advocates are necessarily right. Indeed, as in this case, advocates typically confront contradictory data and must strive to make sense of them long before the whole pattern of the phenomenon is clear. On the issue of pregnancy among teenagers, advocates and policymakers were wrong in several important respects, and their errors had profound implications for social policy.

16. Rosalind Petchesky has made the astute point that social scientists often speak of "revolutions" when only white and middle-class behavior has changed. See Petchesky, *Abortion and Women's Choice: The State, Sexuality and Reproductive Freedom* (Boston: Northeastern University Press, 1990).

17. This figure is adjusted for fringe benefits; see Levy and Michel, *Economic Future*, p. 8, Table 21.

18. Ibid., pp. 9–10; Gary Burtless, ed., *A Future of Lousy Jobs? The Changing Structure of U.S. Wages* (Washington, D.C.: Brookings Institute, 1990).

19. Many of these trends were already visible by the late 1960s and were probably not "caused" in any direct, uncomplicated way by declining real wages. But the decline in real wages probably made these trends steeper and more widespread than they would otherwise have been.

20. Cynthia Taeuber, *Statistical Handbook on Women in America* (Phoenix, Ariz.: Oryx Press, 1991), p. 299.

21. U.S. Bureau of the Census, "Household and Family Characteristics," *Current Population Reports*, Series P-20, various years. Since analysts tend to focus on the vital statistics concerning legal marriage, nonspecialists often assume that the terms "unmarried mother" and "single mother" are interchangeable. However, increases in what the demographers call "cohabitation" (and what everyone else calls "living together") have to some extent offset the decline in marriage. See L. L. Bumpass, J. A. Sweet, and A. J. Cherlin, "The Role of Cohabitation in Declining Rates of Marriage," *Journal of Marriage and the Family* 53, no. 4 (1991): 913–927.

22. Arlie Hochschild, *The Second Shift: Inside the Two-Job Marriage* (New York: Viking, 1989).

23. For an example of how families used sexual choices as an explanation for their children's downward mobility, see Newman, *Declining Fortunes*.

Methods and Theory

INTRODUCTION

Sociology was founded as a discipline of study after the period of tremendous social change that followed the Enlightenment. In Europe, a long, relatively unchanging period of rural, agricultural life was disturbed by the shift to urban, industrial ways. Deep-seated religious beliefs were shaken by scientific inquiry. Democratic rule and beliefs about political individualism reoriented societies built upon aristocracies. Sociologists emerged to essentially ask, "What just happened?" and "What can we expect to happen?" August Comte coined the term sociology in 1838 and defined it as the science of society. What does it mean to be a "science" of society? Sociology seeks some "truth" about the social world, or at the least some understanding about the trends and patterns in social life. Sociologists use a process, a method, to access information to uncover that truth. Calling sociology a social *science* implies that it follows a method of asking questions about the social world, constructing theories that answer the questions, testing those theories to see if they hold up to evidence, and thus coming to logical answers to the questions that are based on verifiable facts. This research process is the same one that is followed in the natural sciences. Theories are tested through empirical observation. Observations lead us to support, refute, or refine theories; and from that point, we continue to build knowledge. This is probably not exactly what Comte meant at the time he defined sociology, but it is much of what is meant by social scientists today. In sociology, we make claims (theories) that we can test with observations (data collected through specific methods). To fully understand the approach to creating sociological knowledge, theory and methods must be understood as they complement each other.

The first piece in the section, from Emile Durkheim's *Suicide: A Study in Sociology*, is one of the first and best-known quantitative approaches to a sociological question. Quantitative research uses numerical data to understand social issues. Quantitative research is sometimes contrasted with qualitative research, which uses non-numerical data to address questions. These two approaches are often used in complementary ways. If you become a sociology major, you will be required to take at least one research methods class that delves more deeply into the relationship between the two. Durkheim is considered one of the three "founding fathers" of sociology. The other two, who you will read in later sections of this book, are Karl Marx and Max Weber. Durkheim held the first formal academic appointment as Professor of Sociology in France where he also offered the first sociology course. He wrote many important foundational pieces in sociology. In this excerpt, he takes what we typically consider a very individual and personal trouble—suicide—and studies it not as an individual problem, but as a social issue having a "social nature." Through an examination of suicide *rates* (comprised in part by aggregations of individual suicides), Durkheim argues that societies have typical propensities for suicide that do not vary much over time. By looking at rates of suicide over time, he shows that some societies have high rates (that don't change much), some have low rates (that don't change much), and so on. Based on this, he makes the claim that there is something very *social* about suicide. In other words, there are certain characteristics of social structures that lead to high rates in some societies and lower rates in others. Through his empirical observation of rates, he generates an initial claim that religion is related to suicide; in particular, he finds patterns that show that societies that are Protestant have higher rates of suicide than societies that are Catholic (in another section of the book, he also looks at Judaism). Not being content just to recognize these differences, he asks why this might be and whether other social causes may be at work. In the passage, he breaks the data down into various configurations to figure it out. In the end, the data confirm that religion is correlated with varying rates of suicides. He moves back and forth between his data (suicide rates) and his claims (about the influence of religion on suicide) to generate an understanding of the social phenomenon of suicide. In the end, he comes to a specific proposition about suicide: The more socially integrated a society is by its religion, the lower suicide rate it will have. The relationship between social integration and deviant actions is one that sociologists have continued to examine. Durkheim's study of suicide has led to hypotheses about other "deviant" acts such as crime. His theory has been retested and his theory reformulated to other social phenomena to improve our understanding of the social world.

The second passage is a contemporary piece by Charles Ragin. Ragin's task is to differentiate social *scientists* from others who write about social life, such as journalists. While he writes about the relationship between theory and data, the thrust of this chapter is about the data collection process. Social scientists differ from journalists in that we are systematic in our processes. Journalists often take a single story and make sweeping generalizations about it. However, sociologists have methods to gather representative pieces of data which allow us to assess which stories (cases) are typical and which ones are atypical. Sociologists are interested in being able to make generalizations based on our research. Our systematic methods of collecting data allow us to do so accurately in ways that journalistic accounts do not. Journalists, audiences, however, do not always think critically about the representativeness of what they are being presented, nor do they critically assess the sources of data, which leads us to the final piece in the section.

Joel Best, who is probably best known for his book, *How to Lie with Statistics*, argues that the public is innumerate. By this he means that we are illiterate when it comes to numbers and we don't really know how to assess quantitative information. The problem with this is that statistics can be used authoritatively by powerful institutions to make arguments to support their views without much opposition. He sees statistics as a double-edged sword: They are tremendously useful for summarizing large amounts of information to see patterns and trends, yet they can be misused because of an uneducated public. His quest is to teach students to analyze statistics critically and to ask, Do these statistics make sense? Who collected them? How were categories defined and labeled? For what purposes? These are questions sociologists ask of data they are presented, as well as data that they collect on their own. Certainly, the questions that Best asks regarding which deaths are labeled "suicide" would be questions that Durkheim would be concerned with were he alive today.

It is difficult to assemble a group of three readings that will give you an idea of the breadth of sociological theory and methods. These just touch the surface. Should you continue as a major or a minor, you will take courses in both of these areas. For now, there are four main points for you to take away from these readings. First, sociologists are in the business of asking questions and making claims about the social world. Second, to answer those questions and assess those claims, sociologists collect data in a systematic manner. There are two types of data: quantitative (numerical) and qualitative. These data are used to answer questions and assess claims. Third, how data are collected, by whom, and for what purposes must be critically evaluated. Finally, sociologists don't just collect data for data's sake, but to engage in answering questions about the social world, such as what is the relationship between religion, social integration, and deviance? If religion plays less of an integrating function over time, what will be the social glue that holds society together?

READING 4

Excerpt from *Suicide: A Study in Sociology*

EMILE DURKHEIM

I

Since the word "suicide" recurs constantly in the course of conversation, it might be thought that its sense is universally known and that definition is

Durkheim, Emile. [translated by John A. Spaulding and George Simpson]. 1951 [1897]. "Introduction" and "Egoistic Suicide" from *Suicide: A Study in Sociology*. New York: The Free Press.

superfluous. Actually, the words of everyday language, like the concepts they express, are always susceptible of more than one meaning, and the scholar employing them in their accepted use without further definition would risk serious misunderstanding. The term *suicide is applied to all cases of death resulting directly or indirectly from a positive or negative act of the victim himself, which he knows will produce this result.* An attempt is an act thus defined but falling short of actual death.

II

Since suicide is an individual action affecting the individual only, it must seemingly depend exclusively on individual factors, thus belonging to psychology alone. Is not the suicide's resolve usually explained by his temperament, character, antecedents and private history?

The degree and conditions under which suicides may be legitimately studied in this way need not now be considered, but that they may be viewed in an entirely different light is certain. If, instead of seeing in them only separate occurrences, unrelated and to be separately studied, the suicides committed in a given society during a given period of time are taken as a whole, it appears that this total is not simply a sum of independent units, a collective total, but is itself a new fact *sui generis*, with its own unity, individuality, and consequently its own nature—a nature, furthermore, dominantly social. Indeed, provided too long a period is not considered, the statistics for one and the same society are almost invariable. This is because the environmental circumstances attending the life of peoples remain relatively unchanged from year to year. To be sure, more considerable variations occasionally occur; but they are quite exceptional. They are also clearly always contemporaneous with some passing crisis affecting the social state.[1] Thus, in 1848 there occurred an abrupt decline in all European states.

If a longer period of time is considered, more serious changes are observed. Then, however, they become chronic; they only prove that the structural characteristics of society have simultaneously suffered profound changes.

At each moment of its history, therefore, each society has a definite aptitude for suicide. The relative intensity of this aptitude is measured by taking the proportion between the total number of voluntary deaths and the population of every age and sex. We will call this numerical datum *the rate of mortality through suicide, characteristic of the society under consideration.* It is generally calculated in proportion to a million or a hundred thousand inhabitants.

EGOISTIC SUICIDE

First let us see how the different religious confessions affect suicide.

I

If one casts a glance at the map of European suicide, it is at once clear that in purely Catholic countries like Spain, Portugal, Italy, suicide is very little developed, while it is at its maximum in Protestant countries, in Prussia, Saxony, Denmark. The following averages compiled by Morselli confirm this first conclusion:

	Average of Suicides per Million Inhabitants
Protestant states	190
Mixed states (Protestant and Catholic)	96
Catholic states	58
Greek Catholic states	40

The low proportion of the Greek Catholics cannot be surely attributed to religion; for as their civilization is very different from that of the other European nations, this difference of culture may be the cause of their lesser aptitude. But this is not the case with most Catholic or Protestant societies. To be sure, they are not all on the same intellectual and moral level; yet the resemblances are sufficiently essential to make it possible to ascribe to confessional differences the marked contrast they offer in respect to suicide.

Nevertheless, this first comparison is still too summary. In spite of undeniable similarities, the social environments of the inhabitants of these different countries are not identical. The civilizations of Spain and Portugal are far below that of Germany, and this inferiority may conceivably be the reason for the lesser development of suicide which we have just mentioned. If one wishes to avoid this source of error and determine more definitely the influence of Catholicism and Protestantism on the suicidal tendency, the two religions must be compared in the heart of a single society.

Of all the great states of Germany, Bavaria has by far the fewest suicides. There have been barely 90 per million inhabitants yearly since 1874, while Prussia has 133 (1871–75), the duchy of Baden 156, Wurttemberg 162, Saxony 300. Now, Bavaria also has most Catholics, 713.2 to 1,000 inhabitants. On the other hand, if one compares the different provinces of Bavaria, suicides are found to be in direct proportion to the number of Protestants and in inverse proportion to that of Catholics (see table on next page). Not only the proportions of averages to one another confirm the law but all the numbers of the first colum [sic] are higher than those of the second and those of the second higher than those of the third without exception.

We shall find these other causes in the nature of these two religious systems. Yet they both prohibit suicide with equal emphasis; not only do they penalize it morally with great severity, but both teach that a new life

Bavarian Provinces (1867–75)*

Provinces with Catholic Minority (less than 50%)	Suicides per Million Inhabitants	Provinces with Catholic Majority (50 to 90%)	Suicides Per Million Inhabitants	Provinces with More Than 90% Catholic	Suicides Per Million Inhabitants
Rhenish Palatinate	167	Lower Franconia	157	Upper Palatinate	64
Central Franconia	207	Swabia	118	Upper Bavaria	114
Upper Franconia	204			Lower Bavaria	19
Average	192	Average	135	Average	75

* The population below 15 years has been omitted.

begins beyond the tomb where men are punished for their evil actions, and Protestantism just as well as Catholicism numbers suicide among them. Finally, in both cults these prohibitions are of divine origin; they are represented not as the logical conclusion of correct reason, but God Himself is their authority. Therefore, if Protestantism is less unfavorable to the development of suicide, it is not because of a different attitude from that of Catholicism. Thus, if both religions have the same precepts with respect to this particular matter, their dissimilar influence on suicide must proceed from one of the more general characteristics differentiating them.

The only essential difference between Catholicism and Protestantism is that the second permits free inquiry to a far greater degree than the first. Of course, Catholicism by the very fact that it is an idealistic religion concedes a far greater place to thought and reflection than Greco-Latin polytheism or Hebrew monotheism. It is not restricted to mechanical ceremonies but seeks the control of the conscience. So it appeals to conscience, and even when demanding blind submission of reason, does so by employing the language of reason. Nonetheless, the Catholic accepts his faith ready made, without scrutiny. He may not even submit it to historical examination since the original texts that serve as its basis are proscribed. A whole hierarchical system of authority is devised, with marvelous ingenuity, to render tradition invariable. All *variation* is abhorrent to Catholic thought. The Protestant is far more the author of his faith. The Bible is put in his hands and no interpretation is imposed upon him. The very structure of the reformed cult stresses this state of religious individualism. Nowhere but in England is the Protestant clergy a hierarchy; like the worshippers, the priest has no other source but himself and his conscience. He is a more instructed guide than the run of worshippers but with no special authority for fixing dogma. But what best proves that this freedom of inquiry proclaimed by the founders of the Reformation has not remained a Platonic affirmation is the increasing multiplicity of all sorts of sects so strikingly in contrast with the indivisible unity of the Catholic Church.

We thus reach our first conclusion, that the proclivity of Protestantism for suicide must relate to the spirit of free inquiry that animates this religion. Let us understand this relationship correctly. Free inquiry itself is only the effect of another cause. When it appears, when men, after having long received their ready made faith from tradition, claim the right to shape it for themselves, this is not because of the intrinsic desirability of free inquiry, for the latter involves as much sorrow as happiness. But it is because men henceforth need this liberty. This very need can have only one cause: the overthrow of traditional beliefs. If they still asserted themselves with equal energy, it would never occur to men to criticize them. If they still had the same authority, men would not demand the right to verify the source of this authority. Reflection develops only if its development becomes imperative, that is, if certain ideas and instinctive sentiments which have hitherto adequately guided conduct are found to have lost their efficacy. Then reflection intervenes to fill the gap that has appeared, but which it has not created. Just as reflection disappears to the extent that thought and action take the form of automatic habits, it awakes only when accepted habits become disorganized. It asserts its rights against public opinion only when the latter loses strength, that is, when it is no longer prevalent to the same extent. If these assertions occur not merely occasionally and as passing crises, but become chronic; if individual consciences keep reaffirming their autonomy, it is because they are constantly subject to conflicting impulses, because a new opinion has not been formed to replace the one no longer existing. If a new system of beliefs were constituted which seemed as indisputable to everyone as the old, no one would think of discussing it any longer. Its discussion would no longer even be permitted; for ideas shared by an entire society draw from this consensus an authority that makes them sacrosanct and raises them above dispute. For them to have become more tolerant, they must first already have become the object of less general and complete assent and been weakened by preliminary controversy.

Thus, if it is correct to say that free inquiry once proclaimed, multiplies schisms, it must be added that it presupposes them and derives from them, for it is claimed and instituted as a principle only in order to permit latent or half-declared schisms to develop more freely. So if Protestantism concedes a greater freedom to individual thought than Catholicism, it is because it has fewer common beliefs and practices. Now, a religious society cannot exist without a collective *credo* and the more extensive the *credo* the more unified and strong is the society. For it does not unite men by an exchange and reciprocity of services, a temporal bond of union which permits and even presupposes differences, but which a religious society cannot form. It socializes men only by attaching them completely to an identical body of doctrine and socializes them in proportion as this body of doctrine is extensive and firm. The more numerous the manners of action and thought of a religious character are, which are accordingly removed from free inquiry, the more the idea of God presents itself in all details of existence and makes individual wills converge to one identical goal. Inversely, the greater concessions a confessional group makes to individual judgment, the less it dominates lives, the less its cohesion and vitality. We thus reach the conclusion that the superiority of Protestantism with respect to suicide results from its being a less strongly integrated church than the Catholic church.

Generally speaking, religion has a prophylactic effect upon suicide. It is not, as has sometimes been said, because it condemns it more unhesitatingly than secular morality, nor because the idea of God gives its precepts exceptional authority which subdues the will, nor because the prospect of a future life and the terrible punishments there awaiting the guilty give its proscriptions a greater sanction than that of human laws. The Protestant believes in God and the immortality of the soul no less than the Catholic. More than this, the religion with least inclination to suicide, Judaism, is the very one not formally proscribing it and also the one in which the idea of immortality plays the least role. Indeed, the Bible contains no law forbidding man to kill himself[2] and, on the other hand, its beliefs in a future life are most vague. Doubtless, in both matters, rabbinical teaching has gradually supplied the omissions of the sacred book; but they have not its authority. The beneficent influence of religion is therefore not due to the special nature of religious conceptions. If religion protects man against the desire for self-destruction, it is not that it preaches the respect for his own person to him with arguments *sui generis*; but because it is a society. What constitutes this society is the existence of a certain number of beliefs and practices common to all the faithful, traditional and thus obligatory. The more numerous and strong these collective states of mind are, the stronger the integration of the religious community, and also the greater its preservative value. The details of dogmas and rites are secondary. The essential thing is that they be capable of supporting a sufficiently intense collective life. And because the Protestant church has less consistency than the others it has less moderating effect upon suicide.

So we reach the general conclusion: suicide varies inversely with the degree of integration of the social groups of which the individual forms a part.

But society cannot disintegrate without the individual simultaneously detaching himself from social life, without his own goals becoming preponderant over those of the community, in a word without his personality tending to surmount the collective personality. The more weakened the groups to which he belongs, the less he depends on them, the more he consequently depends only on himself and recognizes no other rules of conduct than what are founded on his private interests. If we agree to call this state egoism, in which the individual ego asserts itself to excess in the face of the social ego and at its expense, we may call egoistic the special type of suicide springing from excessive individualism.

NOTES

1. The numbers applying to these exceptional years we have put in parentheses.
2. The only penal proscription known to us is that mentioned by Flavius Josephus in his *History of the War of the Jews against the Romans* (III, 25), which says simply that "the bodies of those who kill themselves voluntarily remain unburied until after sunset, although those who have been killed in battle may be buried earlier." This is not even definitely a penal measure.

READING 5

Excerpt from *Constructing Social Research*

CHARLES RAGIN

INTRODUCTION

There are many ways to study and tell about social life. Sometimes it is hard to tell which of these are social research and which are not. Consider a few examples.

Peter Evans spent a lot of time talking to business executives and government officials in Brazil and wrote a book about it called *Dependent Development* (1979). On the basis of his interviews and other work, he found that Brazil's top economic and political leaders were closely enmeshed with some of the world's most powerful multinational corporations, many of which are based in the United States (Union Carbide, for example). He concluded that this "triple alliance" of the Brazilian government, Brazil's economic elites, and multinational corporations shaped Brazil's industrial development in a way that skewed its rewards toward the rich and powerful in Brazil. The bulk of the population benefited only marginally, if at all, and were subjected to intense government repression.

Arlie Hochschild wanted to understand the "commercialization of human feeling." Many jobs in today's economy require what she calls "emotion work"—employees' use of their own feelings to create an outward, public display that supports a particular image (such as friendliness or helpfulness). Such management of a person's emotions can be used to achieve specific ends, especially in service jobs involving interaction with customers or clients. Hochschild studied a lot of different occupations, but devoted special attention to flight attendants and found that emotion

Ragin, Charles. 1994. "What is Social Research?" from *Constructing Social Research.* Thousand Oaks: Pine Forge Press.

work is an essential part of their work. For example, emotion work is often required to keep unruly and sometimes angry passengers in check. Hochschild summarized what she learned from flight attendants and other kinds of service work in a book called *The Managed Heart: Commercialization of Human Feeling* (1983). She found that there was a tendency for certain kinds of emotion work to be assigned to females, thus encouraging the concentration of women in specific occupations.

Douglas Massey was interested in urban poverty in the United States and wanted to find out why conditions deteriorated so rapidly in African-American, inner-city neighborhoods, especially from the 1970s to the present. He studied the largest cities in the United States and found that cities with the most severe housing segregation by race and income level were the ones that experienced the most severe inner-city deterioration. Essentially, he discovered that the greater the degree of housing segregation, the greater the concentration of increases in poverty in specific inner-city neighborhoods. He reported his provocative conclusions in a book titled *American Apartheid* (Massey and Denton 1993).

These three books address important issues. Why do so many people in Third World countries like Brazil still suffer from serious poverty despite the substantial industrialization that has occurred? Why is it that women more than men are required to perform emotion work in their jobs? What factors reinforce this pattern? Why have so many inner-city neighborhoods in the United States suffered such serious deterioration? These questions and the studies that address them are as relevant to the everyday concerns of the informed public as they are to government officials responsible for formulating public policies. The conclusions of any of these three authors could be reported on a television news or magazine show like "Nightline," "60 Minutes," or the "MacNeil/Lehrer NewsHour." The phenomenon of emotion work could even be the basis for a talk show like the "Oprah Winfrey Show."

At first glance, it might appear that these three books were written by journalists or free-lance writers. Yet, all three were written by social researchers trying to make sense of different aspects of social life. What distinguishes these works as social research? More generally, what distinguishes social research from other ways of gathering and presenting evidence about social life? All those who write about society construct **representations** of social life—descriptions that incorporate relevant ideas and evidence about social phenomena. Are the representations constructed by social researchers distinctive in any way from those constructed by nonsocial scientists, and, if so, how?

At the most general level, **social research** includes everything involved in the efforts of social scientists to "tell about society" (Becker 1986). Both parts of this definition of social research—that it involves a *social scientific way* of *telling about society*—are important.

Telling about *society* has special features and some special problems. These problems affect the work of all those who tell about society—from social researchers to novelists to documentary film makers—and separates those who tell about society and social life from those who tell about other things. Social researchers, like others who tell about society, are members of society. They study members of society, and they present the results of their work to members of society. Thus, at a very general level, social researchers overlap with those they study and with the audiences for their work; and those they study—other members of society—also overlap with their audiences.

Among those who consider themselves scientists, this three-way mixing of researcher, subject, and audience exists only in the social and behavioral sciences (anthropology, sociology, political science, and so on) and has an important impact on the nature and conduct of research. For example, it is very difficult to conduct social research without also addressing questions that are fundamentally interpretive or historical in nature—who we are and how we came to be who we are. It is very difficult to neutralize social science in some way and see studying people the same as studying molecules or ants.

The importance of the other part of the definition—that there is a specifically social scientific way of telling—stems from the fact, already noted, that there are lots of people who tell about society. Journalists, for example, do most of the things that social scientists do. They try to collect accurate information (data); they try to organize and analyze the information they gather so that it all makes sense; and they report their conclusions in writing to an audience (typically, the general public). Do journalists conduct social research? Yes, they often do, but they are not considered social scientists. It is important to contrast social research with a variety of other activities so that the special features of the social scientific way of representing social life are clear.

The main concern of this chapter is what is and what isn't social research. I first examine conventional answers to the question of the distinctiveness of social research. Most of these conventional answers are too restrictive—too many social researchers are excluded by these answers. Next, I compare social research to some other ways of telling about society to illustrate important similarities and differences. Too often social researchers are portrayed as ivory tower academics poring over their computer printouts. In fact, social researchers are quite diverse. Some have a lot in common with free-lance writers; others are more like laboratory scientists. Finally, I argue that it is important to focus on how social researchers construct their representations of social life for their audiences, especially for other social scientists. By examining the nature of the representations that social researchers construct, it is possible to see the distinctive features of social research—the social scientific way of representing social life.

JOURNALISM AND SOCIAL RESEARCH: THE SIMILARITIES

Journalists write about what's going on in society; they represent social life. Most often they report on current events, but they also write stories that offer historical perspectives and in-depth interpretations. Journalists also address major trends and social problems, not just the news of the day, and sometimes these reports are very similar to the research reports of social scientists. Also like social researchers, journalists develop special topic areas: some focus on political events; some on economic trends; some on women's issues; some report on everyday life; some analyze major international events and issues; and so on. Virtually all aspects of social life fall within the purview of journalism. If people will read about a topic, journalists will report on it.

Regardless of topic, journalists all face the same problem regarding "evidence" or "facts." This problem parallels that of social researchers facing "data." Like social researchers, journalists collect an enormous amount of information that could become evidence for a report. They have to decide what is relevant as evidence and then identify the most pertinent bits. This process of gathering and selecting evidence goes hand in hand with developing the focus of the investigation and the report. As the report becomes more of a finished product—as it coalesces in the mind of the journalist as a story—the collection of evidence becomes more focused and more selective. Initial ideas become leads; some leads bear fruit and are pursued vigorously; the story takes shape. Lots of potential evidence and potential stories are left behind.

The same holds true for social research. Social scientists must select from the vast amount of information that social life offers and construct their representations from carefully selected bits and slices. Data collection (that is, the process of gathering evidence) is necessarily selective, and becomes much more so as an investigation progresses. The researcher may start with a few ideas (for example, sensitizing concepts) and maybe a working hypothesis or two. These ideas determine the initial data collection efforts. As more is learned about the subject, either through data collection or data analysis, the research becomes more focused and fewer avenues are kept open. As the results take shape in the mind of the investigator, much of what was initially thought to be important may be cast aside as irrelevant.

Both social researchers and journalists find that, in the end, much of the evidence they collected at the start of the investigation was based on false leads, and that they could have been much more efficient in their collection of evidence if only they had known at the start what they learned toward the end of the investigation. The collection of evidence is necessarily selective because potentially there is an infinite quantity of evidence. However, both journalists and social researchers find that in the end they cannot use all the evidence they have collected.

There is great danger in both journalism and social research that follows from this need for *selective* gathering of evidence. Sometimes what may be a false lead is not recognized as such, and it may become the focus or at least an important part of the investigation. False leads pose serious problems in both journalism and social research because they may be biased by accepted knowledge, stereotypes, and common, everyday understandings of social life. For example, there are two common images of the African-American male—the dangerous, inner-city ghetto teenager and the upwardly mobile young professional. As Mitchell Duneier (1992) points out in *Slim's Table*, both of these images are media creations and have little to do with the lives of most African-American men. Research or journalism that uses these images as starting points will fail to arrive at valid representations of the experiences of most African-American males.

Another problem is the simple fact that people questioned or studied by a journalist or a social researcher may unconsciously or deliberately seek to deceive those who study them. Both social researchers and journalists strive to get valid evidence. For journalists, this effort is often described as reporting "just the facts" or at least trying to balance different views of the same facts. Journalists check different sources against each other and maintain constant vigilance in their efforts to detect deception. After all, interested parties may have a lot to gain if their version of "the facts" is accepted by a journalist and then reported as the one true version.

While social researchers are less often the target of outright deception, like journalists they must deal with bias, distortion, and cover-up. For example, while it might seem a simple matter to determine the percentage of homosexuals among adult males in the United States, social researchers have come up with a range of answers, from less than 2% to about 10%. (The more recent studies tend to offer the lower estimates.) There are various reasons for this wide range; one of them is surely people's reluctance to discuss their sexual behavior openly.

"Social facts" can be as elusive as bias-free journalism. Thus, the two fields have comparable obsessions with "truth," or **validity** as it is known to social researchers. For journalism this is expressed by a concern for reporting only verifiable information. Thus, journalists are very concerned with fact-checking and with the authority of their sources of information.

Social researchers' concern for validity is seen in their efforts to verify that their data collection and measurement procedures work the way they claim. Researchers attempting to determine the percentage of homosexuals among adult males in the United States, for example, would have to contend with a variety of threats to the validity of their measurement procedures. People with more varied sex lives, for example, are more likely to agree to talk about their sex lives or to fill out questionnaires on their sexual behavior. This **bias** would surely increase the size of the estimate of the percentage of homosexuals based on survey data. Thus, researchers would have to find some way to address this threat to the validity of their measurement procedures and their estimate of the percentage of homosexuals.

Another similarity between journalists and social researchers is that they must analyze and arrange evidence before they can offer their representations of social life for wider consumption (for example, as news or research reports). As evidence is gathered and selected, the investigator tries to make sense of it. Ongoing analysis of the evidence simplifies the task of what to collect next. Once the gathering and selecting of evidence is complete, the *analysis* of evidence intensifies. A thorough analysis of evidence, in both journalism and social research, is an important preliminary to arranging it for presentation in a report.

When social life is represented, both social researchers and journalists make connections in their data. When a journalist reconstructs the story of a political scandal, for example, connections and timing are crucially important to the representation of the scandal. It matters who said or did what and when. The goal of analysis is to make these connections. In social research, connections are often *causal* in nature. An analysis of a decaying section of a city, for example, might focus on the long-term economic and social forces responsible for the decline.

Journalists analyze their evidence to make sure that the proper connections are made; then they arrange the evidence for presentation in a report. Readers want to know the big picture—the journalist's final synthesis of the evidence—not all the bits of evidence that the journalist collected along the way before arriving at a synthesis. It's the same with social research. It's not possible to include all the evidence the social researcher collected when reporting conclusions. The evidence that is represented in a research report is a select subset of the evidence collected, which of course is a select subset of the vast volume of potential evidence.

The similarities between the work of journalists and the work of social researchers are striking. Of necessity, they both selectively gather evidence relevant to specific questions, analyze it, and then select a subset of the evidence they have gathered for reporting. The report itself is an attempt to construct for the reader the investigator's conclusions regarding the evidence. Evidence is arranged and condensed in a way that illustrates the investigator's conclusions. In effect, the reader is presented with the investigator's arrangement of a fraction of the evidence collected, a small fraction of the potential evidence. Thus, in both social research and journalism representations of social life (the end products of efforts to tell about society) are condensed descriptions structured according to the investigator's ideas. These representations emerge from a systematic dialogue between the investigator's ideas and evidence.

HOW SOCIAL RESEARCH DIFFERS

Journalists write for wide audiences, usually for the literate public as a whole. They hope to reach as many people as possible. The primary audience for social researchers, by contrast, is social scientists and other professionals. Many social researchers hope to reach, eventually, the literate public with their findings and their ideas, and some social researchers write for these audiences. But most social researchers expect to reach these general audiences indirectly—through the work of others such as journalists and free-lance writers who use the work and the ideas of social researchers.

The importance of this difference can be seen clearly in the work of social scientists who write for several different target audiences. When their primary audience is social scientists and other professionals they emphasize, among other things, technical aspects of their research and its place in a specific research literature—that is, its relation to the work of others who have researched the same or similar topics. When these same researchers write for the general public, however, they usually skip over technical aspects of the research and the discussion of the work of others (research literatures) and focus instead on the relevance of their own research findings to the concerns of the general public.

The point is not that the nature of the target audience shapes the nature of the representation, although this is certainly an important consideration. Rather, it is pinpointing the distinctiveness of the social scientific way of representing social life. The distinctiveness of the social scientific way of telling about society is most apparent when representations of social life produced *by* social scientists *for* social scientists are examined, especially given the fact that social scientists consider it their professional responsibility to monitor and evaluate the quality of each other's representations. It is important, therefore, to address how social researchers construct these representations.

What makes a representation of social life especially relevant to a social scientist? Briefly, social scientific audiences expect social scientific representations:

- to address phenomena that are socially significant in some way,
- to be relevant to social theory, either directly or indirectly,
- to be based on or incorporate large amounts of appropriate evidence, purposefully collected, and
- to result from some form of systematic analysis of this evidence.

While *some* of these features are found in many journalistic representations of social life, *all* four features are commonly found together in most social scientific representations. Because social scientific representations of social life have these four features, they tend to be better grounded in *ideas* and *evidence* than other kinds of representations. Ultimately, it is their strong grounding in ideas and evidence that makes these representations especially relevant to social scientists.

Social Researchers Address Phenomena that Are Socially Significant

Many of the things that social researchers address are socially significant simply because they are general. Social scientists address all kinds of rates and percentages, for example, used to characterize large numbers of people (the homicide rate, the percentage of voters, and so on), and they study variation in these rates (for example, why some groups murder more than others, why some groups vote more than others, and so on). Sometimes rates and percentages are compared across whole countries (for example, rates of infant mortality in Asian versus Latin American countries). While a single murder might be relevant to theory in some way, common acts are more often studied across large populations as rates and percentages.

It is not simply generality and the possibility of studying rates that makes phenomena socially significant, however. Some phenomena are significant not because they are common, but because they are rare, unusual, or extreme in some way. A researcher might study a business, for example, that attempts to maintain a completely egalitarian structure, with no one giving orders to anyone else. How do they get things done? Or a researcher might study a country with great ethnic and cultural diversity but little ethnic conflict. How is ethnic competition contained? Another researcher might study a poor immigrant group that assimilated quickly and overcame extreme prejudice while achieving breathtaking economic gains. How did they do it when so many other groups have struggled and failed? Finally, another researcher might study women who dress and pass as men. What do they gain? What do they lose?

These phenomena are worth studying because they are uncommon. However, they are studied not simply because of their interest value, but because they are relevant to how social researchers think about what is more common and thus challenge their basic assumptions about social life.

Social phenomena may also be selected for study because of their historical significance. An understanding of slavery, for example, is vitally important to the understanding and interpretation of race in the United States today. Similarly, an understanding of the relations between the United States and its Latin American neighbors, particularly Mexico and Puerto Rico, is central to an understanding of Hispanic Americans. One key to understanding post–World War II U.S. society is the "Bomb" and other nuclear weapons and the collective perception of their destructive potential. Our thinking about the military and military life in general was strongly influenced by the experience of the Vietnam War and, more recently, the Gulf War. In short, many different aspects of our history have an impact on who we are today. It is difficult to know and understand American society without exploring the impact of its history.

Social Researchers Connect Their Work to Social Theory

Social scientific representations of social life almost always address social theory in some way. A study of homicide rates is relevant to theories of social conflict. A study of women who dress and pass as men is relevant to theories that address gender differences and power. But what is social theory?

Most social scientists participate, in one way or another, in a set of loosely connected, ongoing conversations about abstract ideas with other social scientists and social thinkers. These conversations address basic features and processes of social life and seek to answer enduring questions. These conversations started before any of today's social scientists were born and more than likely will continue long after they have all died. While they often focus on abstract social concepts that have been around a long time (like the concept of equality, or the concept of society), they also shift over time, sometimes taking up new topics (gender and power, for example), sometimes returning to old topics (for example, the degree to which a group's culture can change in the absence of significant changes in material conditions such as level of technology).

These long-term, ongoing conversations provide a background for the development of specific social theories that are spelled out in the research process. A **social theory** is an attempt to specify as clearly as possible a set of ideas that pertain to a particular phenomenon or set of phenomena. Clarity is important because social theory guides research. Sometimes the ideas that make up a theory are expressed clearly at the start of a research project in the form of specific assumptions, concepts, and relationships. Research that seeks to follow the plan of the scientific method needs such clarity from the start. The researcher uses theory as a basis for formulating a specific hypothesis that is then tested with data especially collected for the test.

Sometimes, however, ideas are clarified in the course of the research. This approach is common in research that seeks to use evidence to formulate new ideas. Consider the social researcher who studies something a journalist might study, a new religious cult. More than likely, the researcher will compare this cult to a variety of other cults and in this way show the relevance of the cult to theories of religion. By contrast, a journalist might simply focus on the bizarre or unusual practices that set this cult apart from the rest of society.

The social researcher might also question the label "religious cult." Suppose the cult was also very successful at marketing a particular product, something produced by members of the cult (see Zablocki 1980). Is it a cult or is it a new type of business enterprise? Which set of social theories, those addressing religious cults or those addressing economic organizations, is more useful when trying to understand this group? What are the implications of this group for either set of theories? In most social research, there is a clear *dialogue* with social theory that is an essential part of the research process.

Social Researchers Use Large Amounts of Purposefully Collected Evidence

Most social researchers summarize mountains of evidence in the representations they construct. Social researchers tend to incorporate a lot of in-depth information about a limited number of cases (as in much **qualitative research**) or a limited amount of information about a large number of cases (as in most **quantitative research**) in their representations. Either way, they collect a lot of data. When social researchers construct representations, they try to incorporate as much of this evidence as possible, either by condensing and summarizing it or by highlighting the essential features of the cases they study.

The audiences for social research expect representations to summarize large amounts of evidence. In journalism, investigation is often focused on fact checking—making sure that each piece of a story is correct. Social researchers, by contrast, usually focus on the "weight" of the evidence. For example, in survey research, the investigator expects some respondents to make mistakes when they try to recall how they voted in the last election. Such mistakes are not fatal because the investigator is interested primarily in broad tendencies in the data—in the average voter or in the tendencies of broad categories of voters. Do richer respondents tend to vote more often for Republican candidates? Social researchers *do* strive for precision—they try to get the facts right, but when they construct representations, their primary concern is to present a synthesis of the facts that both makes sense and is true to the evidence.

While large amounts of evidence are incorporated into most social scientific representations, it is important to recognize that the evidence that is used is *purposefully collected*. In much social research, investigators put together a specific research design. An investigator's **research design** is a plan for collecting and analyzing evidence that will make it possible for the investigator to answer whatever questions he or she has posed. The design of an investigation touches almost all aspects of the research. The important ones to consider here are those that pertain to social scientists' use of large amounts of purposefully collected evidence. These include:

1. **Data collection technique**. Social researchers use a variety of different techniques: observation, interviewing, participating in activities, use of telephone and other types of surveys, collection of official statistics or historical archives, use of census materials and other evidence collected by governments, records of historical events, and so on. The choice of data collection technique is in large part shaped by the nature of the research question. All these techniques can yield enormous amounts of evidence.

2. **Sampling**. In most research situations, investigators confront a staggering surplus of data, and they often need to devise strategies for sampling the available data. The survey researcher who wants to study racial differences in voting does not need to know every voter's preference, just enough to make an accurate assessment of tendencies. A **random sample** of 1,000 voters might be sufficient. A researcher who wants to study how protest demonstrations have changed over the last twenty years based on an in-depth investigation of fifty such demonstrations must develop a strategy for selecting which fifty to study.

3. **Sample selection bias**. Whenever researchers use only a subset of the potential evidence, as when they sample, they have to worry about the **representativeness** of the subset they use. A study of poor people that uses telephone interviews is not likely to result in a representative sample because many, many poor people (in addition to thousands of homeless people) cannot afford phones. Likewise, the researcher who

selects fifty protest demonstrations to see how these demonstrations have changed over the last twenty years must make sure that each one selected is sufficiently representative of the period from which it was selected.

4. **Data collection design**. Sometimes researchers collect a lot of evidence but then realize that they don't have the right kinds of evidence for the questions that concern them most. For example, a researcher interested in the differences between upper income whites and upper income blacks may discover all too late that a random sample of a large population typically will not yield enough cases in these two categories, especially upper income blacks, to permit a thorough comparison. Most issues in data collection design concern the *appropriateness* of the data collected for the questions asked. A study of the impact of a new job training program that provides workers with new skills, for example, should follow these workers for several years, not several weeks or months. The *timing* of data collection (or "observation") is an important issue in almost all studies. More generally, social researchers, more than most others who represent social life, recognize that the nature of their evidence constrains the questions that they can ask of it (see especially Lieberson 1985).

Systematic collection of evidence is important even in research that is more open-ended and less structured from the start of the investigation (as in most qualitative research). Often in research of this type, issues of sampling and selection bias are addressed in the course of the research, as the investigator's representation takes shape. A researcher who discovers some new aspect of a group in the course of informal observation will develop a data collection strategy that allows assessment of the generality of the phenomenon (Glaser and Strauss 1967; Strauss 1987).

Social Researchers Analyze Evidence Systematically

The power of the analytic tools social researchers apply to their evidence is sometimes staggering. Powerful computers, for example, are needed to examine the relationship between household income and number of children across the hundreds of thousands of households included in census data banks. Do families with larger incomes have more or fewer children? It's very difficult to answer this question without a computer and sophisticated statistical software. Most social scientific representations result from the application of some systematic technique of data analysis to a large body of evidence. Different procedures for analyzing evidence are used for different kinds of evidence.

Consider the researcher interested in why some women try to dress and pass as men. First, it is clear that to answer this question it would be necessary to interview a substantial number of women who do this. Some effort should be made to talk to women from as many different walks of life as possible. Perhaps women from different ethnic or class backgrounds do it for different reasons. Maybe some are lesbian and some straight, and their reasons differ. It might be necessary to interview thirty to sixty women. Because it is a sensitive topic, and rapport between these women and the researcher is important, these interviews would need to be in depth, perhaps stretching two to four hours each. Assume fifty women are interviewed for 3 hours each. The researcher then would have a total of 150 hours of taped interviews. How can this large body of evidence be shaped into a representation of the social significance and meaning of cross-dressing for these women?

Social scientists have devised a variety of techniques for systematically analyzing this kind of evidence. Most focus on clarifying the concepts and categories that help make sense of this mass of evidence. The issue here is not the specific techniques, but the fact that most audiences for social research expect the representation of this kind of evidence to be based on systematic analysis of the entire body of evidence. A journalistic representation, by contrast, might simply tell the stories of a handful of the most interesting cases.

More generally, techniques for the systematic analysis of data are a central part of research design. As noted, the term *research design* embraces all aspects of the collection and analysis of data. Just as most researchers develop a systematic plan for the collection of data—to make sure that they have evidence that is relevant to the questions they ask—they also develop a plan for analyzing their data. In the cross-dressing study, the plan would involve how to make best use of the hundreds of hours of taped interviews. How does one go about identifying commonalities in the things these women said and how they said them? In a very different type of study, say a survey addressing the relationship between social class and attitudes about abortion, the analysis plan would focus on the measurement of the main variables (social class and attitudes about abortion) and different ways of relating them statistically.

REFERENCES

Becker, Howard S. 1986. "Telling about Society." In *Doing Things Together*, 121–36. Evanston: Northwestern University Press.

Duneier, Mitchell. 1992. *Slim's Table: Race, Respectability, and Masculinity*. Chicago: University of Chicago.

Evans, Peter. 1979. *Dependent Development: The Alliance of Multinational, State, and Local Capital in Brazil*. Princeton: Princeton University Press.

Glaser, Barney G., and Anselm L. Strauss. 1967. *The Discovery of Grounded Theory: Strategies for Qualitative Research*. London: Weidenfeld and Nicholson.

Hochschild, Arlie. 1983. *The Managed Heart*. Berkeley: University of California Press.

Lieberson, Stanley. 1985. *Making It Count: The Improvement of Social Research and Theory*. Berkeley: University of California Press.

Massey, Douglas, and Nancy Denton. 1993. *American Apartheid: Segregation and the Making of the Underclass*. Cambridge, Mass.: Harvard University Press.

Strauss, Anselm. 1987. *Qualitative Analysis for Social Scientists*. New York: Cambridge University Press.

Zablocki, Benjamin David. 1980. *The Joyful Community*. Chicago: University of Chicago Press.

Excerpt from *Damned Lies and Statistics: Untangling Numbers from the Media, Politicians, and Activists*

JOEL BEST

Nineteenth-century Americans worried about prostitution; reformers called it *"the* social evil" and warned that many women prostituted themselves. How many? For New York City alone, there were dozens of estimates: In 1833, for instance, reformers published a report declaring that there were "not less than 10,000" prostitutes in New York (equivalent to about 10 percent of the city's female population); in 1866, New York's Methodist bishop claimed there were more prostitutes (11,000 to 12,000) than Methodists in the city; other estimates for the period ranged as high as 50,000. These reformers hoped that their reports of widespread prostitution would prod the authorities to act, but city officials' most common response was to challenge the reformers' numbers. Various investigations by the police and grand juries produced their own, much lower estimates; for instance, one 1872 police report counted only 1,223 prostitutes (by that time, New York's population included nearly half a million females). Historians see a clear pattern in these cycles of competing statistics: Ministers and reformers "tended to inflate statistics,"[1] while "police officials tended to underestimate prostitution."[2]

Antiprostitution reformers tried to use big numbers to arouse public outrage. Big numbers meant there was a big problem: if New York had tens of thousands of prostitutes, something ought to be done. In response, the police countered that there were relatively few prostitutes—an indication that they were doing a good job. These dueling statistics resemble other, more recent debates. During Ronald Reagan's presidency, for

Best, Joel. 2001. "The Importance of Social Statistics" from *Damned Lies and Statistics: Untangling Numbers from the Media, Politicians, and Activists*. Berkeley: University of California Press.

example, activists claimed that three million Americans were homeless, while the Reagan administration insisted that the actual number of homeless people was closer to 300,000, one-tenth what the activists claimed. In other words, homeless activists argued that homelessness was a big problem that demanded additional government social programs, while the administration argued new programs were not needed to deal with what was actually a much smaller, more manageable problem. Each side presented statistics that justified its policy recommendations, and each criticized the other's numbers. The activists ridiculed the administration's figures as an attempt to cover up a large, visible problem, while the administration insisted that the activists' numbers were unrealistic exaggerations.[3]

Statistics, then, can become weapons in political struggles over social problems and social policy. Advocates of different positions use numbers to make their points ("It's a big problem!" "No, it's not!"). And, as the example of nineteenth-century estimates of prostitution reminds us, statistics have been used as weapons for some time.

THE RISE OF SOCIAL STATISTICS

In fact, the first "statistics" were meant to influence debates over social issues. The term acquired its modern meaning—numeric evidence—in the 1830s, around the time that New York reformers estimated that the city had 10,000 prostitutes. The forerunner of statistics was called "political arithmetic"; these studies—mostly attempts to calculate population size and life expectancy—emerged in seventeenth-century Europe, particularly in England and France. Analysts tried to count births, deaths, and marriages because they believed that a growing population was evidence of a healthy *state;* those who conducted such numeric studies—as well as other, nonquantitative analyses of social and political prosperity—came to be called *statists.* Over time, the statists' social research led to the new term for quantitative evidence: *statistics.*[4]

Early social researchers believed that information about society could help governments devise wise policies. They were well aware of the scientific developments of their day and, like other scientists, they came to value accuracy and objectivity. Counting—quantifying—offered a way of making their studies more precise and let them concisely summarize lots of information. Over time, social research became less theoretical and more quantitative. As the researchers collected and analyzed their data, they began to see patterns. From year to year, they discovered, the numbers of births, deaths, and even marriages remained relatively stable; this stability suggested that social arrangements had an underlying order, that what happened in a society depended on more than simply its government's recent actions, and analysts began paying more attention to underlying social conditions.

By the beginning of the nineteenth century, the social order seemed especially threatened: Cities were larger than ever before; economies were beginning to industrialize; and revolutions in America and France had made it clear that political stability could not be taken for granted. The need for information, for facts that could guide social policy, was greater than ever before. A variety of government agencies began collecting and publishing statistics: the United States and several European countries began conducting regular censuses to collect population statistics; courts, prisons, and police began keeping track of the numbers of crimes and criminals; physicians kept records of patients; educators counted students; and so on. Scholars organized statistical societies to share the results of their studies and to discuss the best methods for gathering and interpreting statistics. And reformers who sought to confront the nineteenth-century's many social problems—the impoverished and the diseased, the fallen woman and the child laborer, the factory workforce and dispossessed agricultural labor—found statistics useful in demonstrating the extent and severity of suffering. Statistics gave both government officials and reformers hard evidence—proof that what they said was true. Numbers offered a kind of precision: Instead of talking about prostitution as a vaguely defined problem, reformers began to make specific, numeric claims (for example, that New York had 10,000 prostitutes).

During the nineteenth century, then, statistics—numeric statements about social life—became an authoritative way to describe social problems. There was growing respect for science, and statistics offered a way to bring the authority of science to debates about social policy. In fact, this had been the main goal of the first statisticians—they wanted to study society through counting and use the resulting numbers to influence social policy. They succeeded; statistics gained widespread acceptance as the best way to measure social problems. Today, statistics continue to play a central role in our efforts to understand these problems. But, beginning in the nineteenth century and continuing through today, social statistics have had two purposes: one public, the other often hidden. Their public purpose is to give an accurate, true description of society. But people also use statistics to support particular views about social problems. Numbers are created and repeated because they supply ammunition for political struggles, and this political purpose is often hidden behind assertions that numbers, simply because they are numbers, must be correct. People use statistics to support particular points of view, and it is naive simply to accept numbers as accurate without examining who is using them and why.

CREATING SOCIAL PROBLEMS

We tend to think of social problems as harsh realities, like gravity or earthquakes, that exist completely independent of human action. But the very term reveals that this is incorrect: *Social* problems are products of what people do.

This is true in two senses. First, we picture social problems as snarls or flaws in the social fabric. Social problems have their causes in society's arrangements; when some women turn to prostitution or some individuals have no homes, we assume that society has failed (although we may disagree over whether that failure involves not providing enough jobs, or not giving children proper moral instruction, or something else). Most people understand that social problems are social in this sense.

But there is a second reason social problems are social. Someone has to bring these problems to our attention, to give them names, describe their causes and characteristics, and so on. Sociologists speak of social problems being "constructed"—that is, created or assembled through the actions of activists, officials, the news media, and other people who draw attention to particular problems.[5] "Social problem" is a label we give to some social conditions, and it is that label that turns a condition we take for granted into something we consider troubling. This means that the processes of identifying and publicizing social problems are important. When we start thinking of prostitution or homelessness as a social problem, we are responding to campaigns by reformers who seek to arouse our concern about the issue.

The creation of a new social problem can be seen as a sort of public drama, a play featuring a fairly standard cast of characters. Often, the leading roles are played by *social activists*—individuals dedicated to promoting a cause, to making others aware of the problem. Activists draw attention to new social problems by holding protest demonstrations, attracting media coverage, recruiting new members to their cause, lobbying officials to do something about the situation, and so on. They are the most obvious, the most visible participants in creating awareness of social problems.

Successful activists attract support from others. The *mass media*—including both the press (reporters for newspapers or television news programs) and entertainment media (such as television talk shows)—relay activists' claims to the general public. Reporters often find it easy to turn those claims into interesting news stories; after all, a new social problem is a fresh topic, and it may affect lots of people, pose dramatic threats, and lead to proposals to change the lives of those involved. Media coverage, especially sympathetic coverage, can make millions of people aware of and concerned about a social problem. Activists need the media to provide that coverage, just as the media depend on activists and other sources for news to report.

Often activists also enlist the support of *experts*—doctors, scientists, economists, and so on—who presumably have special qualifications to talk about the causes and consequences of some social problem. Experts may have done research on the problem and can report their findings. Activists use experts to make claims about social problems seem authoritative, and the mass media often rely on experts' testimonies to make news stories about a new problem seem more convincing. In turn, experts enjoy the respectful attention they receive from activists and the media.[6]

Not all social problems are promoted by struggling, independent activists; creating new social problems is sometimes the work of powerful organizations and institutions. *Government officials* who promote problems range from prominent politicians trying to arouse concern in order to create election campaign issues, to anonymous bureaucrats proposing that their agencies' programs be expanded to solve some social problem. And *businesses, foundations, and other private organizations* sometimes have their own reasons to promote particular social issues. Public and private organizations usually command the resources needed to organize effective campaigns to create social problems. They can afford to hire experts to conduct research, to sponsor and encourage activists, and to publicize their causes in ways that attract media attention.[7]

In other words, when we become aware of—and start to worry about—some new social problem, our concern is usually the result of efforts by some combination of *problem promoters*—activists, reporters, experts, officials, or private organizations—who have worked to create the sense that this is an important problem, one that deserves our attention. In this sense, people deliberately construct social problems.[8]

Efforts to create or promote social problems, particularly when they begin to attract attention, may inspire opposition. Sometimes this involves officials responding to critics by defending existing policies as adequate. Recall that New York police minimized the number of prostitutes in the city, just as the Reagan administration argued that activists exaggerated the number of homeless persons. In other cases, opposition comes from private interests; for example, the Tobacco Institute (funded by the tobacco industry) became notorious for, over decades, challenging every research finding that smoking was harmful.

Statistics play an important role in campaigns to create—or defuse claims about—new social problems. Most often, such statistics describe the problem's size: There are 10,000 prostitutes in New York City, or three million homeless people. When social problems first come to our attention, perhaps in a televised news report, we're usually given an example or two (perhaps video footage of homeless individuals living on city streets) and then a statistical estimate (of the number of homeless people). Typically this is a big number. Big numbers warn us that the problem is a common one, compelling our attention, concern, and action. The media like to report statistics because numbers seem to be "hard facts"—little nuggets of indisputable truth. Activists trying to draw media attention to a new social problem often find that the press demands statistics: Reporters insist on getting estimates of the problem's size—how many people are affected, how much it costs, and so on. Experts, officials, and private organizations commonly report having studied the problem, and they present statistics based on their research. Thus, the key players in creating new social problems all have reason to present statistics.

In virtually every case, promoters use statistics as ammunition; they choose numbers that will draw attention to or away from a problem, arouse or defuse public concern. People use statistics to support their point of view, to bring others around to their way of thinking. Activists trying to gain recognition for what they believe is a big problem will offer statistics that seem to prove that the problem is indeed a big one (and they may choose to downplay, ignore, or dispute any statistics that might make it seem smaller). The media favor disturbing statistics about big problems because big problems make more interesting, more compelling news, just as experts' research (and the experts themselves) seem more important if their subject is a big, important problem. These concerns lead people to present statistics that support their position, their cause, their interests. There is an old expression that captures this tendency: "Figures may not lie, but liars figure." Certainly we need to understand that people debating social problems choose statistics selectively and present them to support their points of view. Gun-control advocates will be more likely to report the number of children killed by guns, while opponents of gun control will prefer to count citizens who use guns to defend themselves from attack. Both numbers may be correct, but most people debating gun control present only the statistic that bolsters their position.[9]

THE PUBLIC AS AN INNUMERATE AUDIENCE

Most claims drawing attention to new social problems aim to persuade all of us—that is, the members of the general public. We are the audience, or at least one important audience, for statistics and other claims about social problems. If the public becomes convinced that prostitution or homelessness is a serious problem, then something is more likely to be done: officials will take action, new policies will begin, and so on. Therefore, campaigns to create social problems use statistics to help arouse the public's concern.

This is not difficult. The general public tends to be receptive to claims about new social problems, and we rarely think critically about social problems statistics. Recall that the media like to report statistics because numbers seem to be factual, little nuggets of truth. The public tends to agree; we usually treat statistics as facts.

In part, this is because we are innumerate. Innumeracy is the mathematical equivalent of illiteracy; it is "an inability to deal comfortably with the fundamental notions of number and chance."[10] Just as some people cannot read or read poorly, many people have trouble thinking clearly about numbers.

One common innumerate error involves not distinguishing among large numbers. A very small child may be pleased by the gift of a penny; a slightly older child understands that a penny or even a dime can't buy much, but a dollar can buy some things, ten dollars considerably more, and a hundred dollars a great deal (at least from a child's point of view). Most adults clearly grasp what one can do with a hundred, a thousand, ten thousand, even one hundred thousand dollars, but then our imaginations begin to fail us. Big numbers blend together: a million, a billion, a trillion— what's the difference? They're all big numbers. (Actually, of course, there are tremendous differences. The difference between a million and a billion is the difference between one dollar and one thousand dollars; the difference between a million and a trillion is the difference between one dollar and a million dollars.)

Because many people have trouble appreciating the differences among big numbers, they tend to uncritically accept social statistics (which often, of course, feature big numbers). What does it matter, they may say, whether there are 300,000 homeless or 3,000,000?—either way, it's a big number. They'd never make this mistake dealing with smaller numbers; everyone understands that it makes a real difference whether there'll be three people or thirty coming by tomorrow night for dinner. A difference (thirty is ten times greater than three) that seems obvious with smaller, more familiar numbers gets blurred when we deal with bigger numbers (3,000,000 is ten times greater than 300,000). If society is going to feed the homeless, having an accurate count is just as important as it is for an individual planning to host three—or thirty—dinner guests.

Innumeracy—widespread confusion about basic mathematical ideas—means that many statistical claims about social problems don't get the critical attention they deserve. This is not simply because an innumerate public is being manipulated by advocates who cynically promote inaccurate statistics. Often, statistics about social problems originate with sincere, well-meaning people who are themselves innumerate; they may not grasp the full implications of what they are saying. Similarly, the media are not immune to innumeracy; reporters commonly repeat the figures their sources give them without bothering to think critically about them.

The result can be a social comedy. Activists want to draw attention to a problem—prostitution, homelessness, or whatever. The press asks the activists for statistics—How many prostitutes? How many homeless? Knowing that big numbers indicate big problems and knowing that it will be hard to get action unless people can be convinced a big problem exists (and sincerely believing that there is a big problem), the activists produce a big estimate, and the press, having no good way to check the number, simply publicizes it. The general public—most of us suffering from at least a mild case of innumeracy—tends to accept the figure without question. After all, it's a big number, and there's no real difference among big numbers.

ORGANIZATIONAL PRACTICES AND OFFICIAL STATISTICS

One reason we tend to accept statistics uncritically is that we assume that numbers come from experts who know what they're doing. Often these experts work for government agencies, such as the U.S. Bureau of the Census, and producing statistics is part of their job. Data that come from the government—crime rates, unemployment rates, poverty rates—are *official statistics*.[11] There is a natural tendency to treat these figures as straightforward facts that cannot be questioned.

This ignores the way statistics are produced. All statistics, even the most authoritative, are created by people. This does not mean that they are inevitably flawed or wrong, but it does mean that we ought to ask ourselves just how the statistics we encounter were created.

Let's say a couple decides to get married. This requires going to a government office, taking out a marriage license, and having whoever conducts the marriage ceremony sign and file the license. Periodically, officials add up the number of marriage licenses filed and issue a report on the number of marriages. This is a relatively straightforward bit of recordkeeping, but notice that the accuracy of marriage statistics depends on couples' willingness to cooperate with the procedures. For example, imagine a couple who decide to "get married" without taking out a license; they might even have a wedding ceremony, yet their marriage will not be counted in the official record. Or consider couples that cohabit—live together—without getting married; there is no official record of their living arrangement. And there is the added problem of recordkeeping: is the system for filing, recording, and generally keeping track of marriages accurate, or do mistakes occur? These examples remind us that the official number of marriages reflects certain bureaucratic decisions about what will be counted and how to do the counting.

Now consider a more complicated example: statistics on suicide. Typically, a coroner decides which deaths are suicides. This can be relatively straightforward: perhaps the dead individual left behind a note clearly stating an intent to commit suicide. But often there is no note, and the coroner must gather evidence that points to suicide—perhaps the deceased is known to have been depressed, the death occurred in a locked house, the cause of death was an apparently self-inflicted gunshot to the head, and so on. There are two potential mistakes here. The first is that the coroner may label a death a "suicide" when, in fact, there was another cause (in mystery novels, at least, murder often is disguised as suicide). The second possibility for error is that the coroner may assign another cause of death to what was, in fact, a suicide. This is probably a greater risk, because some people who kill themselves want to conceal that fact (for example, some single-car automobile fatalities are suicides designed to look like accidents so that the individual's family can avoid embarrassment or collect life insurance benefits). In addition, surviving family members may be ashamed by a relative's suicide, and they may press the coroner to assign another cause of death, such as accident.

In other words, official records of suicide reflect coroners' judgments about the causes of death in what can be ambiguous circumstances. The act of suicide tends to be secretive—it usually occurs in private—and the motives of the dead cannot always be known. Labeling some deaths as "suicides" and others as "homicides," "accidents," or whatever will sometimes be wrong, although we cannot know exactly how often. Note, too, that individual coroners may assess cases differently; we might imagine one coroner who is relatively willing to label deaths suicides, and another who is very reluctant to do so. Presented with the same set of cases, the first coroner might find many more suicides than the second.[12]

It is important to appreciate that coroners view their task as classifying individual deaths, as giving each one an appropriate label, rather than as compiling statistics for suicide rates. Whatever statistical reports come out of coroners' offices (say, total number of suicides in the jurisdiction during the past year) are by-products of their real work (classifying individual deaths). That is, coroners are probably more concerned with being able to justify their decisions in individual cases than they are with whatever over-all statistics emerge from those decisions.

The example of suicide records reveals that all official statistics are prod-ucts—and often by-products—of decisions by various officials: not just cor-oners, but also the humble clerks who fill out and file forms, the exalted supervisors who prepare summary reports, and so on. These people make choices (and sometimes errors) that shape whatever statistics finally emerge from their organization or agency, and the organization provides a context for those choices. For example, the law requires coroners to choose among a specified set of causes for death: homicide, suicide, accident, natural causes, and so on. That list of causes reflects our culture. Thus, our laws do not allow coroners to list "witchcraft" as a cause of death, although that might be considered a reasonable choice in other societies. We can imagine differ-ent laws that would give coroners different arrays of choices: Perhaps there might be no category for suicide; perhaps people who kill themselves might be considered ill, and their deaths listed as occurring from natural causes; or perhaps suicides might be grouped with homicides in a single category of deaths caused by humans. In other words, official statistics reflect what sociologists call *organizational practices*—the organization's culture and struc-ture shape officials' actions, and those actions determine whatever statistics finally emerge.

Now consider an even more complicated example. Police officers have a complex job; they must maintain order, enforce the law, and assist citizens in a variety of ways. Unlike the coroner who faces a relatively short list of choices in assigning cause of death, the police have to make all sorts of decisions. For example, police responding to a call about a domestic dispute (say, a fight between husband and wife) have several, relatively ill-defined options. Perhaps they should arrest someone; perhaps the wife wants her husband arrested—or perhaps she says she does not want that to happen; perhaps the officers ought to encourage the couple to separate for the night; perhaps they ought to offer to take the wife to a women's shelter; perhaps they ought to try talking to the couple to calm them down; perhaps they find that talking doesn't work, and then pick arrest or a shel-ter as a second choice; perhaps they decide that the dispute has already been settled, or that there is really nothing wrong. Police must make deci-sions about how to respond in such cases, and some—but probably not all—of those choices will be reflected in official statistics. If officers make an arrest, the incident will be recorded in arrest statistics, but if the officers decide to deal with the incident informally (by talking with the couple until they calm down), there may be no statistical record of what happens. The choices officers make depend on many factors. If the domestic dispute call comes near the end of the officers' shift, they may favor quick solutions. If their department has a new policy to crack down on domestic disputes, officers will be more likely to make arrests. All these decisions, each shaped by various considerations, will affect whatever statistics eventually summarize the officers' actions.[13]

Like our earlier examples of marriage records and coroners labeling suicides, the example of police officers dealing with domestic disputes reveals that officials make decisions (relatively straightforward for marriage records, more complicated for coroners, and far less clear-cut in the case of the police), that official statistics are by-products of those decisions (police officers probably give even less thought than coroners to the statistical outcomes of their decisions), and that organizational practices form the context for those decisions (while there may be relatively little variation in how marriage records are kept, organizational practices likely differ more among coroners' offices, and there is great variation in how police deal with their complex decisions, with differences among departments, precincts, officers, and so on). In short, even official statistics are social products, shaped by the people and organizations that create them.

THINKING ABOUT STATISTICS AS SOCIAL PRODUCTS

The lesson should be clear: Statistics—even official statistics such as crime rates, unemployment rates, and census counts—are products of social activity. We sometimes talk about statistics as though they are facts that simply exist, like rocks, completely independent of people, and that people gather statistics much as rock collectors pick up stones. This is wrong. All statistics are created through people's actions: People have to decide what to count and how to count it, people have to do the counting and the other calculations, and people have to interpret the resulting statistics, to decide what the numbers mean. All statistics are social products, the results of people's efforts.

Once we understand this, it becomes clear that we should not simply accept statistics by uncritically treating numbers as true or factual. If people create statistics, then those numbers need to be assessed, evaluated. Some statistics are pretty good; they reflect people's best efforts to measure social problems carefully, accurately, and objectively. But other numbers are bad statistics—figures that may be wrong, even wildly wrong. We need to be able to sort out the good statistics from the bad. There are three basic questions that deserve to be asked whenever we encounter a new statistic.

1. *Who created this statistic?* Every statistic has its authors, its creators. Sometimes a number comes from a particular individual. On other occasions, large organizations (such as the Bureau of the Census) claim author-

ship (although each statistic undoubtedly reflects the work of particular people within the organization).

In asking who the creators are, we ought to be less concerned with the names of the particular individuals who produced a number than with their part in the public drama about statistics. Does a particular statistic come from activists, who are striving to draw attention to and arouse concern about a social problem? Is the number being reported by the media in an effort to prove that this problem is newsworthy? Or does the figure come from officials, bureaucrats who routinely keep track of some social phenomenon, and who may not have much stake in what the numbers show?

2. *Why was this statistic created?* The identities of the people who create statistics are often clues to their motives. In general, activists seek to promote their causes, to draw attention to social problems. Therefore, we can suspect that they will favor large numbers, be more likely to produce them and less likely to view them critically. When reformers cry out that there are many prostitutes or homeless individuals, we need to recognize that their cause might seem less compelling if their numbers were smaller. On the other hand, note that other people may favor lower numbers. Remember that New York police officials produced figures showing that there were very few prostitutes in the city as evidence they were doing a good job. We need to be aware that the people who produce statistics often care what the numbers show, they use numbers as tools of persuasion.

3. *How was this statistic created?* We should not discount a statistic simply because its creators have a point of view, because they view a social problem as more or less serious. Rather, we need to ask how they arrived at the statistic. All statistics are imperfect, but some are far less perfect than others. There is a big difference between a number produced by a wild guess, and one generated through carefully designed research. This is the key question. Once we understand that all social statistics are created by someone and that everyone who creates social statistics wants to prove something (even if that is only that they are careful, reliable, and unbiased), it becomes clear that the methods of creating statistics are key.

NOTES

1. Timothy J. Gilfoyle, *City of Eros: New York City, Prostitution, and the Commercialization of Sex, 1790–1920* (New York: Norton, 1992), p. 57.
2. Marilynn Wood Hill, *Their Sisters' Keepers: Prostitution in New York City, 1830–1870* (Berkeley and Los Angeles: University of California Press, 1993), p. 27. The various estimates cited are documented in this book and in Gilfoyle, *City of Eros.*
3. Christopher Hewitt, "Estimating the Number of Homeless: Media Misrepresentation of an Urban Problem," *Journal of Urban Affairs* 18 (1996): 432–47.
4. On statistics' history, see: M. J. Cullen, *The Statistical Movement in Early Victorian Britain: The Foundations of Empirical Social Research* (Sussex: Harvester Press,

1975); and Theodore M. Porter, *The Rise of Statistical Thinking, 1820–1900* (Princeton: Princeton University Press, 1986).

5. There are many studies of the social construction of social problems. For introductions to this approach, see: Malcolm Spector and John I. Kitsuse, *Constructing Social Problems* (Menlo Park, Calif.: Cummings, 1977); Joel Best, ed., *Images of Issues: Typifying Contemporary Social Problems*, 2d ed. (Hawthorne, N.Y.: Aldine de Gruyter, 1995); and Donileen R. Loseke, *Thinking about Social Problems* (Hawthorne, N.Y.: Aldine de Gruyter, 1999).

6. On statistics produced by activists and experts, see Neil Gilbert, "Advocacy Research and Social Policy," *Crime and Justice* 20 (1997): 101–48.

7. On powerful institutions' ability to produce statistics that promote their ends, see Cynthia Crossen, *Tainted Truth: The Manipulation of Fact in America* (New York: Simon & Schuster, 1994).

8. I am not implying that there is anything wrong with calling attention to social problems. In fact, this book can be seen as my effort to construct "bad statistics" as a problem that ought to concern people.

9. Gary Kleck, *Targeting Guns: Firearms and Their Control* (Hawthorne, N.Y.: Aldine de Gruyter, 1997).

10. John Allen Paulos, *Innumeracy: Mathematical Illiteracy and Its Consequences* (New York: Random House, 1988): p. 3.

11. John I. Kitsuse and Aaron V. Cicourel, "A Note on the Uses of Official Statistics," *Social Problems* 11 (1963): 131–39; Robert Bogdan and Margret Ksander, "Policy Data as a Social Process," *Human Organization* 39 (1980): 302–9.

12. On suicide recordkeeping, see Jack D. Douglas, *The Social Meanings of Suicide* (Princeton: Princeton University Press, 1967).

13. There are many studies of the effect of organizational practices on statistics produced by the police; for example, see Richard McCleary, Barbara C. Nienstedt, and James M. Erven, "Uniform Crime Reports as Organizational Outcomes," *Social Problems* 29 (1982): 361–72.

PART 2

WHAT UNITES US?

Culture and Socialization

INTRODUCTION

Humans have the capacity to transmit knowledge from one generation to the next. In theory, this allows us to "progress" over time. Each generation does not have to learn by trial and error which foods are poisonous, for example. We know which foods are safe, how to acquire and prepare them, and which are healthiest for us. The process by which we learn about food (and many other things) is called socialization. We learn the material aspects of life (what to eat, how to dress, what we consider shelter, etc.) and the intangible aspects, including attitudes, values, and actions appropriate to our society. A sociological way to say this is that we learn *culture* through *socialization*. There are numerous agents of socialization; in the earliest stages of life, family is the primary agent of socialization; as we get older, other agents are introduced: peers, teachers, media. Socialization doesn't end when we become adults. Think about becoming a college student, starting a new job, or joining a club or team. Early socialization is called *primary socialization*, and later socialization is called *secondary socialization*. The advantage of socialization is that it teaches us how to behave and how we can expect those around us to act and respond. It is a process that creates continuity of society over time. Our first reading points out, though, that there is also room for change.

The first passage in the section is Howard Becker's take on defining "culture" sociologically. Becker's view differs from an anthropological conception of culture which historically has viewed culture as static, unchanging, and found in artifacts (material culture) and tradition (immaterial culture). Becker counters that culture is adaptive, that we create it through our interactions, and that it is continuously being produced. His view of culture provides a mechanism by which change can occur. He uses the very American and fairly recent (in human times) cultural creation of jazz as a vehicle to explain the process. Unlike lengthy and complex definitions of culture sometimes provided by anthropologists, Becker's definition is simple: Culture is "the shared understandings that people use to coordinate their activities."

The second selection, *The First R: How Children Learn Race and Racism*, is an ethnographic account of pre-schoolers' interactions around race. Pre-school is a time of intense socialization when children are learning, re-creating, and creating culture. The authors of this piece, Debra Van Ausdale and Joe Feagin, agree with Becker's fluid interpretation of culture. They

65

note that there are variations among children in how they respond to social forces and they do not simply accept some pre-packaged "culture." In particular, the children pick and choose varying aspects of their racial roles. In the excerpt, one of the sociologists (Debi) is an observer (ethnographer) in a small pre-school. This is a qualitative account of processes taking place in one small sample in one school. The strength of ethnography is not in its capacity to generalize, but its capacity to give rich detail and uncover specific processes. In this case, we learn that the power of race and ethnicity is known and exerted early on. The evidence shows the perpetuation of racism by the children despite an explicit multicultural curricula at this school. In terms of socialization and culture, it is important to point out that there are multiple sources of learning for the students. In the account provided in the excerpt, when one child behaves in a racist manner, all of the adults involved (teachers and parents) want to deny that they are the source of this learning and instead blame "neighborhood rednecks." While no one wants to take responsibility for teaching racist attitudes, the children in the study have perceived racist roles from some source in society and some of the children are actively re-creating these roles.

Media is often a target of those who claim that our kids are learning the wrong things, such as racism and violence. The piece excerpted from Juliet Schor's book, *Born to Buy: The Commercialized Child and the New Consumer Culture*, details quantitatively the tremendous influence commercials were having on kids at the end of the twentieth century. Unlike the ethnographic work of Van Ausdale and Feagin, Schor uses quantitative data to make generalizations about the widespread presence of media on the lives of children in America. Media socializes children through commercialization. In an era when parents are less authoritative due to social changes in parenting styles, children have a bigger role in family buying. Megacorporations sway children for a profit. They tell the kids what to like and the kids tell their parents what to buy. Though this book was published not too long ago (2004), it probably seriously underestimates the impact of advertising via electronic media today. All of this, Schor argues, has negative impacts on children, such as increases in mental disorders. Over time, there has been a shifting of which institutions have the most influence of socialization. It used to be that most came from the family, when mom was at home (now she's at work). Today, much of it comes from television and electronics. The lessons that kids are learning are about materialism. The trends that Schor lays out suggest that this isn't good for society.

These articles show that socialization and culture create shared meanings and understandings of how to work together in society. The "content" of the culture, as well as the power of various social agents to pass information onto the next generation, changes over time. This is not always for the better; there's not necessarily human "progress." The article on racism and the one on commercialization show pieces of the process of how children are socialized. With regard to racism, we see that even in a school that attempts to create a non-racist environment, it is only one element of a bigger society in which the history of racism is not easily erased, even through intentional socialization efforts. The excerpt on commercialization demonstrates how different social actors can rise and fall in terms of the power they hold in socialization. Culture and socialization are dynamic. Stepping back and "seeing" these social structures allows us to look at these processes and understand them so we might be empowered to choose to use them. Remember what C. Wright Mills said of the sociological imagination: "By the fact of his living [one] contributes, however minutely, to the shaping of this society and to the course of its history, even as [one] is made by society and by its historical push and shove."

READING 7

Excerpt from *Doing Things Together*

HOWARD BECKER

I was for some years what is called a Saturday night musician, making myself available to whoever called and hired me to play for dances and parties in groups of varying sizes, playing everything from polkas through mambos, jazz, and imitations of Wayne King. Whoever called would tell me where the job was, what time it began, and usually would tell me to wear a dark suit and a bow tie, thus ensuring that the collection of strangers he was hiring would at least look like a band because they would all be dressed more or less alike. When we arrived at work we would introduce ourselves—the chances were, in a city the size of Chicago (where I did much of my playing), that we were in fact strangers—and see whom we knew in common and whether our paths had ever crossed before. The drummer would assemble his drums, the others would put together their instruments and tune up, and when it was time to start the leader would announce the name of a song and a key—"Exactly Like You" in B-flat, for instance—and we would begin to play. We not only began at the same time, but also played background figures that fit the melody someone else was playing and, perhaps most miraculously, ended together. No one in the audience ever guessed that we had never met until twenty minutes earlier. And we kept that up all night, as though we had rehearsed often and played together for years. In a place like Chicago, that scene might be repeated hundreds of times during a weekend.

What I have just described embodies the phenomenon that sociologists have made the core problem of their discipline. The social sciences are such

Becker, Howard. 1986. "Culture: A Sociological View" from *Doing Things Together*. Evanston, Illinois: Northwestern University Press.

a contentious bunch of disciplines that it makes trouble to say what I think is true, that they all in fact concern themselves with one or another version of this issue—the problem of collective action, of how people manage to act together. I will not attempt a rigorous definition of collective action here, but the story of the Saturday night musicians can serve as an example of it. The example might have concerned a larger group—the employees of a factory who turn out several hundred automobiles in the course of a day, say. Or it might have been about so small a group as a family. It needn't have dealt with a casual collection of strangers, though the ability of strangers to perform together that way makes clear the nature of the problem. How do they do it? How do people act together so as to get anything done without a great deal of trouble, without missteps and conflict?

We can approach the meaning of a concept by seeing how it is used, what work it is called on to do. Sociologists use the concept of *culture* as one of a family of explanations for the phenomenon of concerted activity; I will consider some of the others below, in order to differentiate culture from them. Robert Redfield defined culture as "conventional understandings made manifest in act and artifact" (1941:132). The notion is that the people involved have a similar idea of things, understand them in the same way, as having the same character and the same potential, capable of being dealt with in the same way; they also know that this idea is shared, that the people they are dealing with know, just as they do, what these things are and how they can be used. Because all of them have roughly the same idea, they can all act in ways that are roughly the same, and their activities will, as a result, mesh and be coordinated. Thus, because all those musicians understood what a Saturday night job at a country club consisted of and acted accordingly, because they all knew the melody and harmony of "Exactly Like You" and hundreds of similar songs, because they knew that the others knew this as they knew it, they could play that job successfully. The concept of culture, in short, has its use for sociologists as an explanation of those musicians and all the other forms of concerted action for which they stand.

I said that culture was not the only way sociologists explain concerted action. It often happens, for example, even in the most stable groups and traditional situations, that things happen which are not fully or even partly covered by already shared understandings. That may be because the situation is unprecedented—a disaster of a kind that has never occurred before—or because the people in the group come from such a variety of backgrounds that, though they all have some idea about the matter at hand and all speak a common language, they do not share understandings. That can easily happen in stratified societies, in ethnically differentiated societies, in situations where different occupational groups meet. Of course, people in such situations will presumably share some understandings which will form the basis of discussion and mediation as they work out what to do. If the Saturday night musicians had not shared as much knowledge as they did, they would have sat down to discuss what kind of music they would play, sketched out parts, and so on. They would have had to negotiate, a process I will consider more fully below.

Culture, however, explains how people act in concert when they *do* share understandings. It is thus a consequence (in this kind of sociological thinking) of the existence of a group of acting people. It has its meaning as one of the resources people draw on in order to coordinate their activities. In this it differs from most anthropological thinking in which the order of importance is reversed, culture leading a kind of independent existence as a system of patterns that makes the existence of larger groups possible.

Most conceptions of culture include a great deal more than the spare definition I offered above. But I think, for reasons made clear later, that it is better to begin with a minimal definition and then to add other conditions when that is helpful.

Many people would insist that, if we are to call something culture, it must be traditional, of long standing, passed on from generation to generation. That would certainly make the concept unavailable as an explanation of the Saturday night musician. While we might conceivably say that these men were engaging in a traditional cultural activity, since a tradition of musicians playing for the entertainment of others goes back centuries and the American tradition of professional musicians playing for dances and parties is decades old, they were not doing it the way people who play for peasant parties in Greece or Mexico do, playing songs their grandparents played, perhaps on the same instruments. No, they were playing songs no more than twenty or thirty years old, songs their grandfathers never knew; in fact, few of their grandfathers had been musicians in whatever countries they came from, and, by becoming musicians themselves, these men were doing something untraditional in their families (and usually something not desired by their families either). They, of course, had learned to do many of the things they were doing from others who were slightly older, as I had learned many of the tricks of being a weekend musician when I was fifteen from people as old as seventeen or eighteen, who had in turn learned them from still older people. But, still, they did not know how to do what they were doing because it was traditional.

Many other people would insist that, if we are to call something culture, it must be part of a larger *system*, in which the various parts not only cohere in the sense of being noncontradictory, but, more than that, harmonize in the sense of being different versions of the same underlying themes. Such people would not use the term "culture" to describe the patterns of cooperation of the weekend musicians unless those patterns were also reflected in the music they played, the clothing they wore, the way they spent their leisure time, and so on. But none of that was true because they were not just musicians, and much of what they did reflected understandings they had acquired by participating in other social arenas in which the musicians' culture was irrelevant and vice versa. Nor, in any event, did they play what they might have played if they had been free to express their cultural understandings, for what they played was largely what they were paid to play (polkas on Friday, mambos on Saturday).

And many people would insist that my example is misleading to begin with, for the kinds of coherence that constitute "real" culture occur only at the level of the whole society. But if we connect culture to activities people carry on with one another, then we have to ask what all the members of a whole society do, or what they all do together, that requires them to share these general understandings. There are such things, but I think they tend to be rather banal and not at the level usually meant in discussions of general cultural themes. Thus, we all use the money of our society and know how many of the smaller units make one of the larger ones. Less trivially, we probably share understandings about how to behave in public, the things Edward T. Hall (1958) and Erving Goffman (1971) have written about— how close to stand to someone when we talk or how much space someone is entitled to in a public place, for example. But, even if for the sake of the argument we imagine that some substantial body of such materials exists, as it might in a relatively undifferentiated or rural society, that would not help us understand how the weekend musicians did their trick, and we would need some other term for what they were able to do and the web of shared understandings they used to do it.

Other people have other requirements for what can be called culture, all of which can be subjected to similar criticisms. Some think that culture, to be "really" culture, must be built in some deep way into the personalities of the people who carry it; others require that culture consist of "basic values," whatever might be meant by that. In neither case would the activities of the Saturday night musicians qualify as culture, however, if those definitional requirements were observed.

Normally, of course, we can define terms any way we want, but in the case of culture, several things seem to limit our freedom. The two most important are the quasi ownership of the term by anthropologists and the ambiguity of the word with respect to the problem of "high culture," to which I will return later. Anthropologists, and most other people, regard culture as anthropology's key concept and assume that the discipline is therefore entitled to make the definition. But anthropologists do not agree on a definition of culture; indeed, they differ spectacularly among themselves, as a famous compendium by Alfred Kroeber and Clyde Kluckhohn (1963) demonstrates. That did not dissuade Kroeber and Talcott Parsons (1958) from signing a jurisdictional agreement (like those by which the building trades decide how much of the work carpenters can do and where electricians must take over) giving "culture" to anthropology and "society" to sociology. But the social sciences, unlike the building trades, have not respected the deal their leaders made.

Which of these additional criteria, if any, should be incorporated into the definition of culture I have already given? Do we need any of them? Do we lose anything by using the most minimal definition of culture, as the shared understandings that people use to coordinate their activities? I think not. We have an inclusive term which describes not only the Saturday night musicians and the way they accomplish their feat of coordination, but all the other combinations of attributes that turn up in real life, raising questions about when they go together and when they do not.

Much depends on what kind of archetypal case you want the definition to cover, since a small Stone Age tribe living at the headwaters of the Amazon, which has never been in contact with European civilization, is obviously quite different from such typical products of twentieth-century urban America as the weekend musicians. The kinds of collective action required in the two situations differ enormously, and, consequently, the kinds of shared understandings participants can rely on vary concomitantly. Many anthropologists have a kind of temperamental preference for the simplicity, order, and predictability of less complicated societies, in which everyone knows what everyone else is supposed to do, and in which there is a "design for living." If you share that preference, then you can turn culture into an honorific term by denying it to those social arrangements which do not "deserve" it, thereby making a disguised moral judgment about those ways of life. But that leaves a good part of modern life, not just the Saturday night musicians, out of the cultural sphere altogether.

THE CULTURAL PROCESS

How does culture—shared understanding—help people to act collectively? People have ideas about how a certain kind of activity might be carried on. They believe others share these ideas and will act on them if they understand the situation in the same way. They believe further that the people they are interacting with believe that they share these ideas too, so everyone thinks that everyone else has the same idea about how to do things. Given such circumstances, if everyone does what seems appropriate, action will be sufficiently coordinated for practical purposes. Whatever was under way will get done—the meal served, the child dealt with, the job finished, all well enough so that life can proceed.

The cultural process, then, consists of people doing something in line with their understanding of what one might best do under the given circumstances. Others, recognizing what was done as appropriate, will then consult their notions of what might be done and do something that seems right to them, to which others in return will respond similarly, and so on. If everyone has the same general ideas in mind, and does something congruent with that image or collection of ideas, then what people do will fit together. If we all know the melody and harmony of "Exactly Like You" and improvise accordingly, whatever comes out will sound reasonable to the players and listeners, and a group of perfect strangers will sound like they know what they are doing.

Consider another common situation. A man and woman meet and find each other interesting. At some stage of their relationship, they may consider any of a variety of ways of organizing their joint activities. Early on, one or the other might propose that they "have a date." Later, one or the other might, subtly or forthrightly, suggest that they spend the night together. Still later, they might try "living together." Finally, they might decide to "get married." They might skip some of these stages and they might not follow that progression, which in contemporary America is a progression of increasingly formal commitment. In other societies and at other times, of course, the stages and the relationships would differ. But, whatever their variety, insofar as there are names for those relationships and stages, and insofar as most or all of the people in a society know those names and have an idea of what they imply as far as continuing patterns of joint activity are concerned, then the man and woman involved will be able to organize what they do by referring to those guideposts. When one or the other suggests one of these possibilities, the partner will know, more or less, what is being suggested without requiring that every item be spelled out in detail, and the pair can then organize their daily lives, more or less, around the patterns suggested by these cultural images.

What they do from day to day will of course not be completely covered by the details of that imagery, although they will be able to decide many details by consulting it together and adapting what it suggests to the problem at hand. None of these images, for instance, really establishes who takes the garbage out or what the details of their sexual activity may be, but the images do, in general, suggest the kind of commitments and obligations involved on both sides in a wide range of practical matters.

That is not the end of the matter, though. Consider a likely contemporary complication: The woman, divorced, has small children who live with her. In this case, the couple's freedom of action is constrained, and no cultural model suggests what they ought to do about the resulting difficulties. The models for pairing and for rearing children suggest incompatible solutions, and the partners have to invent something. They have to improvise.

This raises a major problem in the theory of culture I am propounding. Where does culture come from? The typical cultural explanation of behavior takes the culture as given, as preexisting the particular encounter in which it comes into play. That makes sense. Most of the cultural understandings we use to organize our daily behavior are there before we get there, and we do not propose to change them or negotiate their details with the people we encounter. We do not propose a new economic system every time we go to the grocery store. But those understandings and ways of doing things have not always been there. Most of us buy our food in supermarkets today, and that requires a different way of shopping from the corner grocery stores of a generation ago. How did the new culture of supermarkets arise?

One answer is that the new culture was imposed by the inventors of the concept, the owners of the new stores which embodied it. They created the conditions under which change was more or less inevitable. People might have decided not to shop in supermarkets and chain stores, but changing conditions of urban life caused so many of them to use the new markets that the corner grocery, the butcher shop, the poultry and fish stores disappeared in all but a few areas. Once that happened, supermarkets became the only practical possibility left, and people had to invent new ways of serving themselves.

So, given new conditions, people invent culture. The way they do it was suggested by William Graham Sumner a century ago in *Folkways* (1907). We can paraphrase him this way. A group finds itself sharing a common situation and common problems. Various members of the group experiment with possible solutions to those problems and report their experiences to their fellows. In the course of their collective discussion, the members of the group arrive at a definition of the situation, its problems and possibilities, and develop a consensus as to the most appropriate and efficient ways of behaving. This consensus thenceforth constrains the activities of individual members of the group, who will probably act on it, given the opportunity. In other words, new situations provoke new behavior. But people generally find themselves in company when dealing with these new situations, and since they arrive at their solutions collectively, each assumes that the others share them. The beginnings of a new shared understanding thus come into play quickly and easily.

The ease with which new cultural understandings arise and persist varies. It makes a difference, for one thing, how large a group is involved in making the new understandings. At one extreme, as I have noted, every mating couple, every new family, has to devise its own culture to cover the contingencies of daily interaction. At the other, consider what happens during industrialization when hundreds of thousands—perhaps millions—of people are brought from elsewhere to work in the new factories. They have to come from elsewhere because the area could not support that many people before industrialization. As a result, the newcomers differ in culture from the people already there, and they differ as well in the role they play in the new industries, usually coming in at the bottom. When industrialization takes place on a large scale, not only does a new culture of the workplace have to be devised but also a new culture of the cities in which they all end up living—a new experience for everyone involved.

The range of examples suggests, as I mean it to, that people create culture continuously. Since no two situations are alike, the cultural solutions available to them are only approximate. Even in the simplest societies, no two people learn quite the same cultural material; the chance encounters of daily life provide sufficient variation to ensure that. No set of cultural understandings, then, provides a perfectly applicable solution to any problem people have to solve in the course of their day, and they therefore must remake those solutions, adapt their understandings to the new situation in the light of what is different about it. Even the most conscious and determined effort to keep things as they are would necessarily involve strenuous efforts to remake and reinforce understandings so as to keep them intact in the face of what was changing.

There is an apparent paradox here. On the one hand, culture persists and antedates the participation of particular people in it: Indeed, culture can be said to shape the outlooks of people who participate in it. But cultural understandings, on the other hand, have to be reviewed and remade continually, and in the remaking they change.

This is not a true paradox, however: The understandings last *because* they change to deal with new situations. People continually refine them, changing some here and some there but never changing all of them at once. The emphasis on basic values and coherence in the definition of culture arises because of this process. In making the new versions of the old understandings, people naturally rely on what they already have available, so that consciously planned innovations and revolutions seem, in historical perspective, only small variations on what came before.

To summarize, how culture works as a guide in organizing collective action and how it comes into being are really the same process. In both cases, people pay attention to what other people are doing and, in an attempt to mesh what they do with those others, refer to what they know (or think they know) in common. So culture is always being made, changing more or less, acting as a point of reference for people engaged in interaction.

CULTURE AND COOPERATION

What difference does it make that people continually make culture in the way I have described? The most important consequence is that they can, as a result, cooperate easily and efficiently in the daily business of life, without necessarily knowing each other very well.

Most occupations, for example, operate on the premise that the people who work in them all know certain procedures and certain ways of thinking about and responding to typical situations and problems, and on the premise that such knowledge will make it possible to assemble them to work on a common project without prior team training. Most professional schools operate on the theory that the education they offer provides a basis for work cooperation among people properly trained anywhere. In fact, people probably learn the culture which makes occupational cooperation possible in the workplace itself. It presents them with problems to solve that are common to people in their line of work, and it provides a group of more experienced workers who can suggest solutions. In some occupations, workers change jobs often and move from workplace to workplace often (as do the weekend musicians), and they carry what they have learned elsewhere with them. That makes it easy for them to refine and update their solutions frequently, and thus to develop and maintain an occupational culture. Workers who do not move but spend their work lives in one place may develop a more idiosyncratic work culture, peculiar to that place and its local problems—a culture of IBM or Texas Instruments or (because the process is not limited to large firms) Joe's Diner.

At a different level of cooperative action, Goffman (1971) has described cultural understandings which characterize people's behavior in public. For instance, people obey a norm of "civil inattention," allowing each other a privacy which the material circumstances of, say, waiting for a bus do not provide. Since this kind of privacy is what Americans and many others find necessary before they can feel comfortable and safe in public (Hall [1958] has shown how these rules differ in other cultures), these understandings make it possible for urban Americans to occupy crowded public spaces without making each other uneasy. The point is not trivial, because violations of these rules are at least in part responsible for the currently common fear that some public areas are "not safe," quite apart from whatever assaults have taken place in them. Most people have no personal knowledge of the alleged assaults, but they experience violation of what might be called the "Goffman rules" of public order as the prelude to danger and do not go to places which make them feel that way.

Cultural understandings, if they are to be effective in the organization of public behavior, must be very widely held. That means that people of otherwise varying class, ethnic, and regional cultures must learn them routinely, and must learn them quite young, because even small children can disrupt public order very effectively. That requires, in turn, substantial agreement among people of all segments of the society on how children should be brought up. If no such agreement exists or if some of the people who agree in principle do not manage to teach their children the necessary things, public order breaks down, as it often does.

In another direction, cultural understandings affect and "socialize" the internal experiences people have. By applying understandings they know to be widely accepted to their own perhaps inchoate private experiences, people learn to define those internal experiences in ways which allow them to mesh their activities relevant to those topics with those of others with whom they are involved. Consider the familiar example of falling in love. It is remarkable that one of the experiences we usually consider private and unique—falling in love—actually has the same character for most people who experience it. That is not to say that the experience is superficial, but rather that when people try to understand their emotional responses to others, one available explanation of what they feel is the idea, common in Western culture, of romantic love. They learn that idea from a variety of sources, ranging from the mass media to discussion with their peers, and they learn to see their own experiences as embodiments of it. Because most people within a given culture learn to experience love in the same way from the same sources, two people can become acquainted and successfully fall in love with each other—not an easy trick.

Because shared cultural understandings make it easy to do things in certain ways, moreover, their existence favors those ways of doing things and makes other ways of achieving the same end, which might be just as satisfactory to everyone involved, correspondingly less likely. Random events which might produce innovations desirable to participants occur infrequently. In fact, even when the familiar line of activity is not exactly to anyone's liking, people continue it simply because it is what everyone knows and knows that everyone else knows, and thus is what offers the greatest likelihood of successful collective action. Everyone knows, for instance, that it would be better to standardize the enormous variety of screw threads in this country, or to convert the United States to the metric system. But the old ways are the ones we know, and, of course, in this instance, they are built into tools and machines which would be difficult and costly to change. Many activities exhibit that inertia, and they pose a problem that sociologists have been interested in for many years: Which elements of a society or culture are most likely to change? William Fielding Ogburn (1922), for instance, proposed sixty years ago that material culture (screw threads) changed more quickly than social organization, and that the resultant "lag" could be problematic for human society.

A final consequence: the existence of culture makes it possible for people to plan their own lives. We can plan most easily for a known future, in which the major organizational features of society turn out to be what we expected them to be and what we made allowances for in our planning. We need, most importantly, to predict the actions of other people and of the organizations which consist of their collective actions. Culture makes those actions, individual and collective, more predictable than they would otherwise be. People in traditional societies may not obey in every detail the complex marriage rules held out to them, but those rules supply a sufficiently clear guide for men and women to envision more or less accurately when they will marry, what resources will be available to them when they do, and how the course of their married life will proceed.

In modern industrial societies, workers can plan their careers better when they know what kinds of work situations they will find themselves in and what their rights and obligations at various ages and career stages will be. Few people can make those predictions successfully in this country any more, which indicates that cultural understandings do not always last the twenty or thirty years necessary for such predictability to be possible. When that happens, people do not know how to prepare themselves for their work lives and do not receive the benefits of their earlier investments in hard work. People who seemed to be goofing off or acting irrationally, for example, sometimes make windfall profits as the work world comes to need just those combinations of skills and experiences that they acquired while not following a "sensible" career path. As technical and organizational innovations make new skills more desirable, new career lines open up which were not and could not have been predicted ten years earlier. The first generation of computer programmers benefited from that kind of good luck, as did the first generation of drug researchers, among others.

REFERENCES

Goffman, Erving. 1971. *Relations in Public: Microstudies of the Public Order*. New York: Basic.

Hall, Edward T. 1958. *The Silent Language*. New York: Doubleday.

Kroeber, Alfred, and Clyde Kluckhohn. 1963. *Culture: A Critical Review of Concepts and Definitions*. New York: Vintage Books.

Kroeber, Alfred, and Talcott Parsons. 1958. The Concepts of Culture and of Social System. *American Sociological Review* 23:582–83.

Ogburn, William F. 1922. *Social Change*. New York: Viking.

Redfield, Robert. 1941. *The Folk Culture of Yucatan*. Chicago: University of Chicago Press.

Sumner, William Graham. 1907. *Folkways*. Boston: Ginn and Co.

READING 8

Excerpt from *The First R: How Children Learn Race and Racism*

DEBRA VAN AUSDALE AND JOE R. FEAGIN

OUR FIELD STUDY

In our research the daily lives of children in a racially and ethnically diverse day care center took center stage. We gathered experiential data on how preschool children use racial–ethnic awareness and knowledge in their social relationships.

The preschool had several racially and ethnically diverse classrooms and employed a popular antibias curriculum. The school's official data on children in the classroom we observed was as follows: white (twenty-four); Asian (nineteen); Black (four); biracial (for example, Black and white; three); Middle Eastern (three); Latino (two); and other (three).

As they proceed into preschool settings, young children learn to move from the social field of interaction that is the family to the new social field of the school, a field that most will operate in for the next fifteen or twenty years of their lives.

PLAY GROUPS AND RACIAL–ETHNIC MATTERS

A large portion of the time Debi observed the children was spent outdoors, either on the playground or the deck surrounding the building. The playground contained swings and slides, picnic tables, large concrete tubes lying

Van Ausdale, Debra, and Joe R. Feagin. 2001. *The First R: How Children Learn Race and Racism*. Lanham, MD: Rowman & Littlefield Publishers, Inc.

on the ground, a sandbox, a rowboat, and a small, shed-like building we nicknamed "the playhouse." Benches were placed along the outskirts of the area, primarily to provide teachers with places to sit and watch the children as they played. The following episode took place near the playhouse, while Debi was sitting outside watching the children play.

Using the playhouse to bake pretend muffins, Rita (3.5, white/Latina) and Sarah (4, white) monopolize all the muffin tins. Elizabeth (3.5, Chinese), attempting to join them, stands at the playhouse door and asks the two girls if she can play. Rita shakes her head vigorously, saying, "No, only people who can speak Spanish can come in." Elizabeth frowns and says, "I can come in." Rita counters, "Can you speak Spanish?" Elizabeth shakes her head no, and Rita repeats, "Well, then you aren't allowed in."

Elizabeth scowls and, hinting that Debi intercede, says, "Rita is being mean to me." A plaintive statement like this is often used by children seeking adult intervention. Elizabeth didn't direct her remarks to Debi, or request that Debi intercede, but it was plain that she expected assistance with this matter. After all, Rita was breaking one of the cardinal rules of the center: Sharing was obligatory. Acting within the child-initiated framework, Debi struggles to find a way to help Elizabeth without jeopardizing her status as a nonsanctioning observer. She has to be careful about how and to what extent she interferes in this situation. She decides just to question Rita and Sarah about the rules for play and asks Rita, "If only people who speak Spanish are allowed, then how come Sarah can play? Can you speak Spanish, Sarah?" Sarah shakes her head no. "Sarah can't speak Spanish, and she is playing," Debi remarks to Rita, stating the obvious without suggesting she allow Elizabeth to enter. Rita frowns, amending her original rule. "OK, only people who speak either Spanish or English." "That's great!" Debi responds, "because Elizabeth speaks English, and she wants to play with you guys." Rita's frown deepens. "No," she says. Debi queries in surprise, "But you just said people who speak English can play. Can't you decide?" Rita gazes at Debi, thinking hard. "Well," Rita says triumphantly, "only people who speak two languages."

Elizabeth is waiting patiently to play, apparently hoping for aggressive adult intervention, which Debi does not offer. Debi asks Rita, "Well, Elizabeth speaks two languages, don't you Elizabeth?" Rita is stumped for a moment, then retorts, "She does not. She speaks only English." Debi smiles at Rita. "She does speak two languages: English and Chinese. Don't you?" Debi finally invites Elizabeth into the conversation with Rita, and Elizabeth nods vigorously in affirmation. At this point, Rita turns away and says to Sarah, "Let's go to the store and get more stuff." She and Sarah abandon the playhouse, leaving Elizabeth in sole possession of the area.

Young children often use racial and ethnic ideas and concepts to control interaction with others, maintain their individual space, or establish dominance in interactions with other people. For young children, who are almost always entirely under the direct supervision of adults, the opportunity to gain control over a social situation is rare. When such opportunities occur, the children may take advantage of the situation and sometimes organize their activities around racial or ethnic concepts. They may try out different strategies of interaction or employ the power of racial and ethnic concepts to exercise social control within their play, sometimes working toward including or excluding other children from an activity.

In this society we often use the term "child's play" to denote an activity that is simple, easy, and inconsequential. Child's play, in common usage, describes an activity that adults need not give much heed to, or even notice at all. It also denotes activity that reflects children's fantasy worlds, the assumed unreality of their inner lives. As we see it, these commonsense notions of play are wrongheaded. For most children, play is an essential component in human development, and its critical nature cannot be underestimated. Without play and experimentation with ideas, human beings of any age do not grow and thrive. What young children accomplish in their play helps to create their complex social worlds.

Using Racial and Ethnic Ideas to Exclude

As we saw in the opening account, language is one of the ethnic markers young children can employ in their social lives. Four-year-old Rita clearly knows about languages and explicitly defines rules for entering the play group on the basis of language. She has experience with language as a social marker, since she has been raised in a bilingual household. She has spent her whole life immersed in a world where her first language, Spanish, is not dominant. The power accorded to English is familiar to her. She shows great awareness that each child not only does not look like the others but also speaks a different language. From a traditional child development perspective Rita might be seen as egocentric, strongly resistant to alternative suggestions, and bound to the structure of arbitrary rules. However, a closer look provides a *much* different analysis. Rita did not insist on adhering to rules; she changed the rules and developed new criteria for entry into the play site in response to each of Debi's questions about Rita's standards.

Here we see the crucial importance of the sociocultural context, particularly for the development of racial–ethnic concepts in a collaborative and interpersonal context. Rita creates rules for her social context and acts to defend them. The original rule, requiring the speaking of Spanish, fails. She realizes her preliminary attempts to exclude Elizabeth are not effective. Subsequently, this four-year-old then involves herself in a process of elaborating new rules, based on her significant and advanced understanding of ethnic markers. As challenges are presented, she adapts and extends her control, all the while maintaining her focus on excluding Elizabeth. The final "two languages" rule does not acknowledge the fact that Sarah only speaks English. Rita's choice of language as an exclusionary device is directed entirely at preventing Elizabeth from entering, not at creating or maintaining bilingual play space.

Exclusion of others can involve preventing association with unwanted others, as in the previous case, or removing oneself from the presence of unwanted others. We presented the next account preliminarily in the first chapter and will now recount the entire episode. Carla (3, white/Asian-white) is preparing herself for resting time. She picks up her cot and starts to move it. Karen, the teacher in charge, asks her what she is doing. "I need to move this," explains Carla, offering no more than a simple explanation. "Why?" asks Karen, gently. "Because I can't sleep next to a nigger," Carla says candidly, pointing to Nicole (4, Black), who is stretched out and sleeping on a cot nearby. "Niggers are stinky. I can't sleep next to one." Stunned, the teacher's eyes widen, and her mouth drops open. Karen then frowns in thought and tells Carla to move her cot back and not to use "hurting words." Carla looks amused and puzzled but complies with the teacher's directive and drags her cot back to its assigned place. Nothing more is said to either of the children, but the teacher shakes her head.

Three-year-old Carla made an evaluation of the racial status of another young child that is sophisticated and shows awareness not only of how to use racial epithets but also of one of the numerous negative stigmas attached to Black skin. This is an ancient stereotype. Like most children we observed, Carla is not the unsophisticated, preoperational child of the mainstream literature. She is using social material she has undoubtedly learned from other sources, probably in interaction with other children or adults. Here, Carla is applying this material to a particular interactive circumstance. We see once again the *active* aspect of racism as it operates in the United States. Everyday racism is not just about internalized views, attitudes, and understandings of identity; it is centrally about one person doing something to someone else. It is about action and role performance. The child is acting out her comprehension of what a white person does when they do not wish to be near a Black person—a reactive response common across many sectors of U.S. society. White adults often engage in this type of anti-Black behavior, so it is not surprising that their children should do the same. Adults are usually not quite so forthcoming in their explanations for that behavior, however.

Yet most of the center's adults expressed surprise and shock at the child's actions. Carla's brief action has become a major event. Later that same day, after the children have awakened and gone to the playground, the center's white director approaches Debi. Karen has called his attention to Carla's naptime behavior, and he decides to invite Debi into his plan to address the conduct: "I have called Carla's parents and asked them to come to a meeting with me and Karen about what happened." It is significant that the director felt no need to clarify exactly what he was referring to. He added, "If you want to attend I would really like to have you there. Karen will be there too." Debi then says she will be able to attend. "I suppose this is what you're looking for," he continued with a smile. "Well, no, not exactly," Debi replied, "but of course it is worth noting, and I am interested in anything that the kids do with race." "Well," he quickly replied, "I want you to know that Carla did not learn that here!"

Although the children in this study rarely used explicit racist slurs, the director's remark about the origins of Carla's epithet is typical of the responses adults gave in cases where children did use negative terms. The center's staff members were very interested in keeping children from being exposed to prejudice and discrimination, and they made use of a multicultural curriculum to teach children to value diversity. It often appeared that the center's adults were much more concerned with the origins of children's racialized behavior than with its nuanced content or child-initiated development. One of their goals was to foster in the children acceptance and value of differences. Another was to identify and eliminate the possibility of prejudice and discrimination. Both of these goals informed the process of helping Carla and her parents to deal with her incipient racism.

The meeting with Carla's parents was informative. Eight people were in attendance: the director, his secretary, Carla's parents, two teachers, a psychologist, and Debi. This encounter was clearly important to the people involved. At the beginning of the meeting, Carla's mother notes that she herself is biracial, with white and Asian parents. Carla's father is white. Both the parents were baffled when told about the incident. They feel that because of their own experiences as a mixed-race family they have done a lot to discourage prejudice in their children. They chose this day care center because of its diversity. They wished to foster the value of diversity in their family and were bewildered about their daughter's behavior.

On hearing what happened in the classroom, Carla's father remarked, "Well, she certainly did not learn that sort of crap from us!" Her teacher also insisted that Carla did not learn such words at the center. Carla's father offered this explanation: "I'll bet she got that ["nigger" comment] from Teresa. Her dad is really red." The room was silent for a moment. Puzzled about his remark, Debi asked what he meant. He responded, "You know, he's a real redneck." There is again uncomfortable silence, then the director stepped in: "It's amazing what kids will pick up in the neighborhood. It doesn't really matter where she learned it from. What we need to accomplish is unlearning it." Apparently relieved, the adults involved nod vigorously in agreement. They now have identified a problem that can be solved. The director ended the meeting by suggesting methods for teaching Carla about differences and offered her parents some multicultural storybooks about diversity for them to take home. The parents would be informed if she acted in such a manner again. The educational psychologist offered to help the center and the parents, perhaps with a workshop on diversity conducted with teachers and parents.

The reactions of these key adults illustrate the strength of their beliefs about the conceptual abilities of children. The focus is on child as imitator. A principal concern of the teachers, parents, and administrator was to assure one another that the child did not learn such behavior from *them*. Like the children, interestingly, they shape and reshape their conceptions collaboratively. Acting defensively, several of them exculpate themselves by suggesting another person is responsible. The director ends this blaming exercise by attributing the source of the child's behavior to the "neighborhood," a diffuse and acceptable enemy. From this perspective, once the source is identified, the task of unlearning prejudice can begin. Adult denial takes two forms, both revealed in this incident. Initially, the relevant adults seem to be shocked, and they refused to believe that a young child could know much about racial matters, much less use a racist epithet in a meaningful way. Once the fact of the child's behavior is accepted, all adults turn to denying that they are the source of racist behaviors. Also evident in this story is the lack of attention any of the adults paid to the possible impact of the incident on Black children at the center. Clearly, negative stereotypes are alive and well in the center's child culture. Somehow, racist thinking and action have gained a place there.

CHILDREN LEARNING SOCIAL RULES AND IDENTITY–ROLES

A key finding in our research is that young children quickly learn the racial–ethnic identities and role performances of the larger society. They take the language and concepts of the larger society and experiment with them in their own interactions with other children and adult caregivers. There are, of course, variations between children and over time for a given child. Children may accept these status roles in whole or in part. Their cultural understandings and social performances evolve over time. Many of them play and experiment as they learn and remold the identity–roles of racial superior or inferior. Thus, as white children grow up, they learn, develop, and perform the meanings associated with the white identity–role. Black children and other children of color often must cope with the subordinating expectations imposed on them, expectations that they may accept or resist. In the process most children, like most adults, come to see racial and ethnic categories as more or less permanent parts of their environments.

Modern racism is fundamentally about a severe imbalance of power—the power of whites to control society's social resources. Being white means having power over Blacks and other people of color. Significantly, in our observations *no* child of color used racist epithets to control white children. They did fight back when challenged and sometimes used constructed racial distinctions to create their own exclusive play groups—perhaps as a defensive reaction to the white exclusion they had felt inside and outside the preschool setting.

Obviously, the realities of race and racism do not start with children, and programs to eradicate racism cannot begin there either. Our study of race and racism in the lives of preschoolers is intended to spark a greater awareness of the persistent and perverse racism that pervades, restrains, and limits all those who grow up in this all-too-racist society. It is not a mystery where children this young get their ideas: We adults are a primary source. And they are champions at showing exactly how masterful human beings can be in perpetuating racial–ethnic hatred, discrimination, and inequalities. Attempts to change their behavior, however, may be ineffective until we adults change our own. Watching children at work with racism is like watching ourselves in a mirror. They will not unlearn and undo racism until we do.

READING 9

Excerpt from *Born to Buy:*
The Commercialized Child and the New
Consumer Culture

JULIET SCHOR

> A nation of kids and they Drive purchases; Kids influence 62% of family SUV and minivan purchases! Nickelodeon owns 50% of the K2–11 GRP's [Gross Rating Points] in Kids' Commercial TV.
>
> —From a Nickelodeon ad, with a smiling kid in an SUV

The typical American child is now immersed in the consumer marketplace to a degree that dwarfs all historical experience. At age one, she's watching *Teletubbies* and eating the food of its "promo partners" Burger King and McDonald's. Kids can recognize logos by eighteen months, and before reaching their second birthday, they're asking for products by brand name. By three or three and a half, experts say, children start to believe that brands communicate their personal qualities, for example, that they're cool, or strong, or smart. Even before starting school, the likelihood of having a television in their bedroom is 25 percent, and their viewing time is just over two hours a day. Upon arrival at the schoolhouse steps, the typical first grader can evoke 200 brands. And he or she has already accumulated an unprecedented number of possessions, beginning with an average of seventy new toys a year.

By age six and seven, girls are asking for the latest fashions, using nail polish, and singing pop music tunes. The day after the dELIA*s clothing catalogue arrives in the mail, marketers report that "everyone brings their

Schor, Juliet. 2004. "The Changing World of Children's Consumption" from *Born to Buy: The Commercialized Child and the New Consumer Culture*. New York: Scribner.

catalog to school" to talk about the products in it. (When I wrote those words, dELIA*s was hot; when they appear in print, who knows? Trends move at the speed of light in this world.) Eight-year-old boys are enjoying Budweiser commercials (the consistent favorite ad for this age group), World Wrestling Entertainment, and graphically violent video games. Schools routinely ban the toy fads that sweep the market, from Power Rangers to Pokémon, on the grounds that they lead to fights, antisocial behavior, and disruption. The average eight to thirteen year old is watching over three and a half hours of television a day. American children view an estimated 40,000 commercials annually. They also make approximately 3,000 requests for products and services each year.

As kids age, they turn to teen culture, which is saturated with violence, alcohol, drugs, and guns. Teen media depict a manipulated and gratuitous sexuality, based on unrealistic body images, constraining gender stereotypes, and, all too frequently, the degradation of women. The dominant teen culture is also rife with materialism and preaches that if you're not rich, you're a loser. Adolescents are subjected to unremitting pressure to conform to the market's definition of cool. MTV has been the global leader in promoting these values, and its worldview has become pervasive among youth. And now, teen culture has migrated down to younger children. Eight and nine year olds watch MTV and BET (Black Entertainment Television), reality shows, and other prime-time fare ostensibly aimed at teens and adults. Marketers are deliberately investing children's culture with the themes and sensibilities that have worked with teens. As Betsy Frank, head of research for MTV Networks, explained, "If something works for MTV, it will also work for Nickelodeon." It's a widespread process, known as tweening.

THE EXPLOSION OF YOUTH SPENDING

Companies are advertising because kids are buying. Every half-second, somewhere in the world another Barbie is sold. More than 120 million kids worldwide have watched Children's Television Workshop. McDonald's, despite its current woes, still manages to attract 8 percent of the American population every day, and a fifth of its business is in Happy Meals. Whether it's music, food, movies, video games, apparel, footwear, toys, television, sports, school supplies, retailing, e-tailing, health and beauty products, consumer electronics, entertainment, or travel, there is now a thriving children's market segment.

Children's purchasing power has risen rapidly. McNeal reports that children aged four to twelve made $6.1 billion in purchases in 1989, $23.4 billion in 1997, and $30.0 billion in 2002, an increase of 400 percent. The number one spending category, at a third of the total, is for sweets, snacks, and beverages. Toys are number two and apparel is growing fast. Older kids, aged twelve to nineteen, spend even more: they accounted for $170 billion of personal spending in 2002, or a weekly average of $101 per person. This teen market is important because the children's market tracks it, and because trends and styles now migrate quickly from adolescents to kids. Teens have become a leading indicator for tween and child behavior.

Children are becoming shoppers at an earlier age. Six to twelve year olds are estimated to visit stores two to three times per week and to put six items into the shopping cart each time they go. Eighty percent of them shop regularly with their parents, a change necessitated by the decline of stay-at-home mothers. But kids are also going solo. McNeal estimates that one in four make trips to stores alone before they enter elementary school and that the median age for independent trips is eight. Youthful shoppers are now often buying for family needs, particularly in single-parent households. The proliferation of children in stores is also leading to changes in retail environments. In 1996, the world's first mall catering exclusively to children opened in Alpharetta, Georgia. It has been enormously successful, and its "kids' village" concept has been copied around the country. Expect one on your local interstate before too long.

"KID-FLUENCE"

The more children shop, the more voice they have in parental purchases. In the industry, this is called the influence market, and it is enormous. McNeal estimates that children aged four to twelve directly influenced $330 billion of adult purchasing in 2004 and "evoked" another $340 billion. And he believes that influence spending is growing at 20 percent per year. Global estimates for tween influence topped $1 trillion in 2002. That persuasive power is why Nickelodeon, the number one television channel for kids, has had Ford Motor Company, Target, Embassy Suites, and the Bahamas Ministry of Tourism as its advertisers. (This explains why your child has been asking for an SUV, a vacation in the Bahamas, and a Robert Graves teapot.)

Children's influence is being driven by a number of factors, including changes in parenting style. Older generations were more authoritarian, believing that they knew what was best for their kids. The famous "children should be seen and not heard" adage also meant that parents made most buying decisions. Baby boom and later generations of parents have been far more willing to give voice and choice, to see consumer decisions as "learning opportunities." (Cheerios or Fruit Loops? Cherry Popsicle or grape?) As one marketer explained to me, "When I was a kid I got to pick the color of the car. Kids nowadays get to pick the car." While that may be an exaggeration, there is little doubt that parental attitudes have changed markedly. One industry estimate finds that 67 percent of car purchases by parents are influenced by children. Marketers have put tremendous effort into discovering just how far kid influence has permeated into household purchasing dynamics and for what types of products. And what they have found is that for a growing array of expenditures, children, not parents, are making choices.

What's more, kids' opinions are solicited from the earliest ages. According to a consumer panel run by New York agency Griffin Bacal, 100 percent of the parents of children aged two to five agreed that their children have a major influence on their food and snack purchases. For video and book choices, the rate of major influence was 80 percent, and for restaurants, clothes, and health and beauty products, it stood at 50 percent. The Roper Youth Report has found that among six and seven year olds, 30 percent choose their own grocery store food items, 15 percent choose their toys and games, and 33 percent make fast food and candy decisions. As kids age, their influence grows.

Food is an area where influence marketing and the decline of parental control has been most pronounced. Consider the case of Fruit Roll-ups, a phenomenally successful snack food represented by Saatchi and Saatchi's Kid Connection. When the product was introduced, the ads had both kid and mom appeal. For moms, they called attention to the fruit aspect of the snack. But over time, the agency realized that this "dual messaging" was unnecessary. As a former Saatchi employee explained to me: "For years we used to say 10 percent fruit juice. And finally we're just like, okay, forget it. Who are we kidding? . . . That was also a conscious effort to move toward direct kid marketing and not even worrying about Mom. Just take her out of the equation because the nag factor is so strong on something like that, that you can just take advantage of that."

Parental time pressure and longer working hours have also driven this trend. Time-starved households have become easy prey for marketers, whose research shows that parents who spend less time with their children will spend more money on them. "Guilt money," as they call it, came up in almost all my discussions about why kids have so much influence now. Research done by one of my students is consistent with this view. She found that parents who spent more hours working bought more discretionary items such as toys, videos, and books for their children. This effect is in addition to the fact that the additional income from working more also leads to more spending. By contrast, parents who spent more time with their children bought fewer of these items. The amount of extra spending was larger for mothers than fathers. And it was greater for toys than for other items. In higher-income families, spending was even more sensitive to time spent with children. These results do not show that parental guilt is motivating purchases, but marketers' belief in the power of guilt, and their ability to exploit it, remains strong.

Time pressure operates in other ways as well. Parents have less time to cajole kids to eat products they don't like or to return rejected purchases to stores. This is part of why 89 percent of parents of tweens report that they ask their children's opinions about products they are about to buy for them. Kids are also technologically savvy and eagerly seek out consumer information. Many parents now believe that their children know more about products and brands than they do, and they rely on that knowledge.

"BONDED TO BRANDS"

These days, when kids ask, they ask for particular brands. A 2001 Nickelodeon study found that the average ten year old has memorized 300 to 400 brands. Among eight to fourteen year olds, 92 percent of requests are brand specific, and 89 percent of kids agree that "when I find a brand I like, I tend to stick with it." A 2000 Griffin Bacal study found that nearly two-thirds of mothers thought their children were brand aware by age three, and one-third said it happened at age two. Kids have clear brand preferences, they know which brands are cool, they covet them, and they pay attention to the ads for them. Today's tweens are the most brand-conscious generation in history.

The increased salience of brands is a predictable outcome of kids' greater exposure to ads. Companies spend billions to create positive brand associations for their products, attempting to connect them with culturally valued images, feelings, and sensibilities. This is especially true in the youth marketplace, where so many of the products are hardly differentiable without the labels. There's a copycat sameness to sodas, fast food, candy, athletic shoes, jeans, and even music and films. And in light of that, companies have to work overtime to establish brand identity and loyalty. They turn brands into "signs," pure symbolic entities, detached from specific products and functional characteristics. This has been a winning strategy, and youth have eagerly embraced an ethic of labels and logos. But brand value is a hard quality to sustain, especially in today's supercompetitive environment. The intensification of what scholars Robert Goldman and Stephen Papson have dubbed "sign wars," that is, corporate competition centered on images, has led to an ever-accelerating spiral of changing symbolism and brand vulnerability. And that vulnerability fuels marketing innovation and sometimes desperation.

In what industry insiders call the "kidspace," much of the action has been in what is called brand extension. Products are inserted into a vast matrix of other products. There's the Pokémon TV program, the collectible cards, the handheld electronic game, Pokémon toys at the fast food outlet, Pokémon versions of classic board games, Pokémon clothing, school supplies, plastic cups, backpacks, Pokémon everything and anything. Indeed, the process of extensive branding has become a profoundly normalized part of children's lives. It's now a lack of branding that's out of the ordinary. One of my friends explained to me that her son, a five year old with sophisticated musical tastes, was baffled by the fact that there was no "Talking Heads" stuff—no show, no toys, no logo, no nothing. What was going on, he wondered, with this band he liked so much?

Increasingly the brands kids want aren't just any brands. They crave designer duds and luxury items. By the mid-1990s, parents and buyers reported a sea change as girls aged six to ten became more fashion and label conscious. They wanted trendy styles like platform shoes and black clothing. They started asking for Hilfiger and Donna Karan labels. The designers claim that "kids are driving the trend," but they have been advertising heavily to them. Meanwhile, children's lines have sprung up at fashion houses such as Armani and Calvin Klein. Burberry opened Burberry Kids, and Abercrombie & Fitch, the current bad boy of youth apparel, became tweens' favorite brand. Upscaling has gone beyond designer clothes. By the end of the 1990s, Marianne Szymanski, founder of the Toy Research Institute, reported that "kids are starting to want more expensive toys like computer software, cell phones, VCRs, e-mail, stereos, bedroom microwaves (for making popcorn while they watch movies in their own 'bedroom theater'). And guess what? Parents are buying all these items." Kids are also amassing far more toys than ever before. The number of toys sold annually rose 20 percent between 1995 and 2000. The United States, despite having only 4.5 percent of the world's population, now consumes 45 percent of global toy production.

Consumer experiences are also going luxe, and they're often more adult-like. The London salon MiniKin Kinder offers eight year olds its "Princess Treat," with haircut, manicure, and minifacial. Even cosmetic surgery has begun to reach down into childhood, according to journalist Alissa Quart, who reports that the year between elementary and middle schools is becoming a popular time for aesthetic enhancements for eyes, lips, chins, and ears. For those seeking the ultimate experience, FAO Schwartz offered birthday sleepover parties at a price of $17,500, and they were booked solid. Restauranteurs report that "crayons just won't do it anymore." Now they're providing menus attached to Magna Doodle sets, watercolor paint boxes, and Chinese carryout boxes with chopsticks, fortune cookies, and toys. In perhaps the most dramatic example of restaurant upscaling to come along yet, in 2002 McDonald's gave away Madame Alexander dolls, full-sized versions of which go for $50, with its Happy Meals.

REAL-LIFE MONOPOLY

The commercialization of childhood is certainly being driven by the fact that kids have more money and more say, the explanation most marketers articulate. But there's another side to what scholars Shirley and Joe Kincheloe have insightfully called the "Corporate Construction of Childhood." It's the growing scope, market power, and political influence wielded by the small number of megacorporations that sell most of what kids buy. Far from being a consumers' mecca ruled by diverse and rich choices, children's consumer culture is marked by bigness and sameness. Four companies now dominate the children's media and entertainment market almost entirely. There's Disney, with its global reach, anodyne cultural products, and long history of racial and sexual stereotyping. Number two is Viacom, king of cool, whose MTV Networks is the parent company's most profitable division, whose annual revenue in 2001 exceeded $3 billion. We have MTV to thank for shows such as *Beavis and Butthead*, which has been accused of inspiring copycat antics that led to real-life death and destruction. (Viacom also published this book.) Rupert Murdoch's News Corp is the parent to Fox, which has brought us such contributions to youth culture as *Fear Factor*. And finally, there's AOL Time Warner, owners of WB, Cartoon Network, *Sports Illustrated for Kids*, and DC Comics. In 2002, the company announced it would begin showing paid sponsorship on its CNN-branded school news broadcast, but backed down after criticism. In the midst of these behemoths, PBS is overmatched, and anyway, it has joined up with Nickelodeon (Viacom) to infiltrate the "educational" market.

In the toy category, it's Mattel and Hasbro, which together have gobbled up virtually all the other toy companies. Playskool, Fisher-Price, Parker Brothers, Milton Bradley, Tonka Trucks, Tyco, Hot Wheels, American Girl, Cabbage Patch Dolls, Tinker Toys, Avalon Hill, Wizards of the Coast, and Mr. Potato Head are all owned by the big two. In early 2002, eight of the top-selling ten toys belonged to these two companies. Video games are dominated by a small number of producers—Nintendo, Sony, and Microsoft among them. The big-two model prevails in other markets as well. In candy it's M&M and Hershey. In soft drinks it's Coke and Pepsi. In fast food McDonald's and Burger King. Philip Morris (the tobacco giant, renamed Altria) owns Kraft with its Lunchables product, kids' second favorite lunch choice after pizza, as well as Nabisco and Post cereals. Frito-Lay is part of PepsiCo, as are Tropicana, Gatorade, and Quaker Oats. PepsiCo tries to retain a wholesome oatmeal image with the venerable Quaker on the box, but it's the same company that sells Cap'n Crunch's Choco Donuts cereal. Throughout the world of children's products, the markets are dominated by a few powerful companies.

This matters for a number of reasons. One is that with monopoly comes uniformity. Economic theory predicts that when two opponents face off, the winning strategy for both entails their becoming almost identical. This model explains why gas stations congregate at intersections, why Democrats and Republicans cleave to the political center, and why Coke and Pepsi are hard to tell apart with a blindfold. What it means for consumers is that true variety and diversity of products is hard to find. If you want greasy pizza, sugared drinks, plastic toys, and violent programming for your kids, no problem. It's the other stuff that's missing.

Monopoly also means bigger profits and market power for producers and less value and influence for consumers. That's standard economic reasoning. Finally, many of these companies have spent the past two decades stockpiling money and political influence. At the end of the 1970s, the Federal Trade Commission was investigating practices in children's advertising and didn't like what it saw. It advocated a ban on advertising sugared products to kids, as well as an end to commercials aimed at children under age eight. Today, such a stance seems almost inconceivable, given the tremendous growth in political influence enjoyed by media corporations and food processors. Philip Morris gave more than $9 million in soft money to the two political parties between 1995 and 2002 ($7.8 million of it went to Republicans). AOL Time Warner gave more than $4 million (nearly equally divided). Disney contributed $3.6 million. Coca-Cola gave $2.3 million (mostly to the Republicans). The U.S. Sugar Corporation is also among the top "Double Givers." Two decades of corporate monies have eroded the regulatory, legislative, and judicial environment, making it far harder to protect children.

POSTMODERN CHILDHOOD: THE ELECTRONIC GENERATION

The change that has attracted most attention is kids' heavy involvement with electronic media, prompting some to posit a new, postmodern childhood, driven by television, Internet, video games, movies, and videos.

The Kaiser Family Foundation's 1999 *Kids & Media @ the Millennium*, was a high-quality, large-scale survey that combined a time diary with questions about yesterday's media viewing. It found that daily television viewing for two to eighteen year olds was two hours and forty-six minutes, plus an additional twenty-eight minutes watching videotapes. Viewing is most intense at ages eight to thirteen, when television takes up three hours and thirty-seven minutes a day, plus an additional twenty-nine minutes with videotapes. That's nearly thirty hours per week. The averages conceal wide variations, because there is a substantial group of very heavy watchers: 27.5 percent of kids aged eight to thirteen report more than five hours a day of TV viewing.

These estimates accord with most surveys of media use, including Nielsen's, but are much higher than traditional time diaries, which yield average viewing times of only thirteen to fourteen hours per week. One reason for the difference is that the diaries focus on primary activities, and television is often watched while doing other things. For example, in the Kaiser study, 42 percent of respondents reported that in their house, the television was on "most of the time." In 60 percent of households the television is on during meals.

When we combine all types of media—video games, computers, music, radio, and print—media time almost doubles. The average American child is estimated to spend five hours and twenty-nine minutes a day with media, for a weekly total of more than thirty-eight hours. About forty-five minutes a day is spent with print media. Forty-six percent of eight to thirteen year olds report total media exposure (which double counts media being used simultaneously) of more than seven hours per day.

Television viewing varies significantly by race, income, and parental education, with the racial variations being most pronounced. For example, among eight to eighteen year olds, white children watch an average of two hours and forty-seven minutes a day, Hispanic children watch three hours and fifty minutes, and black children watch four hours and forty-one minutes of television a day. All three groups also watch an additional thirty minutes of video. In households with lower incomes, there is more television watching, especially among younger children. And in households where parents have lower educational levels, viewing times are higher, especially among younger children.

HOW CHILDREN ARE FARING

The conservative take on the trends I've described is that we've produced a generation of couch potato kids, scarfing down chips and soda, driving their parents crazy about those hundred-dollar sneakers. They're spoiled, unable to delay gratification, and headed for trouble. An alternate view stresses the enormous accomplishments of young people today, their volunteer spirit, resiliency, and tolerance. Setting aside these value judgments, what do we know about how children are doing? The past fifteen to twenty years have witnessed big changes in what kids have been eating, drinking, watching, and doing. How are they faring?

Let's start with child nutrition. Historically, poverty has been the major culprit in malnutrition and poor diet. And despite the nation's wealth, we have significant levels of poverty-induced hunger and malnutrition. In 1999, 16.9 percent of children were subject to what is called "food insecurity" and did not have adequate food to live active, healthy lives. Millions of American children still go hungry. But now there's a new problem with food. Diets have gotten far out of line with recommended nutritional standards. Most kids are eating the wrong foods, and too many of them. A 1997 study found that 50 percent of children's calories are from added fat and sugar, and the diets of 45 percent of children failed to meet any of the standards of the USDA's food pyramid. Children eat excessive quantities of advertised food products and not enough fruits, vegetables, and fiber. Among children aged six to twelve, only 12 percent have a healthy diet, and 13 percent eat a poor diet. The rest are in the "needs improvement" category.

As has been widely reported, rates of youth obesity are skyrocketing. Using the eighty-fifth percentile Body Mass Index as a cutoff, about 25 percent of American youth are now overweight or obese. By the stiffer ninety-fifth percentile criterion, 15 percent of children are obese. Since 1980, obesity rates for children have doubled, and those for teens have tripled. Weight-related diseases, such as type II diabetes and hypertension, are rising rapidly. Alongside the rise in obesity is excessive concern with thinness and body image and a host of eating disorders. Record numbers of girls are on diets, and they are beginning to diet at an increasingly young age.

Other forms of consumption are similarly troubling. Kids are smoking, drinking alcohol, and taking illegal drugs at alarming rates. As early as the eighth grade, more than 7 percent of kids are regular smokers, and that number nearly triples by twelfth grade. Despite the tobacco settlement, more than 2,000 children and teens still start smoking every day, a third of whom will die of smoking-related causes. In the eighth grade, 14 percent of kids report that they have taken five alcoholic drinks in a row within the past two weeks. By the twelfth grade, twice as many answer affirmatively. Half of all high schoolers report that they currently drink alcohol. And 12 percent of eighth graders report that they have used illegal drugs within the past thirty days. Among twelfth graders, that percentage rises to 25 percent.

Children and youth are increasingly suffering from emotional and mental health problems. A study published in the *Pediatrics Journal* found that rates of emotional and behavioral problems among children aged four to fifteen soared between 1979 and 1996. Rates of anxiety and depression went from negligible to 3.6 percent; attention deficit hyperactivity disorder rose from 1.4 percent to 9.2 percent. Estimates of major depression are as high as 8 percent for adolescents. In recent decades, suicide rates have climbed, and suicide is now the fourth leading cause of death among ten to fourteen year olds. Suicide rates are highest among racial minorities. In 2001, the annual survey of incoming college freshmen by the University of California at Los Angeles found that self-reports of physical and emotional health reached their worst level in the sixteen years the questions had been asked.

The large-scale MECA study (Methods for the Epidemiology of Child and Adolescent Mental Disorders) yields similar findings. It found that 13 percent of kids aged nine to seventeen suffer from anxiety, 6.2 percent have mood disorders, 10.3 percent have disruptive disorders, and 2 percent suffer from substance abuse. Taken together, about 21 percent of this age group had a "diagnosable mental or addictive disorder with at least minimum impairment." Eleven percent had a significant functional impairment, and 5 percent were reported to have an extreme functional impairment. (See Table 9–1.)

Conclusions from the 1997 Child Development Supplement, which included children aged three to twelve, are also cause for concern. Although parents reported that their children were generally happy and healthy, one in five said that they were fearful or anxious, unhappy, sad, depressed, or withdrawn. Two in five reported that their children were impulsive, disobedient, or moody. All told, nearly 50 percent had at least one of these problems. This survey also asked about the quality of relationships between children and parents. It found that only 59 percent of parents reported that their relationships with their school-aged children are "extremely or very close," and only 57 percent reported engaging in very warm behaviors with their child several times a week. (Warm behaviors are defined as hugging, joking, playing, and telling them they love them.)

Taken together, these findings are not comforting. They show that American children are worse off today than they were ten or twenty years ago. This conclusion is especially notable when we consider that during the past fifteen years, child poverty fell substantially, from a high of 22 percent in the late 1980s to its current rate of 16 percent. The decline in child poverty

Table 9–1 Youth Mental and Addictive Disorders
Children and Adolescents Age 9–17

	Percentage of Youth, Ages 9–17
Anxiety disorders	13.0
Mood disorders	6.2
Disruptive disorders	10.3
Substance use disorders	2.0
Any disorder	20.9

Source: Data cited in U.S. Office of the Surgeon General (1999, Table 3–1).

should have led to improvements in measures of distress, because child poverty is correlated with adverse physical and psychological health outcomes. The deterioration of the well-being indicators suggests that some powerful negative factors are undermining children's well-being.

One of them may be the upsurge in materialist values. Children's top aspiration now is to be rich, a more appealing prospect to them than being a great athlete, or a celebrity, or being really smart, the goals of earlier eras. Forty-four percent of kids in fourth through eighth grades now report that they daydream "a lot" about being rich. And nearly two-thirds of parents report that "my child defines his or her self-worth in terms of the things they own and wear more than I did when I was that age."

Psychologists have found that espousing these kinds of materialist values undermines well-being, leading people to be more depressed, anxious, less vital, and in worse physical health. Among youth, those who are more materialistic are more likely to engage in risky behaviors. In the light of these findings, the survey data are worrisome. One of the few large national surveys of children's materialism found that more than a third of all children aged nine to fourteen would rather spend time buying things than doing almost anything else, more than a third "really like kids that have very special games or clothes," more than half agree that "when you grow up, the more money you have, the happier you are," and 62 percent say that "the only kind of job I want when I grow up is one that gets me a lot of money."

Social Institutions

INTRODUCTION

Social institutions are an important part of how societies organize social relations, define expectations for behavior, establish roles and norms, create meaning, and promote continuity over time. Economy, politics, religion, family, education, medicine, and media are examples of primary institutions in our society. Economy organizes the production and distribution of goods and services. Politics organizes the legitimate exercise of power. Religion organizes our relationship to the spiritual. Family organizes our kinship ties. Education organizes the transmission of knowledge. Medicine organizes our relationship to health. Media organizes our mass communicated culture. These institutions are comprised of powerful organizations or institutional actors, such as corporations in the economy, legislatures in politics, and colleges in education. Social institutions tie us together as a collective, and they impact our lives as individuals. They are the structures with which social worlds are built. If you are reading this text, it's probably because an institutional actor (your college) has required you to do so. You made individual choices to go to college (education), take Introduction to Sociology, and do the required readings. Each of those individual choices that led you to reading this text were shaped in some way by institutional norms. Your decision to go to college may have been shaped by your family. Your valuation of a college education may have been influenced by the interests of potential employers (economy). Your ability to pay for college may have been facilitated by lending organizations (economy or government). Like it or not, you are part of, in, influenced by, and subject to a wide range of social institutions, and so is everyone else. The benefit of social institutions is that we do not have to constantly reinvent the wheel to get routine things done in our social system. Social institutions provide you with established solutions to everyday problems, like how will I house, clothe, and feed myself?

In *The Protestant Ethic and the Spirit of Capitalism*, Max Weber theorizes about the relationship between the institution of religion and the institution of economy at the emergence of the European industrial revolution. As an early foundational sociological theorist, his focus is on the causes and consequences of the great wave of social changes that swept Europe in the nineteenth century. These social changes manifested as a series of institutional rearrangements, as the relative power, roles, and relationships between key institutions like religion, economy, and politics changed rapidly and dramatically. Weber argues that Protestantism (itself a great change in the institution of religion in the west as it challenged Catholicism) laid the ideological foundations for capitalism. By devaluing conspicuous consumption and the "spontaneous enjoyment of life" while valuing productive work and acquisitive activity (to prevent idle hands from being the devil's workshop), the Protestant ethic promoted accumulation of capital as an indicator of God's blessing. Weber believed that Protestantism promoted the impulse to capital accumulation as a religious calling to do God's will by being productive and frugal. This "calling" was ultimately "institutionalized" in our economic structure, roles, norms, and behaviors to the point where the religious foundation has faded, but the rearranging of the institution of economy remains. As social actors in this economy, we now find ourselves embedded in an institutional order that compels and cajoles us into supporting capital accumulation and capitalist economic growth without religious inspiration. Weber views this institutional order as an "Iron Cage" as material goods have gained inexorable power over our lives. We now engage in what often feels like purposeless acquisition and endless work regardless of spiritual goal or individual choice.

In *Corporation Nation*, Charles Derber looks at more recent changes in the institution of economy by analyzing the changed relationship between three large institutional actors: the corporation, the state (or government), and organized labor (unions). Like Weber in his time, Derber is interested in shifting power relations between institutions (like economy and politics), and the consequences that these social institutional shifts have for how people experience social life. In this case, Derber identifies what he calls the "anxious class," those workers who once were socialized to expect relative economic security through hard work and dedication to their employers, but who now find themselves part of a rapidly growing contingent labor force where work is temporary and jobs are fleeting. Derber traces this development to the decreased willingness of the institutional actor of the state to support workers, as the state shifted its allegiance to capital owners and corporations. This institutional shift undermined the power of unions as institutional actors, which had served as a countervailing force to the interests of corporations. The result is that worker protections, wages, benefits, and long-term employment (all of which cost corporations money) declined as the power of corporations increased. The globalization of the economy also facilitated these changes, as corporations found it easier to move employment off shore to escape the wage, benefits, and security demands of U.S. employees. Derber takes a historical approach to understanding how changing relations between institutions and institutional actors created shifting conditions for workers in the Gilded Age (before the rise of unions and state-sponsored worker protections), in the era from the New Deal through the early Post–WWII period (when unions grew strong, partly as a result of strong worker support from the state), and in the late twentieth century, when corporations and the state acted in concert to reduce the relative power of workers. The dynamic flux of institutional power that Derber looks at has important implications for you as you plan an economic course for yourself in a changed economy. Because of these institutional changes, your expectations for your economic future must necessarily be quite different from what your parents' and grandparents' expectations were at your age. The social institutions that impact your life have changed substantially.

Another social institution that has changed substantially from arrangements, norms, structures, and expectations for previous generations is the institution of family. In "The Deinstitutionalization of American Marriage," Andrew Cherlin examines the weakening of social norms defining behavior in a social institution. In looking at statistical trends in American society toward greater rates of cohabitation, remarriage, and same-sex marriage, he notes that the institutional structure, roles, and meaning of marriage have shifted in the late twentieth and early twenty-first centuries. Cherlin points out that clearly defined social roles and norms for step-parenting, unwed families, and same-sex families have not yet emerged and may not emerge. These relationships have not been "institutionalized" as traditional, heterosexual marriage relationships have. This can be liberating in the sense that couples and families are free to make it up as they go along and establish roles as they see fit. Such deinstitutionalization can also be debilitating in that other social institutional actors (schools, hospitals, courts, employers) do not have clearly defined norms and expectations for how to respond to these relationships. The security, normalcy, and social responsivity that we gain from embeddedness in social institutions have been eroded in the case of marriage. Cherlin also points out that the institution of marriage has responded to changes in the institution of economy, as economic norms for women in the workforce shifted in the late twentieth century. He also points out that the institution of politics is grappling with how to respond (legalization of gay marriage, rights of step-parents, etc.) to changes to the institution of marriage. The result for you is that you face far greater choices in the range of socially acceptable family relations than did your parents and grandparents. However, you also face many fewer social definitions of what your family roles, expectations, and behaviors should be.

Institutions are social constructions. They are created and changed. Their power rises and falls. They respond to each other in a series of dynamic relationships that shape our social order. Social institutions impact individual lives and life courses and the social experiences of all social groups. They are changed by individual actions as aggregated (Cherlin) or collective (Derber) efforts. The focus of the readings in this chapter is primarily on two major social institutions: one that operates most obviously on the macro-level (economy), and one that operates most obviously on the micro-level (family). The readings that follow illustrate how both institutions are supported, organized, constrained, and changed by other institutions (like the state). To fully develop and apply your sociological imagination, you need to understand the function, structures, and dynamics of social institutions.

Excerpt from *The Protestant Ethic and the Spirit of Capitalism*

MAX WEBER

Remember, that *time* is *money*. He that can earn ten shillings a day by his labour, and goes abroad, or sits idle one half of that day, though he spends but sixpence during his diversion or idleness, ought not to reckon that the only expense; he has really spent or rather thrown away five shillings besides.

Remember, that *credit* is *money*. If a man lets his money lie in my hands after it is due, he gives me the interest, or so much as I can make of it during that time. This amounts to a considerable sum where a man has good and large credit, and makes good use of it.

Remember, that money is of the *prolific, generating nature*. Money can beget money, and its offspring can beget more, and so on. Five shillings turned is six, turned again it is seven and threepence, and so on, till it becomes a hundred pounds. The more there is of it, the more it produces every turning, so that the profits rise quicker and quicker. He that kills a breeding-sow, destroys all her offspring to the thousandth generation. He that murders a crown, *destroys* all that it might have produced, even scores of pounds....

Remember this saying: The good *paymaster* is lord of another man's purse. He that is known to pay punctually and exactly to the time he promises, may at any time, and on any occasion, raise all the money his friends can spare.

This is sometimes of great use. After industry and frugality, nothing contributes more to the *raising* of a young man in the world than punctuality and justice in all his dealings; therefore never keep borrowed money an hour beyond the time you promised, lest a disappointment shut up your friend's purse for ever.

The most trifling actions that affect a man's *credit* are to be regarded. The sound of your hammer at five in the morning, or nine at night, heard by a creditor, makes him easy six months longer; but if he sees you at a billiard-table, or hears your voice at a tavern, when you should be at work, he sends for his money the next day;... [he] demands it before you are able to pay.

It shows, besides, that you are mindful of what you owe; it makes you *appear* a careful as well as an *honest man*, and that still increases your *credit*.

Weber, Max. 2009 [1905]. *The Protestant Ethic and the Spirit of Capitalism*. Translated by Stephen Kalberg. New York: Oxford University Press.

Beware of thinking that you own all that you possess, and of living accordingly. It is a mistake that many people who have credit fall into. To prevent this, keep an exact account both of your expenses and your income. If you make an effort to attend to particular expenses, it will have this good effect: you will discover how wonderfully small, trifling expenses mount up to large sums, and will discern what might have been, and may for the future be saved, without occasioning any great inconvenience.

> For six pounds a year you may have the use of one hundred pounds if you are a man of known prudence and honesty.
>
> He that spends a groat a day idly, spends idly above six pounds a year, which is the price of using one hundred pounds.
>
> He that wastes idly a groat's worth of his time per day, one day with another, wastes the privilege of using one hundred pounds each year.
>
> He that idly loses five shillings' worth of time, loses five shillings and might as prudently throw five shillings into the sea.
>
> He that loses five shillings not only loses that sum, but all the advantage that might be made by turning it in dealing, which by the time that a young man becomes old, amounts to a comfortable bag of money.

It is *Benjamin Franklin*[1] [1706–90] who preaches to us in these sentences. As the supposed catechism of a Yankee, Ferdinand Kürnberger satirizes these axioms in his brilliantly clever and venomous *Picture of American Culture*.[2] That the spirit of capitalism is here manifest in Franklin's words, even in a characteristic manner, no one will doubt. It will not be argued here, however, that *all aspects* of what can be understood by this spirit are contained in them.

A "drive to acquire goods" has actually nothing whatsoever to do with capitalism, as little as has the "pursuit of profit," money, and the greatest possible gain. Such striving has been found, and is to this day, among waiters, physicians, chauffeurs, artists, prostitutes, corrupt civil servants, soldiers, thieves, crusaders, gambling casino customers, and beggars. One can say that this pursuit of profit exists among "all sorts and conditions of men" [Sir Walter Besant],[3] in all epochs and in all countries of the globe. It can be seen both in the past and in the present wherever the objective possibility for it somehow exists.

This naive manner of conceptualizing capitalism by reference to a "pursuit of gain" must be relegated to the kindergarten of cultural history methodology and abandoned once and for all. A fully unconstrained compulsion to acquire goods cannot be understood as synonymous with capitalism, and even less as its "spirit." On the contrary, capitalism *can* be identical with the *taming* of this irrational motivation, or at least with its rational tempering. Nonetheless, capitalism is distinguished by the striving for *profit*, indeed, profit is pursued in a rational, continuous manner in companies and firms, and then pursued *again and again*, as is *profitability*. There are no choices. If the entire economy is organized according to the rules of the open market, any company that fails to orient its activities toward the chance of attaining profit is condemned to bankruptcy.

We can now seek to clarify those aspects of the Puritan conception of the calling and promotion of an ascetic *organization of life* that must have *directly* influenced the development of the capitalist style of life. As we have seen, asceticism turned with all its force mainly against the *spontaneous enjoyment* of existence and all the pleasures life had to offer.

This aspect of asceticism was expressed most characteristically in the struggle over the *Book of Sports* [1637].[4] James I and Charles I raised its arguments to the level of law in order explicitly to confront Puritanism, and Charles ordered the reading of this law from all pulpits. The fanatic opposition of the Puritans to the king's decree—on Sundays, certain popular amusements would be legally allowed after church services—arose *not* only on account of the resulting disturbance of the Sabbath day of rest. Rather, the more important source of this opposition was the fully premeditated disruption the decree implied of the ordered and organized life practiced by the Puritan saints. Moreover, the king's threat to punish severely every attack on the legality of these sporting activities had a single clear purpose: to banish this Puritan movement that, owing to its *anti-authoritarian ascetic* features, posed a danger to the state. Monarchical-feudal society protected the "pleasure seekers" alike against the crystallizing middle-class morality and the hostility to authority of the ascetic *conventicles*, just as today capitalist society seeks to protect "those willing to work" against the class-specific morality of workers and the trade unions hostile to authority.

In opposition to the feudal-monarchical society, the Puritans held firm to their most central feature in this struggle over the *Book of Sports*, namely, the principle of leading an organized life anchored in asceticism. Actually, Puritanism's aversion to sports was not a fundamental one, even for the Quakers. However, sports must serve a rational end, Puritanism insisted: they must promote the relaxation indispensable for further physical achievement. Hence, sports became suspect whenever they constituted a means for the purely spontaneous expression of unrestrained impulses. They were obviously absolutely reprehensible to the extent that they became means toward pure enjoyment or awakened competitive ambition, raw instincts, or the irrational desire to gamble. Quite simply, the enjoyment of life as if it were only *physical drives*, which pulls one equally away from work in a calling and from piety, was the enemy of rational asceticism as such. This enmity endured, regardless of whether the enjoyment of life presented itself in the form of monarchical-feudal society's sports or in the common man's visits to the dance floor or the tavern.[5]

Correspondingly, Puritanism's position toward those aspects of culture devoid of any direct relevance to religious matters was also one of suspicion and strong hostility. That is not to say that a sombre, narrow-minded scorn for culture was contained in Puritan ideals. Precisely the opposite holds, at least for the sciences (*Wissenschaften*), with the exception of Scholasticism, which was despised.[6] Moreover, the great representatives of Puritanism were deeply submerged in the humanism of the Renaissance; the sermons in the Presbyterian wing drip with references to classical antiquity,[7] and even the radicals (although they took offense at it) did not reject this humanist learning in theological polemics. Perhaps no country was ever so overpopulated with "graduates" as New England in the first generation of its existence. Even the satires of opponents, such as *Hudibras* [1663–78] by [Samuel] Butler [1612–1680], turn quickly to the armchair scholarship and sophomoric dialectics of the Puritans. Their learning *in part* goes together with the high religious esteem for knowledge that followed from the Puritans' rejection of the Catholic *fides implicita*.

Matters are distinctly different as soon as one moves into the arena of non-scientific literature[8] and to the realm of art, which appeals to the senses. Asceticism now blankets like a frost the life of merry old England. Its influence was apparent not only on secular festivals. The angry hatred of the Puritans persecuted all that smacked of "superstition" and all residuals of the dispensation of grace through magic or sacraments, including Christmas festivities, the may pole celebration,[9] and all unrestricted use of art by the church.

In Holland the survival of a public space within which the development of a masterful, often coarse and earthy, realistic art[10] could occur demonstrates in the end that the authoritarian regimentation of morality by the Puritans was not able to exercise a complete domination. The influence of court society and the landlord stratum, as well as members of the lower middle class who had become wealthy and sought joy in life, all contested the impact of Puritanism. This resistance took place after the short domination of the Calvinist theocracy had dissolved into a staid state church. As a consequence of this development, Calvinism in Holland suffered a distinct loss in ascetic energy. Thus its capacity to attract believers perceptibly declined.[11]

The theater was reprehensible to the Puritans.[12] As in literature and art, radical views could not survive once eroticism and nudity had been strictly banned from the realm of the possible. The notions of "idle talk," "superfluities,"[13] and "vain ostentation," all of which designated to the Puritans irrational, aimless, and thus not ascetic, behavior, and surely not conduct serving God's glory but only human goals, surfaced quickly. Hence, dispassionate instrumentalism was given a decisive upper hand over and against every application of artistic tendencies. This purposiveness was especially important wherever the direct decoration of the person was involved, as for example in respect to dress.[14] The foundation in ideas for that powerful tendency to render styles of life uniform, which today supports the capitalist interest in the "standardization" of production,[15] derived from the Puritans' rejection of all "glorification of human wants and desires."[16]

Certainly, in the midst of these considerations, we should not forget that Puritanism contained within itself a world of contradictions. It must be recognized that the instinctive awareness among Puritan leaders of the eternal greatness of art certainly transcended the level of art appreciation found in the milieu of the [feudalism-oriented] "cavaliers."[17] Furthermore, and even though his "conduct" would scarcely have found grace in the eyes of the Puritan God, a unique genius such as Rembrandt was, in the direction of his creativity, fundamentally influenced by his sectarian milieu.[18] These acknowledgments, however, fail to alter the larger picture: the powerful turn of the personality in an inward-looking direction (which the further development of the Puritan milieu could cultivate and, in fact, co-determined) influenced literature for the most part. Even in this realm, however, the impact of ascetic Protestantism would be felt only in later generations.

We cannot here investigate further the influences of Puritanism in all these ways. Nevertheless, we should note that *one* characteristic barrier always opposed ascribing legitimacy to the joy experienced from aspects of culture serving pure aesthetic pleasures or to the pure enjoyment of sports: *this pleasure should not cost anything.* Persons are only administrators of the cultural performances that the grace of God has offered. Hence, every dime expended for them must be justified, just as in the example of the servant in the Bible.[19] It remains doubtful at least whether any part of this money should be spent for a purpose that serves one's own pleasure rather than the glory of God.[20]

Who among us, whose eyes are open, has not seen manifestations of this outlook even at the present time?[21] The idea of a person's *duty* to maintain possessions entrusted to him, to which he subordinates himself as a dutiful steward or even as a "machine for producing wealth," lies upon his life with chilling seriousness. And as one's possessions become more valuable, the more burdensome becomes the feeling of responsibility to maintain them intact for God's glory and to increase their value through unceasing work—*if* the ascetic temper meets the challenge. The roots of this style of life also extend back to the Middle Ages (at least particular roots), as is true of so many components of the modern capitalist spirit.[22] This spirit, however, first found its consistent ethical foundation in the ethic of ascetic Protestantism. Its significance for the development of [modern] capitalism is obvious.[23]

Let us summarize the above. On the one hand, this-worldly Protestant asceticism fought with fury against the spontaneous *enjoyment* of possessions and constricted *consumption*, especially of luxury goods. On the other hand, it had the psychological effect of *freeing* the *acquisition of goods* from the constraints of the traditional economic ethic. In the process, ascetic Protestantism shattered the bonds restricting all striving for gain—not only by legalizing profit but also by perceiving it as desired by God (in the manner portrayed here). The struggle against the desires of the flesh and the attachment to external goods was *not*, as the Puritans explicitly attest (and also the great Quaker apologist, Barclay), a struggle against rational *acquisition*; rather, it challenged the irrational use of possessions. That which remained so familiar to feudal sensibilities—a high regard for the *external* display of luxury consumption—was condemned by the Puritans as a deification of human wants and desires.[24] According to them, God wanted a rational and utilitarian use of wealth on behalf of the basic needs of the person and the community.

Hence, this-worldly asceticism did *not* wish to impose *self-castigation* upon the wealthy.[25] Instead, it wanted that wealth to be used for necessary, *practical*, and *useful* endeavors. The notion of "comfort" [English in original], typically for the Puritans, encompasses the realm of the ethically permissible use of goods. Thus, it is naturally not by chance that one observes the development of the style of life attached to this notion, earliest and most clearly, precisely in those most consistent representatives of the Puritan life outlook: the Quakers. In opposition to the glitter and pretense of feudalism's pomp and display, which rests upon an unstable economic foundation and prefers a tattered elegance to low-key simplicity, the Puritans placed the ideal of the clean and solid comfort of the middle-class "home" [English in original].[26]

In terms of capitalism's *production* of wealth, asceticism struggled against greed. It did so in order to confront both the danger it presented to social order and its *impulsive* character. The Puritans condemned all "covetousness" and "mammonism," for both implied the striving for wealth—becoming rich—as an end in itself. Wealth as such constituted a temptation.

The nature of asceticism again becomes clear at this point. Its methodical-rational organization of life was the power "that perpetually wanted good and perpetually created evil,"[27] namely, evil in the manner conceived by asceticism: wealth and its temptations. For asceticism (together with the Old Testament and completely parallel to the ethical valuation of "good works") defined the pursuit of riches, if viewed as an *end* in itself, as the peak of reprehensibility. At the same time, it also viewed the acquisition of wealth, when it was the *fruit* of work in a vocational calling, as God's blessing. Even more important for this investigation, the religious value set on tireless, continuous, and systematic work in a vocational calling was defined as absolutely the highest of all ascetic means for believers to testify to their elect status, as well as simultaneously the most certain and most visible means of doing so. Indeed, the Puritan's sincerity of belief must have been the most powerful lever conceivable working to expand the life outlook that we are here designating as the spirit of capitalism.[28]

Moreover, if we now combine the strictures against consumption with this unchaining of the striving for wealth, a certain external result [that is, one with an impact outside the realm of religion] now becomes visible: *the formation of capital* through *asceticism's compulsive saving.*[29] The restrictions that opposed the consumption of wealth indeed had their productive use, for profit and gain became used as *investment* capital.

Of course, the strength of this effect cannot be determined exactly in quantitative terms. The connection became so apparent in New England, however, that it did not escape early on the eye of a historian as distinguished as John Doyle.[30] But it was also apparent in Holland, where a strict Calvinism ruled for only seven years. The greater simplicity of life that dominated the Dutch regions of ascetic Protestantism led, among the enormously wealthy, to an excessive desire to accumulate capital.[31]

As far as its power extended, the Puritan life outlook benefited under all circumstances the on-going trend toward a middle-class, economically *rational* organization of life. This outlook was, of course, far more important than the mere facilitating of the formation of capital. Indeed, it was the most substantial and, above all, single consistent social carrier of this middle-class mode of organizing life. Just this rational organization of life stood at the cradle of modern "economic man" (*Wirtschaftsmenschen*).[32]

Our analysis should have demonstrated that one of the constitutive components of the modern capitalist spirit and, moreover, generally of modern civilization, was the rational organization of life on the basis of the *idea of the calling*. It was born out of the spirit of *Christian asceticism*. If we now read again the passages from Benjamin Franklin cited at the beginning of this essay, we will see that the essential elements of the frame of mind described as the "spirit of capitalism" are just those that we have conveyed above as the content of Puritan vocational asceticism.[33] In Franklin, however, this "spirit" exists without the religious foundation, which had already died out.

The idea that modern work in a vocational calling supposedly carries with it an *ascetic* imprint is, of course, also not new. The limitation of persons to specialized work, which necessitates their renunciation of the Faustian multi-dimensionality of the human species, is in our world today the precondition for doing anything of value at all—that is, the "specialized task" and "foreseeking" of multidimensionality irredeemably presuppose and mutually condition one another. *Goethe*, at the peak of his wisdom in his *Wilhelm Meister's Years of Travel* [1829] and in his depiction of Faust's final stage of life [1808], tried to teach us just this:[34] The middle-class way of ordering life, if it wishes to be guided at all rather than to be devoid of continuity, contains a basic component of asceticism. This realization for Goethe implied a resigned farewell to an era of full and beautiful humanity—and a renunciation of it. For such an era will repeat itself, in the course of our civilizational development, with as little likelihood as a reappearance of the epoch in which Athens bloomed.

The Puritan *wanted* to be a person with a vocational calling; we *must* be. For to the extent that asceticism moved out of the monastic cell and was carried over into the life of work in a vocational calling, and then commenced to rule over this-worldly morality, it helped to do its part to build the mighty cosmos of the modern economic order—namely, an economy bound to the technical and economic conditions of mechanized, machine-based production. This cosmos today determines the style of life of all individuals born into this grinding mechanism, and *not* only those directly engaged in economically productive activity. It does so with overwhelming force—and perhaps it will continue to do so until the last ton of fossil fuel has burnt to ashes. The concern for material goods, according to Baxter, should lie on the shoulders of his saints like "a lightweight coat that one can throw off at any time."[35] Yet fate allowed this coat to become a steel-hard casing (*stahlhartes Gehäuse*)[36] To the extent that asceticism undertook to transform and influence the world, the world's material goods acquired an increasing and, in the end, inescapable power over people—as never before in history.

Today the spirit of asceticism has fled from this casing, whether with finality who knows? Victorious capitalism, in any case, ever since it came to rest on a mechanical foundation, no longer needs asceticism as a supporting pillar. Even the optimistic temperament of the Enlightenment, asceticism's joyful heir, appears finally to be fading. And the idea of an "obligation to search for and then accept a vocational calling" now wanders around in our lives as the ghost of beliefs no longer anchored in the substance of religion. The person of today usually rejects entirely all attempts to make sense of a "fulfillment of one's calling" wherever this notion cannot be directly aligned with the highest spiritual and cultural values, or wherever, conversely, it must not be experienced subjectively simply as economic coercion. Then the person of today rejects entirely all attempts to make sense of it at all. The pursuit of gain, in the region where it has become most completely unchained and stripped of its religious-ethical meaning, the United States, tends to be associated with purely competitive passions. Not infrequently, these passions directly imprint this pursuit with the character of a sports event.[37]

No one any longer knows who will live in this casing and whether entirely new prophets or a mighty rebirth of ancient ideas and ideals will stand at the end of this prodigious development. *Or*, however, if neither, whether a mechanized ossification, embellished with a sort of rigidly compelled sense of self-importance, will arise. Then, indeed, if ossification appears, the saying might be true for the "last humans"[38] in this long civilizational development:

> narrow specialists without minds, pleasure-seekers without heart; in its conceit, this nothingness imagines it has climbed to a level of humanity never before attained.[39]

NOTES

1. Compare, for example, Hermann Schell, *Der Katholizismus als Prinzip des Fortschrittes* (Würzburg: Andreas Gobel, 1899), p. 31, and Georg Freiherr von Hertling, *Das Prinzip des Katholizismus und die Wissenschaft* (Freiburg: Herder, 1899), p. 58.
2. One of my students has thoroughly studied the most complete statistical material we possess on this subject: the denominational affiliation statistics of [the state of] Baden. See Martin Offenbacher, "Konfession und soziale Schichtung." *Eine Studie über die wirtschaftliche Lage der Katholiken und Protestanten in Baden* (Tübingen and Leipzig: Mohr, 1901), vol. 4, pt. 5, of the *Volkswirtschaftliche Abhandlungen der badischen Hochschulen*. The facts and figures used for illustrative purposes below all originate from this study.
3. Offenbacher provides for Baden more detailed evidence also on this point in his first two chapters.
4. Printed, for example, in S. R. Gardiner's *Constitutional Documents*. One may draw parallels between this struggle against (anti-authoritarian) asceticism to, for

example, Louis XIV's persecution of the Port Royal settlement and the Jansenists [see ch. 4, note 23]. [On this controversy, see Sharpe, 1992, pp. 351–59.]

5. In this respect the standpoint of *Calvin* was significantly milder, at least to the extent that the finer aristocratic forms of enjoying life were considered. The only limitation is the Bible. The person who stays oriented to it and maintains a good conscience is not required to be suspicious, amidst anxiety, of every stirring in himself to enjoy life. The discussions, which belong here, in chapter 10 of Calvin's *Institutio christianae religionis* (for example, "nec fugere ea quoque possumus quae videntur oblectatione; magis quam necessitat; inservire" [we cannot flee from those things that clearly serve pleasure more than necessity]), might have alone been able to open the floodgates to a very lax praxis. Nonetheless, the distinction between Calvin and Puritanism at this point becomes clear. In addition to an increasing anxiety among the Puritans in regard to the *certitudo salutis* question, it is also the case that, as we will appreciate fully elsewhere, members of the lower *middle-class* became the social carriers of the ethical development of Calvinism in the *ecclesia militans* [militant church] regions.

6. As was common in the German scholarship of his day, Weber here (in contrast to the Anglo-Saxon division between the humanities and the natural sciences) includes in "science," in addition to the natural sciences, literature, history, and languages (the "humanities") [sk].

7. Thomas Adams (*Works of the Puritan Divines*, p. 3) begins a sermon on the three divine sisters ("but love is the greatest of these") with the remark that even Paris gave the golden apple to Aphrodite!

8. Novels and the like, considered as "wastetimes," should not be read (Baxter, *Christian Directory*, vol. 1, p. 51). The decline of lyric poetry and folk music, and not only drama, after the Elizabethan Age in England is well-known. Puritanism did not discover all that much to oppress in the realm of the visual arts. Striking, however, is the decline, from a very good level of musical talent (the role of England in the history of music was not insignificant), to that absolute nothingness in respect to musical giftedness that we later observe among the Anglo-Saxon peoples, and even today. In America, except for the singing in the Negro churches and for the professional singers, who the churches now hire as "attractions" (for $8,000 annually in 1904 in Trinity Church in Boston), one hears mostly "congregational singing"—a noise that is intolerable to German ears. (*Partly analogous developments appeared also in Holland.*)

9. As the proceedings of the synods make clear, the same occurred in Holland. See the resolutions on the may pole in the Reitsma'schen Collection, vol. 6, pt. 78, ch. 139. [J. Reitsma and S. D. van Veen, *Acta der Provinciale en Particuliere Synoden, 1572–1620*, 8 vols. (Groningen: J. B. Walters, 1892–99). The may pole celebration involved a tall, fixed pole. Dancers on May Day, each holding a ribbon attached to the top of the pole, danced around the pole, weaving the ribbons.]

10. It is apparent that the "Renaissance of the Old Testament" and the Pietist orientation to certain Christian sensibilities in art antagonistic to beauty, which in the last analysis refer back to Isaiah [verse 53] and the 22nd Psalm, must have contributed to making *ugliness* more of a possible object of art. It is also evident that, in regard to this development, the Puritan rejection of the deification of human wants and desires played a part. All details, however, appear uncertain. Entirely different motives (demagogical) in the Catholic church brought about developments that, although externally related, led artistically to an entirely different conclusion. Whoever stands in front of Rembrandt's "Saul and David" (in the

Mauritshuis museum) believes he directly experiences the powerful effect of the Puritan sensibility. The inspired analysis of Dutch cultural influences in Karl Neumann's *Rembrandt* (Berlin: Spemann, 1902) probably demarcates the extent to which one *can*, as of today, know the extent to which creative effects in the realm of art can be attributed to ascetic Protestantism.

11. In Holland, a diverse number of pivotal causes (which are impossible to delve into here) were decisive for a comparatively lesser penetration of the Calvinist ethic into everyday life and for a weakening of the ascetic spirit. This situation was visible as early as the beginning of the seventeenth century (the English Congregationalists who fled to Holland in 1608 believed the Dutch sabbath to inadequately uphold the "day of rest" decree); however, it became widely apparent under the [provincial military governor] Friedrich Heinrich [1584–1640]. This decline of the ascetic spirit weakened the expansionary thrust of Dutch Puritanism generally.

The causes for this decline must be located in part in the political constitution (a decentralized federalism of cities and states) and in part in Holland's far lesser development of military forces. (The War of Independence [against Spain, 1568–1648] was early on, for the most part, fought with *money* from Amsterdam and by mercenary soldiers; English preachers illustrated the confusion of tongues among the Babylonians by reference to the Dutch army.) The result was clear: the fervor surrounding the conflict over religious belief was, to a great degree, shifted onto others. As a consequence, however, the chance for participation in political power was flittered away. In contrast, Cromwell's army, although in part conscripted, felt itself to be an army of *citizens*. (To be sure, even more characteristic is that *precisely this* army abolished conscription—because one should fight only for the glory of God and for a cause recognized by the conscience, and not to satisfy the moods of princes. Hence, that English military referred to, according to traditional German views, as possessing an "unethical" constitution, had *historically* very ethical motives at its beginning. Their implementation was demanded by soldiers who had never lost a battle. The ethical values of these soldiers were placed into service in the interest of the Crown only after the Restoration [after 1665].)

As visible in the paintings of [Frans] Hals [1580–1666], the Dutch *schutterijen* [militia], the social carriers of Calvinism in the period of the Great War [1568–1648], appear scarcely "ascetic" as early as one-half generation after the Dordrecht Synod [1574]. Protests in the synods against the organized lives of the *schutterijen* are found repeatedly. The Dutch notion of stiff, haughty formality [*deftigheid*—Weber used a German amalgam: *Deftigkeit*] is a mixture of middle class, rational "respectability" and patrician consciousness of status. This aristocratic character of the Dutch church is evident even today in the allocation of church pews according to class.

The endurance of the city economy in Holland inhibited the development of industry, which expanded only when a new wave of refugees appeared—and therefore only sporadically. Nevertheless, the this-worldly asceticism of Calvinism and Pietism proved effective also in Holland, and in entirely the same direction as elsewhere (even in the sense of an "ascetic compulsion to save," as will be discussed immediately and as G. Groen van Prinsterer demonstrated; see the passage referred to in note 97). The almost entire absence of a belletristic literature in Calvinist Holland is naturally not accidental. [1920]

On Holland see, for example, C. Busken-Huet, *Het Land van Rembrandt*; see also von der Ropp, *Rembrandts Heimat* (Leipzig, 1886–1887).

The understanding of Dutch religious devoutness as involving an "ascetic compulsion to save" is quite apparent even in the eighteenth century; see, for example, the drawings of Albertus Haller. On the characteristic features of Dutch evaluations of art and the motives behind its production, see, for example, the autobiographical remarks of Constantine Huyghens (written 1629–31) in *Oud Holland* (1891). (The work of Groen van Prinsterer, *La Hollande et l'influence de Calvin* [1864], offers for *our* problem nothing pivotal.) The New-Netherlands colony in [New York] involved, viewed in terms of its social composition, a quasi-feudal rulership by "patrons," namely, businessmen who were money-lenders. In contrast to New England, it proved difficult to persuade those near the bottom to emigrate to this region. [1920]

12. It should be remembered that the Puritan city officials closed the Stratford-on-Avon theater even during Shakespeare's time and even when he was, in his later years, still living in Stratford. (His hatred and contempt for the Puritans comes to the surface at every opportunity.) Even in 1777 the city of Birmingham refused to license a theater, arguing that it would promote "slothfulness" and thus adversely influence commerce. See W. J. Ashley, *Birmingham Industry and Commerce* (London, 1913), pp. 7–8. [1920]

13. It is decisive that, for the Puritans, also in this case only an either–or alternative existed: either God's will or the vanity of the flesh. Thus, there could not be, for them, an "Adiaphora" situation [of indifference]. Calvin, as mentioned, in this regard took a different position: as long as an enslavement of the soul under the power of the desires does not take place, what one eats, wears, etc., is a matter of indifference. Freedom from the "world" should be expressed, as for the Jesuits, in indifference; that is, for Calvin, in an undiscriminating, uncovetous usage of whatever goods earthly life offered (see Calvin, *Institutio christianae religionis*, 1st ed. (*op. cit.* [ch. 4, note 19]), p. 409. This position evidently stood closer to Lutheranism than to the precisionism of Calvin's epigones.

14. The behavior of the Quakers is well-known in this regard. Even as early as the beginning of the seventeenth century, tumultuous crowds of pious believers thronged the streets in Amsterdam for a decade in protest against the fashionable hats and apparel of a preacher's wife. (See Dexter's *op. cit.* [ch. 4, note 10], for a charming description). Sanford (*op. cit.* [ch. 4, note 5]) already noted that the male haircut of today is that of the often-mocked "Roundheads." He also observes that the similarly mocked male *apparel* of the Puritans is essentially the same as apparel today, at least in terms of the *principle* at its foundation.

15. [This term, as well as the above three in quotation marks, are in English in the original.] See again on this point Veblen's *Theory of Business Enterprise, op. cit.* [ch. 4, note 221].

16. We will return continuously to this vantage point. Statements such as the following are explained by reference to it: "Every penny which is paid upon yourselves and children and friends must be done as by God's own appointment and to serve and please Him. Watch narrowly, or else that thievish carnal self will leave God nothing" (Baxter, *Chr. Dir., op. cit.*, vol. 1, p. 108). This is decisive: Whatever is turned toward one's *personal* purposes is *withdrawn* from service to God's glory.

17. One is correctly in the habit of remembering (as does Dowden, *op. cit.* [note 4]), for example, that Cromwell saved Raphael's drawings and [Andrea] Mantegna's [1431–1506] *Triumph of Caesar* from extinction while Charles II attempted to sell them. Restoration society, as is well-known, likewise remained thoroughly cool

toward, or directly opposed to, England's national literature. The influence of Versailles among the aristocracy was simply everywhere dominant.

Puritanism uprooted believers from an unreflected enjoyment of everyday life. To analyze in detail the impact of this uprooting on the intellect of the highest types of Puritanism and on those persons influenced by it is a task that cannot be undertaken in the context of this sketch. Washington Irving formulates this influence in the familiar English terms: "It (he means political freedom where we would say Puritanism) evinces less play of the fancy, but more power of the imagination" (*Bracebridge Hall, op. cit.*). One needs only to think of the position of the *Scots* in England in science, literature, technical innovation, and business life in order to sense that this observation strikes the right chord, even though somewhat too narrowly formulated.

We cannot here address the significance of Puritanism for the development of technology and the empirical sciences. The relationship itself between Puritanism and science appears overtly and comprehensively even in daily life [see Robert K. Merton, "Puritanism, Pietism, and Science," in *Social Theory and Social Structure* (New York: Free Press, 1968); F. H. Tenbruck, "Max Weber and the Sociology of Science: A Case Reopened," *Zeitschrift für Soziologie* 3 (1974): 312–20; "Science as a Vocation'—Revisited," *Standorte im Zeitstrom*, ed. by Ernst Forsthoff and Reinhard Hörstel (Frankfurt: Athenäum Verlag, 1974)]. Permitted "recreations" for the Quakers, according to Barclay, are, for example: the visiting of friends, the reading of history, carrying out of experiments in *mathematics and physics*, gardening, the discussion of business and other practical proceedings, etc. The cause of this relationship is that which has been explained earlier.

18. Excellently and beautifully already analyzed in Karl Neumann's *Rembrandt* (*op. cit.*). His analysis should be compared in general with the above remarks.
19. According to Baxter. See the passages cited above [p. 146 and note 49] and *Chr. Dir., op. cit.*, vol. 1, p. 108.
20. See, for example, the well-known description of Colonel Hutchinson (which is often quoted, for example, in Sanford, *op. cit.*, [ch. 4, note 5], p. 57) in the biography written by his widow. After a presentation of all of his chivalrous virtues and his nature inclined toward cheerfulness and an enjoyment of life, she continues: "He was wonderfully neat, cleanly and genteel in his habit, and had a very good fancy in it; but he left off very early the wearing of anything that was costly." According to the description in Baxter's funeral oration for Mary Hammer, the ideal of this cosmopolitan and well-educated Puritan woman is quite similar. However, she is thrifty in regard to time and expenditures for "pomp" and pleasure. See Baxter, *Works of the Puritan Divines (op. cit.* [note 6]), p. 533.
21. In addition to *many* other examples, I remember one in particular. A manufacturer, who had been unusually successful in business and had become very wealthy in his later years, suffered from a stubborn digestive disorder. His physician advised him to enjoy daily a few oysters—yet he complied only after great resistance. That here the issue involved a residual of an "ascetic" disposition (and not simply something related to "stinginess") suspicious of all personal *enjoyment* of wealth becomes apparent *in the end* when one notes that this same manufacturer had made very significant philanthropic contributions throughout his lifetime and had always shown an "open hand" to those in need.
22. The *separation* of workshop, office, and "business" in general from the private residence, of business firm and one's own name, of business capital and private wealth, and the tendency to define the "business" as a *corpus mysticum* [mystical

organization] (at least in the case of corporate assets)—all of these developments go back to the Middle Ages. See my *Handelsgesellschaften im Mittelalter* [in *Gesammelte Aufsätze zur Sozial- und Wirtschaftsgeschichte* (Tübingen: Mohr, 1924/1889), pp. 312–443].

23. In his *Der moderne Kapitalismus*, 1st ed. (Leipzig: Duncker & Humblot, 1902), Sombart has cogently referred occasionally to this characteristic phenomenon. It should be noted, however, that the accumulation of wealth derives psychologically from two very different sources.

   One such source extends far back into the nebulous periods of antiquity and becomes manifest in foundations, family fortunes, trusts, etc. It is just as apparent in these ways, or even in a far more pure and clear form than in the same kind of pursuit, namely, at once to die weighted down with one's own massive accumulation of material possessions and, above all, to insure the continued viability of one's "business," even when doing so violates the personal interests of the majority of the inheriting children. In *these* cases the issue involves, in addition to the wish to lead an ideal life beyond death on the basis of personal achievements that maintain the "splendor familiae," a vanity that takes, so to speak, the expanded personality of the founder as its point of reference. Hence, fundamentally egocentric goals are here apparent.

   It is different when one considers the "middle class" motives with which *we* are here concerned. The maxim of asceticism—"renounce, you should renounce"—holds here and becomes turned toward capitalist activity: "earn, you should earn." And this maxim, with its irrationality, now stands before us plain and pure as a sort of categorical imperative. Only God's glory and one's own duty, not the vanity of human beings, was the motivating force for the Puritans—and *today only* the duty to one's "vocational calling" constitutes one's motivation.

   Whoever derives pleasure from illustrating an idea by looking at its extreme consequences will remember, for example, that theory of certain American millionaires: their earned millions should *not* be left to the children. Doing so would only deny to them the moral task of having to work and earn for themselves. Of course *today* this idea is only "theoretical" bubble-blowing.

24. As must be emphasized repeatedly, *this* is the final, decisive religious motive (in addition to the purely ascetic points of view on the mortification of the flesh). It comes to the forefront especially clearly with the Quakers.

25. Baxter (see *Saints' Everlasting Rest, op. cit.* [ch. 4, note 62], p. 12) completely repudiates this position by reference to the common motive, which is also found normally among the Jesuits: the body must be able to acquire what it needs. Otherwise, one becomes its slave.

26. This ideal, particularly in Quakerism, already clearly existed even in the first period of its development, as has been demonstrated in respect to important points by Hermann Weingarten. See his *Englische Revolutionskirchen (op. cit.* [ch. 4, note 10]). Barclay's detailed discussions also illustrate this point very clearly (*op. cit.* [ch. 4, note 10], pp. 519 ff., 533). To be avoided is bodily vanity thus all ostentation, and sparkling trinkets. This includes the use of things that have no *practical* purpose or that are valued only on account of their rarity (hence, for vanity's sake). Also to be avoided is all unconscientious use of possessions. This takes place when spending occurs, to a *disproportionate degree*, for less necessary needs instead of for the indispensable needs of life and the provision for the future.

   The Quaker life, which was organized according to a living "law of marginal utility," so to speak, exemplified these maxims. "Moderate use of the creature" is completely permitted; *namely*, an emphasis may be placed upon the quality and solidity, etc., of the material used only as long as doing so does not lead to "vanity." On all these matters, see *Morgenblatt für gebildete Leser* (1846), no. 216 ff. (In particular, on the comfort and solidity of materials among the Quakers, see Matthias Schneckenburger, *Vorlesungen, op. cit.* [ch. 4, note 183] (1863), pp. 96 f.)

27. Weber is here playing on the words of Goethe's Mephistopheles, who characterizes himself as "that power which always intends evil, and always creates good" (see *Faust*, Act 1, lines 1336–37) [sk].

28. As already mentioned, the question of the determination of the religious movements' social class cannot be addressed *here* (on this theme see the EEWR essays). However, in order to see that Baxter, for example, who is referred to more than others in this investigation, does not view matters through the eyes of the "bourgeoisie" of his period, it suffices only to note his rank ordering of the vocations pleasing to God: after the teaching vocations, there follows husbandman, and only *then*, in a colorful mix, mariners, clothiers, booksellers, tailors, etc. Even the (characteristically enough) "mariners" are probably at least just as likely thought of as fishermen as ship owners.

In this regard, many statements in the *Talmud* express a different notion. For example, see the, admittedly, not unchallenged sayings of Rabbi Eleasor. All imply that business is better than agriculture. See A. Wünsche, *Der babylonische Talmud*, vol. 2, *op. cit.* [note 67], pp. 20–21. Several later sayings are milder. Here he offers advice for the investing of capital: one-third in land, one-third in merchandise, and one-third in cash (see Wünsche, vol. 2, p. 68).

For those whose conscience remains troubled whenever an economic (or "materialistic" as one, unfortunately, says even today) interpretation is omitted from discussions on causality, let it be noted here that I find the influence of economic development on the destiny of the formation of religious ideas very significant. I will later seek to demonstrate how, in our cases, mutually interacting adaptive processes and relationships produced both economic development on the one hand and religious ideas on the other. [See the Economic Ethics of the World Religions series.] Nonetheless, by no means can the content of religious ideas be *deduced* from "economic" forces. These ideas are, and nothing can change this, actually, *for their part*, the most powerful elements shaping "national character"; they carry purely within themselves an autonomous momentum, lawful capacity (*Eigengesetzlichkeit*), and coercive power. Moreover, the *most important* differences—those between Lutheranism and Calvinism—are predominantly, to the extent that non-religious forces play a part, conditioned by *political* forces.

29. Eduard Bernstein is thinking of this compulsive saving when he says: "Asceticism is a middle-class virtue" (*op. cit.* [ch. 4, note 10], p. 681; see also p. 625). His discussions *are the first* to have suggested these important connections. However, the association is a far more comprehensive one than he suspects. Decisive was not merely capital accumulation; rather, central was the ascetic rationalization of the entire vocational life.

In the case of the American colonies, the contrast between the American North and South was emphasized as early as John Doyle (*The English in America, op. cit.* [ch. 4, note 10]. As a consequence of the "ascetic compulsion to save," capital continuously existed in the Puritan north that needed to be invested. Conditions were quite different in the South. [1920]

30. See Doyle (*ibid.*, vol. 2, ch. 1). The existence of iron works companies (1643) and weaving (1659) for the market (and, by the way, the great prospering of handi-

crafts) in [northern] New England in the first generation after the founding of the colonies are anachronisms if examined from an economic point of view. These developments stand in striking contrast both to conditions in the South and in Rhode Island. In this non-Calvinist state, which enjoyed full freedom of conscience and despite an excellent harbor, a shortage of merchants existed. According to a 1686 report by the "governor and council": "The great obstruction concerning trade is the want of merchants and men of considerable estates amongst us" (S. G. Arnold, *History of the State of Rhode Island*, [Newport, RI: John P. Sanborn & Co., 1876], p. 490.) It can scarcely be doubted that the compulsion repeatedly to invest savings, which resulted from the Puritanical limitation placed upon consumption, played a role here. Church discipline was also important. The role of this factor cannot yet be discussed.

31. The discussion by Busken-Huët indicates that these circles, however, quickly declined in numbers (*op. cit.* [note 77], vol. 2, chs. 3, 4).

    Nevertheless, Groen van Prinsterer notes: "De Nederlanders verkoopen veel en verbruiken wenig" [The Dutch sell much and use little], even in the period *after* the Peace of Westphalia [1648]. See his *Handboek der Geschiedenis* [History] *van het Vaderland*, 3rd ed. (p. 254n.). [1920]

32. The literal translation of Weber's term here, *Wirtschaftsmenschen*—"persons oriented to economic activity"—better conveys his thought. He is seeing, with modernity, an "elevation" of economic activity in people's lives to a position of heretofore unknown salience [sk].

33. That even the components here (which have not yet been traced back to their religious roots)—namely, the maxim honesty is the best policy (Franklin's discussion of *credit*)—are also of Puritan origins is a theme that belongs in a somewhat different context (see the "Protestant Sects" essay below). Only the following observation of J. S. Rowntree (*Quakerism, Past and Present* [London: Smith, Elder and Co., 1859], pp. 95–96), to which Eduard Bernstein called my attention, needs to be repeated:

    Is it merely a *coincidence*, or is it a *consequence*, that the lofty profession of spirituality made by the Friends has gone hand in hand with shrewdness and tact in the transaction of mundane affairs? Real piety favours the success of a trader by insuring his integrity and fostering habits of prudence and forethought. [These are] important items in obtaining that standing and credit in the commercial world, which are requisite for the steady accumulation of wealth (see the "Protestant Sects" essay).

    "Honest as a Huguenot" was as proverbial in the seventeenth century as the respect for law of the Dutch (which Sir W. Temple admired) and, a century later, that of the English. The peoples of the European continent, in contrast, had not moved through this ethical schooling. [1920]

34. This theme is analyzed well in Albert Bielschowsky's *Goethe: sein Leben und seine Werke*, 3rd ed., vol. 2 (Munich: C. H. Beck, 1902–04), ch. 18. A related idea is articulated in regard to the development of the *scientific* "cosmos" by [Wilhelm] Windelband at the end of his *Blütezeit der deutschen Philosophie* (vol. 2 of his *Geschichte der neueren Philosophie* [Leipzig: Breitkopf und Hartel, 1899], pp. 428 ff.).

35. *Saints' Everlasting Rest, op. cit.* [ch. 4, note 62], p. 310. [The text varies slightly from Weber's quote. It reads: "Keep these things loose about thee like thy upper garments, that thou mayest lay them by whenever there is need."]

36. Translated by Parsons as "iron cage," this phrase has acquired near-mythical status in sociology. Weber elaborates upon its meaning in several passages in his

"Parliament and Government in Germany" essay, which was taken by the editors of *Economy and Society* from the corpus of his political writings and incorporated into this analytic treatise (see pp. 1400–03), and in "Prospects for Liberal Democracy in Tsarist Russia" (see *Weber: Selections in Translation*, ed. by W. G. Runciman [Cambridge, UK: Cambridge University Press, 1978], pp. 281–83). Parallel German expressions are translated in these passages as "housing," "shell of bondage," and "casing."

There are many reasons that speak in favor of "steel-hard casing." Not least, it is a literal rendering of the German. Had Weber wished to convey an "iron cage" to his German readership he could easily have done so by employing a commonly used phrase, *eiserner Käfig* (or even *eisenes Gefängnis* [iron prison]; see Stephen Kent, "Weber, Goethe, and the Nietzschean Allusion," *Sociological Analysis* 44 (1983): pp. 297–320 (esp. at pp. 299–300). Let us turn first to the adjective.

Weber's choice of *stahlhart* appropriately conveys (even more than *eisen*) the "hardness" of the constraining casing, as emphasized in the mechanistic images utilized in this passage to describe this new "powerful cosmos." This same image of hardness, however, is visible also in the "lightweight coat" metaphor above: once supple, it has now hardened itself into something (the power of material goods over the individual) that encases persons and cannot be thrown off. Appropriately, because ascetic Protestantism constitutes to Weber a direct precursor to this cosmos, the same adjective is used to describe the Puritan merchant (see p. 111). This lineage is apparent, he argues, even though the dimension foremost for this "merchant saint"—the ethical—has today vanished and left, unforeseeably, in its wake instrumental (or "mechanical") modes of action devoid of genuine brotherhood and resistant to ethical regulation (see, again, the images above and below; see also pp. 426–30). Finally, although not directly apparent in this passage, "steel-hard" conveys a related theme crucial to Weber (as well as Marx and Simmel): the massively impersonal, coldly formal, harsh, and machine-like character of modern public sphere relationships whenever they remain uninfluenced by either traditions or values (see, e.g., the last page of "Science as a Vocation" [Weber, 2005, p. 339]).

Now let us turn to the noun. There are substantive reasons also to prefer "casing" over "cage." Almost without exception, the secondary literature has argued that *stahlhartes Gehäuse* is a phrase intended to call attention to a bleak future inevitably on the horizon. Once in place, this commentary asserts, according to Weber, a nightmare society is putatively permanent. He is then characterized as a dour prophet of doom who, heroically, performs the worthy service of analyzing in a realistic manner a civilization on its deathbed. However, through conditional terms such as "if," "perhaps," "might," "would," "potentially," and "possibly," the usages of this and similar expressions in Weber's other works (as noted above) stress that such a cosmos arises from a series of identifiable economic, religious, political, historical, etc., forces that have become juxtaposed in a unique manner rather than from an unstoppable unfolding of "bureaucratization and rationalization." In other words, if a *stahlhartes Gehäuse* does appear, it must be seen, Weber insists, as a contingent occurrence with, as other occurrences, a period of development and a period of decline.

In my view, this interpretation conforms to the overall tenor of Weber's sociology—a body of work that attends on the one hand to configurations of forces and their contexts rather than to linear historical change and, on the other hand, sees change, conflict, dynamism, and upheaval nearly universally (see 1968 and Kalberg, 1994b, pp. 71–78, 98–117, 168–77, 189–92). Of course, Weber notes that a few civilizations have been quite ossified, such as China for 1500 years and ancient Egypt. Yet their closed character did not result from an "inevitable development" or "evolutionary historical laws" (see above, pp. 87–88, 96–97). Rather, their rigidity must be understood as a consequence of an identifiable constellation of historical, political, etc., forces. (See also the paragraph below on "new prophets…ideas and ideals.") "Cage" implies great inflexibility and hence does not convey this contingency aspect as effectively as "casing" (which, under certain circumstances, can become less restrictive and even peeled off).

In general, in regard to *stahlhartes Gehäuse*, the commentary has vastly exaggerated the importance of this metaphorical image in Weber's works, in the process transforming him from a rigorous comparative-historical sociologist into a social philosopher of modernity (see Lawrence A. Scaff, *Fleeing the Iron Cage* [Berkeley: The University of California Press, 1989]). Notably, *stahlhartes Gehäuse*, and its equivalents, appear in Weber's works either at the end of an empirical study, where he cannot resist the temptation to offer more general speculations (this volume and this volume only), or in his political writings ("Prospects" and "Parliament and Government"), but only once in the body of his sociology; see above (p. 73). Not a single entry can be found in the detailed index to *E&S*, for example, nor in the comprehensive index to the German edition. On the "steel-hard cage" theme generally, see Kalberg, "The Modern World as a Monolithic Iron Cage? Utilizing Max Weber to Define the Internal Dynamics of the American Political Culture Today," in *Max Weber Studies* 1, 2 (2001): 178–97 [sk].

37. "Couldn't the old man be satisfied with his $75,000 a year and retire? No! The frontage of the store must be widened to 400 feet. Why? That beats everything, he says. Evenings, when his wife and daughter read together, he longs for bed. Sundays, in order to know when the day will be over, he checks his watch every five minutes. What a miserable existence!" In this manner the son-in-law (who had emigrated from Germany) of this prosperous dry-goods-man from a city on the Ohio River offered his judgment. Such a judgment would surely appear to the "old man" as completely incomprehensible. It could be easily dismissed as a symptom of the lack of energy of the Germans.

38. This phrase (*letzte Menschen*) is from Friedrich Nietzsche. It could as well be translated as "last people." It is normally rendered as "last men." See *Ecce Homo* (New York: Vintage Books; transl. by Walter Kaufmann, 1967), p. 330; see also *Thus Spoke Zarathustra* (New York: Penguin; transl. by R. J. Hollingdale, 1961), pp. 275–79, 296–311. The "last humans," to Nietzsche, are repulsive figures without emotion. Through their "little pleasures" they render everything small—yet they claim to have "invented happiness." Weber uses this phrase also in "Science as a Vocation." See *Weber*, 2005, p. 325 [sk].

39. Despite thorough investigations by several generations of Weber scholars, the source of this quotation has remained unidentified. Although it appears not to be directly from Nietzsche, as often believed, it is clearly formulated from the tenor of *Thus Spoke Zarathustra*. In full accord with the common usage in academic circles in his time, Weber is using the term *Geist* here to denote a thinker's "multidimensional" capacity to unify and integrate diverse ideas and concepts. This vital capacity was lamented as lacking among specialists (*Fachmenschen*). This passage links back to the above paragraph on Goethe [sk].

LITERATURE CITED

A. WRITINGS OF MAX WEBER

Weber, Max. 1927 (1923). *General Economic History.* Translated by Frank H. Knight. Glencoe, Il.: Free Press.

———. 1930 (1920). *The Protestant Ethic and the Spirit of Capitalism.* Translated by Talcott Parsons. New York: Scribner's.

———. 1936. *Jugendbriefe.* Edited by Marianne Weber. Tübingen: Mohr.

———. 1946a. "Capitalism and Rural Society in Germany." Pp. 363–85 in *From Max Weber: Essays in Sociology (FMW)*, edited and translated by H. H. Gerth and C. Wright Mills. New York: Oxford.

———. 1946b (1919). "Politics as a Vocation." Pp. 77–128 in *FMW.*

———. 1946c (1920). "Religious Rejections of the World." Pp. 323–59 in *FMW.*

———. 1946d (1920). "Science as a Vocation." Pp. 129–56 in *FMW.*

———. 1946e (1920). "The Social Psychology of the World Religions." Pp. 267–301 in *FMW.*

———. 1949 (1922). *The Methodology of the Social Sciences.* Edited and translated by Edward A. Shils and Henry A. Finch. New York: Free Press.

———. 1951 (1920). *The Religion of China.* Edited and translated by Hans H. Gerth. New York: The Free Press.

———. 1952 (1920). *Ancient Judaism.* Edited and translated by Hans H. Gerth and Don Martindale. New York: Free Press.

———. 1958 (1920). *The Religion of India.* Edited and translated by Hans H. Gerth and Don Martindale. New York: The Free Press.

———. 1968 (1921). *Economy and Society.* Edited by Guenther Roth and Claus Wittich. New York: Bedminster Press. [Reprinted 1978; The University of California Press.]

———. 1971a (1910). "Max Weber on Race and Society." Introduction by Benjamin Nelson and translated by Jerome Gittleman. *Social Research*, 38, 1 (Spring): 30–41.

———. 1971b (1924). "Socialism." Pp. 101–219 in *Max Weber*, edited by J. E. T. Eldridge. London: Nelson and Sons.

———. 1973 (1910). "Max Weber, Dr. Alfred Ploetz, and W. E. B. DuBois." Edited and translated by Benjamin Nelson and Jerome Gittleman. *Sociological Analysis*, 34, 4: 308–12.

———. 1976 (1909). *The Agrarian Sociology of Ancient Civilizations.* Translated by R. I. Frank. London: New Left Books.

———. 1978a. "Freudianism." Pp. 383–88 in *Weber: Selections in Translation*, edited by W. G. Runciman. Cambridge: Cambridge University Press.

———. 1978b. (1906). "The Prospects for Liberal Democracy in Tsarist Russia." Pp. 269–84 in *Weber: Selections in Translation*, edited by W. G. Runciman. Cambridge: Cambridge University Press.

———. 1988 (1924). "Diskussionsrede zu W. Sombarts Vortrag über Technik und Kultur. Erste Soziologentagung Frankfurt 1910." Pp. 449–56 in *Gesammelte Aufsätze zur Soziologie und Sozialpolitik*, edited by Marianne Weber. Tübingen: J.C.B. Mohr (Paul Siebeck).

———. 1993 (1904—05/1920). *Die protestantische Ethik und der "Geist" des Kapitalismus* Edited by Klaus Lichtblau and Johannes Weiß. Bodenheim: Athenäum-Hain-Hanstein.

————. 2001 (1907–10). *The Protestant Ethic Debate: Max Weber's Replies to his Critics, 1907–1910.* Edited by David Chalcraft and Austin Harrington and translated by Harrington and Mary Shields. Liverpool: Liverpool University Press.

————. 2002a (1904–1905 and 1907–10). *The Protestant Ethic and the "Spirit" of Capitalism and Other Writings.* Edited, translated, and with an introduction by Peter Baehr and Gordon C. Wells. London: Penguin Books.

————. 2002b (1920). "The Protestant Sects and the Spirit of Capitalism." Translated by H. H. Gerth and C. Wright Mills. Pp. 127–47 in Weber, *The Protestant Ethic and the Spirit of Capitalism.* Translated by Stephen Kalberg. Los Angeles: Roxbury Publ.

————. 2005. *Max Weber: Readings and Commentary on Modernity.* Edited by Stephen Kalberg. Oxford, UK: Blackwell Publishers.

B. SECONDARY LITERATURE CITED

Aptheker, Herbert, ed. 1973. *The Correspondence of W. E. B. Du Bois* (vol. 1, 1877–1934). Amherst, MA: The University of Massachusetts Press.

Becker, George. 1997. "Replication and Reanalysis of Offenbacher's School Enrollment Study: Implications for the Weber and Merton Theses." *Journal for the Scientific Study of Religion,* 36, 4: 483–96.

Collins, Randall. 1980. "Weber's Last Theory of Capitalism." *American Sociological Review,* 45, 6: 925–42.

Groot, Johann Jakob Maria de. 1910. *Religion in China.* New York: Putnam's Sons.

Kaelber, Lutz. 2005. "Rational Capitalism, Traditionalism, and Adventure Capitalism: New Research on the Weber Thesis." Pp. 139–64 in *The Protestant Ethic Turns 100,* edited by William H. Swatos and Kaelber. Boulder, CO: Paradigm Publishers.

Kalberg, Stephen. 1990. "The Rationalization of Action in Max Weber's Sociology of Religion." *Sociological Theory,* 8 (Spring): 58–84.

————. 2001a. "Should the 'Dynamic Autonomy' of Ideas Matter to Sociologists? Max Weber on the Origin of Other-Worldly Salvation Religions and the Constitution of Groups in American Society Today." *Journal of Classical Sociology,* 1,3 (Dec.): 291–327.

————. 2001b. "The Modern World as a Monolithic Iron Cage?" *Max Weber Studies,* 1 (May): 178–95.

————. 2001c. "The 'Spirit' of Capitalism Revisited: On the New Translation of Weber's *Protestant Ethic* (1920)." *Max Weber Studies,* 2, 1 (Dec.): 41–57.

————. 2003a. "Max Weber." Pp. 132–92 in *The Blackwell Companion to Major Social Theorists,* edited by George Ritzer. Oxford: Blackwell Publishers, 2003.

————. 2003b. "The Influence of Political Culture Upon Cross-Cultural Misperceptions and Foreign Policy: The United States and Germany." *German Politics and Society,* 21, 3 (Fall): 1–23.

————. 2004. "The Past and Present Influence of World Views: Max Weber on a Neglected Sociological Concept." *Journal of Classical Sociology,* 4, 2 (July): 139–64.

————. 2005. "Utilizing Max Weber's 'Iron Cage' to Define the Past, Present, and Future of the American Political Culture." Pp. 191–208 in *The Protestant Ethic Turns 100,* edited by William H. Swatos and Lutz Kaelber. Boulder, CO: Paradigm Publishers.

———. 2008. "The Perpetual and Tight Interweaving of Past and Present in Max Weber's Sociology." Pp. 30–54 in *History Matters*, edited by David Chalcraft, Fanon John Howell, Marisol Lopez Menendez, and Hector Vera Martinez. Aldershot, UK: Ashgate Publishers.

———. Forthcoming. *Max Weber's Sociology of Civilizations*.

Keeter, Larry G. 1981. "Max Weber's Visit to North Carolina." *Journal of the History of Sociology*, 3, 2 (Spring): 108–14.

Klages, Ludwig. 1910. *Prinzipien der Charakterologie*. Leipzig: J.A. Barth.

Legge, James. 1861–1872. *The Chinese Classics*. Oxford: Oxford University Press.

Lenger, Friedrich. 1994. *Werner Sombart, 1863–1914: Eine Biographie*. Munich: Beck Verlag.

Lenski, Gerhard. 1974. *The Religious Factor*. New York: Doubleday.

Manasse, Ernst Moritz. 1947. "Max Weber on Race." *Social Research*, 14: 191–221.

Merton, Robert K. 2001 (1938). *Science, Technology and Society in Seventeenth Century England*. New York: Howard Fertig.

Mommsen, Wolfgang. 1974. "Die Vereinigten Staaten von Amerika." Pp. 72–96 in Mommsen, *Max Weber. Gesellschaft, Politik und Geschichte*. Frankfurt: Suhrkamp.

———. 2000. "Max Weber in America." *American Scholar*, 69, 3 (Summer): 103–12.

Nielsen, Donald A. 2005. "*The Protestant Ethic and the "Spirit" of Capitalism* as Grand Narrative: Max Weber's Philosophy of History." Pp. 53–76 in *The Protestant Ethic Turns 100*, edited by William H. Swatos and Lutz Kaelber. Boulder, CO: Paradigm Publishers.

Peukert, Detlev J. K. 1989. *Max Webers Diagnose der Moderne*. Göttingen: Vandenhoeck u. Ruprecht.

Rachfahl, Felix. 1978. "Anti-Critical Last Word on *The Spirit of Capitalism*." Translated by Wallace Davis. *American Journal of Sociology*, 83, 5: 1110–32.

Ringer, Fritz. 1969. *The Decline of the German Mandarins*. Cambridge: Harvard University Press.

———. 2004. *Max Weber*. Chicago: The University of Chicago Press.

Roth, Guenther. 2005. "Transatlantic Connections: A Cosmopolitan Context for Max and Mariannne Weber's New York Visit 1904." *Max Weber Studies*, 5, 1 (January): 81–112.

Salomon, Albert. 1962. *In Praise of Enlightenment*. Cleveland, OH: World Publ. Co.

Scaff, Lawrence. 2005. "Remnants of Romanticism: Max Weber in Oklahoma and Indian Territory." Pp. 77–110 in *The Protestant Ethic Turns 100*, edited by William H. Swatos and Lutz Kaelber. Boulder, CO: Paradigm Publishers.

Schluchter, Wolfgang. 1981. *The Rise of Western Rationalism*. Translated by Guenther Roth. Berkeley: The University of California Press.

Sharpe, Kevin. 1992. *The Personal Rule of Charles I*. New Haven: Yale University Press.

Tawney, R. H. "Foreword." 1958 (1930). Pp. 1–11 in *Max Weber: The Protestant Ethic and the Spirit of Capitalism*. Translated by Talcott Parsons. New York: Charles Scribner's Sons.

Tocqueville, Alexis de. 1945. *Democracy in America*, Vol. 2. New York: Vintage.

Tönnies, Ferdinand. 1957 (1887). *Community and Society*. New York: Harper Torchbooks.

Winter, Elke. 2004. *Max Weber et les relations ethniques. Du refus du biologisme racial a l'Etat multinational*. Quebec: Presses de l'Universite Laval.

Weber, Max. 1927. *General Economic History*. Translated by Frank H. Knight. Glencoe, IL: Free Press. Originally: 1923. *Wirtschaftsgeschichte*. Edited by S. Hellman and M. Palyi. Munich: Duncker & Humblot.

———. 1946a. "Religious Rejections of the World." Pp. 323–59 in *From Max Weber: Essays in Sociology (FMW)*, edited and translated by H. H. Gerth and C. Wright Mills. New York: Oxford. Originally: (1920) 1972. "Zwischenbetrachtung." Pp. 537–73 in *Gesammelte Aufsätze zur Religionssoziologie* (hereafter *GARS*), vol. 1, edited by Johannes Winckelmann. Tübingen: Mohr.

———. 1946b. "The Social Psychology of the World Religions." Pp. 267–301 in *FMW*. Originally: (1920) 1972. Pp. 237–68 in *GARS*, vol. 1.

———. 1949. *The Methodology of the Social Sciences*. Edited and translated by Edward A. Shils and Henry A. Finch. New York: Free Press. Originally: (1922) 1973. Pp. 489–540, 146–214, 215–290 in *Gesammelte Aufsätze zur Wissenschaftslehre*, edited by Johannes Winckelmann. Tübingen: Mohr.

———. 1951. *The Religion of China*. Edited and translated by Hans H. Gerth. New York: The Free Press. Originally: (1920) 1972. "Konfuzianismus und Taoismus." Pp. 276–536 in *GARS*, vol. 1.

———. 1952. *Ancient Judaism*. Edited and translated by Hans H. Gerth and Don Martindale. New York: Free Press. Originally: (1920) 1971. *Das antike Judentum. GARS*, vol. 3, edited by Johannes Winckelmann.

———. 1958. *The Religion of India*. Edited and translated by Hans H. Gerth and Don Martindale. New York: Free Press. Originally: (1920) 1972. *Hinduismus und Buddhismus. GARS*, vol. 2, edited by Johannes Winckelmann.

———. 1968. *Economy and Society*. Edited by Guenther Roth and Claus Wittich. New York: Bedminster Press. Originally: (1921) 1976. *Wirtschaft und Gesellschaft*. Edited by Johannes Winckelmann. Tübingen: Mohr.

———. 1978. "Freudianism." Pp. 383–88 in *Weber: Selections in Translation*, edited by W. G. Runciman and translated by Eric Matthews. Cambridge, UK: University Press. Originally: (unabridged) 1990. *Briefe 1906–1908, Max Weber Gesamtausgabe II, vol. 5*, edited by Rainer Lepsius and Wolfgang J. Mommsen. Tübingen: Mohr.

———. 2001 (1907–10; 1972). *The Protestant Ethic Debate: Max Weber's Replies to his Critics, 1907–1910*. Edited by David Chalcraft and Austin Harrington and translated by Harrington and Mary Shields. Liverpool: Liverpool University Press. Originally: Archiv für Sozialwissenschaft und Sozialpolitik 25 (1907): 243–49; vol. 26 (1908): 275–83; vol. 30 (1910): 176–202; vol. 31 (1910): 554–99.

———. 2002 (1904–1905 and 1907–10). *The Protestant Ethic and the "Spirit" of Capitalism and Other Writings*. Edited, translated, and with an introduction by Peter Baehr and Gordon C. Wells. London: Penguin Books. *PE* originally: *Archiv für Sozialwissenschaft und Sozialpolitik* 20 (1904): 1–54 and 21 (1905): 1–110.

———. 2005. *Max Weber: Readings and Commentary on Modernity*, edited by Stephen Kalberg. Oxford, UK: Blackwell Publishers.

Excerpt from *Corporation Nation*

CHARLES DERBER

THE WANING OF COUNTERVAILING POWER

Our present era is defined by three central tendencies. The first is the rise of giant global corporate empires linking producers, retailers, distributors, and suppliers in integrated worldwide business networks. The second is the downsizing of the federal government and its increasing role as an advocate for, rather than adversary to, business. The third is the erosion of labor unions. Together, these trends mark a great decline of the forces of countervailing power that had developed through much of the twentieth century, and a return to a balance of forces reminiscent of the late 1800s.

Decline should not be confused with collapse. As mentioned, today's corporate ascendancy is taking place in the context of a regulatory regime that sets important limits on business even while buttressing its authority. Labor has been in a near freefall of power and membership, but it still wields significant influence. Moreover, new countervailing forces—including institutional investors, giant competitors, and the financial markets, as well as an array of grassroots social movements—are rising to check corporations in novel ways. Nonetheless the countervailing power of the New Deal has been decisively eroded, and no new countervailing regime—despite the abiding liberal faith in its inevitability—has securely replaced it.

The fate of labor is the most visible sign of the end of the New Deal's countervailing regime—a story that neither Galbraith nor Berle could anticipate in the halcyon days of the 1950s. While total membership began declining by the mid-fifties, the influence of unions continued to grow until at least the late sixties. But by the early seventies globalization and automation had already begun to weaken unions severely, and in the eighties corporations and the federal government moved aggressively to undercut labor's remaining power. Arguing that unions were a threat to global competitiveness, corporate leaders engaged in the most systematic antilabor campaign since the Gilded Age. GM, GE, and other trendsetters routinely broke labor contracts, and demanded wage, benefit, and other concessions. High-tech leaders joined them in creating a new industry of lawyers, personnel specialists, and consultants specializing in union-busting and

Derber, Charles. 1998. "The Curse of the Robber Barons," and "Bye, Bye, American Pie" from *Corporation Nation*. New York: St. Martin's Griffin.

prevention. Universities and hospitals fired organizers and spent millions to tie up certification in legal wrangling. Even when GM was making *concessions* a household word in Michigan, Harvard University was leading a decade-long struggle to prevent clerical unions from getting a foothold in the enlightened groves of academe.[1]

Corporations were getting aid and comfort from Ronald Reagan's Washington. Reagan's devastating assault on PATCO—the air traffic controllers' union—was one of his first presidential acts. FDR used the government to help create organized labor, but in so doing he created a movement deeply vulnerable to the whims of the state's labor bureaucracy. Reagan turned the full weight of that apparatus against the labor movement, appointing regulators to the National Labor Relations Board who sided routinely with corporations on jurisdictional and certification disputes and would make it difficult to contest even blatantly illegal corporate acts such as firing organizers. The Great Communicator also used his bully pulpit to persuade the public, already predisposed to think of unions as corrupt, to see unions as special-interest groups which corrode democracy—a view that many labor leaders contributed to by their own blatant abuse of union power or dues. In tandem with the corporate campaign that pictured unions as subverting competitiveness, Reagan helped turn most Americans into foes of unions, an especially notable achievement while massive downsizing and declining wages were the order of the day.

Combined with changes in market scale and technology, those antilabor campaigns sounded the death knell of labor as a vigorous countervailing force while also signaling the shift of government from countervailing power to corporate booster. Union membership fell precipitously—from its peak of 34 percent in 1954 to its current low of 15 percent of the nation's workforce. The influence of labor plummeted. While there are promising signs of revival in the late nineties, the labor movement has not been so weak since before its takeoff in the New Deal.[2]

The fate of government as a countervailing force is more complex. The Reagan, Bush, and Clinton administrations have all embraced a corporate agenda. Bill Clinton's conversion to corporate priorities such as the balanced budget, international free trade, and privatization is especially notable, since it marked the end of the federal government (under either party) as an aggressive counterweight to business. Nonetheless, the regulatory state remains large and powerful in its contradictory role as a force of both restraint and support for corporate ascendancy. As the two major political parties increasingly act in the interest of business, government's role as an underwriter of business increases, but this has by no means eliminated the regulatory state's countervailing role. President Clinton, who unabashedly solicited corporate contributions and sponsored corporate America's leading policy initiatives, also supported environmental regulation, medical-insurance reform, and family medical-leave programs—all of which were opposed by business. Clinton's administration illustrates mainly the dramatic erosion of government as countervailing power, but also the lingering role of the state as a friendly corporate adversary.

As unions and governments weaken, grassroots social movements are rising, that—if joined with labor and governmental activism—could help create a new countervailing regime. Since the seventies, sociologists have identified feminism, minority-rights groups, and the environmental movement as "new" social movements largely grounded in the middle class. These movements, which might seem unlikely corporate adversaries, increasingly target corporations. In the nineties, minority groups led a series of attacks on Texaco and other leading corporations for racial discrimination, while feminists lambasted the "glass ceiling," the pink-collar ghetto, and widespread sexual harassment in the suites. In 1998, Jesse Jackson went to Wall Street demanding that it was time for America's financial establishment to embrace racial and sexual diversity and redirect its great coffers of wealth to the nation's dispossessed.

The new social movements have already helped write into law constraints that the robber barons never faced, including laws banning sexual or racial discrimination, affirmative-action mandates, and vast environmental regulation. They have shown that corporations both internalize and often promote electrically charged sexual and racial hierarchies in the larger society. Corporations have created specialized "secondary" labor markets for women and minorities, and even when seeking in good faith to implement affirmative action, reproduce, and add new fire to sexual and racial stratification. In beginning to identify corporate power as both gendered and racialized, feminists and minority movements have mobilized opposition that—if linked to a revived labor and populist movement—could shake the corporation to its roots.

Nonetheless, in their current incarnation, the new social movements are an ambiguous and limited countervailing force. Feminists and racial-pride or -rights movements have been far more concerned with issues of identity than economics. Their corporate demands—centered on affirmative action and nondiscrimination—involve fair access to the system rather than systemic transformation. While such demands can change the entry and promotion rules, placing limits on explicit corporate cronyism, they can also subtly legitimate the underlying corporate order, by pitting the sexes and races against each other rather than uniting them around common concerns. Except for small subgroups, the new movements have not challenged corporate ascendancy as an inherent threat to democracy or social justice. Even should they fully realize their aspirations for diversity, affirmative action, and nondiscrimination, they will have barely disturbed a corporate system that already legitimates itself on claims of meritocracy and universalism. If the percentage of female or African-American corporate leaders were to grow dramatically, this would be a major advance. But it would scarcely erode corporate ascendancy, just as promoting more women and African-Americans to the top ranks of the Pentagon does little to subvert militarism.

BYE, BYE, AMERICAN PIE

In the early 1990s, IBM hired a management consultant—call him Bill Phillips—to work on a high-level global project based in Geneva, Switzerland. He was thrilled until he actually got to his job, where he found unexpected tension and distrust among his coworkers. Phillips couldn't understand it until he learned that they all were former IBM engineers and programmers who had been laid off—many after thirty years—and then rehired on a contract basis to do the same work.[3]

They all lived in something like a state of panic. Most were uncertain of whether IBM would keep them on for the duration of this project or hire them for another. Phillips said they reminded him of survivors on a lifeboat jostling to see who would stay on board. Their insecurity and dark mood undermined their ability to cooperate on the team. And these were the winners among the nearly 200,000 IBM employees who had gotten pink slips in recent years. What must the others be like? thought the new man on the job.

All of them, says former labor secretary Robert Reich, are on the same wobbly lifeboat—members of America's new anxious class. The anxious class consists of the millions of Americans, in his words, "who no longer can count on having their jobs next year, or next month, and whose wages have stagnated or lost ground to inflation." Since 50 percent of Americans now say they worry about losing their job, and up to 70 percent of Americans have been seeing stagnant or declining real wages for twenty years, the anxious class is not only anxious but big. It encompasses a huge chunk of the middle class, the entire underclass, at least ten million working poor, and even many professionals such as IBM's dispossessed computer engineers.

The anxious class is making America nervous—keeping an entire industry of analysts in the pink. It is being measured by pollsters, profiled by the media, and addressed by politicians. But despite the deluge of attention, Americans have not learned the real meaning of the cataclysm. Drenched in a dizzying fog of business babble about reengineering, self-reliance, and the new entrepreneurship, the anxious class has been profoundly misled about the causes of its anxiety, blaming itself for its faintness of heart while accepting the rollback of its social protections as the inevitable cost of global competitiveness.

The torrent of analysis about the anxious class has, nonetheless, established two new realities about America. One is that a level of economic insecurity that has not been seen since the Great Depression now permeates the nation—a particularly vexing phenomenon in an economy which is enjoying growth, renewed productivity, and high profits. "For the first time in fifty years," says Richard T. Curtin, director of the University of Michigan's Consumer Surveys, "we are recording a decline in people's expectations. And their uncertainty and anxiety grow the farther you ask them to look into the future." Polls in the mid-1990s, including 1997 surveys carried out at the peak of a remarkable market expansion and economic boom, showed that about two-thirds of Americans saw job security as lower than it was a few years ago, and more than half said they expected this greater insecurity to last for many years.[4]

Louis Uchitelle does not mince words: The anxious class is "the losing class." Caught in America's long-term downsizing blitzkrieg, they are losing their jobs with no assurance of another. Trapped in a quarter-century of wage standstill, they are losing their prosperity.[5] Millions of Americans, former New Jersey senator Bill Bradley agrees, "are adrift on a gigantic river of economic transformation that carries away everything."[6] Bradley hints that Americans are losing more than job security and middle-class wages. Global corporations are bulldozing the economic foundation stones that made a middle class possible.

The most remarkable thing about the anxious class is its empathy with management. Public opinion polls show that most Americans, despite their persistent sense of insecurity, do not blame their employers. Instead, they see business itself as a victim disempowered by the global tide of competition and technological change. Sociologist Joel Rogers says workers tell him: "'My boss is trying hard, but there is nothing he can do either'.... They say he does not have the ability to protect them, which is much different than saying 'He could protect me if he wanted to but he chooses not to.'"

If it sees any enemies, the anxious class has been persuaded to point to politicians and big government rather than the corporate system. Pollster Florence Skelly marvels at the degree of disorientation: "You would think that in a free enterprise system, there would be more criticism of its warts. Instead, we say that government should be run more like a business. And we deal with the boss by ousting the Congressman."[7]

THE ANXIOUS CLASS AND THE ROBBER BARONS: THE SOCIAL CONTRACT AS SOCIAL DARWINISM

Most Americans were part of another anxious class a hundred years ago. Made up mainly of farmers, immigrant workers, and an aspiring middle class who lived close to the brink, its economic insecurity gave rise to the violent labor uprisings and the prairie populist movement that exploded against the robber barons in the 1880s and 1890s. The rebirth of the anxious class today marks the rise of a new era of corporate ascendancy. The new power of the corporate community liberates it from the burden of long-term social obligations to employees and their communities. The anxiety of the anxious class reflects its visceral understanding that the social contract that brought it into being is unraveling.

A social contract is the set of laws and social norms that establishes long-term responsibilities and protective moral covenants among employers, employees, and communities. While it seems the foundation of any society, a social contract is not to be taken for granted in market societies. Again the Gilded Age model is instructive: The robber barons purged social covenants by crushing nonmarket forces and enshrining the amoral ideology of the market as the ultimate morality.

In the Gilded Age, business leaders, politicians, and intellectuals preached the gospel of social Darwinism—a variant of market fundamentalism that has resurfaced today. Herbert Spencer, one of England's leading Darwinist thinkers a century ago, summed up the Gilded Age view of safety nets and social contracts: "The whole effort of nature is to get rid of such [the poor], to clear the world of them, and make room for better... it is best that they die." William Graham Sumner, another of the period's most influential writers, saw the rich as nature's elect—and any effort to distribute wealth to help workers or the poor as contrary to the natural order: "The millionaires are a product of natural selection... if we do not like the survival of the fittest, we have only one possible alternative, and that is the survival of the unfittest. The former is the law of civilization; the latter is the law of anti-civilization." He argued that poor workers were nature's losers and should be treated as such.[8]

Unlike today's business leaders, the robber barons did not have to roll back a social contract so much as ensure that none arose. This meant aborting the rise of unions and activist government, the embryonic countervailing forces at the end of the nineteenth century that sought to limit exploitation of workers and infuse Gilded Age companies and markets with social responsibility. The robber barons rose to the challenge with their customary enthusiasm. Jim Fisk's response to a strike of the Erie railway brakemen was to "send a gang of toughs from New York under orders to shoot down any man who offered resistance." Fisk's stated view of unions as an unacceptable "special interest" resonated among all the robber barons. George F. Baer, a leading industrialist who headed the Philadelphia and Reading Co., said that "the rights and interests of the laboring man will be protected and cared for" not by unions or intrusive legislators but "by the Christian men to whom God has given control of the property rights of the country."[9]

The lack of any Gilded Age social contract beyond social Darwinism created America's first anxious class. Ordinary Americans in the Gilded Age were unprotected by law, self-organization, or the prevailing God. They would be anxious until countervailing forces became powerful enough to create a genuine social contract for twentieth-century Americans.

THE DEATH OF THE ANXIOUS CLASS AND THE RISE OF THE MIDDLE CLASS: THE NEW DEAL SOCIAL CONTRACT

It took the Great Depression to end the agony of America's first anxious class. Desperate circumstances propelled ordinary Americans to take their fate in their own hands. They launched the most powerful challenge to corporate rule ever seen in American history—shutting down factories, marching in the streets, and voting en masse for a new type of political leader. The

Depression led to the creation of America's most powerful labor movement and the election of the activist Democratic government of Franklin Delano Roosevelt.

Roosevelt preserved capitalism, but he was a revolutionary nonetheless, and he created a new American social contract. The New Deal was a genuine alternative to Gilded Age capitalism, and the nation's most decisive repudiation of social Darwinism. It established the protections of the welfare state, giving the anxious class its first dose of guaranteed social security. It also gave legal protection to unions—a dagger in the heart of Gilded Age economics, since it returned some basic rights to workers and institutionalized a modicum of countervailing power among unions. A bold new labor movement and a series of riots among the poor and homeless during the Depression helped force Roosevelt to accept and enact major changes.

For fifty years, the new social contract liberated a majority of ordinary Americans from economic insecurity. The New Deal, to be sure, did not eliminate poverty or create a paradise for the new vast middle class it brought into being. Nor did it dismantle the giant corporations that arose during the Gilded Age. To the contrary, Roosevelt's National Recovery Act institutionalized a close relation between business and government that greatly expanded the public power and character of corporations. Corporate empires built by Rockefeller and J. P. Morgan grew even bigger after the New Deal. But while the New Deal did not shrink the size or influence of the nation's largest corporations, it ended monolithic corporate control of America, giving labor and government itself a seat at the table.[10]

Another decisive shift came after World War II, symbolized by the accommodation made by the big auto companies to a long-term relation with the United Auto Workers. UAW leader Walter Reuther and Charles Wilson, the head of GM in the 1940s, wrote a corporate marriage contract that changed America. While still bureaucratic and authoritarian, the new GM accepted long-term responsibilities to employees and to the nation as the condition of doing business. GM endorsed multiyear agreements, building a corporate safety net that catapulted GM workers out of the anxious class. Guaranteeing annual pay increases and cost-of-living adjustments, as well as an expanding package of benefits, the new GM delivered 3 percent yearly wage increases above inflation for a quarter of a century. The steadily expanding job-security, health-care, vacation, pension and unemployment benefits it offered rivaled those that the European welfare state was delivering to its own new middle class.[11]

Protected by its own dominant position in the auto market GM committed to a primitive version of corporate communitarianism. The company treated employees and their unions as members of the GM family. Both partners acknowledged the legitimate adversarial interests of the other, but also accepted a set of mutual moral obligations. The specific wage, benefit, and seniority arrangements, while balm to the soul of an anxious class were ultimately less important than the simple affirmation that the company owes its workers a share of prosperity and the dignity due a member of the family.[12]

GM found that nonmarket values had long-term market payoffs. Beyond generating an abiding loyalty among its workers, which helped increase productivity, it put money into the American worker's wallet—which helped, in turn, to boost the demand for GM cars.

The GM initiative became a catalyst for national change. America's giant corporations—from AT&T to U.S. Steel—wrote their own new social contracts. These took two forms: an industrial model, which followed the GM blueprint, and a salaried model typified by IBM. Both were based on internal labor markets—instead of hiring from outside, companies would promote from within, institutionalizing the expectation of a long-term marriage between worker and company.[13] In the GM model, workers increased their security by hewing to union-enforced narrow job classifications and rigid rules that decreased the arbitrary power of management to reassign workers and decide whom to hire, promote, or demote.[14] In the IBM model, management resisted narrow work rules and had a freer hand to redeploy workers flexibly, but made a firmer commitment to job security. With its famous lifetime employment policy, Big Blue promised the ultimate antidote to the anxieties of the anxious class.[15]

The new social contract gave birth to a middle class free of the debilitating economic insecurity that is today revisiting their children. This triumph of countervailing forces was made possible both by the political mobilization of the New Deal and by the postwar prosperity and dominance of American corporations. After World War II destroyed the European and Japanese economies, the American century came into full flower. The absence of significant global competition made it far easier for American corporations to treat their unionized employees generously, since higher wages could be passed along to the consumer in higher prices without jeopardizing corporate profitability. But such generosity, which increased employee loyalty and productivity, came into being only through the power of the labor movement and of their liberal allies in postwar governments. Corporations resisted unions and long-term contracts, finally embracing them only because the balance of political forces gave them little alternative.[16]

The limits of the postwar contract should not be forgotten. For one thing, business remained the business of America: Giant corporations still ran the economy. Unions won a foothold in industry and the public sector, but never got a welcome mat in the new high-tech, service-oriented economy. Even in the union sector, New Deal workers won security but not the right to help run the company.

Only one part of the business world, moreover, made a gesture toward a social contract—the biggest corporations such as GM and IBM that couldn't afford not to. Smaller companies—under less pressure from unions and government—continued to treat workers as they always had. The New Deal contract also left out millions of African Americans and women. Three of the New Deal legal linchpins—the National Industrial Recovery Act (1933), the Social Security Act (1935), and the Fair Labor Standards Act (1937)—explicitly excluded agricultural laborers and domestic servants, instantly writing the majority of African Americans out of the New Deal. The New Deal also inherited and perpetuated a dual sexual standard based on the notion of a full-time male worker and a female worker marginally attached to the labor force. Men (and a small number of full-time working women) would gain a form of labor rights and social insurance—including bargained wages and working conditions, unemployment compensation, disability payments, and pensions—designed to promote independence and self-reliance. Women (and a tiny fraction of permanently unemployable men) would receive welfare designed to promote dependency.

While the New Deal thus excluded and disenfranchised many Americans, its accomplishments should not be diminished. It forced business to share power with labor and government and civilize its attitudes toward workers. It weaned a nation from its faith in social Darwinism. And it led America's most powerful corporations to recognize, finally, that good business is more than just a commercial enterprise.

JOB GENOCIDE, THE VIRTUAL CORPORATION, AND THE VIRTUAL WORKER

Nike, the company known by its motto "Just Do It," is living up to its name. A 5-billion-dollar company making almost half a billion dollars in profits, Nike rules the lucrative world of sneakers. But Nike doesn't employ a single worker who makes shoes.

A new class of global contract workers produces Nike's sneakers. While it announced a new policy in 1998, Nike, in the early and mid-1990s, contracted mainly with Indonesian and Vietnamese suppliers, who pay young girls and women about one to two dollars a day to make its footwear—not enough, according to government sources, to keep them adequately fed. In 1992 Nike paid Michael Jordan more for helping market the shoes than the total it paid all 75,000 of its Indonesian contractors. The workers are forced to work overtime; they have no right to strike and no union to represent them. In 1997, Thuyen Nguyen, founder of Vietnam Labor Watch, reported that "Supervisors humiliate women, force them to kneel, to stand in the hot sun, treating them like recruits to boot camp."[17]

Nike is a model of the new virtual corporation that solves the old problem of labor in a new way. While it does have a few thousand employees—all in management, design, and sales—Nike has contracted out all employment in its core line of business. The virtual company is a jobless company. As such, it is practicing job genocide, a strategy for cutting costs and ending long-term corporate obligations to employees by getting rid of jobs as we know them.

While downsizing and automation have brought a great deal of attention to job displacement, these are only symptoms of a far more profound change. "What is disappearing," writes the organizational theorist William

Bridges, "is not just a certain number of jobs—or jobs in certain industries or jobs in some part of the country or even jobs in America as a whole. What is disappearing, is the very thing itself: the job. That much sought after, much maligned social entity, a job, is vanishing like a species that has outlived its evolutionary time."[18]

The end of the job is not, however, a product of natural evolution, but part of an evolving corporate strategy that has more ambitious aims than global competitiveness. The full-time permanent job became the focal point in the New Deal for building a labor movement, regulating the company, and vesting workers with legal rights and economic and moral claims on the company. The labor legislation passed in the New Deal created a framework for ensuring employee representation and legal rights tied to full-time work. This approach to the social contract, based on the assumption that most families would be supported by one full-time wage earner, continued to guide labor law until the present day. Conventional full-time employment remains today the key institution protected by the social contract, with virtually all legal rights and labor representation written to apply to full-time conventional employees.

As long as conventional jobs prevailed, it was difficult for corporations to free themselves from the constraints imposed by both unions and government. The shift toward contract labor is a brilliant maneuver designed to evade the social contract. Without an employment structure based on conventional jobs, workers lose their rights, unions lose their organizing power, and government's ability to protect workers goes into limbo. Contract or "virtual" workers have little meaningful protection under most federal laws governing unionization, collective bargaining, wages and working conditions, discrimination, occupational safety, family and medical leave, or pension and health benefits.[19]

Critics tend to assume that companies shifting toward contract labor are just out to save a buck, mainly on health care and other fringe-benefit costs.[20] The underlying corporate benefits and motives are more far-reaching. Contract labor is a systemic assault on America's Magna Carta of worker rights: the 1935 Wagner Act, which guaranteed the right to unionize and bargain collectively, and the Fair Labor Standards Act of 1937, which governs wages and working conditions. Both these acts remain on the books, but the shift toward contract labor will make them irrelevant for millions of twenty-first-century workers.

Temporary and leased workers are in name still protected, since they can claim their temping or leasing agencies are legally designated employers who must respect their rights to unionization, the minimum wage, and non-discrimination. But since the agencies do not determine their actual conditions of work and the constantly changing corporations in which they work bear no legal liability for violating their rights, such protections are almost meaningless in practice. Temp workers are so widely dispersed, and turn over so rapidly, that it would be nearly impossible to determine who would qualify to vote in a certification election for a union at Manpower, much as it would be an impossible task for union organizers even to identify and locate the temps themselves. Similarly, compliance with overtime or anti-discrimination laws could be theoretically facilitated by the temporary or leasing agency, but the transience of the workforce and the inability of the agencies to determine workplace conditions makes both monitoring and enforcement a prospect that is increasingly remote.[21]

Although the shift to contract labor effectively ends the New Deal social contract for millions of workers, the change cannot be read as purely a matter of conspiratorial strategic planning by heartless corporations. Several studies have suggested that such contingent arrangements have evolved in a far more ad hoc fashion in many companies, driven by unanticipated budgetary pressures or scheduling problems. In an early 1980s study, Richard Belous found that lower-level managers in supermarkets, factories, and department stores frequently experimented with temp labor or contract workers to resolve such problems, without any guidance from senior managers, many of whom had no idea how many of their workers were contingent—nor any theory of how many should be. Only in the nineties, as the radical expansion of their numbers made contingent workers a public issue, did most corporations begin to think systematically about how to restructure their labor markets and consciously design a new model of work organization. Today, as many corporations have moved opportunistically and with greater formal planning to consolidate contingent arrangements in their own interests, corporate motivations cannot be reduced to a simple formula. Nonetheless, the effect has been a radical transformation of New Deal employee social protections, and a systemic shift in risks from companies to workers.[22]

Nike's approach to job genocide—the replacement of workers with contractors—is becoming commonplace. While a relatively small number of corporations—such as Bugle Boy, which makes almost none of its clothes, and Mattel, Inc., which manufactures few of its toys—have joined Nike among the fully virtual corporations, it is hard to find a major corporation in America that is not contracting out jobs in big numbers. Many airlines contract out their cleaning and repair work, computer companies make only a fraction of their electrical components, and auto companies contract out from 30 to 50 percent of their subassembly supply production. Some major corporations, such as Volkswagen, are taking genuinely remarkable steps, creating the first fully virtual auto manufacturing plant in the world. Located in Brazil, it is a VW plant completely operated by contractors, without a single VW employee. All functions in the plant, from sweeping the floor to line assembly to management itself, are carried out by other companies who bring in their own help.

"The reason business executives outsource," says economist Lester Thurow, "is because they can't look a janitor who's been with them for 15 years in the eye and explain why he'll earn $6 and get no medical benefits going forward, rather than $12 he now gets with the same medical benefits as the company vice president."[23] By going virtual, however, the company gains more than just saving the cost of health care. It gains access to a full spectrum of new labor strategies that the New Deal had outlawed. It can refuse to pay benefits, disregard the rights of workers to organize, and in some cases opt for sweatshop labor at home or child labor abroad.

Contractors constitute only one category of the virtual workers who make up America's new contingent labor force. The others include roughly three million temps; a million leased workers, who—like temps—are rented by the hour, day, week, or month, and nearly 25 million part-time workers. Collectively, contingent workers now make up between one-fourth and one-third of all American workers. "If there was a national fear index," says economist Richard Belous about these new charter members of the anxious class, "it would be directly related to the growth of contingent work."[24]

NOTES

1. See Tom Kochan, Harry C. Katz, and Robert B. McKersie, *The Transformation of American Industrial Relations* (Ithaca, NY: ILR Press, 1994).
2. See Kochan et al., *Transformation*. See also Stanley Aronowitz, *Working Class Hero: A New Strategy for Labor* (New York: Pilgrim Press, 1983); Thomas Geoghegan, *Which Side Are You On?* (HarperCollins, 1991), and Jeremy Brecher and Tim Costello, *Global Village or Global Pillage?* (Boston: South End Press, 1994).
3. Reported on *Marketplace*, National Public Radio, December 26, 1995.
4. Richard T. Curtin, quoted in *New York Times*, November 20, 1994, p. 7. See also *Time*, November 22, 1993, p. 35. See also Beth Belton, "Downsizing leaves legacy of insecurity," *USA Today*, August 29, 1997, pp. 1, 1b.
5. Louis Uchitelle, "The Losing Class," *New York Times*, November 20, 1994, p. A6.
6. Bill Bradley, quoted in *Boston Globe*, November 31, 1993, p. A5.
7. Florence Skelly, quoted in *The New York Times*, November 20, 1994, p. 1.
8. Herbert Spencer, *Social Statics* (New York: Appleton and Co., 1864), pp. 414–5. William Graham Sumner, "The Concentration of Wealth," in Stow Pearson (ed.), *Social Darwinism: Selected Essays of William Graham Sumner* (Englewood Cliffs, NJ: Prentice-Hall, 1963). See also Richard Rubenstein, *The Age of Triage* (Boston: Beacon Press, 1983) pp. 220–21.
9. Quoted in Josephson, *Robber Barons*, pp. 364, 374.
10. For a recent reinterpretation of the New Deal, see David Plotke, *Building a Democratic Political Order: Reshaping American Liberalism in the 1930s and 1940s* (New York: Cambridge University Press, 1996).
11. See Barry Bluestone and Irving Bluestone, *Negotiating the Future* (New York: Basic Books, 1992), Chapter 2.
12. See Bluestones, *Negotiating*, Chapters 1–3.
13. See Paul Osterman, *Employment Futures* (New York: Oxford University Press, 1988).
14. The GM model is described in detail by Harry Katz, *Shifting Gears: Changing Relations in the U.S. Automobile Industry* (Cambridge, MA: MIT Press, 1985).
15. See Osterman, *Employment*, Chapters 3 and 4.
16. For a quintessential view of the postwar era as exceptionalist, see Robert Samuelson, *The Good Life and Its Discontents: The American Dream in the Age of Entitlement* (New York: Times Books, 1996). For a brief critique of the exceptional-

ist thesis as ideology, see James Rinehart, "The Ideology of Competitiveness," in Kevin Danaher, *Corporations Are Gonna Get Your Momma* (Monroe, ME: Common Courage Press, 1997).

17. Verena Dobnik, "Group Cites Abuses by Nike Subcontractors," *Boston Globe*, February 28, 1997, p. B2. G. Paschal Zachary, "Just Blew It," *In These Times*, July 28, 1997, (7–9), p. 7.

18. William Bridges, "The End of the Job," *Fortune*, September 19, 1994, (62–74), p. 62. See also William Bridges, *Jobshift* (Boston: Addison Wesley, 1994).

19. Virginia L. duRivage, Françoise J. Carre, and Chris Tilly, "Making Labor Law Work for Part-Time and Contingent Workers," *Russell Sage Foundation Working Paper* #88, 1996. Dorothy Sue Cobble, "Making Postindustrial Unionism Possible," in Sheldon Friedman, Richard W. Hurd, Rudolph A. Oswald, and Ronald L. Seeber (eds.), *Restoring the Promise of American Labor Law* (Ithaca, NY: ILR Press), 285–302. See also Debra Osnowitz, "Policy as Strategy: Labor Law and the Contingent Work Force" (Boston, 1996).

20. See Polly Callaghan and Heidi Hartmann, *Contingent Work: A Chart Book on Part-Time and Temporary Employment* (Washington, D.C.: Economic Policy Institute, 1991).

21. DuRivage et al., "Labor Law." This discussion is also based on conversations with Tim Costello, a Boston-based labor organizer and writer, and with Debra Osnowitz, who has written illuminating papers on the legal problems and new risks faced by contingent workers. See Osnowitz, "Policy as Strategy."

22. See Richard Belous, *The Contingent Economy* (Washington, D.C.: National Planning Association, 1989), Chapters 3 and 4. See also Osterman, *Employment*.

23. Lester Thurow, quoted in Steven Pearlstein, *Washington Post Weekly*, December 18–24, 1996, p. 10.

24. See Belous, *Contingent*.

READING 12

Excerpt from *The Deinstitutionalization of American Marriage*

ANDREW J. CHERLIN

A quarter century ago, in an article entitled "Remarriage as an Incomplete Institution" (Cherlin 1978), I argued that American society lacked norms about the way that members of stepfamilies should act toward each other. Parents and children in first marriages, in contrast, could rely on well-established norms, such as when it is appropriate to discipline a child. I predicted that, over time, as remarriage after divorce became common, norms would begin to emerge concerning proper behavior in stepfamilies—for example, what kind of relationship a stepfather should have with his stepchildren. In other words, I expected that remarriage would become institutionalized, that it would become more like first marriage. But just the opposite has happened. Remarriage has not become more like first marriage; rather, first marriage has become more like remarriage. Instead of the institutionalization of remarriage, what has occurred over the past few decades is the deinstitutionalization of marriage. Yes, remarriage is an incomplete institution, but now, so is first marriage—and for that matter, cohabitation.

By deinstitutionalization I mean the weakening of the social norms that define people's behavior in a social institution such as marriage. In times of social stability, the taken-for-granted nature of norms allows people to go about their lives without having to question their actions or the actions of others. But when social change produces situations outside the reach of established norms, individuals can no longer rely on shared understandings of how to act. Rather, they must negotiate new ways of acting, a process that is a potential source of conflict and opportunity. On the one hand, the development of new rules is likely to engender disagreement and tension among the relevant actors. On the other hand, the breakdown of the old rules of a gendered institution such as marriage could lead to the creation of a more egalitarian relationship between wives and husbands.

This perspective, I think, can help us understand the state of contemporary marriage. It may even assist in the risky business of predicting the future of marriage. To some extent, similar changes in marriage have occurred in the United States, Canada, and much of Europe, but the American situation may be distinctive. Consequently, although I include information about Canadian and European families, I focus mainly on the United States.

Cherlin, Andrew. 2004. "The Deinstitutionalization of American Marriage." *Journal of Marriage and Family* 66: 848–861.

THE DEINSTITUTIONALIZATION OF MARRIAGE

Even as I was writing my 1978 article, the changing division of labor in the home and the increase in childbearing outside marriage were undermining the institutionalized basis of marriage. The distinct roles of homemaker and breadwinner were fading as more married women entered the paid labor force. Looking into the future, I thought that perhaps an equitable division of household labor might become institutionalized. But what happened instead was the "stalled revolution," in Hochschild's (1989) well-known phrase. Men do somewhat more home work than they used to do, but there is wide variation, and each couple must work out their own arrangement without clear guidelines. In addition, when I wrote the article, 1 out of 6 births in the United States occurred outside marriage, already a much higher ratio than at midcentury (U.S. National Center for Health Statistics 1982). Today, the comparable figure is 1 out of 3 (U.S. National Center for Health Statistics 2003). The percentage is similar in Canada (Statistics Canada 2003) and in the United Kingdom and Ireland (Kiernan 2002). In the Nordic countries of Denmark, Iceland, Norway, and Sweden, the figure ranges from about 45% to about 65% (Kiernan). Marriage is no longer the nearly universal setting for childbearing that it was a half century ago.

Both of these developments—the changing division of labor in the home and the increase in childbearing outside marriage—were well under way when I wrote my 1978 article, as was a steep rise in divorce. Here I discuss two more recent changes in family life, both of which have contributed to the deinstitutionalization of marriage after the 1970s: the growth of cohabitation, which began in the 1970s but was not fully appreciated until it accelerated in the 1980s and 1990s, and same-sex marriage, which emerged as an issue in the 1990s and has come to the fore in the current decade.

The Growth of Cohabitation

In the 1970s, neither I nor most other American researchers foresaw the greatly increased role of cohabitation in the adult life course. We thought that, except among the poor, cohabitation would remain a short-term arrangement among childless young adults who would quickly break up or marry. But it has become a more prevalent and more complex phenomenon. For example, cohabitation has created an additional layer of complexity in stepfamilies. When I wrote my article, nearly all stepfamilies were formed by the remarriage of one or both spouses. Now, about one fourth of all stepfamilies in the United States, and one half of all stepfamilies in Canada, are formed by cohabitation rather than marriage (Bumpass, Raley, & Sweet 1995; Statistics Canada 2002). It is not uncommon, especially among the low-income population, for a woman to have a child outside marriage, end her relationship with that partner, and then begin cohabiting with a different partner. This new union is equivalent in structure to a stepfamily but does not involve marriage. Sometimes the couple later marries, and if neither has been married before, their union creates a first marriage with stepchildren. As a result, we now see an increasing number of stepfamilies that do not involve marriage, and an increasing number of first marriages that involve stepfamilies.

More generally, cohabitation is becoming accepted as an alternative to marriage. British demographer Kathleen Kiernan (2002) writes that the acceptance of cohabitation is occurring in stages in European nations, with some nations further along than others. In stage one, cohabitation is a fringe or avant garde phenomenon; in stage two, it is accepted as a testing ground for marriage; in stage three, it becomes acceptable as an alternative to marriage; and in stage four, it becomes indistinguishable from marriage. Sweden and Denmark, she argues, have made the transition to stage four; in contrast, Mediterranean countries such as Spain, Italy, and Greece remain in stage one. In the early 2000s, the United States appeared to be in transition from stage two to stage three (Smock & Gupta 2002). A number of indicators suggested that the connection between cohabitation and marriage was weakening. The proportion of cohabiting unions that end in marriage within 3 years dropped from 60% in the 1970s to about 33% in the 1990s (Smock & Gupta), suggesting that fewer cohabiting unions were trial marriages (or that fewer trial marriages were succeeding). In fact, Manning and Smock (2003) reported that among 115 cohabiting working-class and lower middle-class adults who were interviewed in depth, none said that he or she was deciding between marriage and cohabitation at the start of the union. Moreover, only 36% of adults in the 2002 United States General Social Survey disagreed with the statement, "It is alright for a couple to live together without intending to get married" (Davis, Smith, & Marsden 2003). And a growing share of births to unmarried women in the United States (about 40% in the 1990s) were to cohabiting couples (Bumpass & Lu 2000). The comparable share was about 60% in Britain (Ermisch 2001).

To be sure, cohabitation is becoming more institutionalized. In the United States, states and municipalities are moving toward granting cohabiting couples some of the rights and responsibilities that married couples have. Canada has gone further: Under the Modernization of Benefits and Obligations Act of 2000, legal distinctions between married and unmarried same-sex and opposite-sex couples were eliminated for couples who have lived together for at least a year. Still, the Supreme Court of Canada ruled in 2002 that when cohabiting partners dissolve their unions, they do not have to divide their assets equally, nor can one partner be compelled to pay maintenance payments to the other, even when children are involved (*Nova Scotia [Attorney General] v. Walsh* 2002). In France, unmarried couples may enter into Civil Solidarity Pacts, which give them most of the rights and responsibilities of married couples after the pact has existed for 3 years (Daley 2000). Several other countries have instituted registered partnerships (Lyall 2004).

The Emergence of Same-Sex Marriage

The most recent development in the deinstitutionalization of marriage is the movement to legalize same-sex marriage. It became a public issue in the

United States in 1993, when the Hawaii Supreme Court ruled that a state law restricting marriage to opposite-sex couples violated the Hawaii state constitution (*Baehr* v. *Lewin*, 1993). Subsequently, Hawaii voters passed a state constitutional amendment barring same-sex marriage. In 1996, the United States Congress passed the Defense of Marriage Act, which allowed states to refuse to recognize same-sex marriages licensed in other states. The act's constitutionality has not been tested as of this writing because until recently, no state allowed same-sex marriages. However, in 2003, the Massachusetts Supreme Court struck down a state law limiting marriage to opposite-sex couples, and same-sex marriage became legal in May 2004 (although opponents may eventually succeed in prohibiting it through a state constitutional amendment). The issue has developed further in Canada: In the early 2000s, courts in British Columbia, Ontario, and Quebec ruled that laws restricting marriage to opposite-sex couples were discriminatory, and it appears likely that the federal government will legalize gay marriage throughout the nation. Although social conservatives in the United States are seeking a federal constitutional amendment, I think it is reasonable to assume that same-sex marriage will be allowed in at least some North American jurisdictions in the future. In Europe, same-sex marriage has been legalized in Belgium and The Netherlands.

Lesbian and gay couples who choose to marry must actively construct a marital world with almost no institutional support. Lesbians and gay men already use the term "family" to describe their close relationships, but they usually mean something different from the standard marriage-based family. Rather, they often refer to what sociologists have called a "family of choice": one that is formed largely through voluntary ties among individuals who are not biologically or legally related (Weeks, Heaphy, & Donovan 2001; Weston 1991). Now they face the task of integrating marriages into these larger networks of friends and kin. The partners will not even have the option of falling back on the gender-differentiated roles of heterosexual marriage. This is not to say that there will be no division of labor; one study of gay and lesbian couples found that in homes where one partner works longer hours and earns substantially more than the other partner, the one with the less demanding, lower paying job did more housework and more of the work of keeping in touch with family and friends. The author suggests that holding a demanding professional or managerial job may make it difficult for a person to invest fully in sharing the work at home, regardless of gender or sexual orientation (Carrington 1999).

We might expect same-sex couples who have children, or who wish to have children through adoption or donor insemination, to be likely to avail themselves of the option of marriage. (According to the United States Census Bureau [2003b], 33% of women in same-sex partnerships and 22% of men in same-sex partnerships had children living with them in 2000.) Basic issues, such as who would care for the children, would have to be resolved family by family. The obligations of the partners to each other following a marital dissolution have also yet to be worked out. In these and many other ways, gay and lesbian couples who marry in the near future would need to create a marriage-centered kin network through discussion, negotiation, and experiment.

Two Transitions in the Meaning of Marriage

In a larger sense, all of these developments—the changing division of labor, childbearing outside of marriage, cohabitation, and gay marriage—are the result of long-term cultural and material trends that altered the meaning of marriage during the 20th century. The cultural trends included, first, an emphasis on emotional satisfaction and romantic love that intensified early in the century. Then, during the last few decades of the century, an ethic of expressive individualism—which Bellah, Marsden, Sullivan, Swidler, & Tipton (1985) describe as the belief that "each person has a unique core of feeling and intuition that should unfold or be expressed if individuality is to be realized" (p. 334)—became more important. On the material side, the trends include the decline of agricultural labor and the corresponding increase in wage labor; the decline in child and adult mortality; rising standards of living; and, in the last half of the 20th century, the movement of married women into the paid workforce.

These developments, along with historical events such as the Depression and World War II, produced two great changes in the meaning of marriage during the 20th century. Ernest Burgess famously labeled the first one as a transition "from an institution to a companionship" (Burgess & Locke 1945). In describing the rise of the companionate marriage, Burgess was referring to the single-earner, breadwinner–homemaker marriage that flourished in the 1950s. Although husbands and wives in the companionate marriage usually adhered to a sharp division of labor, they were supposed to be each other's companions—friends, lovers—to an extent not imagined by the spouses in the institutional marriages of the previous era. The increasing focus on bonds of sentiment within nuclear families constituted an important but limited step in the individualization of family life. Much more so than in the 19th century, the emotional satisfaction of the spouses became an important criterion for marital success. However, through the 1950s, wives and husbands tended to derive satisfaction from their participation in a marriage-based nuclear family (Roussel 1989). That is to say, they based their gratification on playing marital roles well: being good providers, good homemakers, and responsible parents.

During this first change in meaning, marriage remained the only socially acceptable way to have a sexual relationship and to raise children in the United States, Canada, and Europe, with the possible exception of the Nordic countries. In his history of British marriages, Gillis (1985) labeled the period from 1850 to 1960 the "era of mandatory marriage." In the United States, marriage and only marriage was one's ticket of admission to a full family life. Prior to marrying, almost no one cohabited with a partner except among the poor and the avant garde. As recently as the 1950s, premarital cohabitation in the United States was restricted to a small minority (perhaps 5%) of the less educated (Bumpass, Sweet, & Cherlin 1991). In the early 1950s, only about 4% of children were born outside marriage (U.S. National Center for Health Statistics, 1982). In fact, during the late 1940s and the 1950s, major changes that increased the importance of marriage occurred in the life course of young adults. More people married—about 95% of young adults in the United States in the 1950s, compared with about 90% early in the century (Cherlin 1992)—and they married at younger ages. Between 1900 and 1960, the estimated median age at first marriage in the United States fell from 26 to 23 for men, and from 22 to 20 for women (U.S. Census Bureau 2003a). The birth rate, which had been falling for a century or more, increased sharply, creating the "baby boom." The post–World War II increase in marriage and childbearing also occurred in many European countries (Roussel 1989).

But beginning in the 1960s, marriage's dominance began to diminish, and the second great change in the meaning of marriage occurred. In the United States, the median age at marriage returned to and then exceeded the levels of the early 1900s. In 2000, the median age was 27 for men and 25 for women (U.S. Census Bureau 2003a). Many young adults stayed single into their mid to late 20s, some completing college educations and starting careers. Cohabitation prior to (and after) marriage became much more acceptable. Childbearing outside marriage became less stigmatized and more accepted. Birth rates resumed their long-term declines and sunk to all-time lows in most countries. Divorce rates rose to unprecedented levels. Same-sex unions found greater acceptance as well.

During this transition, the companionate marriage lost ground not only as the demographic standard but also as a cultural ideal. It was gradually overtaken by forms of marriage (and nonmarital families) that Burgess had not foreseen, particularly marriages in which both the husband and the wife worked outside the home. Although women continued to do most of the housework and child care, the roles of wives and husbands became more flexible and open to negotiation. And an even more individualistic perspective on the rewards of marriage took root. When people evaluated how satisfied they were with their marriages, they began to think more in terms of the development of their own sense of self and the expression of their feelings, as opposed to the satisfaction they gained through building a family and playing the roles of spouse and parent. The result was a transition from the companionate marriage to what we might call the *individualized marriage*.

The transition to the individualized marriage began in the 1960s and accelerated in the 1970s, as shown by an American study of the changing themes in popular magazine articles offering marital advice in every decade between 1900 and 1979 (Cancian 1987). The author identified three themes that characterized beliefs about the post-1960-style marriage. The first was self-development: Each person should develop a fulfilling, independent self instead of merely sacrificing oneself to one's partner. The second was that roles within marriage should be flexible and negotiable. The third was that communication and openness in confronting problems are essential. She then tallied the percentage of articles in each decade that contained one or more of these three themes. About one third of the articles in the first decade of the century, and again at mid-century, displayed these themes, whereas about two thirds displayed these themes in the 1970s. The author characterized this transition as a shift in emphasis "from role to self" (Cancian).

During this second change in the meaning of marriage, the role of the law changed significantly as well. This transformation was most apparent in divorce law. In the United States and most other developed countries, legal restrictions on divorce were replaced by statutes that recognized consensual and even unilateral divorce. The transition to "private ordering" (Mnookin & Kornhauser 1979) allowed couples to negotiate the details of their divorce agreements within broad limits. Most European nations experienced similar legal developments (Glendon 1989; Théry 1993). Indeed, French social demographer Louis Roussel (1989) wrote of a "double deinstitutionalization" in behavior and in law: a greater hesitation of young adults to enter into marriage, combined with a loosening of the legal regulation of marriage.

Sociological theorists of late modernity (or postmodernity) such as Anthony Giddens (1991, 1992) in Britain and Ulrich Beck and Elisabeth Beck-Gernsheim in Germany (1995, 2002) also have written about the growing individualization of personal life. Consistent with the idea of deinstitutionalization, they note the declining power of social norms and laws as regulating mechanisms for family life, and they stress the expanding role of personal choice. They argue that as traditional sources of identity such as class, religion, and community lose influence, one's intimate relationships become central to self-identity. Giddens (1991, 1992) writes of the emergence of the "pure relationship": an intimate partnership entered into for its own sake, which lasts only as long as both partners are satisfied with the rewards (mostly intimacy and love) that they get from it. It is in some ways the logical extension of the increasing individualism and the deinstitutionalization of marriage that occurred in the 20th century. The pure relationship is not tied to an institution such as marriage or to the desire to raise children. Rather, it is "free-floating," independent of social institutions or economic life. Unlike marriage, it is not regulated by law, and its members do not enjoy special legal rights. It exists primarily in the realms of emotion and self-identity.

Although the theorists of late modernity believe that the quest for intimacy is becoming the central focus of personal life, they do not predict that *marriage* will remain distinctive and important. Marriage, they claim, has become a choice rather than a necessity for adults who want intimacy, companionship, and children. According to Beck and Beck-Gernsheim (1995), we will see "a huge variety of ways of living together or apart which will continue to exist side by side" (pp. 141–142). Giddens (1992) even argues that marriage has already become "just one life-style among others" (p. 154), although people may not yet realize it because of institutional lag.

The Current Context of Marriage

Overall, research and writing on the changing meaning of marriage suggest that it is now situated in a very different context than in the past. This is true in at least two senses. First, individuals now experience a vast latitude for choice in their personal lives. More forms of marriage and more alternatives to marriage are socially acceptable. Moreover, one may fit marriage into one's life in many ways: One may first live with a partner, or sequentially with several partners, without an explicit consideration of whether a marriage will occur. One may have children with one's eventual spouse or with someone else before marrying. One may, in some jurisdictions, marry someone of the same gender and build a shared marital world with few guidelines to rely on. Within marriage, roles are more flexible and negotiable, although women still do more than their share of the household work and childrearing.

The second difference is in the nature of the rewards that people seek through marriage and other close relationships. Individuals aim for personal growth and deeper intimacy through more open communication and mutually shared disclosures about feelings with their partners. They may feel justified in insisting on changes in a relationship that no longer provides them with individualized rewards. In contrast, they are less likely than in the past to focus on the rewards to be found in fulfilling socially valued roles such as the good parent or the loyal and supportive spouse. The result of these changing contexts has been a deinstitutionalization of marriage, in which social norms about family and personal life count for less than they did during the heyday of the companionate marriage, and far less than during the period of the institutional marriage. Instead, personal choice and self-development loom large in people's construction of their marital careers.

WHY DO PEOPLE STILL MARRY?

There is a puzzle within the story of deinstitutionalization that needs solving. Although fewer Americans are marrying than during the peak years of marriage in the mid-20th century, most—nearly 90%, according to a recent estimate (Goldstein & Kenney 2001)—will eventually marry. A survey of high school seniors conducted annually since 1976 shows no decline in the importance they attach to marriage. The percentage of young women who respond that they expect to marry has stayed constant at roughly 80% (and has increased from 71% to 78% for young men). The percentage who respond that "having a good marriage and family life" is extremely important has also remained constant, at about 80% for young women and 70%

for young men (Thornton & Young-DeMarco 2001). What is more, in the 1990s and early 2000s, a strong promarriage movement emerged among gay men and lesbians in the United States, who sought the right to marry with increasing success. Clearly, marriage remains important to many people in the United States. Consequently, I think the interesting question is not why so few people are marrying, but rather, why so *many* people are marrying, or planning to marry, or hoping to marry, when cohabitation and single parenthood are widely acceptable options. (This question may be less relevant in Canada and the many European nations where the estimated proportions of who will ever marry are lower.)

The Gains to Marriage

The dominant theoretical perspectives on marriage in the 20th century do not provide much guidance on the question of why marriage remains so popular. The structural functionalists in social anthropology and sociology in the early- to mid-20th century emphasized the role of marriage in ensuring that a child would have a link to the status of a man, a right to his protection, and a claim to inherit his property (Mair, 1971). But as the law began to recognize the rights of children born outside marriage, and as mothers acquired resources by working in the paid work force, these reasons for marriage become less important.

Nor is evolutionary theory very helpful. Although there may be important evolutionary influences on family behavior, it is unlikely that humans have developed an innate preference for marriage as we know it. The classical account of our evolutionary heritage is that women, whose reproductive capacity is limited by pregnancy and lactation (which delays the return of ovulation), seek stable pair bonds with men, whereas men seek to maximize their fertility by impregnating many women. Rather than being "natural," marriage-centered kinship was described in much early- and mid-20th-century anthropological writing as the social invention that solved the problem of the sexually wandering male (Tiger & Fox 1971). Moreover, when dependable male providers are not available, women may prefer a reproductive strategy of relying on a network of female kin and more than one man (Hrdy, 1999). In addition, marriages are increasingly being formed well after a child is born, yet evolutionary theory suggests that the impetus to marry should be greatest when newborn children need support and protection. In the 1950s, half of all unmarried pregnant women in the United States married before the birth of their child, whereas in the 1990s, only one fourth married (U.S. Census Bureau 1999). Finally, evolutionary theory cannot explain the persistence of the formal wedding style in which people are still marrying (see below). Studies of preindustrial societies have found that although many have elaborate ceremonies, others have little or no ceremony (Ember, Ember, & Peregrine 2002; Stephens 1963).

The mid-20th century specialization model of economist Gary Becker (1965, 1981) also seems less relevant than when it was introduced. Becker assumed that women were relatively more productive at home than men, and that men were relatively more productive (i.e., they could earn higher wages) in the labor market. He argued that women and men could increase their utility by exchanging, through marriage, women's home work for men's labor market work. The specialization model would predict that in the present era, women with less labor market potential would be more likely to marry because they would gain the most economically from finding a husband. But several studies show that in recent decades, women in the United States and Canada with less education (and therefore less labor market potential) are *less* likely to marry (Lichter, McLaughlin, Kephart, & Landry 1992; Oppenheimer, Blossfeld, & Wackerow 1995; Qian & Preston 1993; Sweeney 2002; Turcotte & Goldscheider 1998). This finding suggests that the specialization model may no longer hold. Moreover, the specialization model was developed before cohabitation was widespread, and offers no explanation for why couples would marry rather than cohabit.

From a rational choice perspective, then, what benefits might contemporary marriage offer that would lead cohabiting couples to marry rather than cohabit? I suggest that the major benefit is what we might call *enforceable trust* (Cherlin 2000; Portes & Sensenbrenner 1993). Marriage still requires a public commitment to a long-term, possibly lifelong relationship. This commitment is usually expressed in front of relatives, friends, and religious congregants. Cohabitation, in contrast, requires only a private commitment, which is easier to break. Therefore, marriage, more so than cohabitation, lowers the risk that one's partner will renege on agreements that have been made. In the language of economic theory, marriage lowers the transaction costs of enforcing agreements between the partners (Pollak 1985). It allows individuals to invest in the partnership with less fear of abandonment. For instance, it allows the partners to invest financially in joint long-term purchases such as homes and automobiles. It allows caregivers to make relationship-specific investments (England & Farkas 1986) in the couple's children—investments of time and effort that, unlike strengthening one's job skills, would not be easily portable to another intimate relationship.

Nevertheless, the difference in the amount of enforceable trust that marriage brings, compared with cohabitation, is eroding. Although relatives and friends will view a divorce with disappointment, they will accept it more readily than their counterparts would have two generations ago. As I noted, cohabiting couples are increasingly gaining the rights previously reserved to married couples. It seems likely that over time, the legal differences between cohabitation and marriage will become minimal in the United States, Canada, and many European countries. The advantage of marriage in enhancing trust will then depend on the force of public commitments, both secular and religious, by the partners.

In general, the prevailing theoretical perspectives are of greater value in explaining why marriage has declined than why it persists. With more women working outside the home, the predictions of the specialization model are less relevant. Although the rational choice theorists remind us that marriage still provides enforceable trust, it seems clear that its enforcement power is declining. Recently, evolutionary theorists have argued that women who have difficulty finding men who are reliable providers might choose a reproductive strategy that involves single parenthood and kin networks, a strategy that is consistent with changes that have occurred in low-income families. And although the insights of the theorists of late modernity help us understand the changing meaning of marriage, they predict that marriage will lose its distinctive status, and indeed may already have become just one lifestyle among others. Why, then, are so many people still marrying?

The Symbolic Significance of Marriage

What has happened is that although the practical importance of being married has declined, its symbolic importance has remained high, and may even have increased. Marriage is at once less dominant and more distinctive than it was. It has evolved from a marker of conformity to a marker of prestige. Marriage is a status one builds up to, often by living with a partner beforehand, by attaining steady employment or starting a career, by putting away some savings, and even by having children. Marriage's place in the life course used to come before those investments were made, but now it often comes afterward. It used to be the foundation of adult personal life; now it is sometimes the capstone. It is something to be achieved through one's own efforts rather than something to which one routinely accedes.

ALTERNATIVE FUTURES

What do these developments suggest about the future of marriage? Social demographers usually predict a continuation of whatever is happening at the moment, and they are usually correct, but sometimes spectacularly wrong. For example, in the 1930s, every demographic expert in the United States confidently predicted a continuation of the low birth rates of the Depression. Not one forecast the baby boom that overtook them after World War II. No less a scholar than Kingsley Davis (1937) wrote that the future of the family as a social institution was in danger because people were not having enough children to replace themselves. Not a single 1950s or 1960s sociologist predicted the rise of cohabitation. Chastened by this unimpressive record, I will tentatively sketch some future directions.

The first alternative is the reinstitutionalization of marriage, a return to a status akin to its dominant position through the mid-20th century. This would entail a rise in the proportion who ever marry, a rise in the proportion of births born to married couples, and a decline in divorce. It would require a reversal of the individualistic orientation toward family and personal life that has been the major cultural force driving family change over the past several decades. It would probably also require a decrease in women's labor force participation and a return to more gender-typed family roles. I think this alternative is very unlikely—but then again, so was the baby boom.

The second alternative is a continuation of the current situation, in which marriage remains deinstitutionalized but is common and distinctive. It is not just one type of family relationship among many; rather, it is the most prestigious form. People generally desire to be married. But it is an individual choice, and individuals construct marriages through an increasingly long process that often includes cohabitation and childbearing beforehand. It still confers some of its traditional benefits, such as enforceable trust, but it is increasingly a mark of prestige, a display of distinction, an individualistic achievement, a part of what Beck and Beck-Gernsheim (2002) call the "do-it-yourself biography." In this scenario, the proportion of people who ever marry could fall further; in particular, we could see probabilities of marriage among Whites in the United States that are similar to the probabilities shown today by African Americans. Moreover, because of high levels of nonmarital childbearing, cohabitation, and divorce, people will spend a smaller proportion of their adult lives in intact marriages than in the past. Still, marriage would retain its special and highly valued place in the family system.

But I admit to some doubts about whether this alternative will prevail for long in the United States. The privileges and material advantages of marriage, relative to cohabitation, have been declining. The commitment of partners to be trustworthy has been undermined by frequent divorce. If marriage was once a form of cultural capital—one needed to be married to advance one's career, say—that capital has decreased too. What is left, I have argued, is a display of prestige and achievement. But it could be that marriage retains its symbolic aura largely because of its dominant position in social norms until just a half century ago. It could be that this aura is diminishing, like an echo in a canyon. It could be that, despite the efforts of the wedding industry, the need for a highly ritualized ceremony and legalized status will fade. And there is not much else supporting marriage in the early 21st century.

That leads to a third alternative, the fading away of marriage. Here, the argument is that people are still marrying in large numbers because of institutional lag; they have yet to realize that marriage is no longer important. A nonmarital pure relationship, to use Giddens's ideal type, can provide much intimacy and love, can place both partners on an equal footing, and can allow them to develop their independent senses of self. These characteristics are highly valued in late modern societies. However, this alternative also suggests the predominance of fragile relationships that are continually at risk of breaking up because they are held together entirely by the voluntary commitment of each partner. People may still commit morally to a relationship, but they increasingly prefer to commit voluntarily rather than to be obligated to commit by law or social norms. And partners feel free to revoke their commitments at any time.

Therefore, the pure relationship seems most characteristic of a world where commitment does not matter. Consequently, it seems to best fit middle-class, well-educated, childless adults. They have the resources to be independent actors by themselves or in a democratic partnership, and without childbearing responsibilities, they can be free-floating. The pure relationship seems less applicable to couples who face material constraints (Jamieson 1999). In particular, when children are present—or when they are anticipated anytime soon—issues of commitment and support come into consideration. Giddens (1992) says very little about children in his book on intimacy, and his brief attempts to incorporate children into the pure relationship are unconvincing. Individuals who are, or think they will be, the primary caregivers of children will prefer commitment and will seek material support from their partners. They may be willing to have children and begin cohabiting without commitment, but the relationship probably will not last without it. They will be wary of purely voluntary commitment if they think they can do better. So only if the advantage of marriage in providing trust and commitment disappears relative to cohabitation—and I must admit that this could happen—might we see cohabitation and marriage on an equal footing.

In sum, I see the current state of marriage and its likely future in these terms: At present, marriage is no longer as dominant as it once was, but it remains important on a symbolic level. It has been transformed from a familial and community institution to an individualized, choice-based achievement. It is a marker of prestige and is still somewhat useful in creating enforceable trust. As for the future, I have sketched three alternatives. The first, a return to a more dominant, institutionalized form of marriage, seems unlikely. In the second, the current situation continues; marriage remains important, but not as dominant, and retains its high symbolic status. In the third, marriage fades into just one of many kinds of interpersonal romantic relationships. I think that Giddens's (1992) statement that marriage has already become merely one of many relationships is not true in the United States so far, but it could become true in the future. It is possible that we are living in a transitional phase in which marriage is gradually losing its uniqueness. If Giddens and other modernity theorists are correct, the third alternative will triumph, and marriage will lose its special place in the family system of the United States. If they are not, the second alternative will continue to hold, and marriage—transformed and deinstitutionalized, but recognizable nevertheless—will remain distinctive.

NOTE

I thank Frank Furstenberg, Joshua Goldstein, Kathleen Kiernan, and Céline Le Bourdais for comments on a previous version, and Linda Burton for her collaborative work on the Three-City Study ethnography.

REFERENCES

Baehr v. Lewin (74 Haw. 530, 74 Haw. 645, 852 P.2d 44 1993).

Beck, U., & Beck-Gernsheim, E. 1995. *The Normal Chaos of Love*. Cambridge, England: Polity Press.

Beck, U., & Beck-Gernsheim, E. 2002. *Individualization: Institutionalized Individualism and Its Social and Political Consequences*. London: Sage.

Becker, G. S. 1965. A theory of the allocation of time. *Economic Journal*, 75, 493–517.

Becker, G. S. 1981. *A Treatise on the Family*. Cambridge, MA: Harvard University Press.

Bellah, R., Marsden, R., Sullivan, W. M., Swidler, A., & Tipton, S. M. 1985. *Habits of the Heart: Individualism and Commitment in America*. Berkeley: University of California Press.

Bumpass, L. L., & Lu, H.-H. 2000. Trends in cohabitation and implications for children's family contexts in the United States. *Population Studies*. 54, 19–41.

Bumpass, L. L., Raley, K., & Sweet, J. A. 1995. The changing character of stepfamilies: Implications of cohabitation and nonmarital childbearing. *Demography*, 32, 1–12.

Bumpass, L. L., Sweet, J. A., & Cherlin, A. J. 1991. The role of cohabitation in declining rates of marriage. *Journal of Marriage and the Family*, 53, 338–355.

Burgess, E. W., & Locke, H. J. 1945. *The Family: From Institution to Companionship*. New York: American Book.

Cancian, F. M. 1987. *Love in America: Gender and Self-Development*. Cambridge, England: Cambridge University Press.

Carrington, C. 1999. *No Place Like Home: Relationships and Family Life Among Lesbians and Gay Men*. Chicago: University of Chicago Press.

Cherlin, A. 1978. Remarriage as an incomplete institution. *American Journal of Sociology*, 84, 634–650.

Cherlin, A. J. 1992. *Marriage, Divorce, Remarriage* (Rev. ed.) Cambridge, MA: Harvard University Press.

Cherlin, A. J. 2000. Toward a new home socioeconomics of union formation. In L. Waite, C. Bachrach, M. Hindin, E. Thomson, & A. Thomton (Eds.), *Ties that Bind: Perspectives on Marriage and Cohabitation* (pp. 126–144), Hawthome, NY: Aldine de Gruyter.

Daley, S. 2000, April 18. French couples take plunge that falls short of marriage. *The New York Times*, pp. A1, A4.

Davis, J. A., Smith, T. W., & Marsden, P. 2003. *General Social Surveys, 1972–2002 Cumulative Codebook*. Chicago: National Opinion Research Center, University of Chicago.

Davis, K. 1937. Reproductive institutions and the pressure for population. *Sociological Review*, 29, 289–306.

Ember, C. R., Ember, M., & Peregrine, P. N. 2002. *Anthropology* (10th ed.). Upper Saddle River, NJ: Prentice-Hall.

England, P., & Farkas, G. 1986. *Households, Employment, and Gender: A Social, Economic, and Demographic View*. New York: Aldine.

Ermisch, J. 2001. Cohabitation and childbearing outside marriage in Britain. In L. L. Wu & B. Wolfe (Eds.), *Out of Wedlock: Causes and Consequences of Nonmarital Fertility* (pp. 109–139). New York: Russell Sage Foundation.

Giddens, A. 1991. *Modernity and Self-Identity*. Stanford, CA: Stanford University Press.

Giddens, A. 1992. *The Transformation of Intimacy*. Stanford, CA: Stanford University Press.

Gillis, J. R. 1985. *For Better or Worse: British Marriages, 1600 to the Present*. Oxford, England: Oxford University Press.

Glendon, M. A. 1989. *Abortion and Divorce in Western Law*. Cambridge, MA: Harvard University Press.

Goldstein, J. R., & Kenney, C. T. 2001. Marriage delayed or marriage forgone? New cohort forecasts of first marriage for U.S. women. *American Sociological Review*, 66, 506–519.

Hochschild, A. 1989. *The Second Shift: Working Parents and the Revolution at Home*. New York: Viking.

Hrdy, S. B. 1999. *Mother Nature: Maternal Instincts and How They Shape the Human Species*. New York: Ballantine Books.

Jamieson, L. 1999. Intimacy transformed? A critical look at the "pure relationship." *Sociology*, 33, 477–494.

Kieman, K. 2002. Cohabitation in Western Europe: Trends, issues, and implications. In A. Booth & A. C. Crouter (Eds.), *Just Living Together: Implication of Cohabitation on Families, Children, and Social Policy* (pp. 3–31). Mahwah, NJ: Erlbaum.

Lichter, D. T., McLaughlin, D. K., Kephart, G., & Landry, D. J. 1992. Race and the retreat from marriage: A shortage of marriageable men? *American Sociological Review*, 57, 781–799.

Lyall, S. 2004, February 15. In Europe, lovers now propose: Marry me a little. *The New York Times*, p. A3.

Mair, L. 1971. *Marriage*. Middlesex, England: Penguin Books.

Manning, W., & Smock, P. J. 2003, May. *Measuring and Modeling Cohabitation: New Perspectives from Qualitative Data*. Paper presented at the annual meeting of the Population Association of America, Minneapolis, MN.

Mnookin, R. H., & Kornhauser, L. 1979. Bargaining in the shadow of the law: The case of divorce, *Yale Law Journal*, 88, 950–997.

Nova Scotia (Attorney General) v. Walsh. 2002. SCC 83.

Oppenheimer, V. K., Blossfeld, H.-P., & Wackerow, A. 1995. United States of America. In H. P. Blossfeld (Ed.), *The New Role of Women: Family Formation in Modern Societies* (pp. 150–173). Boulder, CO: Westview Press.

Pollak, R. A. 1985. A transaction costs approach to families and households. *Journal of Economic Literature*, 23, 581–608.

Portes, A., & Sensenbrenner, J. 1993. Embeddedness and immigration: Notes on the social determinants of economic action. *American Journal of Sociology*, 98, 1320–1350.

Qian, Z., & Preston, S. H. 1993. Changes in American marriage, 1972 to 1987: Availability and forces of attraction by age and education. *American Sociological Review*, 58, 482–495.

Roussel, L. 1989. *La famille incertaine*. Paris: Editions Odile Jacob.

Smock, P. J., & Gupta, S. 2002. Cohabitation in contemporary North America. In A. Booth & A. C. Crouter (Eds.), *Just Living Together: Implications of Cohabitation on Families, Children, and Social Policy* (pp. 53–84). Mahwah, NJ: Erlbaum.

Statistics Canada. 2002. *Changing conjugal life in Canada* (No. 89–576-XIE). Ottawa, Ontario: Statistical Reference Centre.

Statistics Canada. 2003. *Annual Demographic Statistics, 2002* (No. 91–213-XIB). Ottawa, Ontario: Statistical Reference Centre.

Stephens, William N. 1963. *The Family in Cross-Cultural Perspective*. New York. Holt, Rinehart and Winston.

Sweeney, M. M. 2002. Two decades of family change: The shift in economic foundations of marriage. *American Sociological Review*, 67, 132–147.

Théry, I. 1993. *Le démariage*. Paris: Editions Odile Jacob.

Thomton, A., & Young-DeMarco, L. 2001. Four decades of trends in attitudes toward family issues in the United States: The 1960s through the 1990s. *Journal of Marriage and Family*, 63, 1009–1037.

Tiger, L., & Fox, R. 1971. *The imperial animal*. New York: Holt, Rinehart and Winston.

Turcotte, P., & Goldscheider, F. 1998. Evolution of factors influencing first union formation in Canada. *Canadian Studies in Population*, 25, 145–173.

U.S. Census Bureau. 1999. *Trends in premarital childbearing: 1930–1994* (Current Population Reports No. P23–97). Washington, DC: U.S. Government Printing Office.

U.S. Census Bureau. 2003a. *Estimated median age at first marriage, by sex: 1890 to present*. Retrieved January 11, 2003, from http://www.census.gov/population/www/socdemo/hh-fam.html

U.S. Census Bureau. 2003b. *Married-couple and unmarried-partner households: 2000* (Census 2000 Special Reports, CENSR-5). Washington, DC: U.S. Government Printing Office.

U.S. National Center for Health Statistics. 1982. *Vital Statistics of the United States, 1978* (Volume I—Natality). Washington, DC: U.S. Government Printing Office.

U.S. National Center for Health Statistics. 2003. *Births: Preliminary data for 2002*. Retrieved December 15, 2003, from http://www.cdc.gov/nchs/data/nvsr/nvsr51/nvsr51_11.pdf

Weeks, J., Heaphy, B., & Donovan, C. 2001. *Same Sex Intimacies: Families of Choice and Other Life Experiments*. London: Routledge.

Weston, K. 1991. *Families We Choose: Lesbians, Gays, Kinship*. New York: Columbia University. Press.

PART 3

WHAT DIVIDES US?

Race and Intersectionality

INTRODUCTION

Look around your Introduction to Sociology class. Is the class racially diverse? Why? What racial groups are overrepresented? Which racial groups are underrepresented? How do you know? Do you think of yourself as having a race, or do you think of yourself as racially "neutral"? How does your race (and that of others) impact your identity, your norms of behavior, and the expectations and responses of other individuals, groups, and social institutions? As a social construct, race has been a great source of social division and social conflict, and it often forms a primary dynamic of social relations in racially diverse societies. Although talking about race may make some feel uncomfortable, to understand our social world we must interrogate the source of that discomfort. What is the social meaning of race, and how does the social construct of race impact our social lives and institutions?

In *The Souls of Black Folk*, the early sociological theorist W.E.B. DuBois addresses the social experience of "Negros" at the turn of the last century, forty years after emancipation. Just the fact that DuBois talks about "Negros" rather than "blacks" or "African-Americans" should indicate to you that the way we talk about race changes over time. DuBois articulates America's post-emancipation race problem as it impacts the consciousness of blacks. He poses the searing question, "How does it feel to be a problem?" in addressing the African-American experience in the United States. In doing so, he points out that African-Americans are both a part of, and apart from, the mainstream American social experience. To DuBois, being black in America is to be seen as "other" than the norm as a social being. He points out that African-Americans are led in our society to not just experience themselves as themselves, but to also experience themselves as whites see them. He calls this "double-consciousness," produced by the vast history of racial prejudice that socially constructs blacks as problematic for whites. In DuBois' analysis, blacks must constantly consider how they are viewed by whites, in a way that whites do not have to actively question how they are viewed by blacks. The history and ideology that justified slavery on the basis of racial superiority produced a special socio-cultural burden for blacks post-emancipation. Does this have implications for race relations a century after DuBois' analysis? Does a black man walking or driving down the street still consider how he is being seen by whites as a result of institutional and cultural racism? How does America's racial history impact the individual biographies of blacks today?

One hundred years after the publication of *The Souls of Black Folks*, evidence of the cultural impact of America's racial history can still be found and analyzed by sociologists. In *Racism without Racists: Color-Blind Racism and the Persistence of Racial Inequality in the United States* Eduardo Bonilla-Silva uses interviews with whites to get at racial attitudes that might otherwise be hard to identify. He notes that in contemporary American society, expressing racist attitudes violates social norms, and that survey respondents are likely to try to provide the socially or politically correct answers, rather than revealing their true beliefs or attitudes. In interviewing college students and others, Bonilla-Silva reveals a number of narratives or "stories" that are available in our culture that reinforce and ratify our beliefs and understanding of the social world. The stories about race and racial discrimination he uncovers are probably familiar to you. These include "the past is the past" and "I didn't own any slaves." Such stories are developed to deny the contemporary impact of our social history and to deny that either racial privilege or racial prejudice accrue to us from that history (picture C. Wright Mills making a sad face here). The function of these narratives is to demand that history does not or should not matter and that whites can accept the historic advantages of "whiteness" (i.e., generations of higher education, capital accumulation, and cultural valorization) without any historic responsibility. Another racial story identified is "If other groups have made it, why haven't blacks," which is intended to equate the experience of various immigrant groups with the special experience of blacks that DuBois wrote about. Again, it is a narrative designed to deny or gloss over the weight of history on biography. A final narrative is "I didn't get a job because of a minority," intended to show that affirmative action policies are discriminatory to whites. Bonilla-Silva demonstrates that these stories have cultural authority, despite having little or questionable data to support their claims. He also notes that the institution of the media uses these stories to reinforce the social status quo. While these stories may generate "double-consciousness" for blacks, they also facilitate racial unconsciousness for whites, making it permissible for them to promote racist attitudes and stereotypes without feeling or being perceived as racist.

Do you live in a community that is racially integrated or racially segregated? Is that a result of your individual or family choice, your income, or invisible yet powerful social forces? Could you live in an integrated neighborhood if you wanted to? Is your ability to do so increased or decreased by your racial identity? The answers to these questions have implications for social policy. If it is a matter of wealth and income, economic opportunity can undo segregation. Knowing the social causes of social patterns is necessary to understand (or change) those patterns. In *American Apartheid: Segregation and the Making of the Underclass*, Douglas Massey and Nancy Denton use quantitative analysis to expose and explain the persistence of racially segregated housing patterns in American cities. They ask two important sociological questions about the spatial distribution of housing location by race: (1) Why has housing segregation continued even decades after the end of legal housing discrimination based on race? (2) Is racial segregation in housing a consequence of class or race? By applying a statistical scientific method to the latter question, Massey and Denton are able to demonstrate that race, not class, is the key explanatory variable. They show that, regardless of class status, blacks' level of housing segregation tends to remain substantially unchanged. Controversial questions can sometimes be answered with data, rather than by debating about opinions. To answer the question about the persistence of segregation, Massey and Denton use survey research. Their data reveal that blacks are aware of housing options and prefer to live in integrated communities. Whites, however, prefer less integrated communities. By shedding the cold light of data on the hot topic of race, Massey and Denton are able to understand the social dynamics that lead blacks to remain the most spatially isolated population in the United States.

Media commentators have argued that, after the election of President Barack Obama, we now live in a "post-racial" society where racial identities and conflicts are of no or declining significance. Sociologists are less convinced. We continue to insist that history intersects with biography in ways that make the social construct of race socially significant. We continue to collect data that indicate that racial segregation continues to exist and that racial discrimination is real. And we continue to read and hear in the institutions of media and politics the racial stories and narratives that reinforce historically developed and deeply held cultural beliefs about race. Finally, as sociologists, we do not believe that ignoring social realities, failing to collect and analyze data, and stopping thinking, writing, and talking about the social realities of race would make those realities go away.

READING 13

Excerpt from *The Souls of Black Folk*

W.E.B. DUBOIS

Of Our Spiritual Strivings
O water, voice of my heart, crying in the sand,
All night long crying with a mournful cry,

DuBois, W.E.B. 1990 [1903]. "Of Our Spiritual Strivings" from *The Souls of Black Folk*. New York: Vintage Books.

As I lie and listen, and cannot understand
The voice of my heart in my side or the voice of the sea,
O water, crying for rest, is it I, is it I?
All night long the water is crying to me.

Unresting water, there shall never be rest
Till the last moon droop and the last tide fail,
And the fire of the end begin to burn in the west;
And the heart shall be weary and wonder and cry like the sea,
All life long crying without avail,
As the water all night long is crying to me.

Arthur Symons

Between me and the other world there is ever an unasked question: unasked by some through feelings of delicacy; by others through the difficulty of rightly framing it. All, nevertheless, flutter round it. They approach me in a half-hesitant sort of way, eye me curiously or compassionately, and then, instead of saying directly, How does it feel to be a problem? they say, I know an excellent colored man in my town; or, I fought at Mechanicsville; or, Do not these Southern outrages make your blood boil? At these I smile, or am interested, or reduce the boiling to a simmer, as the occasion may require. To the real question. How does it feel to be a problem? I answer seldom a word.

And yet, being a problem is a strange experience—peculiar even for one who has never been anything else, save perhaps in babyhood and in Europe. It is in the early days of rollicking boyhood that the revelation first bursts upon one, all in a day, as it were. I remember well when the shadow swept across me. I was a little thing, away up in the hills of New England, where the dark Housatonic winds between Hoosac and Taghkanic to the sea. In a wee wooden schoolhouse, something put it into the boys' and girls' heads to buy gorgeous visiting-cards—ten cents a package—and exchange. The exchange was merry, till one girl, a tall newcomer, refused my card—refused it peremptorily, with a glance. Then it dawned upon me with a certain suddenness that I was different from the others; or like, mayhap, in heart and life and longing, but shut out from their world by a vast veil. I had thereafter no desire to tear down that veil, to creep through; I held all beyond it in common contempt, and lived above it in a region of blue sky and great wandering shadows. That sky was bluest when I could beat my mates at examination-time, or beat them at a foot-race, or even beat their stringy heads. Alas, with the years all this fine contempt began to fade; for the worlds I longed for, and all their dazzling opportunities, were theirs, not mine. But they should not keep these prizes, I said; some, all, I would wrest from them. Just how I would do it I could never decide: by reading law, by healing the sick, by telling the wonderful tales that swam in my head—some way. With other black boys the strife was not so fiercely sunny: Their youth shrunk into tasteless sycophancy, or into silent hatred of the pale world about them and mocking distrust of everything white; or wasted itself in a bitter cry, Why did God make me an outcast and a stranger in mine own house? The shades of the prison-house closed round about us all: walls strait and stubborn to the whitest, but relentlessly narrow, tall, and unscalable to sons of night who must plod darkly on in resignation, or beat unavailing palms against the stone, or steadily, half hopelessly, watch the streak of blue above.

After the Egyptian and Indian, the Greek and Roman, the Teuton and Mongolian, the Negro is a sort of seventh son, born with a veil, and gifted with second-sight in this American world—a world which yields him no true self-consciousness, but only lets him see himself through the revelation of the other world. It is a peculiar sensation, this double-consciousness, this sense of always looking at one's self through the eyes of others, of measuring one's soul by the tape of a world that looks on in amused contempt and pity. One ever feels his two-ness—an American, a Negro; two souls, two thoughts, two unreconciled strivings; two warring ideals in one dark body, whose dogged strength alone keeps it from being torn asunder.

The history of the American Negro is the history of this strife—this longing to attain self-conscious manhood, to merge his double self into a better and truer self. In this merging he wishes neither of the older selves to be lost. He would not Africanize America, for America has too much to teach the world and Africa. He would not bleach his Negro soul in a flood of white Americanism, for he knows that Negro blood has a message for the world. He simply wishes to make it possible for a man to be both a Negro and an American, without being cursed and spit upon by his fellows, without having the doors of Opportunity closed roughly in his face.

This, then, is the end of his striving: to be a co-worker in the kingdom of culture, to escape both death and isolation, to husband and use his best powers and his latent genius. These powers of body and mind have in the past been strangely wasted, dispersed, or forgotten. The shadow of a mighty Negro past flits through the tale of Ethiopia the Shadowy and of Egypt the Sphinx. Throughout history, the powers of single black men flash here and there like falling stars, and die sometimes before the world has rightly gauged their brightness. Here in America, in the few days since Emancipation, the black man's turning hither and thither in hesitant and doubtful striving has often made his very strength to lose effectiveness, to seem like absence of power, like weakness. And yet it is not weakness—it is the contradiction of double aims. The double-aimed struggle of the black artisan—on the one hand to escape white contempt for a nation of mere hewers of wood and drawers of water, and on the other hand to plough and nail and dig for a poverty-stricken horde—could only result in making him a poor craftsman, for he had but half a heart in either cause. By the poverty and ignorance of his people, the Negro minister or doctor was tempted toward quackery and demagogy; and by the criticism of the other world, toward ideals that made him ashamed of his lowly tasks. The would-be black *savant* was confronted by the paradox that the knowledge his people needed was a twice-told tale to his white neighbors, while the knowledge which would teach the white world was Greek to his own flesh and blood. The innate love of harmony and beauty that set the ruder souls of his people a-dancing and a-singing raised but confusion and doubt in the soul of the black artist; for the beauty revealed to him was the soul-beauty of a race which his larger audience despised, and he could not articulate the message of another people. This waste of double aims, this seeking to satisfy two unreconciled ideals, has wrought sad havoc with the courage and faith and deeds of ten thousand thousand people—has sent them often wooing false gods and invoking false means of salvation, and at times has even seemed about to make them ashamed of themselves.

Away back in the days of bondage they thought to see in one divine event the end of all doubt and disappointment; few men ever worshipped Freedom with half such unquestioning faith as did the American Negro for two centuries. To him, so far as he thought and dreamed, slavery was indeed the sum of all villainies, the cause of all sorrow, the root of all prejudice; Emancipation was the key to a promised land of sweeter beauty than ever stretched before the eyes of wearied Israelites. In song and exhortation swelled one refrain—Liberty; in his tears and curses the God he implored had Freedom in his right hand. At last it came—suddenly, fearfully, like a dream. With one wild carnival of blood and passion came the message in his own plaintive cadences:

> "Shout, O children!
> Shout, you're free!
> For God has bought your liberty!"

Years have passed away since then—ten, twenty, forty; forty years of national life, forty years of renewal and development, and yet the swarthy spectre sits in its accustomed seat at the Nation's feast. In vain do we cry to this our vastest social problem:

> "Take any shape but that, and my firm nerves
> Shall never tremble!"

The Nation has not yet found peace from its sins; the freedman has not yet found in freedom his promised land. Whatever of good may have come in these years of change, the shadow of a deep disappointment rests upon the Negro people—a disappointment all the more bitter because the unattained ideal was unbounded save by the simple ignorance of a lowly people.

The first decade was merely a prolongation of the vain search for freedom, the boon that seemed ever barely to elude their grasp—like a tantalizing will-o'-the-wisp, maddening and misleading the headless host. The holocaust of war, the terrors of the Ku-Klux Klan, the lies of carpet-baggers, the disorganization of industry, and the contradictory advice of friends and foes, left the bewildered serf with no new watchword beyond the old cry for freedom. As the time flew, however, he began to grasp a new idea. The ideal of liberty demanded for its attainment powerful means, and these the Fifteenth Amendment gave him. The ballot, which before he had looked upon as a visible sign of freedom, he now regarded as the chief means of gaining and perfecting the liberty with which war had partially endowed him. And why not? Had not votes made war and emancipated millions? Had not votes enfranchised the freedmen? Was anything impossible to a power that had done all this? A million black men started with renewed zeal to vote themselves into the kingdom. So the decade flew away, the revolution of 1876 came, and left the half-free serf weary, wondering, but still inspired. Slowly but steadily, in the following years, a new vision began gradually to replace the dream of political power—a powerful movement, the rise of another ideal to guide the unguided, another pillar of fire by night after a clouded day. It was the ideal of "book-learning"; the curiosity, born of compulsory ignorance, to know and test the power of the cabalistic letters of the white man, the longing to know. Here at last seemed to have been discovered the mountain path to Canaan; longer than the highway of Emancipation and law, steep and rugged, but straight, leading to heights high enough to overlook life.

Up the new path the advance guard toiled, slowly, heavily, doggedly; only those who have watched and guided the faltering feet, the misty minds, the dull understandings, of the dark pupils of these schools know how faithfully, how piteously, this people strove to learn. It was weary work. The cold statistician wrote down the inches of progress here and there, noted also where here and there a foot had slipped or some one had fallen. To the tired climbers, the horizon was ever dark, the mists were often cold, the Canaan was always dim and far away. If, however, the vistas disclosed as yet no goal, no resting-place, little but flattery and criticism, the journey at least gave leisure for reflection and self-examination; it changed the child of Emancipation to the youth with dawning self-consciousness, self-realization, self-respect. In those sombre forests of his striving his own soul rose before him, and he saw himself—darkly as through a veil; and yet he saw in himself some faint revelation of his power, of his mission. He began to have a dim feeling that, to attain his place in the world, he must be himself, and not another. For the first time he sought to analyze the burden he bore upon his back, that dead-weight of social degradation partially masked behind a half-named Negro problem. He felt his poverty; without a cent, without a home, without land, tools, or savings, he had entered into competition with rich, landed, skilled neighbors. To be a poor man is hard, but to be a poor race in a land of dollars is the very bottom of hardships. He felt the weight of his ignorance—not simply of letters, but of life, of business, of the humanities; the accumulated sloth and shirking and awkwardness of decades and centuries shackled his hands and feet. Nor was his burden all poverty and ignorance. The red stain of bastardy, which two centuries of systematic legal defilement of Negro women had stamped upon his race, meant not only the loss of ancient African chastity, but also the hereditary weight of a mass of corruption from white adulterers, threatening almost the obliteration of the Negro home.

A people thus handicapped ought not to be asked to race with the world, but rather allowed to give all its time and thought to its own social problems. But alas! while sociologists gleefully count his bastards and his prostitutes, the very soul of the toiling, sweating black man is darkened by the shadow of a vast despair. Men call the shadow prejudice, and learnedly explain it as the natural defence of culture against barbarism, learning against ignorance, purity against crime, the "higher" against the "lower" races. To which the Negro cries Amen! and swears that to so much of this strange prejudice as is founded on just homage to civilization, culture, righteousness, and progress, he humbly bows and meekly does obeisance. But before that nameless prejudice that leaps beyond all this he stands helpless, dismayed, and well-nigh speechless; before that personal disrespect and mockery, the ridicule and systematic humiliation, the distortion of fact and wanton license of fancy, the cynical ignoring of the better and the boisterous welcoming of the worse, the all-pervading desire to inculcate disdain for everything black, from Toussaint to the devil—before this there rises a sickening despair that would disarm and discourage any nation save that black host to whom "discouragement" is an unwritten word.

But the facing of so vast a prejudice could not but bring the inevitable self-questioning, self-disparagement, and lowering of ideals which ever accompany repression and breed in an atmosphere of contempt and hate. Whisperings and portents came borne upon the four winds: Lo! we are diseased and dying, cried the dark hosts; we cannot write, our voting is vain; what need of education, since we must always cook and serve? And the Nation echoed and enforced this self-criticism, saying: Be content to be servants, and nothing more; what need of higher culture for half-men? Away with the black man's ballot, by force or fraud—and behold the suicide of a race! Nevertheless, out of the evil came something of good—the more careful adjustment of education to real life, the clearer perception of the Negroes' social responsibilities, and the sobering realization of the meaning of progress.

So dawned the time of *Sturm und Drang*: storm and stress today rocks our little boat on the mad waters of the world-sea; there is within and without the sound of conflict, the burning of body and rending of soul; inspiration strives with doubt, and faith with vain questionings. The bright ideals of the past—physical freedom, political power, the training of brains and the training of hands—all these in turn have waxed and waned, until even the last grows dim and overcast. Are they all wrong—all false? No, not that, but each alone was over-simple and incomplete—the dreams of a credulous race-childhood, or the fond imaginings of the other world which does not know and does not want to know our power. To be really true, all these ideals must be melted and welded into one. The training of the schools we need to-day more than ever—the training of deft hands, quick eyes and ears, and above all the broader, deeper, higher culture of gifted minds and pure hearts. The power of the ballot we need in sheer self-defence—else what shall save us from a second slavery? Freedom, too, the long-sought, we still seek—the freedom of life and limb, the freedom to work and think, the freedom to love and aspire. Work, culture, liberty—all these we need, not singly but together, not successively but together, each growing and aiding each, and all striving toward that vaster ideal that swims before the Negro people, the ideal of human brotherhood, gained through the unifying ideal of Race; the ideal of fostering and developing the traits and talents of the Negro, not in opposition to or contempt for other races, but rather in large conformity to the greater ideals of the American Republic, in order that some day on American soil two world-races may give each to each those characteristics both so sadly lack. We the darker ones come even now not altogether empty-handed: there are to-day no truer exponents of the pure human spirit of the Declaration of Independence than the American Negroes; there is no true American music but the wild sweet melodies of the Negro slave; the American fairy tales and folk-lore are Indian and African; and, all in all, we black men seem the sole oasis of simple faith and reverence in a dusty desert of dollars and smartness. Will America be poorer if she replace her brutal dyspeptic blundering with light-hearted but determined Negro humility? or her coarse and cruel wit with loving jovial good-humor? or her vulgar music with the soul of the Sorrow Songs?

Merely a concrete test of the underlying principles of the great republic is the Negro Problem, and the spiritual striving of the freedmen's sons is the travail of souls whose burden is almost beyond the measure of their strength, but who bear it in the name of an historic race, in the name of this the land of their fathers' fathers, and in the name of human opportunity.

And now what I have briefly sketched in large outline let me on coming pages tell again in many ways, with loving emphasis and deeper detail, that men may listen to the striving in the souls of black folk.

Excerpt from *Racism without Racists: Color-Blind Racism and the Persistence of Racial Inequality in the United States*

EDUARDO BONILLA-SILVA

HOW TO STUDY COLOR-BLIND RACISM

I will rely mostly on interview data to make my case. This choice is based on important conceptual and methodological considerations. Conceptually, my focus is examining whites' racial ideology, and ideology, racial or not, is produced and reproduced in communicative interaction.[1] Hence, although surveys are useful instruments for gathering general information on actors' views, they are severely limited tools for examining how people explain, justify, rationalize, and articulate racial viewpoints. People are less likely to express their positions and emotions about racial issues by answering "yes" and "no" or "strongly agree" and "strongly disagree" to questions. Despite the gallant effort of some survey researchers to produce methodologically correct questionnaires, survey questions still restrict the free flow of ideas and unnecessarily constrain the range of possible answers for respondents.[2]

Methodologically, I argue that because the normative climate in the post–Civil Rights era has made illegitimate the public expression of racially based feelings and viewpoints,[3] surveys on racial attitudes have become like multiple-choice exams in which respondents work hard to choose the "right" answers (i.e., those that fit public norms). For instance, although a variety of data suggest racial considerations are central to whites' residential choices, more than 90 percent of whites state in surveys that they have no problem with the idea of blacks moving into their neighborhoods.[4] Similarly, even though about 80 percent of whites claim they would not have a problem if a member of their family brought a black person home for dinner, research shows that (1) very few whites (fewer than 10 percent) can legitimately claim the proverbial "some of my best friends are blacks" and (2) whites rarely fraternize with blacks.[5]

Of more import yet is the insistence by mainstream survey researchers' on using questions developed in the 1950s and 1960s to assess changes in

Bonilla-Silva, Eduardo. 2003. "The Strange Enigma of Race in Contemporary America," "Color-Blind Racism's Racial Stories," and "Conclusion" from *Racism without Racists: Color-Blind Racism and the Persistence of Racial Inequality in the United States*. Lanham, MD: Rowman & Littlefield.

racial tolerance. This strategy is predicated on the assumption that "racism" (what I label here racial ideology) does not change over time. If instead one regards racial ideology as in fact changing, the reliance on questions developed to tackle issues from the Jim Crow era will produce an artificial image of progress and miss most of whites' contemporary racial nightmares.

Despite my conceptual and methodological concerns with survey research, I believe well-designed surveys are still useful instruments to glance at America's racial reality. Therefore, I report survey results from my own research projects as well as from research conducted by other scholars whenever appropriate. My point, then, is not to deny attitudinal change or to condemn to oblivion survey research on racial attitudes, but to understand whites' new racial beliefs and their implications as well as possible.

COLOR-BLIND RACISM'S RACIAL STORIES

Storytelling is central to communication. To a large degree, all communication is about telling stories.[6] We tell stories to our spouses, children, friends, and coworkers. Through stories we present and represent ourselves and others.[7] Stories have been defined as "social events that instruct us about social processes, social structures, and social situations."[8] We literally narrate status ("When we were at the Gold Golf Club..."), biases ("This guy, who was not even a member of the GG Club..."), and beliefs about the social order ("...had the audacity of asking me out, even though he just drives a Cavalier"). Stories are also important because they help us reinforce our arguments; they assist us in our attempt of persuading listeners that we are "right."

Thus, the stories we tell are not random, as they evince the social position of the narrators and belong to what Moscovici labels as "social representations."[9] Storytelling often represents the most ideological moments when we tell stories we tell them as if there was *only one way* of telling them, as the "of course" way of understanding what is happening in the world. These are moments when we are "least aware that [we] are using a particular framework, and that if [we] used another framework the things we are talking about would have different meaning."[10] This is also the power of storytelling—that the stories seem to lie in the realm of the given, in the matter-of-fact world. Hence stories help us make sense of the world but in ways that reinforce the status quo, serving particular interests without appearing to do so.

Not surprisingly, then, since stories are a normal part of social life, they are a central component of color-blind racism.

"The Past Is the Past"

"The past is the past" story line is central to color-blind racism since it fits well with the minimization of discrimination frame. Thus more than

50 percent (21 of 41) of the college students and most DAS (Detroit Area Study) respondents used the story line most often when discussing affirmative action or government programs targeted for blacks. The core of this story line is that we must put the past behind us and that programs such as affirmative action do exactly the opposite by keeping the racial flame alive. A perfect example of how students inserted this story line was provided by Andy, a student at WU. Andy's answer to the question, "Do you believe that the history of oppression endured by minorities merits the intervention of the government on their behalf?" was:

> I almost—I think that the past is kind of the past and so, history of oppression?[11] I don't know if anyone [is] owed anything because of the, like, past [is] really past history, but to look at things, the way things are right at this moment and to try to move forward from there. Then I support some things, maybe affirmative action, so long as it wasn't a run away sort of....

Emily, a student at SU, used the story line in an exchange with the interviewer on the meaning of affirmative action:

> I have, I just have a problem with the discrimination, you're gonna discriminate against a group and what happened in the past is horrible and it should never happen again, but I also think that to move forward you have to let go of the past and let go of what happened, you know? And it should really start equaling out 'cause I feel that some of, some of it will go too far and it'll swing the other way. One group is going to be discriminated against, I don't, I don't believe in that. I don't think one group should have an advantage over another regardless of what happened in the past.

Very few DAS respondents who expressed their displeasure with programs they believe benefit blacks solely because of their racial background did not use a version of this story line. For instance, Jennifer, a school-district personnel director in her forties, expressed her opposition to affirmative action in a straightforward manner: "In general I am against it. I think it had its place. It was necessary." She later reaffirmed her position using a version of the story line in response to a hypothetical case dealing with a company that decides to hire a black over a white applicant because of past discrimination:

> Again, I don't think that we can make retribution for things that happened in the past. I don't think it serves any purpose today to try to fix something that happened a long time ago that doesn't affect anyone today. All it does is bring up to the surface that there was a problem.

Jennifer's last statement ("All it does is bring up to the surface that there was a problem") is the central ideological component of this story line. For whites, remedial policies are inherently divisive and hence whites' insistence in forgetting the past.

Kate, a salesperson and part-time college student in her twenties, used the story line to explain her opposition to government programs for blacks. Kate first stated: "To make up for what we did in the past, I'd say no. I mean, we can't still punish the Germans for what happened to the Jews so if that is to make up for what they did, then I'd say no." Since her answer left open the possibility there may be cases in which compensatory assistance was reasonable, the interviewer asked for clarification. After the interviewer read the question to Kate again, she answered:

> Am I not elaborating enough? [*Interviewer: Oh, no, no, no, no, we're just...*] No, I don't think that the government should because I think that's saying "OK, we made a mistake a hundred of years ago so no we're gonna try to make up for it." But yet, you know, I think that is the past and you have to move along; I mean, should they admit that they made a mistake? Yes! But should there be programs for blacks that aren't for whites if they're in the same position, you know? If they're hurting or they're battered or they're starving should it be any different because they're not black? No!

Some respondents used the story line while venting lots of anger at the idea of affirmative action or reparations. John II, for instance; a retired architect and home builder in his late sixties, vented anger in his response to the question on reparations.

> Not a nickel, not a nickel! I think that's ridiculous. I think that's a great way to go for the black vote. But I think that's a ridiculous assumption because those that say we should pay them because they were slaves back in the past and yet, how often do you hear about the people who were whites that were slaves and ah, the whites that were ah? Boy, we should get reparations, the Irish should get reparations from the English....

But what is ideological about this story? Is it not true that "the past is the past"? First, whites interpreted the past as slavery, even when in some questions we left it open (e.g., questions regarding the "history of oppression") or specified we were referring to "slavery *and* Jim Crow." Since Jim Crow died slowly in the country (1960s to 1970s), their constant reference to a remote past distorts the fact about how recent overt forms of racial oppression impeded black progress. This also means that most whites are still connected to parents and grandparents who participated in Jim Crow in some fashion. Second, the effects of historic discrimination have limited blacks' capacity to accumulate wealth at the same rate as whites. According to Melvin L. Oliver and Thomas M. Shapiro, the "cumulation of disadvantages" has "sedimented" blacks economically so that, even if all forms of economic discrimination blacks face ended today, they would not catch up with whites for several hundred years![12] Third, believing discrimination is a thing of the past helps whites reinforce their staunch opposition to all race-based compensatory programs. This story line, then, is used to deny the enduring effects of historic discrimination as well as to deny the significance of contemporary discrimination. Thus, when one considers the combined effects of historic and contemporary discrimination, the anchor holding minorities in place weighs a ton and cannot be easily dismissed.

"I Didn't Own Any Slaves"

The essence of the "I didn't own any slaves" story line is that present generations are not responsible for the ills of slavery. This story line was used frequently in conjunction with the story line of "The past is the past," but it was inserted less often (nine students and a third of DAS respondents). As with the previous story line, this one was usually invoked in discussions about affirmative action. For instance, Carol, a student at SU, said in response to the question on government intervention: "I mean, I almost kind of have the 'what happened, happened' attitude. You know, I mean, my generation certainly didn't inflict any of this onto your generation, I mean, if anyone should pay it's the generation that did the inflicting." Because the generation who "did the inflicting" is long gone, her suggestion would not have any impact on blacks today.

Lynn, an MU student, used the story line to explain her opposition to a hypothetical company hiring a black candidate over a white candidate because of past discrimination:

> I think I would, I would, I'd disagree, I think. I mean, yeah, I think I'd disagree because, I mean, even though it's kinda what affirmative action—well, it's not really because I don't think like my generation should have to—I mean, in a way, we should, but we shouldn't be punished real harshly for the things that our ancestors did, on the one hand, but on the other hand, I think that now we should try and change the way we do things so that we aren't doing the same things that our ancestors did.

Using the story line here gave credence to Lynn's stance on this case because she had stated before she supported affirmative action and she realized that this case was "kinda what affirmative action" is. It also helped Lynn to regain her composure after a serious bout of rhetorical incoherence ("I think I would, I would, I'd disagree, I think. I mean, yeah, I think I'd disagree because, I mean").

Finally, Sara, a student at SU, used the story line to state her view on government intervention on blacks' behalf.

> Hm [long exhalation], maybe just—Well, I don't know 'cause it seems like people are always wondering if, you know, do we, like do we as white people owe people as black something their ancestors were, you know, treated so badly. But then, I mean, it wasn't really us that did that, so I don't know. I mean, I think that the race or that culture should, you know, be paid back for something in some way. But I don't think that....I don't know [laughs].

DAS respondents used this story line in ways similar to students. For example, Dina, an employment manager for an advertising agency in her early thirties, used the story line to answer the question on government compensation to blacks for past discrimination.

> No, and I, you know, I have to say that I'm pretty supportive of anything to help people, but I don't know why that slavery thing has a—I've got a chip on my shoulder about that. It's like it happened so long ago and you've got these sixteen-year-old kids saying, "Well, I deserve because great great granddaddy was a slave." Well, you know what, it doesn't affect you. Me, as white person, I had nothing to do with slavery. You, as a black person, you never experienced it. It was so long ago I just don't see how that pertains to what's happening to the race today so, you know, that's one thing that I'm just like "God, shut up!"

Roland, an electrical engineer in his forties, also used the story line to oppose the idea of reparations.

> I think they've gotten enough. I don't think we need to pay them anything or I think as long as they are afforded opportunities and avail themselves to the opportunities like everybody else, I, I don't know why we should give them any reparation for something that happened, you know....I can't, I *can't* help what happened in the 1400s, the 1500s, or the 1600s, when the blacks were brought over here and put into slavery. I mean, I had no control over that, neither did you, so I don't think we should do anything as far as reparations are concerned.

Although most Detroit-area whites used this story line as part of their argumentative repertoire to explain their opposition to or doubts about affirmative action, occasionally they used them in odd places. For instance, Monica, a medical transcriber in her fifties with a strong commitment to the Jehovah's Witnesses religious viewpoint, used the story line while discussing discrimination. After a long statement arguing that because of past discrimination, blacks developed a cultural outlook based on the idea that they can't succeed because of discrimination, Monica then proceeded to argue: "It's, it's become such a mess and it's perpetuated again by media and by these special interest groups. You and I aren't responsible for what our ancestors did in slavery, that we didn't initiate that slavery."

As can be seen, these two story lines served whites as instruments to object to blacks' demands for compensatory policies. Furthermore, they helped whites stand on a high moral ground while objecting to these policies. But, again, what is ideological about this particular story line? It is a fact that most whites did not participate directly[13] in slavery or came to the country years after slavery had ended.[14] However, this story line ignores the fact that prowhite policies ("preferential treatment") in jobs, housing, elections, and access to social space ("No blacks and Mexicans allowed here!") have had (and continue to have) a positive multiplier effect for all those deemed "white." Thus, not surprisingly, "suspect" racial groups such as the Irish, Italians, and Jews,[15] among others, struggled to become "white" because by doing so, they could receive the manifold "wages of whiteness." Hence, the "It wasn't me"[16] approach of this story line does not fit the reality of how racial privilege operated and still operates in America. Although specific whites may not have participated directly in the overt discriminatory practices that injured blacks and other minorities in the past, they all have received unearned privileges[17] by virtue of being regarded as "white" and have benefited from the various incarnations of white supremacy in the United States.

"If Jews, Italians, and Irish Have Made It, How Come Blacks Have Not"?

Another story line that has become quite popular is "If (ethnic groups such as Japanese, Chinese, Jews, and Irish) have made it, how come blacks have not?" This story line is used by whites to suggest blacks' status in America is their own doing, because other groups who experienced discrimination in the past are doing quite well today. Few college students, but ten DAS respondents, used this story line. However, it is important to point out that 35 percent of the students agreed with the premise of this story line when it was asked in the survey.

One example of a student who used this story line is Kim, a student at SU. She inserted a version of the story line in combination with the "The past is the past" story line to explain why she does not favor government intervention on behalf of minorities.

> Um no. I think that, you know, a lot of bad things happened to a lot of people, but you can't sit there and dwell on that. I mean, like the Jewish people, look what happened to them. You know, do you hear them sitting around complaining about it, you know, and attributing, you know, anything bad that happens to them? I've never heard anyone say, "Oh, it's because I'm Jewish." You know, and I know it's a little different because, you know, a black, I mean, you can't really, a lot of, you can't really tell on the outside a lot of times, but, I mean, they don't wallow in what happened to them a long time ago. I mean, it was a horrible thing, I admit, but I think that you need to move on and try to put that behind, you know, put that behind you.

Although DAS respondents were more likely than students to use this story line, they did not use it as frequently as they did the previous two. An example of how they used this story line was provided by Henrietta, a transvestite school teacher in his fifties. Henrietta used the story line in his answer to the question on government spending on blacks' behalf:

> [5 seconds pause] As a person who was once reversed discriminated against, I would have to say no. Because the government does not need programs if they, if people would be motivated to bring themselves out of the poverty level. When we talk about certain programs, when the Irish came over, when the Italians, the Polish, and the East European Jews, they all were immigrants

who lived in terrible conditions, who worked in terrible conditions, too. But they had one thing in common: they all knew that education was the way out of that poverty. And they did it. I'm not saying the blacks were brought over here maybe not willingly, but if they realize education's the key, that's it. And that's based on individuality.

Mandy, a registered nurse in her forties, used the story line to address the issue of whether or not blacks' standing in this country is due to their values and laziness:

MANDY: Generally, I think that's probably true. Now are you talking about *all minorities*? [*Interviewer: Umhumm.*] 'Cause I don't—when you look at the people coming from Asia, Japan, and China . . . they're making the honor roll. When you look at the honor [roll] here in Rochester, they're all foreign names. You know, some of those kids from minority families figured out that they had to work and strive and work harder if they were going to make it all the way to the top.

INTERVIEWER: Okay. So you're saying that you would classify minorities by race and go from there?

MANDY: Not all minorities are lazy and lay on the couch all the time.

This story line equates the experiences of immigrant groups with that of involuntary "immigrants" (such as enslaved Africans). But as Stephen Steinberg has perceptively pointed out in his *The Ethnic Myth*, most immigrant groups were able to get a foothold on certain economic niches or used resources such as an education or small amounts of capital to achieve social mobility. "In contrast, racial minorities were for the most part relegated to the preindustrial sectors of the national economy and, until the flow of immigration was cut off by the First World War, were denied access to the industrial jobs that lured tens of millions of immigrants. All groups started at the bottom, but as Blauner points out, 'the bottom' has by no means been the same for all groups."[18] Thus, comparing these groups, as this story line does, is comparing apples and pears as a way to "blame the victims" (many minority groups).

"I Did Not Get a Job (or a Promotion), or Was Not Admitted to a College, Because of a Minority"

This story line is extremely useful to whites rhetorically and psychologically. When whites do not get a job or promotion, it must be because of a minority. If they are not admitted into a college, it must be because of a minority. This story line allows whites to never consider the possibility that they are not qualified for a job, promotion, or college. Curiously, the number of actual cases filed on reverse discrimination before the Equal Employment Opportunity Commission is quite small and the immense majority of them are dismissed as lacking any foundation.[19] Furthermore, as I will show, most versions of this story line lack substance, are based on limited data, and rely on less than credible information.[20] This lack of specificity, however, does not detract from the usefulness of this story line, since its sense of veracity is not based on facts, but on commonly held beliefs by whites. Hence, when whites use this story line, precise information needs not be included. And because this story line is built upon a personal moral tale, many whites vent personal frustrations or resentment toward minorities while using it.

Almost a quarter of the students (10 of 41) and more than a third of the DAS respondents used this story line. For instance, Bob, the SU student cited above, opposed providing unique opportunities to minorities to be admitted into universities. After anchoring his view in the abstract liberalism frame ("you should be judged on your qualifications, your experience, your education, your background, not of your race"), Bob added:

> I had a friend, he wasn't—I don't like him that much, I think it's my brother's friend, a good friend of my brother's, who didn't get into law school here and he knows for a fact that other students less qualified than him *did*. And that really, and he was considering a lawsuit against the school. But for some reason, he didn't. He had better grades, better LSAT, better everything, and he—other people got in up above him, I don't care who it is, if it's Eskimo, or Australian, or what it is, you should have the best person there.

This is a classic example of this story line. Bob "had a friend" (who was not his friend, but his brother's friend and whom he did not "like that much") who claimed to know "for a fact" (facts he never documents) that minority students who were less qualified than his brother[21] were admitted into SU Law School. Bob uses the story line here to reinforce his view that admission to colleges ought to be strictly based on merits.

Kara, a student from MU, inserted the story line when she was asked if she had been a victim of "reverse discrimination."

> I think applying to schools. I know a couple of people, like, schools like Notre Dame that are, you know, very, like, competitive to get into. Like, I was put on the wait list where this kid in my school who was black was admitted and, like, for me, you know, like, I almost had a four point, you know, I did well on my SATs, and he was kind of a slacker, grade-point-wise, and I always thought it *could* have been something else, but it didn't make sense to me and that was the only thing I could put it to.

When asked if she knew of other cases of "reverse discrimination," Kara added, "Yeah, especially my friends that applied to the Ivy League schools." They really felt that they were discriminated against.

Kara claims that while she was not admitted to Notre Dame, a black "kid" in her school who was "kind of a slacker" was. She believes the only logical explanation for this is "reverse discrimination" and that many of her friends experienced it, too. But we do not get any data on how she did on her SAT (she reports doing "well," but does not indicate her score) and, more significantly, we get absolutely no information on how well the black student did on the SAT. Regarding her friends' claims, Kara provides even less information.

This story line was also important for white DAS respondents, since more than a third of them used it. One example is Ann, a young unemployed wom[a]n. She used the story line in her answer to the question, "Do you think that being white is an advantage or a disadvantage in contemporary America?"

> No. It's, I don't know. [*Interviewer: Why do you think that?*] I don't know, it's [*laughs*], it's weird because my friend that is there, she went for a job interview with two of her white girlfriends. It was her and those three white females and the rest were black. Well, when they were done with the testing they took their scores and they all had the same scores, the three white girls. and they come out and they hire, they said that the two white girls didn't pass their math test, but they said that she passed hers and then they hired her....

Ann claims that a black friend of hers experienced preferential treatment in a job search. As usual in the iterations of this story line, the story is very fuzzy and refers to third parties. In Ann's narrative it is very difficult to assess any of the particularities of the case. How many people went for the job? How many tests did they take? What scores did all the applicants get? Were the applicants interviewed after they were tested? What kind of job were they applying for? The answers to all these questions are uncertain.

Marie, a homemaker in her late thirties, used the story line to explain her position on affirmative action.

> Ah, I'm puzzled a little bit by that. I'm for making sure everybody gets equal opportunity. I think that there are points, though, where it is inappropriate. Just as an example, my sister has a good student that applied for a teaching position at a university and was told that she was one of three final candidates for the position, but the other two candidates, one was a Mexican American and the other was a black female. Unless she could prove she had some active minority in her background, she could not be considered for the position because they had to hire a minority.

Although Marie's story seems more robust than usual, the details do not square with what we know of the academic job market. First, based on the peculiar list of final candidates (peculiar because it is very unusual to have two minority scholars as finalists in a job search), it seems this job required expertise on racial matters. This does not disqualify the white applicant, but it adds some complexity to the story. Second, the argument that she had to prove some minority background to qualify for this position (after she made the final cut) is not credible. Had that been the case, this applicant could have successfully sued this university for discrimination. An alternative reading of the events is that this white applicant lost out to a minority candidate and explained this to herself, her professor, and her peers as many whites do, as a case of reverse discrimination.

Many of the workers in the sample vented lots of anger against what they regarded as "preferential treatment" for minorities, although few knew what affirmative action was. Not surprisingly, many used the story line in its most generic sense. The following two cases illustrate my point. First is Darren, a bus driver in his late forties. He opposed affirmative action by stating that "two wrongs don't make a right" and used the story line to supply evidence on which to base his opinion.

> Ah no, other than I have applied at jobs and been turned down because I was white. *Now, I have nothing* against the black person [if he] was qualified better than I was. But when the guy comes into the interview and I'm off on the side and I can hear them talking and he can't even speak good English, he doesn't know how to read a map, and they're gonna make him a bus driver and hire him over me. I've been doing bus driving off and on since 1973 and I know the guy well enough that [I know] he's a lousy driver. I know why he got the job, and I don't think that's fair.

Darren believed he was turned down for a job as a bus driver because he was white. Furthermore, he claimed that he overheard the interview and that his black competitor could not "even speak good English." But his story is as loose as the others. Both applicants now work in the same company, which suggests Darren got the job there at some point in time. And Darren failed to mention two other factors that may account—besides driving skills, which we cannot ascertain based on the information he provided—for why this other driver may have gotten the job before Darren did. First, this company is located in Detroit and it makes business sense to hire black bus drivers. Second, and more important, Darren has moved a lot in his life and has had more than twelve jobs. Hence, any rational manager must look at his record with some trepidation and wonder why this person has moved so much and whether he would be a reliable worker.

Tony, a carpet installer in his twenties used a very unusual version of the story line to explain why he believes being white is no longer an advantage in America: "Oh yeah. Like when my girlfriend went to get on aid, the lady told her if she was black, she could have got help, but she wasn't black and she wasn't getting no help." Tony's account can be translated as "I did not get welfare because of blacks."

These racial stories "make" whites, but also help them navigate the turbulent waters of contemporary public discussions on race. The four story lines I analyzed, "The past is the past," "I did not own slaves," "If (other ethnic groups such as Italians or Jews) have made it, how come blacks have not?" and "I did not get a (job or promotion) because of a black man," help whites discursively since they provide "evidence" to solidify their viewpoints. For example, if whites object to the idea of affirmative action or reparations, they can insert "The past is the past" or "I did not own any slaves" story lines to strengthen the apparent reasonableness of their argument. If the issue at hand is explaining blacks' status in America, the story line of "If (other ethnic groups such as Italians or Jews) have made it, how come blacks have not?" is very appropriate. Finally, because the story line of "I did not get a (job or promotion) because of a black man" seems personal (in truth, the facts included in this story line tend to be secondhand or based on racialized impressions of social outcomes), it has become a powerful rhetorical weapon to win arguments ("I know for a *fact* that...").

In addition to the rhetorical role filled by story lines, they also serve whites as vehicles to vent deep-seated emotions[22] about racial matters. In case after case, whether students or whites from the Detroit area, respondents vented anger about what they interpreted as blacks' whining ("I didn't own any slaves and I do not understand why they keep asking for things when slavery ended 200 hundred *God-damned* years ago!") or about not getting into certain jobs or universities because of minorities ("A friend of mine was not admitted into SU Law School, but many *unqualified* black students were and that's *wrong*"). The story lines then serve whites as legitimate conduits for expressing anger, animosity, and resentment toward racial minorities.

A final point on story lines and testimonies: because these story lines are *social* products, the media play an important role in reinforcing them.[23] News reports on affirmative action seldom address the whiteness of academia or the workplace and its implications[24]; sensational reports on welfare cheats never address the reality of welfare, that people on welfare live below the poverty line[25]; stories of "bad" behavior by black and Latino youths are presented as "normal," whereas stories depicting "bad" behavior by white youths are not.[26] News reports on minorities thus tend to be presented as morality tales that support the various racial stories of the color-blind era. These reports are then recycled by the white audience as absolute truths ("Didn't you hear about that black guy who couldn't read and was admitted into Harvard? It was in the news."). Therefore, the media uses the racial stories we create and makes them as if they were independent creations that validate our racial angst.[27]

EXPOSING THE WHITENESS OF COLOR BLINDNESS

"I thought racism died in the sixties? But you guys keep talking, and talking, and talking about racism. Please stop using racism as a crutch!"

"Don't you think the best way of dealing with America's racial problems is by not talking about them? By constantly talking about racism you guys add wood to the racial fire, which is almost extinguished!"

"Race is a myth, an invention, a socially constructed category. Therefore, we should not make it 'real' by using it in our analyses. People are people, not black, white, or Indian. White males are just people."[28]

"A&M's tradition of focusing on race is a terrible mentality to teach a new generation. Dr. Eduardo Bonilla-Silva's book *White Supremacy & Racism in the Post–Civil Rights Era* is the latest evolution in this ritual that should have collapsed with the 1960s."[29]

Statements such as these have become standard examples of how most whites think and talk about racism in contemporary America. Those of us who are minority professors in the academic trenches hear statements like these from students, staff, and colleagues. I personally have been accused of being a "racist" because I use the category race in my analysis (as if by closing our eyes, racial fractures would disappear from society and we would all just be "Americans") and of spreading "racist propaganda"[30] (in the color-blind era, those of us who write about race and racism are the ones accused of fostering racial divisions). These statements are all emblematic of the racial ideology that I labeled "color-blind racism." At the heart of these statements—and of color blindness—lies a myth: the idea that race has all but disappeared as a factor shaping the life chances of all Americans. This myth is the central column supporting the house of color blindness. Remove this column and the house will collapse.

The interview data in this book demonstrated that color-blind racism is central to old and young whites alike. Although older, working-class white respondents (mostly in the DAS sample) were less adept at using softer, more efficient versions of the frames and style of color-blind racism than were younger, middle-class, educated ones (mostly among the college students sample), both groups were attuned to this new ideology. Yet the fact that some whites are "compassionate conservatives" on race does not change in any way the reality that all are baptized in the waters of color-blind racism. Besides, even though younger, middle-class, educated whites seem better adept at using the arsenal of color blindness, many—particularly those who were already in the labor market or close to entering it—were as crude and unsophisticated as their poorer, less-educated brethren. To examine this matter more accurately, we need a panel study to follow college students over a ten-year period or so to assess whether or not, as they mature and deal with central life issues (e.g., getting a job, purchasing a house, getting married, having children), their color blindness becomes cruder.

The data also evinced color-blind racism forms an impregnable yet elastic ideological wall that barricades whites off from America's racial reality. An impregnable wall because it provides them a safe, color-blind way to state racial views without appearing to be irrational or rabidly racist. And an elastic wall—and hence a stronger one—because this ideology does not rely on absolutes (it prefers statements such as "Most blacks are" rather than "All blacks are"), admits a variety of ways of using its frames (from crude and direct to kinder and indirect), and allows whites to employ a variety of emotional tones for stating their views (from the angry "Darned lazy blacks" to the compassionate conservative "Poor blacks are trapped in their inferior schools in their cycle of poverty; what a pity").

Accordingly, my answer to the strange enigma of "racism without racists" is as follows. The United States does not depend on Archie Bunkers to defend white supremacy. (In truth, it never did, but that is *otros veinte pesos*.[31]) Modern racial ideology does not thrive on the ugliness of the past or on the language and tropes typical of slavery and Jim Crow. Today there is a sanitized, color-blind way of calling minorities niggers, Spics, or Chinks. Today most whites justify keeping minorities from having the good things of life with the language of liberalism ("I am all for equal opportunity; that's why I oppose affirmative action!"). And today, as yesterday, whites do not feel guilty about the plight of minorities (blacks in particular). Whites believe minorities have the opportunities to succeed and that, if they do not, it is because they do not try hard. And if minorities dare talk about discrimination, they are rebuked with statements such as "Discrimination ended in the sixties, man" or "You guys are hypersensitive."

The analysis of the interview data also sheds light on the methodological importance of using this kind of data for examining racial ideology. Had I relied on my survey results to analyze whites' racial views, it would have been difficult. Depending on which questions I had used to make my case, I seemingly could have argued three totally different positions.[32] Moreover, I could not have extracted from the survey data the stylistic and narrative elements of color blindness. Although this does not mean that surveys on racial attitudes are useless, it does mean that survey researchers must strive to develop research projects with a qualitative dimension. Otherwise they may either produce an artificial image of racial progress or miss central components of the contemporary racial ideological constellation.

NOTES

1. Vološinov, the great Russian psychologist, stated a long time ago that ideology, and even self-awareness and consciousness, are "always verbal [communicative], always a matter of finding some specifically suitable verbal complex." Vladimir N. Vološinov, *Freudianism: A Marxist Critique* (New York: Academic, 1976), 86. For treatises on how language is embedded in ideology, see Norman Fairclough, *Language and Power* (London: Longman, 1989) and *Critical Discourse Analysis: The Critical Study of Language* (London: Longman, 1995).
2. For an example of the efforts of survey researchers to craft better survey instruments, see Judith Tanur, ed., *Questions About Questions* (New York: Russell Sage Foundation, 1994).
3. Teun A. van Dijk, *Prejudice in Discourse*. (Philadelphia: Benjamins, 1984). See also Howard Schuman et al., *Racial Attitudes in America*.
4. The specific wording of this survey question is: "If a black family with about the same income as you moves into your neighborhood, would you mind it a little, a lot, or not at all?" See Schuman et al., *Racial Attitudes in America*.
5. For data on traditional social distance questions, see chapter 3 in Schuman et al., *Racial Attitudes in America*. For data on the limited level of white-black friendship, see Mary R. Jackman and Marie Crane, "'Some of My Best Friends are Black...': Interracial Friendship and Whites' Racial Attitudes," *Public Opinion Quarterly* 50 (Winter 1986): 459–86.
6. For an interesting discussion of stories and a superb story on how affirmative action is being undercut from within in academia, see Adalberto Aguirre Jr.,

"Academic Storytelling: A Critical Race Theory Story of Affirmative Action," *Sociological Perspectives*, 43, no. 2 (2000): 319–39.

7. On this issue, see Margaret Somers, "The Narrative Constitution of Identity; A Relational and Network Approach," *Theory and Society* 23, no. 3 (1994): 605–49.

8. Aguirre, "Academic Storytelling," 320.

9. Stuart Hall, "The Narrative Construction of Reality," *Southern Review* 17, no. 2 (1984): 8.

10. Hall, "Narrative Construction," 8.

11. I set off the pertinent phrase with a different font not to signify emphasis from the respondents, but to help readers identify the racial story.

12. Melvin L. Oliver and Thomas Shapiro, *Black Wealth/White Wealth* (New York: Routledge, 1995). For an estimate of how much America owes blacks, see Richard F. America, *Paying the Social Debt: What White America Owes Black America* (Westport, Conn.: Praeger, 1993).

13. Most of the white population in the South participated in slavery as a social institution, for example by participating in the patrol system, which sought to catch runaway slaves. See George P. Rawick, *From Sundown to Sunup: The Making of the Black Community* (Westport, Conn.: Greenwood, 1972).

14. Jim Goad, in his *The Redneck Manifesto* (New York: Touchstone, 1998), states that at the peak of slavery (1860), only one out of every fifteen whites was a slaveholder. However, Goad, whose manifesto includes a number of interesting ideas, fails to analyze how slavery formed a social system in which all whites participated (in patrols, in the war effort, in catching fugitives).

15. See David Roediger, *The Wages of Whiteness* (London: Verso, 1994); Noel Ignatiev, *How the Irish Became White* (New York: Routledge, 1995); and Karen Brodkin, *How Jews Became White Folks and What That Says About Race in America* (New Brunswick, N.J.: Rutgers University Press, 1998).

16. Eduardo Bonilla-Silva, Tyrone A. Forman, Amanda E. Lewis, and David G. Embrick, "'It Wasn't Me': Race and Racism in 21st Century America," *Research in Political Sociology* (forthcoming).

17. On this point, see Joe R. Feagin, *Racist America: Roots, Realities, and Future Reparations* (New York: Routledge, 2000).

18. Stephen Steinberg, *The Ethnic Myth* (Boston: Beacon, 1989).

19. See Tom Wicker, *Tragic Failure* (New York: Morrow, 1996).

20. For a similar finding based on data from the Los Angeles Study of Urban Inequality (part of the Multi City Study of Urban Inequality), see chapter 14, by Lawrence Bobo and Susan Suh, "Surveying Racial Discrimination: Analyses from a Multiethnic Labor Market," in *Prismatic Metropolis: Inequality in Los Angeles*, edited by Laurence Bobo et al., 523–60 (New York: Russell Sage Foundation, 2000).

21. As Beverly Daniel Tatum points out, "When these stories are told, I wonder how the speaker knows so much about the person of color's résumé." Tatum, *Why Are All the Black Kids Sitting Together in the Cafeteria? And Other Conversations about Race.* (New York: Basic Books, 1990).

22. In his recent *Racist America*, Feagin has forcefully argued that emotions are a central part of "systemic racism."

23. The classic study on racism and the media is Paul Hartmann, *Racism and the Mass Media: A Study of the Role of the Mass Media in the Formation of White Beliefs and Attitudes in Britain* (Totowa, N.J.: Rowman & Littlefield, 1974). See also the important contributions of Teun van Dijk, in *News as Discourse* (Hillsdale, N.J.: Erlbaum,

1988) and *Racism and the Press* (London: Routledge, 1991), and by Darnell Hunt, in *Screening the Los Angeles "Riots": Race, Seeing, and Resistance* (New York: Cambridge University Press, 1996) and *O. J. Simpson Facts and Fictions: News Rituals in the Construction of Reality* (Cambridge: Cambridge University Press, 1999).

24. On this point, see Joe R. Feagin and Nikitah Imani, *The Agony of Education: Black Students at White Colleges and Universities* (New York: Routledge, 1996).

25. On the realities of how women survive on welfare, see Kathryn Edin, *Making Ends Meet: How Single Mothers Survive Welfare and Low-Wage Work* (New York: Russell Sage Foundation, 1997). For a discussion on the limited supply of good jobs and its implications, see Gordon Lafer, *The Job Training Charade* (Ithaca, N.Y.: Cornell University Press, 2002).

26. For example, whereas gang-related activity in urban areas is naturalized, gang-like activity in the suburbs (such as drug selling and drug use, the many recent mass murders in schools, prostitution) is presented as exceptional behavior that we need to think long and hard about to prevent. For an example of the latter, see "Born to Be Bad," *Dateline NBC*, April 27, 1999.

27. Here I am borrowing Marx's idea of "commodity fetishism" to explain how these media stories operate.

28. A colleague said something like this to me almost verbatim a few years ago in response to a presentation I gave about racism in sociology. Later on, the same colleague uttered a statement along the same lines to challenge a graduate student's presentation on whiteness. Denying the *social reality* of race because of its constructed nature, unfortunately, has become respectable in academia. This position, which has been uttered by conservatives such as David Horowitz, has now been adopted by liberals such as Todd Gitlin and even radicals (or former radicals) such as Paul Gilroy. For the latter, see Paul Gilroy, *Against Race* (Cambridge, Mass.: Belknap, 2000).

29. Matthew Maddox, "Institutionalized Racism Continues at A&M: Sociology Professor's Book Will Continue Tradition of Racist Ideology on Campus," *Battalion*, October 2, 2002.

30. Maddox, "Institutionalized Racist Ideology."

31. "Otros veinte pesos" is a Puerto Rican expression that literally means "another twenty dollars" and is used to suggest that a side argument will take a long time to make and, therefore, that making it will distract from the main one.

32. See Eduardo Bonilla-Silva and Tyrone A. Forman, "'I Am Not a Racist, But...': Mapping White Students' Racial Ideology in the USA," *Discourse and Society* 11, no. 1 (2000): 50–85.

READING 15

Excerpt from *American Apartheid: Segregation and the Making of the Underclass*

DOUGLAS MASSEY AND NANCY DENTON

> Residential segregation has proved to be the most resistant to change of all realms—perhaps because it is so critical to racial change in general.
>
> Thomas Pettigrew, 1966
> review of *Negroes in Cities*
> by Karl and Alma Taeuber

The spatial isolation of black Americans was achieved by a conjunction of racist attitudes, private behaviors, and institutional practices that disenfranchised blacks from urban housing markets and led to the creation of the ghetto.[1] Discrimination in employment exacerbated black poverty and limited the economic potential for integration, and black residential mobility was systematically blocked by pervasive discrimination and white avoidance of neighborhoods containing blacks. The walls of the ghetto were buttressed after 1950 by government programs that promoted slum clearance and relocated displaced ghetto residents into multi-story, high-density housing projects.

In theory, this self-reinforcing cycle of prejudice, discrimination, and segregation was broken during the 1960s by a growing rejection of racist sentiments by whites and a series of court decisions and federal laws that banned discrimination in public life. The Civil Rights Act of 1964 outlawed racial discrimination in employment, the Fair Housing Act of 1968 banned discrimination in housing, and the *Gautreaux* and *Shannon* court decisions prohibited public authorities from placing housing projects exclusively in black neighborhoods. Despite these changes, however, the nation's largest black communities remained as segregated as ever in 1980. Indeed, many urban areas displayed a pattern of intense racial isolation that could only be described as hypersegregation.

Although the racial climate of the United States improved outwardly during the 1970s, racism still restricted the residential freedom of black Americans; it just did so in less blatant ways. In the aftermath of the civil

Massey, Douglas S., and Nancy A. Denton. 1993. "The Continuing Causes of Segregation" from *American Apartheid*. Cambridge, MA: Harvard University Press.

rights revolution, few whites voiced openly racist sentiments; realtors no longer refused outright to rent or sell to blacks; and few local governments went on record to oppose public housing projects because they would contain blacks. This lack of overt racism, however, did not mean that prejudice and discrimination had ended; although racist attitudes and behaviors went underground, they did not disappear. Despite whites' endorsement of racial equality in principle, prejudice against blacks continued in subtle ways; in spite of the provisions of the Fair Housing Act, real estate agents continued to practice surreptitious but widespread discrimination; and rather than conform to court decrees, local authorities stopped building projects.

RACE VERSUS CLASS: AN UNEQUAL CONTEST

Before exploring the continuing causes of segregation, we assess the extent to which the geographic separation of blacks and whites may be attributed to economic differences between the two groups. In the market-driven, status-conscious society of the United States, affluent families live in different neighborhoods than poor families, and to the extent that blacks are poor and whites are affluent, the two groups will tend to be physically separated from one another. Is what appears to be racial segregation actually segregation on the basis of social class?

Economic arguments can be invoked to explain why levels of black–white segregation changed so little during the 1970s. After decades of steady improvement, black economic progress stalled in 1973, bringing about a rise in black poverty and an increase in income inequality.[2] As the black income distribution bifurcated, middle-class families experienced downward mobility and fewer households possessed the socioeconomic resources necessary to sustain residential mobility and, hence, integration. If the economic progress of the 1950s and 1960s had been sustained into the 1970s, segregation levels might have fallen more significantly. William Clark estimates that 30%–70% of racial segregation is attributable to economic factors, which, together with urban structure and neighborhood preferences, "bear much of the explanatory weight for present residential patterns."[3]

Arguments about whether racial segregation stems from white racism or from economic disadvantages are part of a larger debate on the relative importance of race and class in American society. Some observers hold that black social and economic problems now stem from the unusually disadvantaged class position of African Americans; they argue that black poverty has become divorced from race per se and is now perpetuated by a complex set of factors, such as joblessness, poor schooling, and family instability, that follow from the transformation of cities from manufacturing to service centers.[4] Other investigators place greater emphasis on racism; they argue that because white prejudice and discrimination have persisted in a variety of forms, both overt and subtle, skin color remains a powerful basis of stratification in the United States.[5]

Since the mid-1970s, the race-class debate has gone on without definitive resolution with respect to a variety of socioeconomic outcomes: employment, wealth, family stability, education, crime. But when one considers residential segregation, the argument is easily and forcefully settled: Race clearly predominates. Indeed, race predominates to such an extent that speculations about what would have happened if black economic progress had continued become moot. Even if black incomes had continued to rise through the 1970s, segregation would not have declined: No matter how much blacks earned, they remained spatially separated from whites. In 1980, as in the past, money did not buy entry into white neighborhoods of American cities.

The dominance of race over class is illustrated by Table 15–1, which presents black–white dissimilarity indices for three income groups within the thirty largest black communities of the United States. These data show the degree of residential segregation that blacks experience as their family income rises from under $2,500 per year to more than $50,000 per year. Although we computed segregation indices for all income categories between these two extremes, in the interest of brevity we only show one middle category ($25,000–$27,500). Little is added by including other income groups, because black segregation does not vary by affluence.[6]

Among northern metropolitan areas, for example, blacks, no matter what their income, remain very highly segregated from whites. As of 1980, black families earning under $2,500 per year experienced an average segregation index of 86, whereas those earning more than $50,000 had an average score of 83; blacks in the middle category displayed a score of 81. This pattern of constant, high segregation was replicated in virtually all northern urban areas. In Chicago, for example, the poorest blacks displayed an index of 91; the most affluent blacks had an index of 86. In New York the respective figures were 86 and 79, and in Los Angeles they were 85 and 79. In no northern metropolitan area did blacks earning more than $50,000 per year display a segregation index lower than 72.

Although southern areas generally evinced lower levels of racial segregation, the basic pattern by income was the same: rising economic status had little or no effect on the level of segregation that blacks experienced. On average, segregation moved from 74 in the lowest income category to 73 in the highest, with a value of 67 in between. Segregation was particularly high and resistant to change in Atlanta, Baltimore, Dallas, Miami, and Tampa; but even in southern cities with relatively low levels of segregation, there was little evidence of a meaningful differential by income: the poorest blacks in Birmingham, Alabama, displayed a segregation index of 46, whereas the most affluent black families had a segregation index of 45.

One possible explanation for this pattern of constant segregation irrespective of income is that affluent blacks are not well informed about the cost and availability of housing opportunities in white neighborhoods. Reynolds Farley examined this possibility using special data collected in the University of Michigan's Detroit Area Survey. He found that blacks were

Table 15-1 Segregation by Income in Thirty Metropolitan Areas with the Largest Black Populations, 1980

Metropolitan Area	INCOME CATEGORY		
	Under $2,500	$25,000–$27,500	$50,000
Northern Areas			
Boston	85.1	83.9	89.1
Buffalo	85.2	80.0	90.0
Chicago	91.1	85.8	86.3
Cincinnati	81.7	70.9	74.2
Cleveland	91.6	87.1	86.4
Columbus	80.3	74.6	83.4
Detroit	88.6	85.0	86.4
Gary–Hammond–E. Chicago	90.6	89.5	90.9
Indianapolis	80.8	76.6	80.0
Kansas City	86.1	79.3	84.2
Los Angeles–Long Beach	85.4	79.8	78.9
Milwaukee	91.3	87.9	86.3
New York	86.2	81.2	78.6
Newark	85.8	79.0	77.5
Philadelphia	84.9	78.6	81.9
Pittsburgh	82.1	80.6	87.9
St. Louis	87.3	78.4	83.2
San Francisco–Oakland	79.9	73.7	72.1
Average	85.8	80.7	83.2
Southern Areas			
Atlanta	82.2	77.3	78.2
Baltimore	82.4	72.3	76.8
Birmingham	46.1	40.8	45.2
Dallas–Ft. Worth	83.1	74.7	82.4
Greensboro–Winston Salem	63.2	55.1	70.8
Houston	73.8	65.5	72.7
Memphis	73.8	66.8	69.8
Miami	81.6	78.4	76.5
New Orleans	75.8	63.1	77.8
Norfolk–Virginia Beach	70.1	63.3	72.4
Tampa–St. Petersburg	81.8	76.0	85.7
Washington, D.C.	79.2	67.0	65.4
Average	74.4	66.7	72.8

Source: Nancy A. Denton and Douglas S. Massey, "Residential Segregation of Blacks, Hispanics, and Asians by Socioeconomic Status and Generation," *Social Science Quarterly* 69 (1988):811.

quite knowledgeable about housing costs throughout the metropolitan area, even in distant white suburbs, and were well aware that they could afford to live outside the ghetto.[7] Whatever was keeping affluent blacks out of white areas, it was not ignorance.

The uniqueness of this pattern of invariant high segregation is starkly revealed when blacks are compared with Hispanics or Asians. In the Los Angeles metropolitan area, for example, the segregation index for Hispanics earning under $2,500 in 1979 was 64, and it declined to a moderate value of 50 among those earning $50,000 or more. In the largest Latino barrio in the United States, therefore, the *poorest* Hispanics were less segregated than the *most affluent* blacks (whose score was 79). Similarly, in the San Francisco–Oakland metropolitan area, which contains the largest concentration of Asians in the United States, the Asian–white segregation index fell from 64 in the lowest income category to 52 in the highest (compared with respective black–white indices of 86 and 79). These contrasts were repeated in cities throughout the United States: Hispanic and Asian segregation generally begins at a relatively modest level among the poor and falls steadily as income rises.[8]

Similar patterns are observed when segregation is examined by education and occupation. No matter how socioeconomic status is measured, therefore, black segregation remains universally high while that of Hispanics and Asians falls progressively as status rises. Only blacks experience a pattern of constant, high segregation that is impervious to socioeconomic influences. The persistence of racial segregation in American cities, therefore, is a matter of race and not class. The residential segregation of African Americans cannot be attributed in any meaningful way to the socioeconomic disadvantages they experience, however serious these may be.[9]

ATTITUDES IN BLACK AND WHITE

Even if the segregation of African Americans cannot be linked to black socioeconomic disadvantages, it does not necessarily follow that current residential patterns are involuntary. It is conceivable, for example, that high levels of segregation reflect black preferences for racial separation, and that these desires for residential homogeneity are merely expressed through urban housing markets. If most black people prefer to live in neighborhoods that are largely black, then high levels of racial segregation may correspond to black desires for self-segregation and not discrimination or prejudice.[10]

This line of reasoning does not square with survey evidence, however. The vast majority of black Americans express strong support for the ideal of integration, and when asked on national surveys whether they favor "desegregation, strict segregation, or something in-between" they generally answer "desegregation" in large numbers. Although support for the "in-between" option rose during the 1970s, an average of 68% favored desegregation across the decade.[11] Moreover, 98% of black respondents have consistently agreed that "black people have a right to live wherever they can afford to," and in 1978 71% said they would be willing to vote for a community-wide law to ban racial discrimination in housing.[12]

In both principle and action, therefore, blacks strongly favor the desegregation of American society. They endorse the ideal of integration, they unanimously state that people should be able to move wherever they want to regardless of skin color, and they support the passage of laws to enforce these principles. But the endorsement of abstract principles and laws does not really get at the kinds of neighborhoods that blacks actually prefer to live in, or the degree of neighborhood integration they find attractive and comfortable. The most widely cited source of information on this issue is the Detroit Area Survey.

Respondents to the survey were shown drawings of hypothetical neighborhoods with homes colored in either black or white. The percentage of black homes was systematically varied and respondents were asked how they felt about different racial compositions. Blacks expressed a strong preference for racial parity in neighborhoods: 63% chose a neighborhood that was half-black and half-white as most desirable, and 20% selected this option as their second choice (see Table 15–2). Virtually all blacks (99%) said they would be willing to live in such a neighborhood. At the same time, blacks appeared to resist strongly complete segregation: nearly a third would not be willing to move into a neighborhood that was all black, and 62% would be unwilling to enter an area that was all white. Nearly 90% ranked all-white neighborhoods as their fourth or fifth preference, and 62% placed all-black neighborhoods into one of these rankings.

Among racially mixed neighborhoods, blacks seem to prefer those with a relatively higher black percentage, other things equal. Thus the second

Table 15–2 Neighborhood Preferences of Black Respondents to Detroit Area Survey, 1976

| Neighborhood Composition | PREFERENCE RANKING | | | | | Percentage Willing to Enter Such a Neighborhood |
	First Choice	Second Choice	Third Choice	Fourth Choice	Last Choice	
All black	12%	5%	21%	35%	27%	69%
70% black	14	55	18	10	2	99
50% black	63	20	14	2	1	99
15% black	8	17	40	32	3	95
All white	2	3	7	21	66	38
Total	100%	100%	100%	100%	100%	

Sources: Reynolds Farley, Suzanne Bianchi, and Diane Colasanto, "Barriers to the Racial Integration of Neighborhoods: The Detroit Case," *Annals of the American Academy of Political and Social Science* 441 (1979):104; Reynolds Farley, Howard Schuman, Suzanne Bianchi, Diane Colasanto, and Shirley Hatchett, "'Chocolate City, Vanilla Suburbs': Will the Trend toward Racially Separate Communities Continue?" *Social Science Research* 7 (1978):330.

choice of most blacks (55%) was a neighborhood that was 70% black, and only 17% selected an area where whites clearly predominated; neighborhoods that were 15% black were generally chosen as the third most desirable neighborhood. Even though blacks prefer a racial mixture of 50% black or higher, however, they are comfortable with almost any level of integration: 95% would be willing to live in any neighborhood with a black percentage lying between 15% and 70%.

We may summarize white neighborhood preferences using data from the Detroit Area Survey (see Table 15–3). As with blacks, whites were asked how they felt about hypothetical neighborhoods that contained black and white homes in different proportions. In their responses, whites indicated they were still quite uncomfortable with the prospect of black neighbors in practice, despite their endorsement of open housing in principle. Roughly a fourth of whites said they would feel uncomfortable in a neighborhood where 8% of the residents were black, and about the same percentage would be unwilling to enter such an area. When the black percentage reached 21%, half of all whites said they would be unwilling to enter, 42% would feel uncomfortable, and 24% would seek to leave. Once a neighborhood reached about one-third black, the limits of racial tolerance were reached for the majority of whites: 73% would be unwilling to enter, 57% would feel uncomfortable, and 41% would try to leave. At the 50–50 threshold, a neighborhood became unacceptable to all but a small minority of whites: 84% said they would not wish to enter a neighborhood that was 57% black, 64% would try to leave, and 72% would feel uncomfortable.

Whereas 63% of blacks picked a 50–50 racial mixture as the most desirable, the great majority of whites would not be willing to enter such a neighborhood and most would try to leave. Although blacks and whites may share a common commitment to "integration" in principle, this word connotes very different things to people in the two racial groups. For blacks, integration means racial mixing in the range of 15% to 70% black, with 50% being most desirable; for whites, it signifies much smaller black percentages.

Table 15–3 Neighborhood Preferences of White Respondents to Detroit Area Survey, 1976

Neighborhood Composition	Percentage Who Would Feel Uncomfortable in Neighborhood	Percentage Who Would Try to Move Out of Neighborhood	Percentage Unwilling to Move Into Neighborhood
8% black	24%	7%	27%
21% black	42	24	50
36% black	57	41	73
57% black	72	64	84

Source: Reynolds Farley, Howard Schuman, Suzanne Bianchi, Diane Colasanto, and Shirley Hatchett, "'Chocolate City, Vanilla Suburbs': Will the Trend toward Racially Separate Communities Continue?" *Social Science Research* 7 (1978):335.

This fundamental disparity between blacks and whites has been confirmed by surveys conducted in Milwaukee, Omaha, Cincinnati, Kansas City, and Los Angeles, all of which show that blacks strongly prefer a 50–50 mixture and that whites have little tolerance for racial mixtures beyond 20% black.[13] When the New York newspaper *Newsday* asked whites and blacks on suburban Long Island what "integration" meant to them, 64% of black respondents chose a neighborhood composition that was 40% black or higher, whereas 52% of whites selected a mixture that was 40% black or lower.[14] On a nationwide survey carried out by Lou Harris in 1988, 69% of blacks said the races were better off living next to each other "in the long run," but only 53% of whites shared this sentiment.[15]

The absence of overt discrimination does not mean that exclusionary practices have ended, however; rather, the character of discrimination has changed. Black homeseekers now face a more subtle process of exclusion. Rather than encountering "white only" signs, they face a covert series of barriers. Instead of being greeted with the derisive rejection "no niggers allowed," they are met by a realtor with a smiling face who, through a series of ruses, lies, and deceptions, makes it hard for them to learn about, inspect, rent, or purchase homes in white neighborhoods.

Black clients who inquire about an advertised unit may be told that it has just been sold or rented; they may be shown only the advertised unit and told that no others are available; they may be shown only houses in black or racially mixed areas and led systematically away from white neighborhoods; they may be quoted a higher rent or selling price than whites; they may be told that the selling agents are too busy and to come back later; their phone number may be taken but a return call never made; they may be shown units but offered no assistance in arranging financing; or they may be treated brusquely and discourteously in hopes that they will leave.[16]

Although each individual act of discrimination may be small and subtle, together they have a powerful cumulative effect in lowering the probability of black entry into white neighborhoods. Because the discrimination is latent, however, it is usually unobservable, even to the person experiencing it. One never knows for sure. It may be true, for example, that the agent has no additional units to show the client right then, or that all agents are indeed busy. The only way to confirm whether or not discrimination has occurred is to compare the treatment of black and white clients who have similar social and economic characteristics. If white clients receive systematically more favorable treatment, then we conclude that discrimination has taken place.

Differences in the treatment of white and black homeseekers are determined by means of a housing audit. Teams of white and black auditors are paired and sent to randomly selected realtors to pose as clients seeking a home or apartment. The auditors are trained to present comparable housing needs and family characteristics, and to express similar tastes, they are assigned equivalent social and economic traits by the investigator. Typically the order of presentation is varied so that half the time the black auditor goes first, and the other half of the time the white auditor leads off. A sufficient span of time is left between encounters to prevent realtors from growing suspicious and linking the two cases. After each encounter, the auditors fill out a detailed report of their experiences and the results are tabulated and compared to determine the nature and level of discrimination.[17]

Local fair housing organizations began to carry out audit studies toward the end of the 1960s, and these efforts quickly revealed that discrimination against blacks continued despite the Fair Housing Law. A 1969 audit of realty companies in St. Louis, for example, documented a pattern and practice of discrimination that was sufficient to force four realtors to sign a consent decree with the U.S. Department of Justice wherein they agreed to change their behavior. A 1971 audit study carried out in Palo Alto, California, found that blacks were treated in a discriminatory fashion by 50% of the area's apartment complexes; and a 1972 audit of apartments in suburban Baltimore uncovered discrimination in more than 45% of the cases.[18]

Systematic housing discrimination apparently continued into the 1980s. A series of audits carried out in the Chicago metropolitan area, for example, confirmed that realtors still employed a variety of exclusionary tactics to keep blacks out of white neighborhoods. In one 1983 study, suburban realtors showed homes to 67% of white auditors but to only 47% of black auditors.[19] Another study done in 1985 revealed that whites were offered financial information at nearly twice the rate of blacks.[20] One developer working near Chicago's South Side black community refused to deal with blacks at all: blacks were *always* told that no properties were available, even though 80% of whites were shown real estate.[21] In the same 1988 study, realtors told 92% of whites that apartments were available but gave this information to only 46% of blacks.

Given its unusual history of racial animosity, Chicago might be dismissed as an extreme case, but audit studies of other metropolitan areas reveal similar patterns of racial discrimination. According to John Yinger's review of audit studies carried out in metropolitan Boston and Denver during the early 1980s, black homeseekers had between a 38% and a 59% chance of receiving unfavorable treatment compared with whites on any given real estate transaction.[22] Through various lies and deceptions, blacks were informed of only 65 units for every 100 presented to whites, and they inspected fewer than 54 for every 100 shown to whites.

In 1987 George Galster wrote to more than two hundred local fair housing organizations and obtained written reports of seventy-one different audit studies carried out during the 1980s: twenty-one in the home sales market and fifty in the rental market.[23] Despite differences in measures and methods, he concluded that "racial discrimination continues to be a dominant feature of metropolitan housing markets in the 1980s."[24] Using a very conservative measure of bias, he found that blacks averaged a 20% chance of experiencing discrimination in the sales market and a 50% chance in the rental market.

Studies have also examined the prevalence of "steering" by real estate agents in different urban areas. Racial steering occurs when white and black clients are guided to neighborhoods that differ systematically with respect to social and economic characteristics, especially racial composition. A study carried out in Cleveland during the early 1970s found that 70% of companies engaged in some form of racial steering:[25] and an examination of realtors in metropolitan Detroit during the mid-1970s revealed that, compared to whites, blacks were shown homes in less-expensive areas that were located closer to black population centers.[26]

Galster studied six real estate firms located in Cincinnati and Memphis and found that racial steering occurred in roughly 50% of the transactions sampled during the mid-1980s. As in the Detroit study, homes shown to blacks tended to be in racially mixed areas and were more likely to be adjacent to neighborhoods with a high percentage of black residents. White auditors were rarely shown homes in integrated neighborhoods unless they specifically requested them, and even after the request was honored, they continued to be guided primarily to homes in white areas. Sales agents also made numerous positive comments about white neighborhoods to white clients but said little to black home buyers.[27] In a broader review of thirty-six different local audit studies, Galster discovered that such selective commentary by agents is probably more common than overt steering.[28]

These local studies, however suggestive, do not provide a comprehensive assessment of housing discrimination in contemporary American cities. The only entity capable of undertaking this task is the federal government, and the first such effort was mounted by the U.S. Department of Housing and Urban Development (HUD) in 1977. The study covered forty metropolitan areas chosen to represent those areas with central cities that were at least 11% black. The study confirmed the results of earlier local housing audits and demonstrated that discrimination was not confined to a few isolated cases. Nationwide, whites were favored on 48% of transactions in the sales market and on 39% of those in the rental market.[29]

The HUD audit was large enough to develop measures of racial discrimination for a variety of different metropolitan areas. Among the thirty metropolitan areas discussed twelve were audited by HUD and the results are summarized in Table 15–4. Our index of discrimination is the percentage of real estate transactions in which whites were clearly favored.[30] Corresponding to overall patterns of segregation, discrimination appears to be more severe in the north than in the south. On average, whites in northern urban areas received more favorable treatment from realtors in 52% of rental transactions and in 54% of sales transactions, whereas in southern cities the figures were 45% and 41%, respectively.[31] Blacks experienced an especially high degree of bias in the rental markets of Detroit, Indianapolis, and Los Angeles and in the sales markets of Cincinnati, Columbus, and Detroit. Blacks in these areas had at least a 60% chance of receiving unfavorable treatment on any given real estate transaction.

Table 15–4 Probability of Encountering Racial Discrimination in Selected U.S. Metropolitan Housing Markets, 1977

Metropolitan Area	PERCENTAGE OF ENCOUNTERS WHERE WHITES ARE FAVORED		NUMBER OF AUDITS	
	Rental Units	Sales Units	Rental Units	Sales Units
Northern Areas				
Boston	46%	43%	119	78
Cincinnati	48	65	29	48
Columbus	52	63	29	40
Detroit	67	64	30	51
Indianapolis	64	54	28	50
Los Angeles	63	42	30	50
Milwaukee	32	53	108	80
New York	45	50	29	50
Average	52	54	50	56
Southern Areas				
Atlanta	45	42	110	73
Dallas	40	41	114	80
Louisville	40	46	30	39
Tampa—St. Petersburg	53	34	30	44
Average	45	41	71	59

Source: Ronald Wienk, Cliff Reid, John Simonson, and Fred Eggers, *Measuring Racial Discrimination in American Housing Markets: The Housing Market Practices Survey* (Washington, D.C.: U.S. Department of Housing and Urban Development, 1979), pp. ES-21, ES-23.

Note: White favoritism defined to occur when white auditor receives favorable treatment on at least one of the following items and black auditors receive favorable treatment on none: housing availability, courtesy to client, terms and conditions of sale or rental, information requested of client, information supplied to client.

When it comes to housing and residential patterns, therefore, race is the dominant organizing principle. No matter what their ethnic origin, economic status, social background, or personal characteristics, African Americans continue to be denied full access to U.S. housing markets. Through a series of exclusionary tactics, realtors limit the likelihood of black entry into white neighborhoods and channel black demand for housing into areas that are within or near existing ghettos. White prejudice is such that when black entry into a neighborhood is achieved, that area becomes unattractive to further white settlement and whites begin departing at an accelerated pace. This segmentation of black and white housing demand is encouraged by pervasive discrimination in the allocation of mortgages and home improvement loans, which systematically channel money away from integrated areas. The end result is that blacks remain the most spatially isolated population in U.S. history.

NOTES

1. Epigraph from Thomas Petigrew, Book Review of *Negroes in Cities: Residential Segregation and Neighborhood Change, American Journal of Sociology* 82 (1966):112–13.

2. Douglas S. Massey and Mitchell L. Eggers, "The Ecology of Inequality: Minorities and the Concentration of Poverty, 1970–1980," *American Journal of Sociology* 95 (1990):1153–89.

3. William A. V. Clark, "Residential Segregation in American Cities: A Review and Interpretation," *Population Research and Policy Review* 5 (1986):95–127.

4. The most forceful exposition of the argument is by William Julius Wilson, *The Declining Significance of Race: Blacks and Changing American Institutions* (Chicago: University of Chicago Press, 1978); see also William Julius Wilson, *The Truly Disadvantaged: The Inner City, the Underclass, and Public Policy* (Chicago: University of Chicago Press, 1987).

5. See Douglas S. Glasgow, *The Black Underclass: Poverty, Unemployment, and the Entrapment of Ghetto Youth* (New York: Vintage, 1980); Alphonso Pinkney, *The Myth of Black Progress* (Cambridge: Cambridge University Press, 1984); Bettylou Valentine, *Hustling and Other Hard Work* (New York: Macmillan, 1978); Charles V. Willie, "The Inclining Significance of Race," *Society* 15 (1978):10–15.

6. Nancy A. Denton and Douglas S. Massey, "Residential Segregation of Blacks, Hispanics, and Asians by Socioeconomic Status and Generation," *Social Science Quarterly* 69 (1988):797–818.

7. Reynolds Farley, "Can Blacks Afford to Live in White Residential Areas? A Test of the Hypothesis That Subjective Economic Variables Account for Racial Residential Segregation," paper presented at the annual meetings of the Population Association of America, Philadelphia, April 1979.

8. Denton and Massey, "Residential Segregation by Socioeconomic Status and Generation"; Douglas S. Massey, "Effects of Socioeconomic Factors on the Residential Segregation of Blacks and Spanish Americans in United States Urbanized Areas," *American Sociological Review* 44 (1979):1015–22.

9. Socioeconomic variables have also been entered into multivariate regression equations in an effort to explain away intergroup differences in segregation, but the very high degree of black segregation persists even when education, income, and occupational status are controlled statistically; see Douglas S. Massey and Nancy A. Denton, "Trends in the Residential Segregation of Blacks, Hispanics, and Asians: 1970–1980," *American Sociological Review* 52 (1987):802–25; and Douglas S. Massey and Nancy A. Denton, "Suburbanization and Segregation in U.S. Metropolitan Areas," *American Journal of Sociology* 94 (1988):592–626.

10. See the arguments in Clark, "Residential Segregation in American Cities"; and Stanley Lieberson and Donna K. Carter, "A Model for Inferring the Voluntary and Involuntary Causes of Residential Segregation," *Demography* 19 (1982):511–26.

11. Howard Schuman, Charlotte Steeh, and Lawrence Bobo, *Racial Attitudes in America: Trends and Interpretations* (Cambridge: Harvard University Press, 1985), pp. 144–45.

12. Lawrence Bobo, Howard Schuman, and Charlotte Steeh, "Changing Racial Attitudes toward Residential Integration," in John M. Goering, ed., *Housing Desegregation and Federal Policy* (Chapel Hill: University of North Carolina Press, 1986), pp. 152–69.

13. William A. V. Clark, "Residential Preferences and Neighborhood Racial Segregation: A Test of the Schelling Segregation Model," *Demography* 28 (1991):1–19.

14. "A World Apart: Segregation on Long Island," *Newsday*, Monday, September 24, 1990.

15. Louis Harris and Associates, *The Unfinished Agenda on Race in America* (New York: NAACP Legal Defense and Education Fund, 1989).

16. Rose Helper, *Racial Policies and Practices of Real Estate Brokers* (Minneapolis: University of Minnesota Press, 1969), pp. 277–304, 349–52.

17. See Urban Institute, *Housing Discrimination Study: Methodology and Data Documentation* (Washington, D.C.: U.S. Department of Housing and Urban Development, Office of Policy Development and Research, 1991); John Yinger, "Measuring Discrimination in Housing Availability," Final Research Report No. 2 to the U.S. Department of Housing and Urban Development (Washington, D.C.: Urban Institute, 1989); and John Yinger, "Measuring Racial Discrimination with Fair Housing Audits: Caught in the Act," *American Economic Review* 76 (1986):991–93.

18. Juliet Saltman, "Housing Discrimination: Policy Research, Methods, and Results," *Annals of the American Academy of Political and Social Science* 441 (1979):186–96.

19. Hans Hintzen, *Report of an Audit of Real Estate Sales Practices of 15 Northwest Chicago Real Estate Sales Offices* (Chicago: Leadership Council for Metropolitan Open Communities, 1983); results are also reviewed in Douglas S. Massey, "Segregation and the Underclass in Chicago," in The Chicago Community Trust Human Relations Task Force, *A Report on Race, Ethnic, and Religious Tensions in Chicago* (Chicago: Chicago Community Trust, 1989), pp. 111–27.

20. Ann Schroeder, *Report on an Audit of Real Estate Sales Practices of Eight Northwest Suburban Offices* (Chicago: Leadership Council for Metropolitan Open Communities, 1985); see also Massey, "Segregation and the Underclass in Chicago."

21. Susan Bertram, *An Audit of the Real Estate Sales and Rental Markets of Selected Southern Suburbs* (Homewood, Ill.: South Suburban Housing Center, 1988); see also Massey, "Segregation and the Underclass in Chicago."

22. John Yinger, "The Racial Dimension of Urban Housing Markets in the 1980s," in Gary A. Tobin, ed., *Divided Neighborhoods: Changing Patterns of Racial Segregation* (Newbury Park, Calif.: Sage Publications, 1987), pp. 43–67; see also John Yinger, "Measuring Racial Discrimination with Fair Housing Audits."

23. George C. Galster, "Racial Discrimination in Housing Markets during the 1980s: A Review of the Audit Evidence," *Journal of Planning Education and Research* 9 (1990):165–75.

24. Ibid., p. 172.

25. Juliet Saltman, "Housing Discrimination."

26. Diana M. Pearce, "Gatekeepers and Homeseekers: Institutional Patterns in Racial Steering," *Social Problems* 26 (1979):325–42.

27. George C. Galster, "Racial Steering by Real Estate Agents: Mechanisms and Motives," *Review of Black Political Economy* 19 (1990):39–63.

28. George C. Galster, "Racial Steering in Urban Housing Markets: A Review of the Audit Evidence," *Review of Black Political Economy* 18 (1990):105–129.

29. Ronald Wienk, Cliff Reid, John Simonson, and Fred Eggers, *Measuring Racial Discrimination in American Housing Markets: The Housing Market Practices Survey* (Washington, D.C.: U.S. Department of Housing and Urban Development, 1979).

30. White favoritism was defined to occur when whites received favorable treatment on at least one of five items and blacks received favorable treatment on none. The five items included overall availability of housing, courtesy shown to client, terms and conditions of sale or rental, and amount of information supplied to the client.

31. In the past, housing researchers have reported "net discrimination scores" from the 1977 HUD survey. These scores were obtained by subtracting the percentage of cases in which blacks were favored from those in which whites were favored. Recent research has shown, however, that this procedure understates the real incidence of discrimination, for a variety of technical reasons. The figures reported in the table are gross discrimination scores, or the percentage of encounters in which whites were favored, which still tend to understate the amount of discrimination, but not as severely as net scores; this issue is explained in John Yinger, *Housing Discrimination Study: Incidence of Discrimination and Variations in Discriminatory Behavior* (Washington, D.C.: U.S. Department of Housing and Urban Development, Office of Policy Development and Research, 1991), pp. 6–12; and John Yinger, *Housing Discrimination Study: Incidence and Severity of Unfavorable Treatment* (Washington, D.C.: U.S. Department of Housing and Urban Development, Office of Policy Development and Research, 1991), pp. 14–20.

Class and Intersectionality

INTRODUCTION

Right from its inception, sociology has focused analytical attention on issues of social class. We have asked questions such as, What are social classes? How do relationships between classes change? How do they persist? Why do new classes emerge and old classes wane? Social classes are formed by differing roles in economic production. In agriculture there are often land owners (a class) and farm workers (another class). These social groups are bound together in a relationship by their common connection to the process of producing agricultural goods. In that relationship, they have different degrees and forms of power, as well as different interests, and they receive different benefits from the production process. It is not uncommon for the landowner class to receive more of the profits of production than the farm worker class. It is also likely for the landowners to have power over the agricultural workers, since without access to the land, the farm workers can't make a living. Landowners want more profits, and farm workers want better wages, and so they are often in conflict over the distribution of the benefits of production. Everyone involved in economic production is part of a social class and is locked into a relationship with other classes. These social relationships between classes are central to sociologists' analysis and understanding of how societies are organized and change.

As one of sociology's earliest theorists, Karl Marx focused his attention on the social transformation of Europe in the industrial revolution. As society reorganized from rural to urban, as well as from agricultural production to industrial production, new social classes emerged, old social classes went into decline, and new economic and power relationships were formed. In *The Manifesto of the Communist Party*, Marx and his collaborator Frederick Engels present an analysis of these sweeping changes, one that places the concepts and dynamics of social class centrally. They view industrial capitalism as bringing into being two great conflicting social classes, the bourgeoisie (capitalists) and the proletariat (industrial workers). Marx and Engels view the relationship between these classes as fundamentally antagonistic because their interests are diametrically opposed. What is good for capitalists, like keeping wages low so profits can be higher, is bad for workers. What is good for workers, like better wages, benefits, and working conditions, is bad for capitalists, because all of those things cost money and that reduces profits. Marx sees the dynamic relationship between a relatively small number of capital owners and a relatively large number of industrial workers as the primary source of social conflict in society and as the primary engine of social change. He argues that such conflict must ultimately be resolved by the industrial workers banding together as a social class and seizing control of the means of production (the capital, and factories the owners control as private property). He argues that production should be controlled socially and operated for the benefit of all rather than controlled privately for the good of a single, small yet powerful social class. While Marx and Engels' prescription for resolving class conflict has not been realized, the dynamic tension between capital owners (the 1%) and dependent workers (the 99%) persists and is manifest in current social structures and institutions. Class relations continue to be an object of great sociological interest.

In *Class Acts*, Rachel Sherman uses qualitative research methods to look at the relationship between classes in the service industry. Just as Marx in his time was interested in class formations and relations in a period of major transformation of the economy from agrarian to industrial, so Sherman is interested in class relations as the U.S. economy transforms from industrial to service production. She looks at how work is connected to class in the luxury hotel industry. Luxury service depends on unequal entitlements to material resources by social class. Perhaps you have either provided or received luxury service where you were "entitled" to act like you were in a superior class position, or "required" to act like you were in a subservient class position. Sherman looks at the social norms and expectations of behavior in class unequal social situations to explore how we "do class," acting out our class roles in ways that normalize and legitimize differential class entitlements. She chooses an arena of study, the luxury hotel industry, in which class entitlements are particularly pronounced. The service provided in the luxury hotel industry is making the guests feel that their every need is catered to. Luxury hotel service workers' job is to meet guests' needs and make them feel that having their needs met is something that they are unquestionably entitled to (based on their ability to pay). The performance of class roles in service work helps to keep the social structural basis of vast economic inequality unquestioned so that the social system that divides us into "the served" and "the servers" can operate smoothly and without social friction.

Like Rachel Sherman, Erik Olin Wright is interested in the economic shift from an industrial economy to a service economy in the United States. In *Class Counts*, he employs quantitative methods to do a class analysis of post-industrialism or deindustrialization. He asks questions derived from Karl Marx's understanding of what was happening in industrializing societies in the nineteenth century. Is the working-class continuing to expand? Is it continuing to be "de-skilled"? Is the working-class increasingly dominated by a growing managerial class? That is, is the proletariat continuing to get larger as a share of the working population? He contrasts Marx's theory with the view of more recent post-industrial theorists who see the service and information-based economy in the late twentieth century as providing more skilled work and workers gaining more autonomy and control over their work lives. After analyzing the quantitative data on employment over time, Wright concludes that the working class in the United States got smaller starting in the 1970s. The data indicate that, within the United States, the proletarianization hypothesis does not hold true. In conducting this analysis, Wright illustrates the relationship between theory and data, testing theory against contemporary conditions and using the results to further theorize. In this case, Wright goes on to note that, while the working class has gotten smaller in the United States since the 1970s, the working class may have actually gotten larger globally, as industrial production (the basis for the working class) was moved by corporations in recent decades out of the United States and into lower-wage countries. He questions whether it is appropriate to attempt this kind of class analysis within a single country in an economy that is organized globally. What Wright's analysis certainly reveals is that, counter to Marx's view, class structures are becoming more, not less, complex.

Whether we are looking at agricultural, industrial, or service economies, production processes organize class divisions and class relations. These relations take many forms, can be simple or complex, can lead to routine overt political conflict, or can operate without apparent friction for decades on end. In every case, the social organization of production and the interests that they structure for each group in each role in the production process are important to our sociological understanding of how societies are organized, maintained, and changed. The structure of the institution of economy, which generates social classes, impacts the institution of politics, even without revolutionary impulse. Workers negotiate and bargain (collectively or individually) with employers. They often try to organize unions, and employers often try to prevent unionization. Each class appeals to elected officials to support or oppose workers' rights to organize and collectively bargain. Questions about the way the wealth produced by an economy is distributed among the population—How much should go to the top 1%? How much should go to the working poor? Should the government intervene?—remain running themes in political discussions. How does race impact class? How does gender impact class? Does the social meaning of race and gender differ in different social classes? Such questions are fundamental to the sociological research agenda.

READING 16

Excerpt from *The Manifesto of the Communist Party*

KARL MARX AND FREDERICK ENGELS

A spectre is haunting Europe—the spectre of communism.

I. BOURGEOISIE AND PROLETARIANS

The history of all hitherto existing societies is the history of class struggles.

Freeman and slave, patrician and plebeian, lord and serf, guild-master and journeyman—in a word, oppressor and oppressed—stood in constant opposition to one another, carried on an uninterrupted, now hidden, now open fight, a fight that each time ended, either in a revolutionary re-consti- tution of society at large, or in the common ruin of the contending classes.

In the earlier epochs of history, we find almost everywhere a complicated arrangement of society into various orders, a manifold gradation of social rank. In ancient Rome we have patricians, knights, plebeians, slaves; in the Middle Ages, feudal lords, vassals, guild-masters, journeymen, apprentices, serfs; in almost all of these classes, again, subordinate gradations.

The modern bourgeois society that has sprouted from the ruins of feudal society has not done away with class antagonisms. It has but established new classes, new conditions of oppression, new forms of struggle in place of the old ones. Our epoch, the epoch of the bourgeoisie, possesses, how- ever, this distinctive feature: It has simplified the class antagonisms. Society as a whole is more and more splitting up into two great hostile camps, into two great classes, directly facing each other: Bourgeoisie and Proletariat.

From the serfs of the Middle Ages sprang the chartered burghers of the earliest towns. From these burgesses the first elements of the bourgeoisie were developed.

The feudal system of industry, under which industrial production was monopolised by closed guilds, now no longer sufficed for the growing wants of the new markets. The manufacturing system took its place. The guild-masters were pushed on one side by the manufacturing middle class; division of labour between the different corporate guilds vanished in the face of division of labour in each single workshop.

Meantime the markets kept ever growing, the demand ever rising. Even manufacture no longer sufficed. Thereupon, steam and machinery revo- lutionised industrial production. The place of manufacture was taken by

Marx, Karl, and Frederick Engels. 1848. *The Manifesto of the Communist Party.*

the giant, Modern Industry, the place of the industrial middle class, by industrial millionaires, the leaders of whole industrial armies, the modern bourgeois.

Modern industry has established the world-market, for which the discovery of America paved the way. This market has given an immense development to commerce, to navigation, to communication by land. This development has, in its time, reacted on the extension of industry; and in proportion as industry, commerce, navigation, railways extended, in the same proportion the bourgeoisie developed, increased its capital, and pushed into the background every class handed down from the Middle Ages.

We see, therefore, how the modern bourgeoisie is itself the product of a long course of development, of a series of revolutions in the modes of production and of exchange.

The bourgeoisie, historically, has played a most revolutionary part.

The bourgeoisie, wherever it has got the upper hand, has put an end to all feudal, patriarchal, idyllic relations. It has pitilessly torn asunder the motley feudal ties that bound man to his "natural superiors," and has left remaining no other nexus between man and man than naked self-interest, than callous "cash payment." It has drowned the most heavenly ecstasies of religious fervour, of chivalrous enthusiasm, of philistine sentimentalism, in the icy water of egotistical calculation. It has resolved personal worth into exchange value, and in place of the numberless and indefeasible chartered freedoms, has set up that single, unconscionable freedom—Free Trade. In one word, for exploitation, veiled by religious and political illusions, naked, shameless, direct, brutal exploitation.

The bourgeoisie has stripped of its halo every occupation hitherto honoured and looked up to with reverent awe. It has converted the physician, the lawyer, the priest, the poet, the man of science, into its paid wage labourers.

The bourgeoisie has torn away from the family its sentimental veil, and has reduced the family relation to a mere money relation.

The bourgeoisie cannot exist without constantly revolutionising the instruments of production, and thereby the relations of production, and with them the whole relations of society. Conservation of the old modes of production in unaltered form, was, on the contrary, the first condition of existence for all earlier industrial classes. Constant revolutionizing of production, uninterrupted disturbance of all social conditions, everlasting uncertainty, and agitation distinguish the bourgeois epoch from all earlier ones. All fixed, fast-frozen relations, with their train of ancient and venerable prejudices and opinions, are swept away; all new-formed ones become antiquated before they can ossify. All that is solid melts into air, all that is holy is profaned, and man is at last compelled to face with sober senses, his real conditions of life, and his relations with his kind.

The need of a constantly expanding market for its products chases the bourgeoisie over the whole surface of the globe. It must nestle everywhere, settle everywhere, establish connexions everywhere.

The bourgeoisie has through its exploitation of the world-market given a cosmopolitan character to production and consumption in every country. To the great chagrin of Reactionists, it has drawn from under the feet of industry the national ground on which it stood. All old-established national industries have been destroyed or are daily being destroyed. They are dislodged by new industries, whose introduction becomes a life and death question for all civilised nations, by industries that no longer work up indigenous raw material, but raw material drawn from the remotest zones; industries whose products are consumed, not only at home, but in every quarter of the globe. In place of the old wants, satisfied by the productions of the country, we find new wants, requiring for their satisfaction the products of distant lands and climes. In place of the old local and national seclusion and self-sufficiency, we have intercourse in every direction, universal interdependence of nations. And as in material, so also in intellectual production. The intellectual creations of individual nations become common property. National one-sidedness and narrow-mindedness become more and more impossible, and from the numerous national and local literatures, there arises a world literature.

The bourgeoisie, by the rapid improvement of all instruments of production, by the immensely facilitated means of communication, draws all, even the most barbarian, nations into civilisation. The cheap prices of its commodities are the heavy artillery with which it batters down all Chinese walls, with which it forces the barbarians' intensely obstinate hatred of foreigners to capitulate. It compels all nations, on pain of extinction, to adopt the bourgeois mode of production; it compels them to introduce what it calls civilisation into their midst—i.e., to become bourgeois themselves. In one word, it creates a world after its own image.

The bourgeoisie has subjected the country to the rule of the towns. It has created enormous cities, has greatly increased the urban population as compared with the rural, and has thus rescued a considerable part of the population from the idiocy of rural life. Just as it has made the country dependent on the towns, so it has made barbarian and semi-barbarian countries dependent on the civilised ones, nations of peasants on nations of bourgeois, the East on the West.

Modern bourgeois society with its relations of production, of exchange and of property, a society that has conjured up such gigantic means of production and of exchange, is like the sorcerer, who is no longer able to control the powers of the nether world whom he has called up by his spells. For many a decade past the history of industry and commerce is but the history of the revolt of modern productive forces against modern conditions of production, against the property relations that are the conditions for the existence of the bourgeoisie and of its rule. It is enough to mention the commercial crises that by their periodical return put on its trial, each time more threateningly, the existence of the entire bourgeois society. In these crises a great part not only of the existing products, but also of the previously created productive forces, are periodically destroyed. In these crises there breaks out an epidemic that, in all earlier epochs, would have seemed an absurdity—the epidemic of over-production. Society suddenly finds itself put back into a state of momentary barbarism; it appears as if a famine, a universal war of devastation had cut off the supply of every means of subsistence; industry and commerce seem to be destroyed; and why? Because there is too much civilisation, too much means of subsistence, too much industry, too much commerce. The productive forces at the disposal of society no longer tend to further the development of the conditions of bourgeois property; on the contrary, they have become too powerful for these conditions, by which they are fettered, and so soon as they overcome these fetters, they bring disorder into the whole of bourgeois society, endanger the existence of bourgeois property. The conditions of bourgeois society are too narrow to comprise the wealth created by them. And how does the bourgeoisie get over these crises? On the one hand by inforced destruction of a mass of productive forces; on the other, by the conquest of new markets, and by the more thorough exploitation of the old ones. That is to say, by paving the way for more extensive and more destructive crises, and by diminishing the means whereby crises are prevented.

The weapons with which the bourgeoisie felled feudalism to the ground are now turned against the bourgeoisie itself.

But not only has the bourgeoisie forged the weapons that bring death to itself; it has also called into existence the men who are to wield those weapons—the modern working class—the proletarians.

In proportion as the bourgeoisie, i.e., capital, is developed, in the same proportion is the proletariat, the modern working class, developed—a class of labourers, who live only so long as they find work, and who find work only so long as their labour increases capital. These labourers, who must sell themselves piece-meal, are a commodity, like every other article of commerce, and are consequently exposed to all the vicissitudes of competition, to all the fluctuations of the market.

Owing to the extensive use of machinery and to division of labour, the work of the proletarians has lost all individual character, and consequently, all charm for the workman. He becomes an appendage of the machine, and it is only the most simple, most monotonous, and most easily acquired knack, that is required of him. Hence, the cost of production of a workman is restricted, almost entirely, to the means of subsistence that he requires for his maintenance, and for the propagation of his race. But the price of a commodity, and therefore also of labour, is equal to its cost of production. In proportion therefore, as the repulsiveness of the work increases, the wage decreases. Nay more, in proportion as the use of machinery and division of labour increases, in the same proportion the burden of toil also increases, whether by prolongation of the working hours, by increase of the work exacted in a given time or by increased speed of the machinery, etc.

Modern industry has converted the little workshop of the patriarchal master into the great factory of the industrial capitalist. Masses of labourers, crowded into the factory, are organised like soldiers. As privates of the industrial army they are placed under the command of a perfect hierarchy of officers and sergeants. Not only are they slaves of the bourgeois class, and of the bourgeois State; they are daily and hourly enslaved by the machine, by the over-looker, and, above all, by the individual bourgeois manufacturer himself. The more openly this despotism proclaims gain to be its end and aim, the more petty, the more hateful and the more embittering it is.

The less the skill and exertion of strength implied in manual labour—in other words, the more modern industry becomes developed—the more is the labour of men superseded by that of women. Differences of age and sex have no longer any distinctive social validity for the working class. All are instruments of labour, more or less expensive to use, according to their age and sex.

No sooner is the exploitation of the labourer by the manufacturer—so far at an end, that he receives his wages in cash—than he is set upon by the other portions of the bourgeoisie—the landlord, the shopkeeper, the pawnbroker, etc.

The lower strata of the middle class—the small tradespeople, shopkeepers, retired tradesmen generally, the handicraftsmen and peasants—all these sink gradually into the proletariat, partly because their diminutive capital does not suffice for the scale on which Modern Industry is carried on, and is swamped in the competition with the large capitalists, partly because their specialized skill is rendered worthless by the new methods of production. Thus the proletariat is recruited from all classes of the population.

The proletariat goes through various stages of development. With its birth begins its struggle with the bourgeoisie. At first the contest is carried on by individual labourers, then by the workpeople of a factory, then by the operatives of one trade, in one locality, against the individual bourgeois who directly exploits them. They direct their attacks not against the bourgeois conditions of production, but against the instruments of production themselves; they destroy imported wares that compete with their labour, they smash to pieces machinery, they set factories ablaze, they seek to restore by force the vanished status of the workman of the Middle Ages.

But with the development of industry the proletariat not only increases in number; it becomes concentrated in greater masses, its strength grows, and it feels that strength more. The various interests and conditions of life within the ranks of the proletariat are more and more equalised, in proportion as machinery obliterates all distinctions of labour, and nearly everywhere reduces wages to the same low level. The growing competition among the bourgeois, and the resulting commercial crises, make the wages of the workers ever more fluctuating. The unceasing improvement of machinery, ever more rapidly developing, makes their livelihood more and more precarious; the collisions between individual workmen and individual bourgeois take more and more the character of collisions between two classes. Thereupon the workers begin to form combinations (Trades Unions) against the bourgeois; they club together in order to keep up the rate of wages; they found permanent associations in order to make provision beforehand for these occasional revolts. Here and there the contest breaks out into riots.

Now and then the workers are victorious, but only for a time. The real fruit of their battles lies, not in the immediate result, but in the ever-expanding union of the workers. This union is helped on by the improved means of communication that are created by modern industry and that place the workers of different localities in contact with one another. It was just this contact that was needed to centralise the numerous local struggles, all of the same character, into one national struggle between classes. But every class struggle is a political struggle. And that union, to attain which the burghers of the Middle Ages, with their miserable highways, required centuries, the modern proletarians, thanks to railways, achieve in a few years.

This organisation of the proletarians into a class, and consequently into a political party, is continually being upset again by the competition between the workers themselves. But it ever rises up again, stronger, firmer, mightier. It compels legislative recognition of particular interests of the workers, by taking advantage of the divisions among the bourgeoisie itself. Thus the ten-hours' bill in England was carried.

Of all the classes that stand face to face with the bourgeoisie today, the proletariat alone is a really revolutionary class. The other classes decay and finally disappear in the face of Modern Industry; the proletariat is its special and essential product. The lower middle class, the small manufacturer, the shopkeeper, the artisan, the peasant, all these fight against the bourgeoisie, to save from extinction their existence as fractions of the middle class. They are therefore not revolutionary, but conservative. Nay more, they are reactionary, for they try to roll back the wheel of history. If by chance they are revolutionary, they are so only in view of their impending transfer into the proletariat; they thus defend not their present, but their future interests, they desert their own standpoint to place themselves at that of the proletariat.

In the conditions of the proletariat, those of old society at large are already virtually swamped. The proletarian is without property; his relation to his wife and children has no longer anything in common with the bourgeois family-relations; modern industrial labour, modern subjection to capital, the same in England as in France, in America as in Germany, has stripped him of every trace of national character. Law, morality, religion, are to him so many bourgeois prejudices, behind which lurk in ambush just as many bourgeois interests.

All the preceding classes that got the upper hand, sought to fortify their already acquired status by subjecting society at large to their conditions of appropriation. The proletarians cannot become masters of the productive forces of society, except by abolishing their own previous mode of appropriation, and thereby also every other previous mode of appropriation. They have nothing of their own to secure and to fortify; their mission is to destroy all previous securities for, and insurances of, individual property.

All previous historical movements were movements of minorities, or in the interests of minorities. The proletarian movement is the self-conscious, independent movement of the immense majority, in the interests of the immense majority. The proletariat, the lowest stratum of our present society, cannot stir, cannot raise itself up, without the whole superincumbent strata of official society being sprung into the air.

The essential condition for the existence, and for the sway of the bourgeois class, is the formation and augmentation of capital; the condition for capital is wage-labour. Wage-labour rests exclusively on competition between the laborers. The advance of industry, whose involuntary promoter is the bourgeoisie, replaces the isolation of the labourers, due to competition, by their revolutionary combination, due to association. The development of Modern Industry, therefore, cuts from under its feet the very foundation on which the bourgeoisie produces and appropriates products. What the bourgeoisie, therefore, produces, above all, is its own grave-diggers. Its fall and the victory of the proletariat are equally inevitable.

II. PROLETARIANS AND COMMUNISTS

In this sense, the theory of the Communists may be summed up in the single sentence: Abolition of private property.

We Communists have been reproached with the desire of abolishing the right of personally acquiring property as the fruit of a man's own labour; which property is alleged to be the groundwork of all personal freedom, activity and independence.

Hard-won, self-acquired, self-earned property! Do you mean the property of the petty artisan and of the small peasant, a form of property that preceded the bourgeois form? There is no need to abolish that; the development of industry has to a great extent already destroyed it, and is still destroying it daily.

Or do you mean modern bourgeois private property?

But does wage-labour create any property for the labourer? Not a bit. It creates capital, i.e., that kind of property which exploits wage-labour, and which cannot increase except upon condition of begetting a new supply of wage-labour for fresh exploitation. Property, in its present form, is based on the antagonism of capital and wage-labour. Let us examine both sides of this antagonism.

To be a capitalist, is to have not only a purely personal, but a social status in production. Capital is a collective product, and only by the united action of many members, nay, in the last resort, only by the united action of all members of society, can it be set in motion.

Capital is, therefore, not a personal, it is a social power.

When, therefore, capital is converted into common property, into the property of all members of society, personal property is not thereby transformed into social property. It is only the social character of the property that is changed. It loses its class-character.

Let us now take wage-labour.

The average price of wage-labour is the minimum wage—i.e., that quantum of the means of subsistence, which is absolutely requisite in bare existence as a labourer. What, therefore, the wage-labourer appropriates by means of his labour, merely suffices to prolong and reproduce a bare existence. We by no means intend to abolish this personal appropriation of the products of labour, an appropriation that is made for the maintenance and reproduction of human life, and that leaves no surplus wherewith to command the labour of others. All that we want to do away with, is the miserable character of this appropriation, under which the labourer lives merely to increase capital, and is allowed to live only in so far as the interest of the ruling class requires it.

In bourgeois society, living labour is but a means to increase accumulated labour. In Communist society, accumulated labour is but a means to widen, to enrich, to promote the existence of the labourer.

In bourgeois society, therefore, the past dominates the present; in Communist society, the present dominates the past. In bourgeois society capital is independent and has individuality, while the living person is dependent and has no individuality.

And the abolition of this state of things is called by the bourgeois, abolition of individuality and freedom! And rightly so. The abolition of bourgeois individuality, bourgeois independence, and bourgeois freedom is undoubtedly aimed at.

By freedom is meant, under the present bourgeois conditions of production, free trade, free selling and buying.

But if selling and buying disappears, free selling and buying disappears also. This talk about free selling and buying, and all the other "brave words" of our bourgeoisie about freedom in general, have a meaning, if any, only in contrast with restricted selling and buying, with the fettered traders of the Middle Ages, but have no meaning when opposed to the Communistic abolition of buying and selling, of the bourgeois conditions of production, and of the bourgeoisie itself.

You are horrified at our intending to do away with private property. But in your existing society, private property is already done away with for nine-tenths of the population; its existence for the few is solely due to its non-existence in the hands of those nine-tenths. You reproach us, therefore, with intending to do away with a form of property, the necessary condition for whose existence is the non-existence of any property for the immense majority of society.

In one word, you reproach us with intending to do away with your property. Precisely so; that is just what we intend.

From the moment when labour can no longer be converted into capital, money, or rent, into a social power capable of being monopolised—i.e., from the moment when individual property can no longer be transformed into bourgeois property, into capital—from that moment, you say individuality vanishes.

You must, therefore, confess that by "individual" you mean no other person than the bourgeois, than the middle-class owner of property. This person must, indeed, be swept out of the way, and made impossible.

Communism deprives no man of the power to appropriate the products of society; all that it does is to deprive him of the power to subjugate the labour of others by means of such appropriation.

It has been objected that upon the abolition of private property all work will cease, and universal laziness will overtake us.

According to this, bourgeois society ought long ago to have gone to the dogs through sheer idleness; for those of its members who work, acquire nothing, and those who acquire anything, do not work. The whole of this objection is but another expression of the tautology: that there can no longer be any wage-labour when there is no longer any capital.

All objections urged against the Communistic mode of producing and appropriating material products, have, in the same way, been urged against the Communistic modes of producing and appropriating intellectual products. Just as, to the bourgeois, the disappearance of class property is the disappearance of production itself, so the disappearance of class culture is to him identical with the disappearance of all culture.

That culture, the loss of which he laments, is, for the enormous majority, a mere training to act as a machine.

But don't wrangle with us so long as you apply, to our intended abolition of bourgeois property, the standard of your bourgeois notions of freedom, culture, law, etc. Your very ideas are but the outgrowth of the conditions of your bourgeois production and bourgeois property, just as your jurisprudence is but the will of your class made into a law for all, a will, whose essential character and direction are determined by the economical conditions of existence of your class.

The selfish misconception that induces you to transform into eternal laws of nature and of reason, the social forms springing from your present mode of production and form of property—historical relations that rise and disappear in the progress of production—this misconception you share with every ruling class that has preceded you. What you see clearly in the case of ancient property, what you admit in the case of feudal property, you are of course forbidden to admit in the case of your own bourgeois form of property.

The Communists are further reproached with desiring to abolish countries and nationality.

The working men have no country. We cannot take from them what they have not got. Since the proletariat must first of all acquire political supremacy, must rise to be the leading class of the nation, must constitute itself the nation, it is, so far, itself national, though not in the bourgeois sense of the word.

National differences and antagonisms between peoples are daily more and more vanishing, owing to the development of the bourgeoisie, to freedom of commerce, to the world-market, to uniformity in the mode of production and in the conditions of life corresponding thereto.

The proletariat will use its political supremacy to wrest, by degrees, all capital from the bourgeoisie, to centralise all instruments of production in the hands of the State, i.e., of the proletariat organised as the ruling class; and to increase the total of productive forces as rapidly as possible.

Of course, in the beginning, this cannot be effected except by means of despotic inroads on the rights of property, and on the conditions of bourgeois production; by means of measures, therefore, which appear economically insufficient and untenable, but which, in the course of the movement, outstrip themselves, necessitate further inroads upon the old social order, and are unavoidable as a means of entirely revolutionising the mode of production.

These measures will of course be different in different countries.

Nevertheless in the most advanced countries, the following will be pretty generally applicable.

1. Abolition of property in land and application of all rents of land to public purposes.
2. A heavy progressive or graduated income tax.
3. Abolition of all right of inheritance.
4. Confiscation of the property of all emigrants and rebels.
5. Centralisation of credit in the hands of the State, by means of a national bank with State capital and an exclusive monopoly.
6. Centralisation of the means of communication and transport in the hands of the State.
7. Extension of factories and instruments of production owned by the State; the bringing into cultivation of waste-lands; and the improvement of the soil generally in accordance with a common plan.
8. Equal liability of all to labour. Establishment of industrial armies, especially for agriculture.
9. Combination of agriculture with manufacturing industries; gradual abolition of the distinction between town and country, by a more equable distribution of the population over the country.
10. Free education for all children in public schools. Abolition of children's factory labour in its present form. Combination of education with industrial production, &c., &c.

When, in the course of development, class distinctions have disappeared, and all production has been concentrated in the hands of a vast association of the whole nation, the public power will lose its political character. Political power, properly so called, is merely the organised power of one class for oppressing another. If the proletariat during its contest with the bourgeoisie is compelled, by the force of circumstances, to organise itself as a class, if, by means of a revolution, it makes itself the ruling class, and, as such, sweeps away by force the old conditions of production, then it will, along with these conditions, have swept away the conditions for the existence of class antagonisms and of classes generally, and will thereby have abolished its own supremacy as a class.

In place of the old bourgeois society, with its classes and class antagonisms, we shall have an association, in which the free development of each is the condition for the free development of all.

Working men of all countries, unite!

Excerpt from *Class Acts:*
Service and Inequality in Luxury Hotels

RACHEL SHERMAN

LUXURY SERVICE AND THE NEW ECONOMY

When Mr. Jones, a guest at the five-star Luxury Garden hotel, began to prepare for an early business meeting, he realized he had forgotten to pack his dress shoes. Panicked, he called the concierge desk. Not to worry, said Max, the concierge. Max called a local department store, asked the security guard to help him contact the manager, and convinced the manager to open the store two hours early for the desperate guest. At the same hotel, room service workers know that when Mrs. Smith orders breakfast, they must slice her papaya along a straight line, forgoing the usual serrated edge. At the Royal Court, a small luxury hotel nearby, Mrs. Frank looks forward to the hazelnut butter on her French toast, which the chef whips up just for her. In a third upscale hotel, the gift shop does not carry the Silk Cut cigarettes Mr. White prefers. No problem, he is told; we can send someone to get them. Each time the guest returns thereafter, the cigarettes await him in his room. A legendary housekeeper in the same hotel has a habit of rifling through guests' wastebaskets; she is trying to identify their favorite candy bars and magazines in order to enter these into a computer database that helps workers keeps track of guests' preferences for the future.

I heard these stories from luxury hotel managers I interviewed in the late 1990s as part of my preliminary research on this book. I talked with mid- and upper-level managers in all different kinds of urban hotels—economy, mid-price, convention, and so on—about the challenges of running the hotel, the service they offered, the types of guests they catered to, changes in the economic climate and the structure of the industry, and their views about unions. But managers in *luxury* hotels recounted especially captivating anecdotes. Like

Sherman, Rachel. 2007. *Class Acts: Service and Inequality in Luxury Hotels*. Berkeley, CA: University of California Press.

the examples above, these tales described hotel staff going to great lengths to observe guests' preferences, recognize each guest's individuality, and meet—even anticipate—the guests' wishes. These hotels promised, in the words of an ad for the Four Seasons, "service that cares for your every need."[1]

Managers and hospitality industry literature insisted that this caring service is more important than the physical characteristics of the hotel or its amenities. Asked what differentiated the Luxury Garden from its competition, for example, the hotel's sales director told me, "The service, because we all have beds and bathrooms." It was, managers said, the main reason guests paid daily rates as high as eight hundred dollars for rooms and three thousand dollars for suites. The staff played a crucial role in this enterprise. One manager commented, for instance, "The room helps, the views help, but it's really the people."

Managers characterized the guests who consume luxury service as "truly wealthy." As one manager put it, "They're not looking for discount coupons." Another told me that guest wealth "blows my mind." I wondered: if it blew the *managers'* minds, what did the *workers* think about it? Workers in these hotels earned ten to fifteen dollars per hour and in some cases tips and commissions; that could add up to a substantial wage, but it was nothing compared with guest wealth. And managers talked about the services their hotels offered as providing *care*. But *caring for* guests appeared also to mean *catering to* them. What was it like when your job was to ensure that the guest's every desire, no matter how insignificant, was fulfilled? Did workers feel subordinated by guests' seemingly unlimited entitlement to the workers' personalized labor and attention? And how did guests feel about luxury service, which seemed to involve a fair amount of potentially intrusive surveillance of personal preferences and habits, and about the workers who served them? Finally, I was curious about how managers tried to guide the production of this intangible, interactive service, especially given its dependence on the workers themselves.

Customized contacts with workers are a major part of what clients are paying for in many luxury sites, including high-end hotels, restaurants, spas, resorts, retail shops, and first-class airline cabins. However, the limited sociological literature on hotels and other service industry organizations has rarely focused on luxury.[2] And few sociologists since Thorstein Veblen, over a century ago, have investigated the luxury sector at all, let alone luxury service specifically.[3]

To understand luxury service, I decided I needed to participate in its production, which led me to conduct twelve months of ethnography in two luxury hotels. Based on the data I gathered and on interviews I conducted, this book looks at how managers, guests, and interactive workers negotiated unequal entitlement to resources, recognition, and labor as they produced and consumed luxury service. These issues matter for two reasons. First, they are important for our understanding of interactive work and its links to relationships and to selfhood. Second, they are significant for our conception of how work is connected to class. These questions are particularly important given the rise of both service work and economic inequality in the United States.

LOOKING AT LUXURY

Luxury service, in particular the luxury hotel, is a good place to explore in more depth the connections among work, class, and self. First, the worker's self is deeply implicated in the highly personalized and attentive service she provides. And it is a self-subordinating service, as guests' every wish must be workers' command. Research has established that workers value dignity on the job above most other considerations,[4] but their dignity, in this case, seems constantly compromised by their subservience to guests. If any interactive workplace is likely to produce alienated and resentful workers, the luxury hotel is the one. On the other hand, the importance of service is a source of worker autonomy vis-à-vis managers, because the success of the guest's intangible experience rests largely on workers' shoulders. The discretion that interactive workers must exercise makes them hard to control, monitor, and standardize.[5] Thus, workers might have more power and autonomous selfhood in these sites.

The upscale hotel is also a good place to look at customers and class. Like other luxury establishments, this site is structured by the unequal distribution of resources. Workers and guests nearly always occupy different class positions, by any definition.[6] Furthermore, asymmetries in power, authority, and entitlement also inhere in the relationships between workers and guests. Workers demonstrate deference and subordination; guests enact entitlement to human attention and labor.[7] As a result, both are constantly performing class differences, or "doing class."[8] Each actor must occupy her position appropriately in these classed interactions, thus also "doing self" in a classed context. Furthermore, in the luxury setting, both the structural inequality in which the interaction is embedded and the interactive inequality of which the luxury product consists are totally visible to both workers and hotel guests.

Thus, the following questions remain: How do workers reconcile their desire for dignity and power with the self-subordinating imperatives of their work? How do managers organize the production of this intangible, self-subordinating relation? How are workers' and guests' selves constituted or compromised? How do workers and guests make sense of their class differences and negotiate their unequal entitlements? Finally, what can the process of production-consumption of this interactive product, marked by inequality, tell us about classed identities and the legitimacy of class inequality more broadly? These are the questions that guided my research.

"They Zero in on You": Personalization

Consistent with the luxury hotel's emphasis on distinctiveness, service in these hotels is highly personalized.[9] First and foremost, managers and workers literally recognize the guest; consistent name use is one of the main

204 / THIRTY READINGS IN INTRODUCTORY SOCIOLOGY

tenets of service at any luxury hotel. The Luxury Garden's first service standard, for example, was "recognize guests personally through the use of their name, naturally and appropriately."[10] Management in both my sites encouraged workers to learn not only guests' names but also the names of their children or pets. (Another dimension of luxury service, of course, is to know when the guest prefers *not* to be recognized, at moments when he might want privacy or would be embarrassed at being acknowledged by staff.)[11]

Workers customize contact in other ways as well. To individualize their conversations with first-time guests, workers use information they already have or whatever they can glean. They might remember where the guest dined the previous night or that he is in the city for the first time. Or they might wish him a happy birthday or a happy anniversary. Luxury hotels also mark special occasions by providing complimentary champagne or other amenities.

For frequent guests, personalization goes even further. Workers greet returning guests on arrival with "welcome back." They remember details about guests' lives, families, and preferences. Upscale hotels devote significant energy to gathering and acting on information about the desires of repeat guests, including the type of room they want, particular services they require (such as ionizing the room to purify the air or not using chemicals when cleaning), special requests for blankets or pillows, favorite newspapers, and food preferences. These hotels also keep track of guest conditions such as alcoholism and diabetes in order to avoid offering inappropriate amenities.

Beyond customizing these basic elements of the guest's stay (some of which are also noted in nonluxury hotels),[12] the staff of upscale hotels observe preferences spanning a wide and unpredictable range. At the Mandarin Oriental hotel in Hong Kong, for example, a frequent guest's toy monkey always awaits her on the bed; in another Hong Kong hotel, workers iron one guest's shirt near his door "because he likes the feeling of warm cloth when dressing in the morning."[13] One repeat guest at the Royal Court required that a rented red Jaguar convertible be waiting when he checked in; another guest insisted on always being addressed as "Doctor." A guest at the Luxury Garden requested that laundry workers avoid putting starch in his clothes; another demanded that the head of his bed be elevated six inches off the ground; still another thought of a particular chair as "his" (he had reportedly carved his initials on it) and requested that it always be in his room when he was staying in the hotel.

Sometimes preferences are observed as a result of the guest's explicit request, as in the examples above. Yet luxury service also means fulfilling preferences when the guest has not explicitly articulated them. One manager at the Luxury Garden said that for him, luxury service was exemplified by a housekeeper's noticing that a guest had eaten a peanut butter cookie provided for him one evening but had left the chocolate chip one untouched; the next night she left him two peanut butter cookies. In fact, workers there were given forms to record any guest preferences they became aware of, to keep them on file for future stays. A Royal Court standard of the week exhorted workers hotelwide to "please tell the front desk anything you know to put in the guest history."

Many luxury hotels use additional strategies to recognize repeat customers. Some offer frequent guests gifts to mark significant stays (such as the fifth, tenth, twentieth, and so on). Often these emphasize the guest's individuality, such as personally monogrammed stationery at the Luxury Garden and monogrammed pillowcases at the Ritz-Carlton and the Peninsula Beverly Hills.[14] These hotels even make major structural modifications in order to meet the needs of repeat guests. For example, one Ritz-Carlton hotel installed a wood floor in a room for a frequent guest who was allergic to carpeting.[15] The Royal Court provided a shower curtain for Ms. Parker, a frequent visitor who did not like the open shower in the recently renovated bathrooms.

Research suggests that personalized attention is indeed an important element of creating customer loyalty. One industry study found four factors related to recognition, personal attention, and customized service to be among the top eight factors (of eighteen) that clients said engendered loyalty to a particular hotel; 87.5 percent of clients surveyed rated "the hotel uses information from your prior stays to customize services for you" as either 6 or 7 on a 7-point scale of important factors (with a mean rating of 6.4). The factors "the staff recognizes you by name" and "the staff recognizes you when you arrive" achieved a mean score of 5.6.[16] Other research has identified personal attention and recognition as two of the three factors determining the choice of a hotel brand.[17] Marketing research reveals that affluent frequent travelers in particular look for recognition by name and, in making reservations, "a direct line to the general manager, who inquires about a recent family triumph or tragedy, as any old friend would do."[18]

Most guests I interviewed likewise described personal attention as important to them. Many enjoyed being called by name; Christina, a young leisure traveler, appreciatively told me that at a Four Seasons hotel the staff had remembered not only her name and her husband's but also the names of her two dogs. Tom, a business traveler, had been "dumbfounded" when his preferences were observed at another Four Seasons hotel; upon arrival, he had received plain strawberries instead of chocolate-covered ones, because on an earlier visit he had mentioned that he was "a low-fat eater."

Guests appreciated being distinguished from others and having their personhood acknowledged, often describing this treatment in terms of "care" and feeling "at home." Betty, a training consultant, preferred luxury hotels because, she said, "they treat you like you're a person" and "they respect me as a person." Adam, a retired businessman, said of himself and his wife, "We feel [being called by name is] more a guest relationship and a human thing, that you're not simply a number or a unit. You're a person who is recognized and you can have a little conversation." Andrew, the president of a major manufacturing firm, echoed these ideas: "I think that that changes the whole equation for the entire hotel, when somebody who's at the door in the lobby—there's at least a sense of recognition. If he doesn't know your name, he might say—like if you are coming back from dinner, he says, 'Did you have a nice evening this evening,' like he really cares, 'I care about you as a person.' "

By the same token, guests frequently complained if they did not get the personalized attention to which they felt they were entitled. On several occasions at both the Royal Court and the Luxury Garden, guests lamented, "No one here knows me anymore," or asked, "What happened to everyone that knew me?" A frequent guest at the Royal Court complained that during the recent renovation "they destroyed my room." One return guest at the Luxury Garden mentioned on a comment card that she felt "ignored" because the personalized stationery she and her husband received was always in his name.

A few guests I interviewed, all women, said they did not care if the staff used their names or appeared interested in their lives. They spoke of being "embarrassed" when they were treated this way, and they suspected that recognition was not authentic. These guests were more likely to consider recognition facilitated by technology as less meaningful, saying, for example, "I'm sure they have it in the computer or something." These guests cared more about the design and décor of the hotel and that the service be efficient rather than personalized. Some of them also mentioned a sense of surveillance or intrusion associated with recognition; one woman told me of a friend who was shocked when hotel staff knew something about her that she felt they could have found out only by listening in on her private conversations. Nonetheless, most of these women also said they would notice if the staff failed to provide this kind of attention, indicating that recognition was still part of their expectation of luxury service.[19]

"They Go Out of Their Way": Anticipation and Legitimation of Needs

In Robert Altman's 2001 film *Gosford Park*, Helen Mirren's character, the head housekeeper in an English country mansion in the 1930s, says to a young lady's maid: "What gift do you think a good servant has that separates him from the others? It's the gift of anticipation. I'm a good servant. I'm better than good; I'm the best. I'm the perfect servant. I know when they'll be hungry, and the food is ready. I know when they'll be tired, and the bed is turned down. I know it before they know it themselves."

Workers in the luxury hotel are likewise expected to anticipate guests' needs, a process in which the definition of "needs" expands to include what might otherwise be considered "desires." The Ritz-Carlton's credo, for example, includes the commitment to fulfill even the guest's "unexpressed wishes and needs." The general manager of the Peninsula Beverly Hills, Ali Kasikci, told a reporter, "Waiting for customers to tell you what they need is like driving your car by looking in the rearview mirror."[20] Workers must be on the lookout for needs the guest might not articulate or even be aware of. Concierges, for example, stood armed with umbrellas for guests who were on their way out and might not know that it was raining. Antonio, a guest services manager at the Luxury Garden, advised me always to offer soup to guests who mentioned they were not feeling well, thereby actually creating a need rather than anticipating an existing need. Needs anticipation may also include withholding information or refraining from taking some kind of action; for example, I was cautioned not to tell a guest that he had been upgraded when the person he was traveling with had not been.

Needs anticipation also entails reading the guest's demeanor, picking up subtle cues to predict her needs and desires. Sydney, a guest services manager at the Luxury Garden, told me, "You have to know what they want that they aren't telling you, because if you don't they won't like what you get them." When a guest asks the concierge to recommend a restaurant, the concierge must (in addition to asking the guest about his tastes, of course) take into account factors such as where he is from, how old he is, and how sophisticated he appears, in order to increase the chances of making an appropriate choice. If the guest is older and appears unschooled in upscale dining, he may receive a reservation at a chain steakhouse; if a visitor from New York requests information on local entertainment, the concierge will not recommend the traveling version of the latest Broadway hit. In employee training sessions at the Luxury Garden, Alice, the human resources manager, encouraged workers to use visual clues to offer the guests something they might need. On one occasion she role-played a woman massaging her neck and seeming tired and another guest arriving with a crying baby, then asked what we would do to meet the needs they were not expressing verbally (the answers: offer the tired guest a place to sit down and give the mother a private space even if her room is not ready).

Guests appreciate needs anticipation. One visitor to the Luxury Garden wrote on a comment card: "Housekeeper apparently saw cold medicine next to the rollaway bed for our 10 year old daughter and thoughtfully left an extra box of tissues! Great attention to detail!!" Herbert, a businessman in food manufacturing, recounted approvingly that after hearing that his young son was going to a baseball game, workers at an upscale hotel left cookies, milk, and a baseball hat in the room for him. Shirley, a leisure traveler, was amazed when tea was delivered unexpectedly upon her arrival at one fancy hotel:

> We'd checked into our room, and there was a knock on the door, and they brought chamomile tea and cookies. It was just those sorts of things, those unanticipated, delightful little things. You didn't even know you wanted chamomile tea, and it was the perfect thing....I think it's a combination of anticipating your needs but doing it in a way that's sort of invisible, that doesn't draw attention to itself, that it sort of magically happens without you seeing how it happens, but it's as if they knew what you were thinking two seconds before you thought of it.

Although these practices are known in the industry as *needs* anticipation, these examples demonstrate that the process also creates *desires*, by providing things "you didn't even know you wanted," and then codes them as needs.

Workers also recognize clients by responding to the individual needs and problems they express. Managers in training sessions and in industry literature stress that the guest must be able to get whatever she wants, including having prescriptions picked up, salon shampoo delivered to the room, and a cell phone retrieved from the restaurant where she had lunch. But more extreme examples abound. At one Four Seasons property, for instance, the maitre d' lent his tuxedo to a guest who did not have one for a black tie event, and even had the trousers altered for him.[21] As I have mentioned, on two separate occasions, Max, the Luxury Garden concierge, convinced the manager of a local department store to open early for guests with urgent needs for clothing. Another concierge, Alec, literally lent the shoes off his feet to a guest whose own shoes had been misplaced by the housekeeping department. When a group of incoming guests at the Royal Court wanted to rent two new-model Mercedes SUVs, front desk workers found a rental agency that could provide them, though it entailed having the vehicles delivered from several hundred miles away. At the same hotel, I was asked to find a gauze bandage for a woman who had recently undergone knee surgery and then to assist her in dressing her leaky wound.

In both hotels, my coworkers and I were asked to perform many services for guests. A partial list, culled from my field notes, illustrates the broad range: "Find doctor; find live crab, feathers, balloons; find white truffles; take shoes to be fixed; take luggage to be fixed; find gown; reserve spa for six, rental van, all-day limo; obtain video of local performance; arrange babysitting; get cell phones, Japanese furniture, cigars; find sheet music; find blue roses; find jade jewelry; plan out-of-town day trip; find pediatrician; give directions to local farmer's market; find out about tea set used in hotel's restaurant; arrange for local golf; get kosher takeout menu; find Greek Orthodox church; arrange camera equipment rental; open package arriving for departed guest and send back to him; arrange for spa, watsu treatment, shiatsu; get symphony tickets; find yoga clothes, particular designer furniture; find computer equipment; find map store; arrange helicopter tour; find and make appointment with German-speaking dentist; get shoelaces; find tailor; make hotel reservations in New Orleans; get coat left at restaurant and send to guest; get birthday cake for tonight; find Catholic church; place T-shirts and welcome packages in incoming guests' rooms; get ginger root for tea; send champagne to incoming guests on behalf of a friend; find out about lobby furniture; find out about duvet cover in room; find artificial orchids; get baseball tickets; mail knife; put rose petals on bed; find lost child."

The list for one especially demanding Luxury Garden guest, Dr. Kramer, compiled over several visits, included "get electronics; get cotton jogging clothes; make hotel reservation; make copies; get stapler; get sushi;

fix e-mail access; find battery for cell phone; get luggage fixed; get rental car exchanged; find access to Internet for his computer; fix luggage; get temps; get more temps; find Indian food; change room; fix cell phone; find CDs; get newspaper; give message to models waiting for him in lobby; find cell phone help; rent convertible; find directions to state park; make laptop work."

Recognition work also entails that the worker legitimate these needs by responding sympathetically. Workers are expected to show concern about any situation the guest finds difficult, from a missed flight to a cloudy day. This standard extends to moments when the guest is dissatisfied with the hotel service itself. Alice, the Luxury Garden human resources manager, emphasized five elements of responding to guest complaints, the second of which was "apologize first." She said that when she studied guest complaints, most guests claimed, "All I wanted was someone to listen and care," or said, "No one apologized." She said the appropriate emotional response was especially important in the luxury hotel because "we don't have clientele that count pennies," so monetary compensation when something went wrong was less meaningful to them. Sebastian, the general manager, told me in an interview that guests were most likely to complain that "their needs weren't met" and that "they weren't heard."

Guests value worker responsiveness to their needs and problems, seeing it as a key dimension of luxury service. For example, one guest at the Luxury Garden wrote in a letter to the general manager, "Antonio [the guest services manager] and his staff were extremely courteous and helpful when we needed to locate our lost luggage. I am sure that we seemed very high maintenance at one point when several calamities occurred at once. But Antonio and his people never complained nor seemed in any way reticent to attack each challenge as it arose." Asked in an interview what he meant by "caring service," Herbert invoked both recognition of needs and their legitimation, as well as personalization:

> When you're in the hotel and you order room service and—because I get up early, and I make a motion to the room service waiter that my wife and son are still asleep in the next room. The next morning the same waiter comes and delivers the breakfast and taps so quietly on the door I almost didn't know he was there because he noticed—that's sort of a very concrete example. He really did care that he didn't want to wake them and knew I wanted to have coffee in the room, and that's really legitimate.

Guests also see it as a failure of service when workers do not acknowledge their problems. Christina described a stay at a hotel where "everything" had gone wrong; among other things, she and her husband were given a room much smaller than the suite they had reserved. She said, "If they had put flowers in the small room or a fruit basket or whatever, all would have been forgiven, but we were totally ignored."[22] Shirley described a bad experience in which the staff upgraded her but did not respond to her complaint that the room smelled musty: "They kind of pooh-poohed my concern and acted as if I wasn't being appreciative enough of the upgrade." Here staff failed to legitimate the guest's need, assuming that the bigger room would be more important to her than the odor.

Legitimation of guests' needs carries another dimension: a sense of unlimitedness. The imperative to "never say no to a guest" is a mantra in luxury hotels. Check-in and check-out times were rarely enforced at the Luxury Garden, for example; if a guest decided to stay another night, he was not refused, even if that meant overbooking the hotel. One manager told me that imposing these rules would violate "five-star service," especially given the rates guests were paying. The general manager at the Royal Court stressed several times in an all-employee meeting that "the guest needs to be able to get anything he wants." He said, "We can't let rules get in the way," berating the staff for turning a guest away from the restaurant because he had arrived five minutes late for breakfast. "For four hundred dollars," he said sarcastically, "we should be able to find a piece of bacon somewhere in this building."

Guests approved of this idea that rules could be bent or broken for them, and they often saw a willingness to transgress as a defining feature of luxury establishments in contrast to midrange hotels. One couple wrote a comment card to the Luxury Garden praising the hotel for providing breakfast at 10:30 P.M. On comment cards, several guests at both hotels lauded the chef for making vegetarian meals available. Tom, after citing an instance in which a Four Seasons had accommodated his request for a special meeting room, said of luxury hotels, "You just don't have problems. You just don't hear about rules and stuff—you know, they solve [problems]. They basically do everything humanly possible in these nicer hotels to meet whatever you want and make it a wonderful stay for you and your family." Betty, the consultant, described her experience:

> If I ask—like the Ritz-Carlton in Boston is one of my favorite hotels, and if I ask for something there they'll do whatever they need to do to fix it, to accommodate me. But if I would go to, say—I was staying in some [nonluxury] place in Washington about four months ago and all I needed was some pens for my room and I got an argument at the desk....You know they're not going to go out of their way for anything unless you have an argument with them, and that bothers me.... [In luxury hotels] you don't hear, "We don't do it that way," or "We can't do it that way," or "We don't have that here," that kind of thing.

Again, the guest is given the sense of unlimited entitlement in the fulfillment of her needs.

SERVICE WORK AND CLASS ENTITLEMENTS

I have argued that interactive service complicates the traditional view of class in work. The traditional approach takes the point of (factory) production as the paradigmatic site of class exploitation and focuses on how labor processes generate alienation and resistance among workers. Even analyses of the service sector have drawn on this paradigm. But, in fact, the service sector—especially service that features class asymmetry between customers and workers—is different. New forms of inequality come into play, adding a further object of criticism to the traditional one of exploitation. At stake in the hotel is not only the production of inequality through the appropriation of labor effort but also workers' and clients' unequal entitlement to material and emotional resources. I have therefore focused not on relations of *exploitation in production* but on relations of *entitlement in production-consumption*.

These entitlements are class based, arising from the class positions of workers and clients, including their locations in global and local divisions of labor. Such entitlements have two aspects. First, unequal entitlements to material resources that exist outside the hotel determine workers' and guests' relative positions inside the hotel (guests pay to consume the hotel's product, while workers are paid to produce it). Second, by virtue of their greater material resources, guests receive more personal attention and labor than workers receive. Luxury service thus both *depends on* unequal entitlements to material resources and *guarantees* unequal entitlements to recognition.

Class not only structures these sites but is also "accomplished" interactively within them. As Amy Hanser writes, "Service interactions that involve acts of deference...become practical enactments of relative social locations, a 'doing' of social difference."[23] Workers and guests perform class in their appearance and demeanor as well as in their interactions. This "doing" of class is not unlike the doing of gender that many scholars have analyzed.[24] It is performative but not necessarily inauthentic; rather, this "acting" of class can feel genuine and natural for both workers and guests in the hotel.[25]

Furthermore, the effects of the luxury workplace—now the service theater—on workers differ from those usually described in the literature. Rather than foster resistance or alienate the worker from himself, relations of production-consumption here primarily *normalize* class entitlements, leading both workers and guests to take them for granted. This normalization is a paradoxical result of workers' and guests' strategies of self. Workers construct and defend nonsubordinate selves, drawing on local, organizationally and culturally inflected repertoires of selfhood to create and emphasize autonomy, authority, competence, prestige, benevolence, discernment, morality, and privilege. These self-constructions are not coping mechanisms that workers create to protect "authentic" selves that arise outside the labor process; rather, they depend on consenting participation in work. Guests, for their part, also work to create needy, deserving, and generous selves in order to overcome their fears of not belonging or of exploiting workers.

But these strategies for mitigating class entitlements also lead these actors to begin to take them for granted. Catering to guests' every need comes to seem reasonable to workers, just as having their needs catered to seems appropriate to guests. The material inequalities in which both are embedded recede into the background and are normalized.

NOTES

1. Four Seasons advertisement, *New York Times Magazine*, September 26, 2004.
2. The sociological literature on work in hotels is surprisingly limited. Hayner (1936) offers an early discussion of residential hotels and anomie. Contemporary researchers have tended to focus on manager-worker relations and control strategies (Jones, Taylor, and Nixon 1997; Madsen Camacho 1996; Mason 1989); characteristics of workers, jobs, and relations among workers (Prus and Irini 1980; Lennon and Wood 1989; Wood 1992, 1994; Stepick and Grenier 1994); and union representation and organizing (Zamudio 1996; Wells 2000; Bernhardt, Dresser, and Hatton 2003). These researchers do not explore the specificity of worker–guest relations or the particularities of luxury service. In their multiyear ethnographic study of Hawaiian resorts, Adler and Adler (2004) provide a comprehensive analysis of the types of workers and the organization of work in these sites and of workers' backgrounds and careers in the industry. However, much of their analysis is specific to the Hawaiian resort context, and they do not focus on worker-guest relations.
3. Veblen [1899] (1994). See Frank (1999) for a critique of luxury consumption, Twitchell (2002) for a celebration of the "democratization of luxury," and Brooks (2000) for the claim that changes in the nature of high-end consumption indicate shifts in the nature of the upper class. None of these authors are sociologists.
4. Hughes ([1971] 1984), Hodson (2001).
5. See Benson (1986) and Leidner (1993: 24–31).
6. To take a gradational definition focused on socioeconomic status: guests in luxury hotels (and consumers of luxury services generally) have higher incomes, more education, more prestigious occupations, more wealth, and more social connections (which we could also call, following Bourdieu, economic, cultural, and social capital) than workers. From a relational standpoint, they are much more likely than workers to own capital and not to have to sell their labor for a wage. To use Weber's terminology, these workers and guests have unequal life chances in the market (as well as unequal status defined by consumption). Some guests would not be able to afford to stay in luxury hotels aside from their expense accounts, but even these guests are, on balance, better off than workers. And these less affluent guests are in the minority; most guests are either rich leisure travelers or well-compensated corporate executives, as I will describe in more detail later.
7. See Derber (1979) on the asymmetrical distribution of attention in society generally.
8. West and Fenstermaker (1995). See also Jackson (2002); and Bettie (2003). The questions of class that arise here are not about class location or exploitation of workers' labor effort for profit. Nor am I looking at class consciousness, manifested in individual attitudes, workers' self-identifications, or collective action (Halle 1984; Fantasia 1988; Freeman 2000).
9. See Mars and Nicod (1984).
10. Both hotels posted service standards guiding worker behavior.
11. Mann (1993); Dev and Ellis (1991). See also Bearman (2005) for a discussion of the tensions surrounding residential doormen's awareness of tenants' personal affairs.

12. In nonluxury hotels, personalization is usually limited to tracking repeat clients' preferences in terms of what type of room or newspaper they want.
13. Lipper (2000).
14. Maxa (2001); Rosenfeld (2001).
15. Keates (1998).
16. Bowen and Shoemaker (1998).
17. Dev and Ellis (1991).
18. Mann (1993: 56).
19. Although I did not explore the reasons for the gender dimension of this phenomenon in interviews, it may occur because women are more conscious of the labor involved in the service, having themselves performed domestic services similar to those offered in the hotel (or directed their own servants to perform them). For research on the gender and class contradictions among wealthy women, see Ostrander (1984); Rollins (1985); Daniels (1988); Odendahl (1990); and Kendall (2002).
20. Rosenfeld (2001).
21. Byrne (1998). See also Lipper (2000); and Jones, Taylor, and Nickson (1997).
22. In contrast, she appreciatively described a situation in which she had arrived hours late at a luxury hotel because the staff had given her bad directions; she told the front desk agent what had happened, and the woman came out from behind the desk, put her arm around Christina, and petted her dogs. Notably, Christina saw this incident as exemplifying *good* service, although it was the hotel's fault that she had gotten lost in the first place.
23. Hanser (2005a).
24. See West and Zimmerman (1987); for specific analyses of work in this vein, see Leidner (1993); and Hanser (2005b).
25. For similar notions of class performance, see Jackson (2002); and Bettie (2003).

REFERENCES

Adler, Patricia, and Peter Adler. 2004. *Paradise Laborers: Hotel Work in the Global Economy*. Ithaca, NY: ILR Press.

Bearman, Peter. 2005. *Doormen*. Chicago: University of Chicago Press.

Benson, Susan Porter. 1986. *Counter Cultures: Saleswomen, Managers, and Customers in American Department Stores 1890–1940*. Urbana: University of Illinois Press.

Bernhardt, Annette, Laura Dresser, and Erin Hatton. 2003. "The Coffee Pot Wars: Unions and Firm Restructuring in the Hotel Industry." In *Low-Wage America: How Employers Are Reshaping Opportunity in the Workplace*, ed. E. Appelbaum, A. Bernhardt, and R. Murnane. New York: Russell Sage Foundation.

Bettie, Julie. 2003. *Women without Class: Girls, Race, and Identity*. Berkeley: University of California Press.

Bowen, John, and Stowe Shoemaker. 1998. "Loyalty: A Strategic Commitment." *Cornell Hotel and Restaurant Administration Quarterly* 39 (February):12–25.

Brooks, David. 2000. *Bobos in Paradise*. New York: Simon and Schuster.

Byrne, Harlan. 1998. "The Secret: Service." Barron's Online, May 11.

Daniels, Arlene Kaplan. 1988. *Invisible Careers: Women Civic Leaders from the Volunteer World*. Chicago: University of Chicago Press.

Derber, Charles. 1979. *The Pursuit of Attention: Power and Individualism in Everyday Life*. New York: Oxford University Press.

Dev, Chekitan, and Bernard Ellis. 1991. "Guest Histories: An Untapped Service Resource." *Cornell Hotel and Restaurant Administration Quarterly* 32 (August):29–37.

Fantasia, Rick. 1988. *Cultures of Solidarity: Consciousness, Action, and Contemporary American Workers*. Berkeley: University of California Press.

Frank, Robert. 1999. *Luxury Fever: Money and Happiness in an Era of Excess*. Princeton, NJ: Princeton University Press.

Freeman, Carla. 2000. *High Tech and High Heels in the Global Economy: Women, Work, and Pink-Collar Identities in the Caribbean*. Durham: Duke University Press.

Halle, David. 1984. *America's Working Man*. Chicago: University of Chicago Préss.

Hanser, Amy. 2005a. "Is the Customer Always Right? Class, Service and the Production of Distinction in Chinese Department Stores." Unpublished paper.

———. 2005b. "The Gendered Rice Bowl." *Gender and Society* 19:581–600.

Hayner, Norman S. 1936. *Hotel Life*. Chapel Hill: University of North Carolina Press.

Hodson, Randy. 2001. *Dignity at Work*. Cambridge: Cambridge University Press.

Hughes, Everett C. 1952. "The Sociological Study of Work: An Editorial Foreword." *American Journal of Sociology* 57(5):423–26.

———. [1971] 1984. *The Sociological Eye*. New Brunswick, NJ: Transaction Publishers.

Jackson, John. 2002. *Harlemworld*. Chicago: University of Chicago Press.

Jones, Carol, George Taylor, and Dennis Nickson. 1997. "Whatever It Takes? Managing 'Empowered' Employees and the Service Encounter in an International Hotel Chain." *Work, Employment and Society* 11(September):541–54.

Keates, Nancy. 1998. "Summer Travel: The New Perks." *Wall Street Journal*, May 29.

Kendall, Diana. 2002. *The Power of Good Deeds*. Lanham, MD: Rowman and Littlefield.

Leidner, Robin. 1993. *Fast Food, Fast Talk: Service Work and the Routinization of Everyday Life*. Berkeley: University of California Press.

Lennon, J. John, and Roy C. Wood. 1989. "The Sociological Analysis of Hospitality Labour and the Neglect of Accommodation Workers." *International Journal of Hospitality Management* 8(3):227–35.

Lipper, Hal. 2000. "Personalized Service at Top Hotels Gets Mixed Results, Survey Says." *Wall Street Journal*, January 21.

Madsen Camacho, Michelle. 1996. "Dissenting Workers and Social Control: A Case Study of the Hotel Industry in Huatulco, Oaxaca." *Human Organization* 55(1):33–40.

Mann, Irma S. 1993. "Marketing to the Affluent: A Look at Their Expectations and Service Standards." *Cornell Hotel and Restaurant Administration Quarterly* 34(October):54–58.

Mars, Gerald, and Michael Nicod. 1984. *The World of Waiters*. London: Allen and Unwin.

Mason, Simon. 1989. "Technology and Change in the Hotel Industry." Ph.D. thesis, Department of Sociology and Social Policy, University of Durham, England.

Maxa, Rudy. 2001. "The Savvy Traveler." Marketplace. National Public Radio, April 3–4.

Odendahl, Teresa. 1990. *Charity Begins at Home*. New York: Basic Books.

Ostrander, Susan. 1984. *Women of the Upper Class*. Philadelphia: Temple University Press.

Prus, Robert, and Styllianoss Irini. 1980. *Hookers, Rounders, and Desk Clerks: The Social Organization of a Hotel Community*. Toronto: Gage Publishing.

Rollins, Judith. 1985. *Between Women*. Philadelphia: Temple University Press.

Romero, Mary. 1992. *Maid in the USA*. New York: Routledge.

Rosenfeld, Jill. 2001. "No Room for Mediocrity." *Fast Company* 50(September):160.

Stepick, Alex, and Guillermo Grenier. 1994. "The View from the Back of the House: Restaurants and Hotels in Miami." With Hafidh A. Hafidh, Sue Chaffee, and Debbie Draznin. In *Newcomers in the Workplace: Immigrants and the Restructuring of the U.S. Economy*, ed. Louise Lamphere, Alex Stepick, and Guillermo Grenier. Philadelphia: Temple University Press.

Turrell, Carter. 2004. "Luxury for the Masses." www.Forbes.com, July 13.

Twitchell, James B. 2002. *Living It Up: Our Love Affair with Luxury*. New York: Columbia University Press.

Urban Land Institute (PKF Consulting). 1996. *Hotel Development*. San Francisco: PKF Consulting.

Veblen, Thorstein. [1899] 1994. *The Theory of the Leisure Class*. New York: Penguin.

Wells, Miriam. 2000. "Immigration and Unionization in the San Francisco Hotel Industry." In *Organizing Immigrants*, ed. Ruth Milkman. Ithaca, NY: ILR/Cornell University Press.

West, Candace, and Sarah Fenstermaker. 1995. "Doing Difference." *Gender and Society* 9(1):8–37.

West, Candace, and Don Zimmerman. 1987. "Doing Gender." *Gender and Society* 1:125–51.

Wood, Roy C. 1992. *Working in Hotels and Catering*. London: Routledge.

———. 1994. "Hotel Culture and Social Control." *Annals of Tourism Research* 21:65–80.

Zamudio, Margaret. 1996. "Organizing the New Otani Hotel in Los Angeles: The Role of Ethnicity, Race, and Citizenship in Class Formation." Ph.D. dissertation, Department of Sociology, University of California, Los Angeles.

READING 18

Excerpt from *Class Counts*

ERIK OLIN WRIGHT

Two opposed images have dominated discussions of the transformation of class structures in developed capitalist societies. The first of these is associated with the idea that contemporary technological changes are producing a massive transformation of social and economic structures that are moving us towards what is variously called a "post-industrial society" (Bell 1973), a "programmed society" (Touraine 1971), a "service society" (Singelmann 1978; Fuchs 1968), or some similar designation. The second image, rooted in classical Marxist visions of social change, argues that in

Wright, Erik Olin. 2000. "The transformation of the American class structure, 1960–1990" from *Class Counts* (student edition). Cambridge, UK: Cambridge University Press.

spite of these transformations of the "forces of production," we remain a capitalist society and the changes in that class structure thus continue to be driven by the fundamental "laws of motion" of capitalism.

The post-industrial scenario of social change generally envisions the class structure becoming increasingly less proletarianized, requiring higher and higher proportions of workers with technical expertise and demanding less mindless routine and more responsibility and knowledge. For some of these theorists, the central process underwriting this tendency is the shift from an economy centered on industrial production to one based on services. Other theorists have placed greater stress on the emancipatory effects of the technical-scientific revolution within material production itself. In either case the result is a trajectory of changes that undermines the material basis of alienation within production by giving employees progressively greater control over their conditions of work and freedom within work. In class terms, this augurs a decline in the working class and an expansion of various kinds of expert and managerial class locations.

The classical Marxist image of transformation of class relations in capitalism is almost the negative of post-industrial theory: Work is becoming more proletarianized; technical expertise is being confined to a smaller and smaller proportion of the labor force; routinization of activity is becoming more and more pervasive, spreading to technical and even professional occupations; and responsibilities within work are becoming less meaningful. This argument was most clearly laid out in Braverman's (1974) influential book, *Labor and Monopoly Capital*. The basic argument runs something like this: Because the capitalist labor process is a process of exploitation and domination and not simply a technical process of production, capital is always faced with the problem of extracting labor effort from workers. In the arsenal of strategies of social control available to the capitalist class, one of the key weapons is the degradation of work, that is, the removal of skills and discretion from direct producers. The result is a general tendency for the proletarianzed character of the labor process to intensify over time. In terms of class structure, this implies that the working class will tend to expand, skilled employees and experts decline, and supervisory labor to increase as the demands of social control intensify.

This chapter attempts to use quantitative data on the changes in distributions of people in the American class structure from 1960 to 1990 as a way of intervening in this debate. In section 1 I will lay out a series of alternative hypotheses about the expected changes in different class locations based on the arguments of post-industrial theory and traditional Marxist theory. Section 2 will explain the empirical strategy we will adopt. Section 3 will then present the basic results.

1. CONTRASTING EXPECTATIONS OF POST-INDUSTRIAL AND MARXIST THEORY

The debate between post-industrial and Marxist conceptions of social change can be seen as a set of competing claims about the relative expansion and contraction of different locations within the class structure.

The classical Marxist theory of capitalist development posits three trends which directly affect the class distribution of the labor force. First, the expansion of capitalism tends to destroy independent, self-employed producers. In the nineteenth century and the first half of the twentieth century this process massively affected self-employed farmers in the agricultural sector, but the process is a general one affecting all sectors of the economy. This yields the prediction of a steadily declining petty bourgeoisie. Second, the dynamics of capital accumulation tend to generate increasing concentration and centralization of capital as small capitalist firms are destroyed and larger firms grow. This trend yields the prediction of a decline in small employers and an expansion of managers, especially expert managers, to staff the administrative bureaucracies of corporations. Third, as noted above, in order to increase control over the labor force and the extraction of labor effort, capitalists have an incentive to reduce the autonomy of skilled labor and, where possible, replace skilled with unskilled labor. This, in turn, requires an expansion of the social control apparatus within production to monitor and supervise workers increasingly deprived of a knowledge about production. The appropriation by management of knowledge from skilled workers should also lead to the expansion of the expert-manager category. These trends of intensified proletarianization in the labor process generate the prediction of an expansion of the working class, an expansion of supervisors, managers and expert-managers, and a decline of (nonmanagerial) experts and skilled workers.

Post-industrial theory does not contain as systematic a set of hypotheses about transformations of the petty bourgeoisie and small employers, and therefore I will not impute formal predictions for these categories. The expectations for the changes in various categories of employees can be more clearly derived from the logic of post-industrialism. The expectation in post-industrial theory of a world of work with much more self-direction and autonomy than industrial capitalism suggests the prediction of a relative decline in purely supervisory labor (i.e., positions of social control within work which are not part of the managerial decision-making apparatus). On the other hand, managerial positions would be expected to increase as the complexity of organizations and decision-making increases.

Where post-industrial theory differs most sharply from the Marxist arguments outlined above is in the predictions about experts, skilled workers and workers. As a concomitant of the move to a knowledge- and service-based economy, post-industrial theorists would generally expect a pervasive expansion of jobs requiring high levels of expertise and autonomy. This implies a process of gradual *de*proletarianization of labor in which there was steady expansion of the expert and expert-manager class location and a corresponding decline of the core working class. Insofar as manual labor is still required, it would have an increasingly skilled and technical character to it, and thus highly skilled workers should also expand. The basic

Table 18–1 Hypotheses for Transformations of the American Class Structure

	PREDICTED CHANGES IN CLASS DISTRIBUTIONS	
Class location	Traditional Marxist Prediction	Post-Industrial Theory Prediction
Class locations for which the two theories make different predictions		
Workers	Increase	Decrease
Skilled workers	Decrease	Increase
Supervisors	Increase	Decrease
Experts (nonmanager)	Small decrease	Big increase
Class locations for which the two theories have similar predictions		
Managers	Increase	Increase
Expert-managers	Increase	Big increase
Class locations for which there is not a clear divergence of predictions		
Petty bourgeoisie	Decrease	No prediction
Small employers	Decrease	No prediction

hypotheses of Marxist and post-industrial perspectives are summarized in Table 18–1.

2. METHODOLOGICAL STRATEGY

The analytical technique used in this chapter is sometimes referred to as "shift/share" analysis (Wright 1997: 97). This procedure divides overall changes (shifts) over time in the class composition of the labor force into three components: a "sector shift" component, a "class shift" component and an interaction component. The first of these identifies the contribution to changes in the class structure that comes from the changing distribution of the labor force *across* economic sectors. For example, historically the agricultural sector has had an especially high concentration of the petty bourgeoisie in the form of small farmers. A decline in the relative size of the agricultural sector would thus, all other things being equal, have an adverse effect on the relative size of the petty bourgeoisie. In our analysis this would appear as a "negative sector shift" for the petty bourgeoisie. The "class shift" refers to changes in the class structure that result from a changing class composition *within* economic sectors, independent of changes in the relative size of these sectors. For example, the gradual replacement of Mom and Pop grocery stores by chain supermarkets would be reflected in a negative class shift for the petty bourgeoisie and small employers within the retail trade sector and a positive class shift for managers and supervisors within that sector. Finally, some changes in the class structure cannot be uniquely attributed either to changes within sectors or to changes in the sectoral composition of the labor force. Rather, they result from the interaction of these two forces. This contribution to the overall change in class distributions is thus referred to as the interaction component.

Because of limitations of sample size, for the analyses of this chapter the 12 categories of the class structure matrix have been collapsed into a simpler, eight-category model: employers (combining capitalists and small employers); petty bourgeoisie; expert-managers; managers (combining skilled and nonskilled managers); supervisors (combining skilled and nonskilled supervisors); experts (combining expert supervisors and nonsupervisory experts); skilled workers; and workers. We will also examine the results for workers and skilled workers combined. This eight-category typology drops the distinction between nonskilled and skilled within the two categories in the authority hierarchy, and the distinction between nonmanagers and supervisors within the expert category.[1]

Throughout the analysis which follows our focus will be primarily on the various class categories among wage-earners rather than on employers and the petty bourgeoisie.

3. RESULTS

The basic time series data for class distributions between 1960 and 1990 appear in Table 18–2.[2] The results of the shift-share analysis for the class shift components for selected class locations appear in Figure 18–1.[3] The numbers in this figure indicate the rate of change of the labor force in a particular class location that can be attributed to the changes in the number of people in that class *within* economic sectors. For example, consider the expert-manager category in the 1970s. This category increased from 4.41% of the labor force to 5.06% of the labor force in this decade (see Table 18–2). This represents a 14.7% increase in the relative size of this class location during the 1970s. Some of this change was due to the movement of people into sectors that already had a higher proportion of expert-managers than in other sectors, but most of it (in fact, nearly 14% of the total rate of expansion of 14.7%) was due to the expansion of expert-managers within sectors, or what we are calling the "class shift component."

The results of the shift-share analysis in Figure 18–1 are much more con-sistent with the predictions of the post-industrial society thesis than the traditional Marxist view of changes in class structures. While in the 1960s, as predicted by Marxist theory, there was a small expansion of the working class within sectors (i.e. a small positive class-shift component), this expan-sion was reversed in the 1970s. By the 1980s, the class shift for the work-ing class was –5%, meaning that the proportion of the labor force in the working class declined by an average 5% within sectors during that decade. There was also a small negative *sector* shift for the working class in all three decades (indicating that the sectors with relatively high concentrations of

Table 18–2 Class Distributions in the United States, 1960–1990

Class Location	1960	1970	1980	1990
Nonowners				
1 Managers	7.50	7.57	7.95	8.25
2 Supervisors	13.66	14.86	15.23	14.82
3 Expert-managers	3.87	4.41	5.06	5.99
4 Experts	3.53	4.53	5.49	6.90
5 Skilled workers	13.46	14.08	12.92	12.77
6 Workers	44.59	45.13	44.05	41.38
All workers (5, 6)	58.05	59.21	56.97	54.15
Owners				
7 Petty bourgeoisie	5.54	4.09	4.53	5.19
8 Employers	7.86	5.33	4.77	4.71

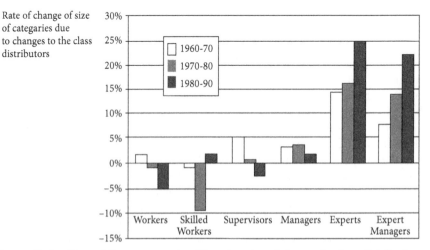

Figure 18–1 Class-shift components of decade rates of change in class distributions for class locations among employees.

workers were declining in relative importance). In contrast, the class-shift component for expert-managers and nonmanagerial experts was increasingly large and positive across the three decades. This is in keeping with the predictions of the post-industrial theory, especially those versions that emphasize technological change rather than sectoral change (since the class-shift components are much bigger and more consistent than the sector-shift components).

Overall, then, the main thrust of these results runs directly counter to the principal expectations of classical Marxism and formalized as hypotheses in Table 18–1. What is more, given that the 1970s and 1980s were a period of relative economic stagnation compared to the 1960s, classical Marxism would have predicted that the pressures towards degradation of labor would have intensified. The evidence in these results indicates that, if anything, there was an acceleration in the trend of *deproletarianization* in the 1970s and 1980s. While these results hardly indicate that the working class is in the process of dissolution—the core working class in the United States remains over 40% of the labor force in 1990, and, when combined with skilled workers, the extended working class is 54% of the labor force—nevertheless, the trajectory of change is more in keeping with the expectations of post-industrial theory than traditional Marxism.

Refined Sectoral Analysis

One final step in the data analysis is needed, however, to add force to this conclusion. It is important to know whether or not the class-shift components in Figure 18–1 are largely contained within particular sectors or are diffused throughout the economy, since this might affect the overall interpretation of the results. To check this out, I therefore disaggregated the class-shift components into six sectors: extractive, transformative (mainly manufacturing and related sectors), distributive services (mainly retail and wholesale trade), business services, personal services and social-political services (see Wright 1997: 105–107 for detailed results).

For the working class, the negative class-shift component in the 1970s and 1980s—the deproletarianization process within economic sectors—is not simply a result of a massive change in one sector, but is present in 4 of the 6 aggregated sectors. In both decades, the biggest contributor to the negative class shift for the working class is the transformative sector (manufacturing and processing). This is also the one sector in the 1960s within which there was a negative class shift for workers. Thus, while overall the direction of the class shift component for the working-class changes from positive (proletarianization) in the 1960s to negative (deproletarianization) in the 1970s and 1980s, in the case of the transformative sector the 1970s and 1980s represent a continuation and acceleration of a deproletarianization process already in place in the 1960s.

In this more refined analysis, the positive class-shift component for experts and for expert-managers occurs within nearly all of these broad sectors. The only consistent exception is for the distributive services sector in which there is a negative component for expert-managers in all three decades. The expansion of class locations involving significant credentials and expertise, therefore, is pervasive across sectors in keeping with post-industrial theory.

Not only are the patterns of class-shift components fairly consistent with the expectations of post-industrial theory, so also are the broad patterns of sectoral shifts: the expansion of managers, experts, and expert-managers is most closely linked to the expansion of social and political services in the 1960s and the expansion of business services in the 1970s and 1980s, while the decline of the working class, skilled workers and supervisors through-out these decades is most linked to the decline of employment in the trans-formative sector.

Finally, the specific pattern of sectoral and class shifts for experts and expert-managers is consistent with the expectations of those post-indus-trial theorists who emphasize the increasing importance of knowledge and information in post-industrial economies. In the 1960s, the expansion of experts and expert-managers in the class structure was driven almost equally by sectoral shifts in the employment structure centered on the expansion of social-political services (especially medical services) and the expansion of these class locations within sectors. In contrast, by the 1980s the relative expansion of these class locations was almost entirely a product of changes in the class composition within sectors, especially in the trans-formative sector and the social-political service sector. This is in keeping with the idea of the increasing centrality of knowledge and information within the production processes of post-industrial society, even within the manufacturing sectors of the economy.

4. INTERPRETATIONS AND IMPLICATIONS

The results presented in this chapter pose a real challenge to traditional Marxist expectations about the trajectory of development of the class struc-ture of advanced capitalist societies in general and particularly about the pro-cess of intensive proletarianization. Contrary to the traditional Marxist expec-tation, the working class in the United States modestly declined in the period 1960–1990, and this decline appears if anything to be accelerating. What is especially noteworthy is that this decline is not simply a question of the shift of employment from manufacturing to services; the decline is accelerating *within the transformative sector itself*. While it may also be true in recent decades that within the working class itself working conditions may have deteriorated and exploitation may have increased as real wages have declined, neverthe-less within the class structure as a whole the evidence does not support the prediction of increasing and deepening proletarianization.

One response to this challenge is to question the validity of the results themselves by arguing that they are artifacts of the measurements employed. The procedure for estimating class structures in 1960 and 1970 is certainly open to question (see Wright 1997: 109). These could conceivably have led to systematic over- or underestimation of changes in working class in the period under study. Nevertheless, in the absence of specific evidence that measurement biases exist in sufficient magnitude to alter significantly our estimates, the results remain a sharp challenge to traditional Marxist expectations of continuing proletarianization.

A second line of response is to accept the results, but to argue that the transnational character of capitalism in the world today makes it inappropriate to study transformations of class distributions within single national units. The last twenty-five years have certainly witnessed a significant growth of multinational corporate industrial investment in the Third World and an accompanying expansion of the industrial working class in Third World countries. The Marxist theory of proletarianization is a theory about the trajectory of changes in class structures in capitalism as such, not in national units of capitalism. In a period of rapid internationalization of capital, therefore, national statistics are likely to give a distorted image of transformations of capitalist class structures.

If these arguments are correct, then one would expect that changes in the class structure of world capitalism would be unevenly distributed globally. In particular, there should be at least some tendency for managerial class locations and expert class locations to expand more rapidly in the core capitalist countries and proletarian positions to expand more rapidly in the Third World. It is hard to get meaningful data directly on this hypothesis. There are some indirect data in our results, however, which are at least suggestive. The economic sector within which globalization is likely to have the biggest impact on class structure is the transformative sector (principally manufacturing), since this is the sector within which, many people argue, multinational corporations are shifting large numbers of working-class jobs to less developed regions of the world. If this is true, then one would expect to find a large, positive class shift within this sector for manager experts (i.e. they should very substantially increase as a proportion of the labor force within this sector), combined with a large negative sector shift (as overall employment in this sector declines). This is in fact what we find in the disaggregated decompositions for the 1960s and 1980s (see Wright 1997: Table 3–4): the largest positive class-shift component for manager experts is in the transformative sector. It could thus be the case that, if it were possible to measure the global class structure of multinational capitalism, the decades of the 1970s and 1980s would have been a period of proletarianization worldwide.

A final line of response to these results is to acknowledge that capitalist class relations are changing in ways unexpected by the traditional Marxist theory of deepening proletarianization. While the problem of extracting labor effort from workers remains an issue within class relations, under conditions of highly developed forces of production this no longer generates an inherent tendency towards the degradation of labor. Instead, as

Piore and Sabel (1984) have argued, we may be in the midst of a "second industrial divide" which requires labor with much higher levels of technical training and work autonomy than characterized "Fordist" production, training which makes workers capable of flexibly adapting to rapid changes in technology and the organization of work. The positive class shift for skilled workers within the transformative sector in the 1980s (+2.17), reversing the considerable negative class shift (−5.41) in that sector for this category in the 1970s, is consistent with this account.

These trends do not imply that "post-Fordist" capitalism is any less capitalistic than its predecessors—surplus is still appropriated by capitalists; investments are still allocated on the basis of profit-maximizing in capitalist markets; workers are still excluded from control over the overall process of production. And they also do not imply the immanent demise of the working class. In spite of the decline we have observed, the working class remains around 40% of the labor force in 1990; and when skilled workers are added, the extended working class is still over 50%. What these results do suggest, however, is a trajectory of change within developed capitalist societies towards an expansion, rather than a decline, of contradictory locations within class relations. Unless these trends are a temporary detour, it thus appears that the class structure of capitalism continues to become increasingly complex rather than simplified around a single, polarized class antagonism.

NOTES

1. The method for estimating these class distributions within economic sectors for the period 1960–90 is discussed in Wright (1997: 112–113).
2. For a discussion of the method for measuring class structure used here, see Wright (1997: 112–113).
3. The detailed results of the shift share analysis can be found in Wright (1997: 100).

REFERENCES

Bell, Daniel. 1973. *The Coming of Post-Industrial Society*. New York: Harper and Row.

Braverman, Harry. 1974. *Labor and Monopoly Capital: The Degradation of Work in the Twentieth Century*. New York: Monthly Review Press.

Fuchs, Victor R. 1968. *The Service Economy*. New York: Columbia University Press.

Piore, Michael, and Charles Sabel. 1984. *The Second Industrial Divide*. New York: Basic Books.

Singelmann, Joachim. 1978. *From Agriculture to Services*. Beverly Hills: Sage Publications.

Touraine, Alain. 1971. *The Post Industrial Society*. New York: Random House.

Wright, Erik Olin. 1997. *Class Counts: Comparative Studies in Class Analysis*. Cambridge, UK: Cambridge University Press.

Gender and Intersectionality

INTRODUCTION

When C. Wright Mills advised readers wishing to develop their sociological imaginations to look around yourselves, and evaluate how well others in your social group are doing to make predictions about how well you will do in your life, his focus was probably more on class and race than on gender. Historically, the main theorists taught in sociology have been male theorists. Using our sociological imaginations, we could argue that their position at the top of the sex and gender hierarchy made it more difficult for them to see any problems with sex and gender stratification. Some theorists did analyze sex early on. For instance, Friedrich Engels (Marx's collaborator), published *The Origin of the Family, Private Property, and the State* in 1884, which looks at the historical evolution of sex roles in the family. There were also female sociologists who wrote about sexual division of labor, notably, Charlotte Perkins Gilman who wrote *Women and Economics* (1898) and argued that women should gain economic power by working outside the home. Analyzing gender is not just about including women writers or adding women to the discussion; it is about recognizing the organizing role that gender has in social life. The divisions of female/male and feminine/masculine shape social attitudes and behaviors. Early academic attempts to analyze gender started with "women's studies" and today that has matured into "gender studies," which also includes analysis of men and of masculinity.

The first piece in this section, which in a short time has become a classic, is "Doing Gender," by Candace West and Don H. Zimmerman. You might notice that this article has a strong tie to Becker's piece on culture, in that West and Zimmerman argue that we "do" gender (i.e., create it through interactions) in much the same way that Becker suggests that we "do" culture (i.e., via social interaction). Sociologists call this school of thought *social (or symbolic) interactionism*. Neither culture nor gender are "essential" (i.e., natural)—they vary geographically and over time, which suggests they can change and adapt. "Doing Gender" is an important article for this field because it defines and outlines the relationships between the concepts of sex, sex category, and gender. While sex is defined by biology, and sex categorization is determined by sex, they argue that "gender itself is constituted by interaction." Gender is not a set of traits or a role; one must "accomplish gender." The article argues that individuals *do* gender over and over again through their interactions, and that *doing*, not some essential biological set of traits, is what produces femininity and masculinity.

The second passage is by the past president of the American Sociological Association, Patricia Hill Collins. Collins is known for developing the concept of "intersectionality," which you've been reading about in the prior two sections as well. She developed this in reference to black feminist thought. The idea is that oppressions in society based on race, class, and gender are not separate from each other, but are interrelated, intersect with each other, and often compound each other. The excerpt outlines the binaries of oppression evident in U.S. society that define some groups as "normal" and stereotypes those outside the limits of "normal" as "other." Collins examines the stereotypical roles of African American women, whose place in society lies at the overlapping bottom halves of two binaries: male/female and white/black. Stereotypes (controlling images) of African American women, such as "mammies" and "hoochies," link gender domination and racism in a "matrix of domination" that is used to control this group. Collins illustrates the complexity of this position at the end of the selection when she explains how institutions that have explicit goals to support African Americans, such as the church, have often gone against the empowerment of black women. This piece demonstrates how society's ideas (stereotypes/controlling images) have an impact on social behavior.

The final selection looks at the American family. Why do we include a passage on the family when talking about gender and intersectionality? Well, there are at least four messages we'd like you to take away from this piece by Janet C. Gornick and Marcia K. Meyers. The first is that families are gendered. Typically, a gendered division of labor exists in the family as well as in the workplace. Think about who is expected to do which jobs in the family. Second, this piece uses a quantitative approach which allows us to see broad patterns in family life and make generalizations to larger populations. This is important for the third and fourth lessons. The third lesson is that in recent history there has been a large shift in the social institution of economy. This shift has driven women into the workforce. It has also created a public problem: Who will care for the children? Gornick and Meyers take a decidedly sociological approach to the problems of families, by demonstrating the "problem of private solutions" (recall again C. Wright Mills' sociological imagination). In the United States, in response to a public problem, each family has independently and privately tried to solve their family's problem. Rather than deal with this question collectively (publicly), Americans have tried to deal with it on their own, with varying degrees of success. The fourth and final lesson is that there are other ways to deal with this; namely, through a public solution: policy. The authors compare policies that other industrial societies have implemented in the face of similar economic shifts and how their policies have generated better outcomes for families and children. The United States, with its individualistic ideologies, has not used policy to improve outcomes for families. Most funds spent for caregiving in the United States are private, unlike many countries in Europe and Canada. The workforce consequences of private solutions to caregiving are that men earn more than women and that women do more work at home (reinforcing traditional gender stereotypes). The private solutions are gendered. Women get wage penalties and men get less time with their children.

In sum, these passages are intended to show the following: (1) Gender, like culture, is practiced through interaction. While it is based on sex (biology), it is socially constructed and, thus, malleable. (2) Gender cannot be understood in isolation, but as a construct that interacts and overlaps with other social categories, such as race and class. (3) The consequences of a gendered society are real. Men and women earn different amounts of money and are expected to carry out different roles and tasks based on their gender. Finally, (4) public policies that address the gendered division of labor in the home and in the workforce can produce different outcomes than the private solutions that the United States currently uses.

READING 19

Excerpt from *Doing Gender*

CANDACE WEST AND DON H. ZIMMERMAN

In the beginning, there was sex and there was gender. Those of us who taught courses in the area in the late 1960s and early 1970s were careful to distinguish one from the other. Sex, we told students, was what was ascribed by biology: anatomy, hormones, and physiology. Gender, we said, was an achieved status: that which is constructed through psychological, cultural, and social means. To introduce the difference between the two, we drew on singular case studies of hermaphrodites (Money 1968, 1974; Money and Ehrhardt 1972) and anthropological investigations of "strange and exotic tribes" (Mead 1963, 1968).

Inevitably (and understandably), in the ensuing weeks of each term, our students became confused. Sex hardly seemed a "given" in the context of research that illustrated the sometimes ambiguous and often conflicting criteria for its ascription. And gender seemed much less an "achievement" in the context of the anthropological, psychological, and social imperatives we studied—the division of labor, the formation of gender identities, and the social subordination of women by men. Moreover, the received doctrine of gender socialization theories conveyed the strong message that while

West, Candace, and Don H. Zimmerman. 1987. *"Doing Gender."* Gender and Society 1(2):125–151.

gender may be "achieved," by about age five it was certainly fixed, unvarying, and static—much like sex.

Since about 1975, the confusion has intensified and spread far beyond our individual classrooms. For one thing, we learned that the relationship between biological and cultural processes was far more complex—and reflexive—than we previously had supposed (Rossi 1984, especially pp. 10–14). For another, we discovered that certain structural arrangements, for example, between work and family, actually produce or enable some capacities, such as to mother, that we formerly associated with biology (Chodorow 1978 versus Firestone 1970). In the midst of all this, the notion of gender as a recurring achievement somehow fell by the wayside.

Our purpose in this article is to propose an ethnomethodologically informed, and therefore distinctively sociological, understanding of gender as a routine, methodical, and recurring accomplishment. We contend that the "doing" of gender is undertaken by women and men whose competence as members of society is hostage to its production. Doing gender involves a complex of socially guided perceptual, interactional, and micropolitical activities that cast particular pursuits as expressions of masculine and feminine "natures."

When we view gender as an accomplishment, an achieved property of situated conduct, our attention shifts from matters internal to the individual and focuses on interactional and, ultimately, institutional arenas. In one sense, of course, it is individuals who "do" gender. But it is a situated doing, carried out in the virtual or real presence of others who are presumed to be oriented to its production. Rather than as a property of individuals, we conceive of gender as an emergent feature of social situations: both as an outcome of and a rationale for various social arrangements and as a means of legitimating one of the most fundamental divisions of society.

To elaborate our proposal, we suggest at the outset that important but often overlooked distinctions be observed among *sex, sex category,* and *gender. Sex* is a determination made through the application of socially agreed upon biological criteria for classifying persons as females or males.[1] The criteria for classification can be genitalia at birth or chromosomal typing before birth, and they do not necessarily agree with one another. Placement in a *sex category* is achieved through application of the sex criteria, but in everyday life, categorization is established and sustained by the socially required identificatory displays that proclaim one's membership in one or the other category. In this sense, one's sex category presumes one's sex and stands as proxy for it in many situations, but sex and sex category can vary independently; that is, it is possible to claim membership in a sex category even when the sex criteria are lacking. *Gender,* in contrast, is the activity of managing situated conduct in light of normative conceptions of attitudes and activities appropriate for one's sex category. Gender activities emerge from and bolster claims to membership in a sex category.

PERSPECTIVES ON SEX AND GENDER

In Western societies, the accepted cultural perspective on gender views women and men as naturally and unequivocally defined categories of being (Garfinkel 1967, pp. 116–18) with distinctive psychological and behavioral propensities that can be predicted from their reproductive functions. Competent adult members of these societies see differences between the two as fundamental and enduring—differences seemingly supported by the division of labor into women's and men's work and an often elaborate differentiation of feminine and masculine attitudes and behaviors that are prominent features of social organization. Things are the way they are by virtue of the fact that men are men and women are women—a division perceived to be natural and rooted in biology, producing in turn profound psychological, behavioral, and social consequences. The structural arrangements of a society are presumed to be responsive to these differences.

Analyses of sex and gender in the social sciences, though less likely to accept uncritically the naive biological determinism of the view just presented, often retain a conception of sex-linked behaviors and traits as essential properties of individuals (for good reviews, see Hochschild 1973; Tresemer 1975; Thorne 1980; Henley 1985). The "sex differences approach" (Thorne 1980) is more commonly attributed to psychologists than to sociologists, but the survey researcher who determines the "gender" of respondents on the basis of the sound of their voices over the telephone is also making trait-oriented assumptions. Reducing gender to a fixed set of psychological traits or to a unitary "variable" precludes serious consideration of the ways it is used to structure distinct domains of social experience (Stacey and Thorne 1985, pp. 307–8).

Taking a different tack, role theory has attended to the social construction of gender categories, called "sex roles" or, more recently, "gender roles" and has analyzed how these are learned and enacted. Beginning with Linton (1936) and continuing through the works of Parsons (Parsons 1951; Parsons and Bales 1955) and Komarovsky (1946, 1950), role theory has emphasized the social and dynamic aspect of role construction and enactment (Thorne 1980; Connell 1983). But at the level of face-to-face interaction, the application of role theory to gender poses problems of its own (for good reviews and critiques, see Connell 1983, 1985; Kessler, Ashendon, Connell, and Dowsett 1985; Lopata and Thorne 1978; Thorne 1980; Stacey and Thorne 1985). Roles are *situated* identities—assumed and relinquished as the situation demands—rather than *master identities* (Hughes 1945), such as sex category, that cut across situations. Unlike most roles, such as "nurse," "doctor," and "patient" or "professor" and "student," gender has no specific site or organizational context.

Moreover, many roles are already gender marked, so that special qualifiers—such as "female doctor" or "male nurse"—must be added to exceptions to the rule. Thorne (1980) observes that conceptualizing gender as a role makes it difficult to assess its influence on other roles and reduces its explanatory usefulness in discussions of power and inequality. Drawing on Rubin (1975), Thorne calls for a reconceptualization of women and men as distinct social groups, constituted in "concrete, historically changing—and generally unequal—social relationships" (Thorne 1980, p. 11).

We argue that gender is not a set of traits, nor a variable, nor a role, but the product of social doings of some sort. What then is the social doing of gender? It is more than the continuous creation of the meaning of gender through human actions (Gerson and Peiss 1985). We claim that gender itself is constituted through interaction.

SEX, SEX CATEGORY, AND GENDER

Garfinkel's (1967, pp. 118–40) case study of Agnes, a transsexual raised as a boy who adopted a female identity at age 17 and underwent a sex reassignment operation several years later, demonstrates how gender is created through interaction and at the same time structures interaction. Agnes, whom Garfinkel characterized as a "practical methodologist," developed a number of procedures for passing as a "normal, natural female" both prior to and after her surgery. She had the practical task of managing the fact that she possessed male genitalia and that she lacked the social resources a girl's biography would presumably provide in everyday interaction. In short, she needed to display herself as a woman, simultaneously learning what it was to be a woman. Of necessity, this full-time pursuit took place at a time when most people's gender would be well-accredited and routinized. Agnes had to consciously contrive what the vast majority of women do without thinking. She was not "faking" what "real" women do naturally. She was obliged to analyze and figure out how to act within socially structured circumstances and conceptions of femininity that women born with appropriate biological credentials come to take for granted early on. As in the case of others who must "pass," such as transvestites, Kabuki actors, or Dustin Hoffman's "Tootsie," Agnes's case makes visible what culture has made invisible—the accomplishment of gender.

Garfinkel's (1967) discussion of Agnes does not explicitly separate three analytically distinct, although empirically overlapping, concepts—sex, sex category, and gender.

Sex

Agnes did not possess the socially agreed upon biological criteria for classification as a member of the female *sex*. Still, Agnes regarded herself as a female, albeit a female with a penis, which a woman ought not to possess. The penis, she insisted, was a "mistake" in need of remedy (Garfinkel 1967, pp. 126–27, 131–32). Like other competent members of our culture, Agnes honored the notion that there *are* "essential" biological criteria that unequivocally distinguish females from males. However, if we move away from the commonsense viewpoint, we discover that the reliability of these criteria is not beyond question (Money and Brennan 1968; Money and Erhardt 1972; Money and Ogunro 1974; Money and Tucker 1975). Moreover, other cultures have acknowledged the existence of "cross-genders" (Blackwood 1984; Williams 1986) and the possibility of more than two sexes (Hill 1935; Martin and Voorhies 1975, pp. 84–107; but see also Cucchiari 1981, pp. 32–35).

More central to our argument is Kessler and McKenna's (1978, pp. 1–6) point that genitalia are conventionally hidden from public inspection in everyday life; yet we continue through our social rounds to "observe" a world of two naturally, normally sexed persons. It is the *presumption* that essential criteria exist and would or should be there if looked for that provides the basis for sex categorization. Drawing on Garfinkel, Kessler and McKenna argue that "female" and "male" are cultural events—products of what they term the "gender attribution process"—rather than some collection of traits, behaviors, or even physical attributes. Illustratively they cite the child who, viewing a picture of someone clad in a suit and a tie, contends, "It's a man, because he has a pee-pee" (Kessler and McKenna 1978, p. 154). Translation: "He must have a pee-pee [an essential characteristic] because I see the *insignia* of a suit and tie." Neither initial sex assignment (pronouncement at birth as a female or male) nor the actual existence of essential criteria for that assignment (possession of a clitoris and vagina or penis and testicles) has much—if anything—to do with the identification of sex category in everyday life. There, Kessler and McKenna note, we operate with a moral certainty of a world of two sexes. We do not think, "Most persons with penises are men, but some may not be" or "Most persons who dress as men have penises." Rather, we take it for granted that sex and sex category are congruent—that knowing the latter, we can deduce the rest.

Sex Categorization

Agnes's claim to the categorical status of female, which she sustained by appropriate identificatory displays and other characteristics, could be *discredited* before her transsexual operation if her possession of a penis became known and after by her surgically constructed genitalia (see Raymond 1979, pp. 37, 138). In this regard, Agnes had to be continually alert to actual or potential threats to the security of her sex category. Her problem was not so much living up to some prototype of essential femininity but preserving her categorization as female. This task was made easy for her by a very powerful resource, namely, the process of commonsense categorization in everyday life.

The categorization of members of society into indigenous categories such as "girl" or "boy," or "woman" or "man," operates in a distinctively social way. The act of categorization does not involve a positive test, in the sense of a well-defined set of criteria that must be explicitly satisfied prior to making an identification. Rather, the application of membership categories relies on an "if-can" test in everyday interaction (Sacks 1972, pp. 332–35). This test stipulates that if people *can be seen* as members of relevant categories, *then categorize them that way.* That is, use the category that seems appropriate, except in the presence of discrepant information or obvious features that would rule out its use. This procedure is quite in keeping with the attitude of everyday life, which has us take appearances at face value unless we have special reason to doubt (Schutz 1943; Garfinkel 1967, pp. 272–77; Bernstein 1986).[2] It should be added that it is precisely when we have special reason to doubt that the issue of applying rigorous criteria arises, but it is rare, outside legal or bureaucratic contexts, to encounter insistence on positive tests (Garfinkel 1967, pp. 262–83; Wilson 1970).

Agnes's initial resource was the predisposition of those she encountered to take her appearance (her figure, clothing, hair style, and so on), as the undoubted appearance of a normal female. Her further resource was our cultural perspective on the properties of "natural, normally sexed persons." Garfinkel (1967, pp. 122–28) notes that in everyday life, we live in a world of two—and only two—sexes. This arrangement has a moral status, in that we include ourselves and others in it as "essentially, originally, in the first place, always have been, always will be, once and for all, in the final analysis, either 'male' or 'female' " (Garfinkel 1967, p. 122).

Consider the following case:

> This issue reminds me of a visit I made to a computer store a couple of years ago. The person who answered my questions was truly a *salesperson.* I could not categorize him/her as a woman or a man. What did I look for? (1) Facial hair: She/he was smooth skinned, but some men have little or no facial hair. (This varies by race, Native Americans and Blacks often have none.) (2) Breasts: She/he was wearing a loose shirt that hung from his/her shoulders. And, as many women who suffered through a 1950s' adolescence know to their shame, women are often flat-chested. (3) Shoulders: His/hers were small and round for a man, broad for a woman. (4) Hands: Long and slender fingers, knuckles a bit large for a woman, small for a man. (5) Voice: Middle range, unexpressive for a woman, not at all the exaggerated tones some gay males affect. (6) His/her treatment of me: Gave off no signs that would let me know if I were of the same or different sex as this person. There were not even any signs that he/she knew his/her sex would be difficult to categorize and I wondered about that even as I did my best to hide these questions so I would not embarrass him/her while we talked of computer paper. I left still not knowing the sex of my salesperson, and was disturbed by that unanswered question (child of my culture that I am). (Diane Margolis, personal communication)

What can this case tell us about situations such as Agnes's (cf. Morris 1974; Richards 1983) or the process of sex categorization in general? First, we infer from this description that the computer salesclerk's identificatory display was ambiguous, since she or he was not dressed or adorned in an unequivocally female or male fashion. It is when such a display *fails* to provide grounds for categorization that factors such as facial hair or tone of voice are assessed to determine membership in a sex category. Second, beyond the fact that this incident could be recalled after "a couple of years," the customer was not only "disturbed" by the ambiguity of the salesclerk's category but also assumed that to acknowledge this ambiguity would be embarrassing to the salesclerk. Not only do we want to know the sex category of those around us (to see it at a glance, perhaps), but we presume that others are displaying it for us, in as decisive a fashion as they can.

Gender

Agnes attempted to be "120 percent female" (Garfinkel 1967, p. 129), that is, unquestionably in all ways and at all times feminine. She thought she could protect herself from disclosure before and after surgical intervention by comporting herself in a feminine manner, but she also could have given herself away by overdoing her performance. Sex categorization and the accomplishment of gender are not the same. Agnes's categorization could be secure or suspect, but did not depend on whether or not she lived up to some ideal conception of femininity. Women can be seen as unfeminine, but that does not make them "unfemale." Agnes faced an ongoing task of *being* a woman—something beyond style of dress (an identificatory display) or allowing men to light her cigarette (a gender display). Her problem was to produce configurations of behavior that would be seen by others as normative gender behavior.

Agnes's strategy of "secret apprenticeship," through which she learned expected feminine decorum by carefully attending to her fiancé's criticisms of other women, was one means of masking incompetencies and simultaneously acquiring the needed skills (Garfinkel 1967, pp. 146–147). It was through her fiancé that Agnes learned that sunbathing on the lawn in front of her apartment was "offensive" (because it put her on display to other men). She also learned from his critiques of other women that she should not insist on having things her way and that she should not offer her opinions or claim equality with men (Garfinkel 1967, pp. 147–48). (Like other women in our society, Agnes learned something about power in the course of her "education.")

Popular culture abounds with books and magazines that compile idealized depictions of relations between women and men. Those focused on the etiquette of dating or prevailing standards of feminine comportment are meant to be of practical help in these matters. However, the use of any such source *as a manual of procedure* requires the assumption that doing gender merely involves making use of discrete, well-defined bundles of behavior that can simply be plugged into interactional situations to produce recognizable enactments of masculinity and femininity. The man "does" being masculine by, for example, taking the woman's arm to guide her across a street, and she "does" being feminine by consenting to be guided and not initiating such behavior with a man.

Agnes could perhaps have used such sources as manuals, but, we contend, doing gender is not so easily regimented (Mithers 1982; Morris 1974). Such sources may list and describe the sorts of behaviors that mark or display gender, but they are necessarily incomplete (Garfinkel 1967, pp. 66–75; Wieder 1974, pp. 183–214; Zimmerman and Wieder 1970, pp. 285–98). And to be successful, marking or displaying gender must be finely fitted to situations and modified or transformed as the occasion demands. Doing gender consists of managing such occasions so that, whatever the particulars, the outcome is seen and seeable in context as gender-appropriate or, as the case may be, gender-*in*appropriate.

RESOURCES FOR DOING GENDER

Doing gender means creating differences between girls and boys and women and men, differences that are not natural, essential, or biological. Once the differences have been constructed, they are used to reinforce the "essentialness" of gender. In a delightful account of the "arrangement between the sexes," Goffman (1977) observes the creation of a variety of institutionalized frameworks through which our "natural, normal sexedness" can be enacted. The physical features of social setting provide one obvious resource for the expression of our "essential" differences. For example, the sex segregation of North American public bathrooms distinguishes "ladies" from "gentlemen" in matters held to be fundamentally biological, even though both "are somewhat similar in the question of waste products and their elimination" (Goffman 1977, p. 315). These settings are furnished with dimorphic equipment (such as urinals for men or elaborate grooming facilities for women), even though both sexes may achieve the same ends through the same means (and apparently do so in the privacy of their own homes). To be stressed here is the fact that:

> The *functioning* of sex-differentiated organs is involved, but there is nothing in this functioning that biologically recommends segregation; *that* arrangement is a totally cultural matter... toilet segregation is presented as a natural consequence of the difference between the sex classes when in fact it is a means of honoring, if not producing, this difference. (Goffman 1977, p. 316)

Standardized social occasions also provide stages for evocations of the "essential female and male natures." Goffman cites organized sports as one such institutionalized framework for the expression of manliness. There, those qualities that ought "properly" to be associated with masculinity, such as endurance, strength, and competitive spirit, are celebrated by all parties concerned—participants, who may be seen to demonstrate such traits, and spectators, who applaud their demonstrations from the safety of the sidelines (1977, p. 322).

Assortative mating practices among heterosexual couples afford still further means to create and maintain differences between women and men. For example, even though size, strength, and age tend to be normally distributed among females and males (with considerable overlap between them), selective pairing ensures couples in which boys and men are visibly bigger, stronger, and older (if not "wiser") than the girls and women with whom they are paired. So, should situations emerge in which greater size, strength, or experience is called for, boys and men will be ever ready to display it and girls and women, to appreciate its display (Goffman 1977, p. 321; West and Iritani 1985).

Gender may be routinely fashioned in a variety of situations that seem conventionally expressive to begin with, such as those that present "helpless" women next to heavy objects or flat tires. But, as Goffman notes, heavy, messy, and precarious concerns can be constructed from *any* social situation, "even though by standards set in other settings, this may involve something that is light, clean, and safe" (Goffman 1977, p. 324). Given these resources, it is clear that *any* interactional situation sets the stage for depictions of "essential" sexual natures. In sum, these situations "do not so much allow for the expression of natural differences as for the production of that difference itself" (Goffman 1977, p. 324).

Many situations are not clearly sex categorized to begin with, nor is what transpires within them obviously gender relevant. Yet any social encounter can be pressed into service in the interests of doing gender. Thus, Fishman's (1978) research on casual conversations found an asymmetrical "division of labor" in talk between heterosexual intimates. Women had to ask more questions, fill more silences, and use more attention-getting beginnings in order to be heard. Her conclusions are particularly pertinent here:

> Since interactional work is related to what constitutes being a woman, with what a woman *is*, the idea that it is work is obscured. The work is not seen as what women do, but as part of what they are. (Fishman 1978, p. 405)

We would argue that it is precisely such labor that helps to constitute the essential nature of women *as* women in interactional contexts (West and Zimmerman 1983, pp. 109–11; but see also Kollock, Blumstein, and Schwartz 1985).

Individuals have many social identities that may be donned or shed, muted or made more salient, depending on the situation. One may be a friend, spouse, professional, citizen, and many other things to many different people—or, to the same person at different times. But we are always women or men—unless we shift into another sex category. What this means is that our identificatory displays will provide an ever-available resource for doing gender under an infinitely diverse set of circumstances.

Some occasions are organized to routinely display and celebrate behaviors that are conventionally linked to one or the other sex category. On such occasions, everyone knows his or her place in the interactional scheme of things. If an individual identified as a member of one sex category engages in behavior usually associated with the other category, this routinization is challenged. Hughes (1945, p. 356) provides an illustration of such a dilemma:

> [A] young woman...became part of that virile profession, engineering. The designer of an airplane is expected to go up on the maiden flight of the first plane built according to the design. He [sic] then gives a dinner to the engineers and workmen who worked on the new plane. The dinner is naturally a stag party. The young woman in question designed a plane. Her co-workers urged her not to take the risk—for which, presumably, men only are fit—of the maiden voyage. They were, in effect, asking her to be a lady instead of an engineer. She chose to be an engineer. She then gave the party and paid for it like a man. After food and the first round of toasts, she left like a lady.

On this occasion, parties reached an accommodation that allowed a woman to engage in presumptively masculine behaviors. However, we note that in the end, this compromise permitted demonstration of her "essential" femininity, through accountably "ladylike" behavior.

Hughes (1945, p. 357) suggests that such contradictions may be countered by managing interactions on a very narrow basis, for example, "keeping the relationship formal and specific." But the heart of the matter is that even—perhaps, especially—if the relationship is a formal one, gender is still something one is accountable for. Thus a woman physician (notice the special qualifier in her case) may be accorded respect for her skill and even addressed by an appropriate title. Nonetheless, she is subject to evaluation in terms of normative conceptions of appropriate attitudes and activities for her sex category and under pressure to prove that she is an "essentially" feminine being, despite appearances to the contrary (West 1984, pp. 97–101). Her sex category is used to discredit her participation in important clinical activities (Lorber 1984, pp. 52–54), while her involvement in medicine is used to discredit her commitment to her responsibilities as a wife and mother (Bourne and Wikler 1978, pp. 435–37). Simultaneously, her exclusion from the physician colleague community is maintained and her accountability *as a woman* is ensured.

In this context, "role conflict" can be viewed as a dynamic aspect of our current "arrangement between the sexes" (Goffman 1977), an arrangement that provides for occasions on which persons of a particular sex category can "see" quite clearly that they are out of place and that if they were not there, their current troubles would not exist. What is at stake is, from the standpoint of interaction, the management of our "essential" natures, and from the standpoint of the individual, the continuing accomplishment of gender. If, as we have argued, sex category is omnirelevant, then any occasion, conflicted or not, offers the resources for doing gender.

We have sought to show that sex category and gender are managed properties of conduct that are contrived with respect to the fact that others will judge and respond to us in particular ways. We have claimed that a person's gender is not simply an aspect of what one is, but, more fundamentally, it is something that one *does*, and does recurrently, in interaction with others.

What are the consequences of this rheoretical formulation? If, for example, individuals strive to achieve gender in encounters with others, how does a culture instill the need to achieve it? What is the relationship between the production of gender at the level of interaction and such institutional arrangements as the division of labor in society? And, perhaps most important, how does doing gender contribute to the subordination of women by men?

NOTES

1. This definition understates many complexities involved in the relationship between biology and culture (Jaggar 1983, pp. 106–13). However, our point is that the determination of an individual's sex classification is a *social* process through and through.
2. Bernstein (1986) reports an unusual case of espionage in which a man passing as a woman convinced a lover that he/she had given birth to "their" child, who, the lover thought, "looked like" him.

REFERENCES

Bernstein, Richard. 1986. "France Jails 2 in Odd Case of Espionage." *New York Times* (May 11).

Blackwood, Evelyn. 1984. "Sexuality and Gender in Certain Native American Tribes: The Case of Cross-Gender Females." *Signs: Journal of Women in Culture and Society* 10:27–42.

Bourne, Patricia G., and Norma J. Wikler. 1978. "Commitment and the Cultural Mandate: Women in Medicine." *Social Problems* 25:430–40.

Chodorow, Nancy. 1978. *The Reproduction of Mothering: Psychoanalysis and the Sociology of Gender.* Los Angeles: University of California Press.

Connell, R.W. 1983. *Which Way Is Up?* Sydney: Allen & Unwin.

——— 1985. "Theorizing Gender." *Sociology* 19:260–72.

Cucchiari, Salvatore. 1981. "The Gender Revolution and the Transition from Bisexual Horde to Patrilocal Band: The Origins of Gender Hierarchy." Pp. 31–79 in *Sexual Meanings: The Cultural Construction of Gender and Sexuality*, edited by S. B. Ortner and H. Whitehead. New York: Cambridge.

Firestone, Shulamith. 1970. *The Dialectic of Sex: The Case for Feminist Revolution.* New York: William Morrow.

Fishman, Pamela. 1978. "Interaction: The Work Women Do." *Social Problems* 25:397–406.

Garfinkel, Harold. 1967. *Studies in Ethnomethodology.* Englewood Cliffs, NJ: Prentice-Hall.

Gerson, Judith M., and Kathy Peiss. 1985. "Boundaries, Negotiation, Consciousness: Reconceptualizing Gender Relations." *Social Problems* 32:317–31.

Goffman, Erving. 1977. "The Arrangement Between the Sexes." *Theory and Society* 4:301–31.

Henley, Nancy M. 1985. "Psychology and Gender." *Signs: Journal of Women in Culture and Society* 11:101–119.

Hill, W. W. 1935. "The Status of the Hermaphrodite and Transvestite in Navaho Culture." *American Anthropologist* 37:273–79.

Hochschild, Arlie R. 1973. "A Review of Sex Roles Research." *American Journal of Sociology* 78:1011–29.

—1983. *The Managed Heart: Commercialization of Human Feeling*. Berkeley: University of California Press.

Hughes, Everett C. 1945. "Dilemmas and Contradictions of Status." *American Journal of Sociology* 50:353–59.

Jaggar, Alison M. 1983. *Feminist Politics and Human Nature*. Totowa, NJ: Rowman & Allanheld.

Kessler, S., D. J. Ashendon, R. W. Connell, and G. W. Dowsett. 1985. "Gender Relations in Secondary Schooling." *Sociology of Education* 58:34–48.

Kessler, Suzanne J., and Wendy McKenna. 1978. *Gender: An Ethnomethodological Approach*. New York: Wiley.

Kollock, Peter, Philip Blumstein, and Pepper Schwartz. 1985. "Sex and Power in Interaction." *American Sociological Review* 50:34–46.

Komarovsky, Mirra. 1946. "Cultural Contradictions and Sex Roles." *American Journal of Sociology* 52:184–89.

——— 1950. "Functional Analysis of Sex Roles." *American Sociological Review* 15:508–16.

Linton, Ralph. 1936. *The Study of Man*. New York: Appleton-Century.

Lopata, Helen Z., and Barrie Thorne. 1978. "On the Term 'Sex Roles.' " *Signs: Journal of Women in Culture and Society* 3:718–21.

Lorber, Judith. 1984. *Women Physicians: Careers, Status and Power*. New York: Tavistock.

——— 1986. "Dismantling Noah's Ark." *Sex Roles* 14:567–80.

Martin, M. Kay, and Barbara Voorheis. 1975. *Female of the Species*. New York: Columbia University Press.

Mead, Margaret. 1963. *Sex and Temperment*. New York: Dell.

——— 1968. *Male and Female*. New York: Dell.

Mithers, Carol L. 1982. "My Life as a Man." *The Village Voice* 27 (October 5):1ff.

Money, John. 1968. *Sex Errors of the Body*. Baltimore: Johns Hopkins.

——— 1974. "Prenatal Hormones and Postnatal Sexualization in Gender Identity Differentiation." Pp. 221–95 in *Nebraska Symposium on Motivation*, Vol. 21, edited by J. K. Cole and R. Dienstbier. Lincoln: University of Nebraska Press.

——— and John G. Brennan. 1968. "Sexual Dimorphism in the Psychology of Female Transsexuals." *Journal of Nervous and Mental Disease* 147:487–99.

——— and Anke, A. Erhardt. 1972. *Man and Woman/Boy and Girl*. Baltimore: Johns Hopkins.

——— and Charles Ogunro. 1974. "Behavioral Sexology: Ten Cases of Genetic Male Intersexuality with Impaired Prenatal and Pubertal Androgenization," *Archives of Sexual Behavior* 3:181–206.

——— and Patricia Tucker. 1975. *Sexual Signatures*. Boston: Little, Brown.

Morris, Jan. 1974. *Conundrum*. New York: Harcourt Brace Jovanovich.

Parsons, Talcott. 1951. *The Social System*. New York: Free Press.

——— and Robert F. Bales. 1955. *Family, Socialization and Interaction Process*. New York: Free Press.

Raymond, Janice G. 1979. *The Transsexual Empire*. Boston: Beacon.

Richards, Renee (with John Ames). 1983. *Second Serve: The Renee Richards Story*. New York: Stein and Day.

Rossi, Alice. 1984. "Gender and Parenthood." *American Sociological Review* 49:1–19.

Rubin, Gayle. 1975. "The Traffic in Women: Notes on the 'Political Economy' of Sex." Pp. 157–210 in *Toward an Anthropology of Women*, edited by R. Reiter. New York: Monthly Review Press.

Sacks, Harvey. 1972. "On the Analyzability of Stories by Children." Pp. 325–45 in *Directions in Sociolinguistics*, edited by J. J. Gumperz and D. Hymes. New York: Holt, Rinehart & Winston.

Schutz, Alfred. 1943. "The Problem of Rationality in the Social World." *Economics* 10:130–49.

Stacey, Judith, and Barrie Thorne. 1985. "The Missing Feminist Revolution in Sociology." *Social Problems* 32:301–16.

Thorne, Barrie. 1980. "Gender...How Is It Best Conceptualized?" Unpublished manuscript.

Tresemer, David. 1975. "Assumptions Made About Gender Roles." Pp. 308–39 in *Another Voice: Feminist Perspectives on Social Life and Social Science*, edited by M. Millman and R. M. Kanter. New York: Anchor/Doubleday.

West, Candace. 1984. "When the Doctor is a 'Lady': Power, Status and Gender in Physician-Patient Encounters." *Symbolic Interaction* 7:87–106.

——— and Bonita Iritani. 1985. "Gender Politics in Mate Selection: The Male-Older Norm." Paper presented at the Annual Meeting of the American Sociological Association, August, Washington, DC.

——— and Don H. Zimmerman. 1983. "Small Insults: A Study of Interruptions in Conversations Between Unacquainted Persons." Pp. 102–17 in *Language, Gender and Society*, edited by B. Thorne, C. Kramarae, and N. Henley. Rowley, MA: Newbury House.

Wieder, D. Lawrence. 1974. *Language and Social Reality: The Case of Telling the Convict Code*. The Hague: Mouton.

Williams, Walter L. 1986. *The Spirit and the Flesh: Sexual Diversity in American Indian Culture*. Boston: Beacon.

Wilson, Thomas P. 1970. "Conceptions of Interaction and Forms of Sociological Explanation." *American Sociological Review* 35:697–710.

Zimmerman, Don H., and D. Lawrence Wieder. 1970. "Ethnomethodology and the Problem of Order: Comment on Denzin." Pp. 287–95 in *Understanding Everyday Life*, edited by J. Denzin. Chicago: Aldine.

Excerpt from *Black Feminist Thought*

PATRICIA HILL COLLINS

> Called Matriarch, Emasculator and Hot Momma. Sometimes Sister, Pretty Baby, Auntie, Mammy and Girl. Called Unwed Mother, Welfare Recipient and Inner City Consumer. The Black American Woman has had to admit that while nobody knew the troubles she saw, everybody, his brother and his dog, felt qualified to explain her, even to herself.
>
> —Trudier Harris (1982, 4)

Collins, Patricia Hill. 2000. "Mammies, Matriarchs, and Other Controlling Images" from *Black Feminist Thought* (2nd edition). New York: Routledge.

Intersecting oppressions of race, class, gender, and sexuality could not continue without powerful ideological justifications for their existence. As Cheryl Gilkes contends, "Black women's assertiveness and their use of every expression of racism to launch multiple assaults against the entire fabric of inequality have been a consistent, multifaceted threat to the status quo. As punishment, Black women have been assaulted with a variety of negative images" (1983, 294). Portraying African-American women as stereotypical mammies, matriarchs, welfare recipients, and hot mommas helps justify U.S. Black women's oppression. Challenging these controlling images has long been a core theme in Black feminist thought.

As part of a generalized ideology of domination, stereotypical images of Black womanhood take on special meaning. Because the authority to define societal values is a major instrument of power, elite groups, in exercising power, manipulate ideas about Black womanhood. They do so by exploiting already existing symbols, or creating new ones. Hazel Carby suggests that the objective of stereotypes is "not to reflect or represent a reality but to function as a disguise, or mystification, of objective social relations" (1987, 22). These controlling images are designed to make racism, sexism, poverty, and other forms of social injustice appear to be natural, normal, and inevitable parts of everyday life.

Even when the initial conditions that foster controlling images disappear, such images prove remarkably tenacious because they not only subjugate U.S. Black women but are key in maintaining intersecting oppressions (Mullings 1997, 109–30). African-American women's status as outsiders becomes the point from which other groups define their normality. Ruth Shays, a Black inner-city resident, describes how the standpoint of a subordinate group is discredited: "It will not kill people to hear the truth, but they don't like it and they would much rather hear it from one of their own than from a stranger. Now, to white people your colored person is always a stranger. Not only that, we are supposed to be dumb strangers, so we can't tell them anything!" (Gwaltney 1980, 29). As the "Others" of society who can never really belong, strangers threaten the moral and social order. But they are simultaneously essential for its survival because those individuals who stand at the margins of society clarify its boundaries. African-American women, by not belonging, emphasize the significance of belonging.

THE OBJECTIFICATION OF BLACK WOMEN AS THE OTHER

Black feminist critic Barbara Christian asserts that in the United States, "the enslaved African woman became the basis for the definition of our society's *Other*" (1985, 160). Maintaining images of U.S. Black women as the Other provides ideological justification for race, gender, and class oppression. Certain basic ideas crosscut these and other forms of oppression. One such idea is binary thinking that categorizes people, things, and ideas in terms of their difference from one another (Keller 1985, 8). For example, each term in the binaries white/black, male/female, reason/emotion, culture/nature, fact/opinion, mind/body, and subject/object gains meaning only in *relation* to its counterpart (Halpin 1989).

Another basic idea concerns how binary thinking shapes understandings of human difference. In such thinking, difference is defined in oppositional terms. One part is not simply different from its counterpart; it is inherently opposed to its "other." Whites and Blacks, males and females, thought and feeling are not complementary counterparts—they are fundamentally different entities related only through their definition as opposites. Feeling cannot be incorporated into thought or even function in conjunction with it because in binary oppositional thinking, feeling retards thought and values obscure facts.

Objectification is central to this process of oppositional difference. In binary thinking, one element is objectified as the Other, and is viewed as an object to be manipulated and controlled. Social theorist Dona Richards (1980) suggests that Western thought requires objectification, a process she describes as the "separation of the 'knowing self' from the 'known object'" (p. 72). Intense objectification is a "prerequisite for the despiritualization of the universe," Richards writes, "and through it the Western cosmos was made ready for ever increasing materialization" (p. 72). A Marxist assessment of the culture/nature binary argues that history can be seen as that in which human beings constantly objectify the natural world in order to control and exploit it (Brittan and Maynard 1984, 198). Culture is defined as the opposite of an objectified nature. If undomesticated, this wild and primitive nature might destroy more civilized culture.[1] Feminist scholarship points to the identification of women with nature as being central to women's subsequent objectification and conquest by men (McClintock 1995). Black studies scholarship and postcolonial theory both suggest that defining people of color as less human, animalistic, or more "natural" denies African and Asian people's subjectivity and supports the political economy of domination that characterized slavery, colonialism, and neo-colonialism (Torgovnick 1990; Chow 1993, 27–54; Said 1993; Bannerji 1995, 55–95).

Domination always involves attempts to objectify the subordinate group. "As subjects, people have the right to define their own reality, establish their own identities, name their history," asserts bell hooks (1989, 42). "As objects, one's reality is defined by others, one's identity created by others, one's history named only in ways that define one's relationship to those who are subject" (p. 42). The treatment afforded U.S. Black women domestic workers exemplifies the many forms that objectification can take. Making Black women work as if they were animals or "mules uh de world" represents one form of objectification. Deference rituals such as calling Black domestic workers "girls" enable employers to treat their employees like children, as less capable human beings. Objectification can be so severe that the Other simply disappears.

Finally, because oppositional binaries rarely represent different but equal relationships, they are inherently unstable. Tension may be temporarily relieved by subordinating one half of the binary to the other. Thus Whites rule Blacks, men dominate women, reason is thought superior to emotion in ascertaining truth, facts supersede opinion in evaluating knowledge, and subjects rule objects. The foundations of intersecting oppressions become grounded in interdependent concepts of binary thinking, oppositional difference, objectification, and social hierarchy. With domination based on difference forming an essential underpinning for this entire system of thought, these concepts invariably imply relationships of superiority and inferiority, hierarchical bonds that mesh with political economies of race, gender, and class oppression.

African-American women occupy a position whereby the inferior half of a series of these binaries converge, and this placement has been central to our subordination. The allegedly emotional, passionate nature of Black women has long been used to justify Black women's sexual exploitation. Similarly, restricting Black women's literacy, then claiming that we lack the facts for sound judgment, relegates African-American women to the inferior side of the fact/opinion binary. Denying Black women status as fully human subjects by treating us as the objectified Other within multiple binaries demonstrates the power that binary thinking, oppositional difference, and objectification wield within intersecting oppressions.

Despite its seeming permanence, this way of thinking, by fostering injustice, can also stimulate resistance. For example, U.S. Black women have long recognized the fundamental injustice of a system that routinely and from one generation to the next relegates U.S. Black women to the bottom of the social hierarchy. When faced with this structural injustice targeted toward the group, many Black women have insisted on our right to define our own reality, establish our own identities, and name our history. One significant contribution of work on domestic workers is that it documents Black women's everyday resistance to this attempted objectification.

Analyzing the particular controlling images applied to African-American women reveals the specific contours of Black women's objectification as well as the ways in which oppressions of race, gender, sexuality, and class intersect. Moreover, since the images themselves are dynamic and changing, each provides a starting point for examining new forms of control that emerge in a transnational context, one where selling images has increased in importance in the global marketplace.

CONTROLLING IMAGES AND BLACK WOMEN'S OPPRESSION

"Black women emerged from slavery firmly enshrined in the consciousness of white America as 'Mammy' and the 'bad black woman,'" contends Cheryl Gilkes (1983, 294). The dominant ideology of the slave era fostered the creation of several interrelated, socially constructed controlling images of Black womanhood, each reflecting the dominant group's interest in maintaining Black women's subordination. Moreover, since Black and White women were both important to slavery's continuation, controlling images of Black womanhood also functioned to mask social relations that affected all women.

According to the cult of true womanhood that accompanied the traditional family ideal, "true" women possessed four cardinal virtues: piety, purity, submissiveness, and domesticity. Propertied White women and those of the emerging middle class were encouraged to aspire to these virtues. African-American women encountered a different set of controlling images.

The first controlling image applied to U.S. Black women is that of the mammy—the faithful, obedient domestic servant. Created to justify the economic exploitation of house slaves and sustained to explain Black women's long-standing restriction to domestic service, the mammy image represents the normative yardstick used to evaluate all Black women's behavior. By loving, nurturing, and caring for her White children and "family" better than her own, the mammy symbolizes the dominant group's perceptions of the ideal Black female relationship to elite White male power. Even though she may be well loved and may wield considerable authority in her White "family," the mammy still knows her "place" as obedient servant. She has accepted her subordination.

Black women intellectuals have aggressively criticized the image of African-American women as contented mammies. Literary critic Trudier Harris's (1982) volume *From Mammies to Militants: Domestics in Black American Literature* investigates prominent differences in how Black women have been portrayed by others in literature and how they portray themselves. In her work on the difficulties faced by Black women leaders, Rhetaugh Dumas (1980) describes how Black women executives are hampered by being treated as mammies and penalized if they do not appear warm and nurturing. Striking a similar chord, Barbara Omolade's (1994) description of the "mammification" of Black professional women also takes aim at the imagined Black woman mammy. But despite these works, the mammy image lives on in scholarly and popular culture. Audre Lorde's account of a shopping trip offers a powerful example of its tenacity: "I wheel my two-year-old daughter in a shopping cart through a supermarket in…1967, and a little white girl riding past in her mother's cart calls out excitedly, 'Oh look, Mommy, a baby maid!' " (1984, 126).[2]

The mammy image is central to intersecting oppressions of race, gender, sexuality, and class. Regarding racial oppression, controlling images like the mammy aim to influence Black maternal behavior. As the members of African-American families who are most familiar with the skills needed for Black accommodation, Black mothers are encouraged to transmit to their own children the deference behavior that many are forced to exhibit in their mammified jobs. By teaching Black children their assigned place in White power structures, Black women who internalize the mammy image potentially become effective conduits for perpetuating racial oppression. Ideas about mammy buttress racial hierarchies in other ways. Employing Black women in mammified occupations supports the racial superiority of White employers, encouraging middle-class White women in particular to identify more closely with the racial and class privilege afforded their fathers, husbands, and sons. In a climate where, as Patricia Williams (1995) puts it, "those blacks who do indeed rise into the middle class end up being figured only as those who were *given* whatever they enjoy, and the black 'underclass' becomes those whose sole life activity is *taking*" (p. 61), no wonder that working-class Whites expect Black women to exhibit deferential behavior, and deeply resent those who do not. Mammy is the public face that Whites expect Black women to assume for them.

The mammy image also serves a symbolic function in maintaining oppressions of gender and sexuality. Black feminist critic Barbara Christian argues that images of Black womanhood serve as a reservoir for the fears of Western culture, "a dumping ground for those female functions a basically Puritan society could not confront" (1985, 2). Juxtaposed against images of White women, the mammy image as the Other symbolizes the oppositional difference of mind/body and culture/nature thought to distinguish Black women from everyone else. Christian comments on the mammy's gender significance: "All the functions of mammy are magnificently physical. They involve the body as sensuous, as funky, the part of woman that white southern America was profoundly afraid of. Mammy, then, harmless in her position of slave, unable because of her all-giving nature to do harm, is needed as an image, a surrogate to contain all those fears of the physical female" (1985, 2). The mammy image buttresses the ideology of the cult of true womanhood, one in which sexuality and fertility are severed. "Good" White mothers are expected to deny their female sexuality. In contrast, the mammy image is one of an asexual woman, a surrogate mother in blackface whose historical devotion to her White family is now giving way to new expectations. Contemporary mammies should be completely committed to their jobs.

No matter how loved they were by their White "families," Black women domestic workers remained poor because they were economically exploited workers in a capitalist political economy. The restructured post–World War II economy, in which African-American women moved from service in private homes to jobs in the low-paid service sector and to jobs in clerical work and mammified professions, has produced similar yet differently organized economic exploitation. Historically, many White families in both the middle class and working class were able to maintain their class position because they used Black women domestic workers as a source of cheap labor (Rollins 1985; Byerly 1986). The mammy image was designed to mask this economic exploitation of social class (King 1973). Currently, while the mammy image becomes more muted as Black women move into better jobs, the basic economic exploitation where U.S. Black women either make less for the same work or work twice as hard for the same pay persists. U.S. Black women and African-American communities pay a price for this exploitation. Removing Black women's labor from African-American families and exploiting it denies Black extended family units the benefits of both decent wages and Black women's emotional labor in their homes. Moreover, as the attention to issues of stress in Black feminist analyses of U.S. Black women's health suggest, participating in this chronically undercompensated and unrecognized labor takes its toll (White 1994, 11–14).

For reasons of economic survival, U.S. Black women may play the mammy role in paid work settings. But within African-American families and neighborhoods these same women often teach their own children something quite different. Bonnie Thornton Dill's (1980) work on child-rearing patterns among Black domestics shows that while the participants in her study showed deference behavior at work, they discouraged their children from believing that they should be deferential to Whites and encouraged their children to avoid domestic work. Barbara Christian's analysis of the mammy in Black slave narratives reveals that, "unlike the white southern image of mammy, she is cunning, prone to poisoning her master, and not at all content with her lot" (1985, 5).

The fact that the mammy image by itself cannot control Black women's behavior is tied to the creation of the second controlling image of Black womanhood. Though a more recent phenomenon, the image of the Black matriarch fulfills similar functions in explaining Black women's placement in intersecting oppressions. Ironically, Black scholars such as William E. B. DuBois (1969) and E. Franklin Frazier (1948) described the connections among higher rates of female-headed households in African-American communities, the importance that women assume in Black family networks, and the persistence of Black poverty. However, neither scholar interpreted Black women's centrality in Black families as a *cause* of African-American social class status. Both saw so-called matriarchal families as an *outcome* of racial oppression and poverty. During the eras when DuBois and Frazier wrote, the political disenfranchisement and economic exploitation of African-Americans was so entrenched that control over Black women could be maintained without the matriarchal stereotype. But what began as a muted theme in the works of these earlier African-American scholars grew into a full-blown racialized image in the 1960s, a time of significant political and economic mobility for African-Americans. Racialization involves attaching racial meaning to a previously racially unclassified relationship, social practice, or group (Omi and Winant 1994). Prior to the 1960s, Black communities contained higher percentages of families maintained by single mothers than White ones, but an ideology that racialized female-headedness as one important cause of Black poverty had not emerged. Interestingly, the insertion of the Black matriarchy thesis into discussions of Black poverty came in the midst of considerable Black activism. Moreover, the public depiction of U.S. Black women as unfeminine matriarchs came at precisely the same moment that the women's movement advanced its critique of U.S. patriarchy (Gilkes 1983, 296).

While the mammy typifies the Black mother figure in White homes, the matriarch symbolizes the mother figure in Black homes. Just as the mammy represents the "good" Black mother, the matriarch symbolizes the "bad" Black mother. Introduced and widely circulated via a government report titled *The Negro Family: The Case for National Action*, the Black matriarchy thesis argued that African-American women who failed to fulfill their traditional "womanly" duties at home contributed to social problems in Black civil society (Moynihan 1965). Spending too much time away from home, these working mothers ostensibly could not properly supervise their children and thus were a major contributing factor to their children's failure at school. As overly aggressive, unfeminine women, Black matriarchs allegedly emasculated their lovers and husbands. These men, understandably, either deserted their partners or refused to marry the mothers of their children. From the dominant group's perspective, the matriarch represented a failed mammy, a negative stigma to be applied to African-American women who dared reject the image of the submissive, hardworking servant.

Black women intellectuals who study African-American families and Black motherhood typically report finding few matriarchs and even fewer mammies (Myers 1980; Sudarkasa 1981; Dill 1988). Instead they portray African-American mothers as complex individuals who often show tremendous strength under adverse conditions, or who become beaten down by the incessant demands of providing for their families. In *A Raisin in the Sun*, the first play presented on Broadway written by a Black woman, Lorraine Hansberry (1959) examines the struggles of widow Lena Younger to actualize her dream of purchasing a home for her family. In *Brown Girl, Brownstones*, novelist Paule Marshall (1959) presents Mrs. Boyce, a Black mother negotiating a series of relationships with her husband, her daughters, the women in her community, and the work she must perform outside her home. Ann Allen Shockley's *Loving Her* (1974) depicts the struggle of a lesbian mother trying to balance her needs for self-actualization with the pressures of child-rearing in a homophobic community.

Like these fictional analyses, Black women's scholarship on Black single mothers also challenges the matriarchy thesis, but finds far fewer Lena Youngers or Mrs. Boyces (Ladner 1972; Brewer 1988; Jarrett 1994; Dickerson 1995; Kaplan 1997). In her study of Black teenage mothers, Elaine Bell Kaplan (1997) learned that the reactions of mothers to their teenaged daughters' pregnancies were far from the image of the superstrong Black mother. Mothers in the new working poor felt their pregnant teenage daughters had failed them. Until their daughters' pregnancies, these mothers hoped that their daughters would do better with their lives. The mothers who came from humble beginnings and who had worked hard to achieve a modicum of middle-class respectability felt cheated when their daughters became pregnant. Among both groups of mothers, adjusting to their daughters' pregnancies brought on much hardship.

Like the mammy, the image of the matriarch is central to intersecting oppressions of class, gender, and race. While at first glance the matriarch may appear far removed from issues in U.S. capitalist development, this image is actually important in explaining the persistence of Black social class outcomes. Assuming that Black poverty in the United States is passed on intergenerationally via the values that parents teach their children, dominant ideology suggests that Black children lack the attention and care allegedly lavished on White, middle-class children. This alleged cultural deficiency seriously retards Black children's achievement. Such a view diverts attention from political and economic inequalities that increasingly characterize global capitalism. It also suggests that anyone can rise from poverty if he or she only received good values at home. Inferior housing, underfunded schools, employment discrimination, and consumer racism all but disappear from Black women's lives. In this sanitized view of American society, those African-Americans who remain poor cause their own victimization. In this context, portraying African-American women as matriarchs allows White men and women to blame Black women for their children's failures in school and with the law, as well as Black children's subsequent poverty. Using images of bad Black mothers to explain Black economic disadvantage links gender ideology to explanations for extreme distributions of wealth that characterize American capitalism.

One source of the matriarch's failure is her inability to model appropriate gender behavior. Thus, labeling Black women unfeminine and too strong works to undercut U.S. Black women's assertiveness. Many U.S. Black women who find themselves maintaining families by themselves often feel that they have done something wrong. If only they were not so strong, some reason, they might have found a male partner, or their sons would not have had so much trouble with the law. This belief masks the culpability of the U.S. criminal justice system, described by Angela Davis (1997) as an "out of control punishment industry" that locks up a disproportionate number of U.S. Blacks. African-Americans are almost eight times more likely to be imprisoned than Whites (p. 267), a social policy that leaves far fewer men for Black women to marry than the proportion of White men available to White women. Moreover, not only does the image of the Black matriarch seek to regulate Black women's behavior, it also seems designed to influence White women's gendered identities. In the post–World War II era, increasing numbers of White women entered the labor market, limited their fertility, and generally challenged their proscribed roles as subordinate helpmates in their families and workplaces. In this context, the image of the Black matriarch serves as a powerful symbol for both Black and White women of what can go wrong if White patriarchal power is challenged. Aggressive, assertive women are penalized—they are abandoned by their men, end up impoverished, and are stigmatized as being unfeminine. The matriarch or overly strong Black woman has also been used to influence Black men's understandings of Black masculinity. Many Black men reject Black women as marital partners, claiming that Black women are less desirable than White ones because we are too assertive.

The image of the matriarch also supports racial oppression. Much social science research implicitly uses gender relations in African-American communities as one seeming measure of Black cultural disadvantage. For example, the Moynihan Report (1965) contends that slavery destroyed Black families by creating reversed roles for men and women. Black family structures are seen as being deviant because they challenge the patriarchal assumptions underpinning the traditional family ideal. Moreover, the absence of Black patriarchy is used as evidence for Black cultural inferiority (Collins 1989). Under scientific racism, Blacks have been construed as inferior, and their inferiority has been attributed either to biological causes or cultural differences. Thus, locating the source of cultural difference in flawed gender relations provides a powerful foundation for U.S. racism. Black women's failure to conform to the cult of true womanhood can then be identified as one fundamental source of Black cultural deficiency. Advancing ideas about Black cultural disadvantage via the matriarchal image worked to counter efforts by African-Americans who identified political and social policies as one important source of Black economic disadvantage. The image of Black women as dangerous, deviant, castrating mothers divided the Black community at a critical period in the Black liberation struggle. Such images fostered a similar reaction within women's political activism and created a wider gap between the worlds of Black and White women at an equally critical period in women's history (Gilkes, 1983).

Taken together, images of the mammy and the matriarch place African-American women in an untenable position. For Black women workers in service occupations requiring long hours and/or substantial emotional labor, becoming the ideal mammy means precious time and energy spent away from husbands and children. But being employed when Black men have difficulty finding steady work exposes African-American women to the charge that Black women emasculate Black men by failing to be submissive, dependent, "feminine" women. This image ignores gender-specific patterns of incorporation into the capitalist economy, where Black men have greater difficulty finding work but make higher wages when they do work, and Black women find work with greater ease yet earn much less. Moreover, Black women's financial contributions to Black family well-being have been cited as evidence supporting the matriarchy thesis (Moynihan 1965). Many Black women are the sole support of their families, and labeling these women "matriarchs" erodes their self-confidence and ability to confront oppression. In essence, African-American women who must work encounter pressures to be submissive mammies in one setting, then are stigmatized again as matriarchs for being strong figures in their own homes.

A third, externally defined, controlling image of Black womanhood—that of the welfare mother—appears tied to working-class Black women's increasing access to U.S. welfare state entitlements. At its core, the image of the welfare mother constitutes a class-specific, controlling image developed for poor, working-class Black women who make use of social welfare benefits to which they are entitled by law. As long as poor Black women were denied social welfare benefits, there was no need for this stereotype. But when U.S. Black women gained more political power and demanded equity in access to state services, the need arose for this controlling image.

Essentially an updated version of the breeder woman image created during slavery, this image provides an ideological justification for efforts to harness Black women's fertility to the needs of a changing political economy. During slavery the breeder woman image portrayed Black women as more suitable for having children than White women. By claiming that Black women were able to produce children as easily as animals, this image provided justification for interference in enslaved Africans' reproductive lives. Slave owners wanted enslaved Africans to "breed" because every slave child born represented a valuable unit of property, another unit of labor, and, if female, the prospects for more slaves. The controlling image of the breeder woman served to justify slave owners' intrusion into Black women's decisions about fertility (King 1973; Davis 1981; D. White 1985).

In the post–World War II political economy, African-Americans struggled for and gained rights denied them in former historical periods (Squires 1994). Contrary to popular belief, U.S. Black women were not "given" unearned entitlements, but instead had to struggle for rights routinely offered to other American citizens (Amott 1990; Quadagno 1994). African-Americans successfully acquired basic political and economic protections from a greatly expanded social welfare state, particularly Social Security, unemployment compensation, school feeding programs, fellowships and loans for higher education, affirmative action, voting rights, antidiscrimination legislation, child welfare programs, and the minimum wage. Despite sustained opposition by Republican administrations in the 1980s, these social welfare programs allowed many African-Americans to reject the subsistence-level, exploitative jobs held by their parents and grandparents. However, these Black citizenship rights came at a time of shrinking economic opportunities in U.S. manufacturing and agriculture. Job export, de-skilling, and increased use of illegal immigrants have all been used to replace the cheap, docile labor force that U.S. Blacks used to be (Nash and Fernandez-Kelly 1983; Brewer 1993; Squires 1994). Until the mid-1990s, the large numbers of undereducated, unemployed African-Americans ghettoized in U.S. inner cities, most of whom were women and children, could not be forced to work. This surplus population no longer represented cheap labor but instead, from the perspective of elites, signified a costly threat to political and economic stability. African-American men increasingly became targeted by a growing punishment industry (Davis 1997). In the absence of legitimate jobs, many men worked in the informal sector, serving as low-level employees of a growing, global drug industry that introduced crack cocaine into U.S. Black neighborhoods in the 1980s. For many, becoming entangled with the punishment industry was one cost of doing business.

Controlling Black women's fertility in this political and economic context became important to elite groups. The image of the welfare mother fulfills this function by labeling as unnecessary and even dangerous to the values of the country the fertility of women who are not White and middle class. A closer look at this controlling image reveals that it shares some important features with its mammy and matriarch counterparts. Like the matriarch, the welfare mother is labeled a bad mother. But unlike the matriarch, she is not too aggressive—on the contrary, she is not aggressive enough. While the matriarch's unavailability contributed to her children's poor socialization, the welfare mother's accessibility is deemed the problem. She is portrayed as being content to sit around and collect welfare, shunning work and passing on her bad values to her offspring. The image of the welfare mother represents another failed mammy, one who is unwilling to become "de mule uh de world."

The image of the welfare mother provides ideological justifications for intersecting oppressions of race, gender, and class. African-Americans can be racially stereotyped as being lazy by blaming Black welfare mothers for failing to pass on the work ethic. Moreover, the welfare mother has no male authority figure to assist her. Typically portrayed as an unwed mother, she violates one cardinal tenet of White, male-dominated ideology: She is a woman alone. As a result, her treatment reinforces the dominant gender ideology positing that a woman's true worth and financial security should occur through heterosexual marriage. Finally, on average, in the post–World War II political economy, one of every three African-American families has been officially classified as poor. With such high levels of Black poverty, welfare state policies supporting poor Black mothers and their children have become increasingly expensive. Creating the controlling image of the welfare mother and stigmatizing her as the cause of her own poverty and that of African-American communities shifts the angle of vision away from structural sources of poverty and blames the victims themselves. The image of the welfare mother thus provides ideological justification for the dominant group's interest in limiting the fertility of Black mothers who are seen as producing too many economically unproductive children (Davis 1981).

With the election of the Reagan administration in 1980, the stigmatized welfare mother evolved into the more pernicious image of the welfare queen (Lubiano 1992). To mask the effects of cuts in government spending on social welfare programs that fed children, housed working families, assisted cities in maintaining roads, bridges, and basic infrastructure, and supported other basic public services, media images increasingly identified and blamed Black women for the deterioration of U.S. interests. Thus, poor Black women simultaneously become symbols of what was deemed wrong with America and targets of social policies designed to shrink the government sector. Wahneema Lubiano describes how the image of the welfare queen links Black women with seeming declines in the quality of life:

"Welfare queen" is a phrase that describes economic dependency—the lack of a job and/or income (which equal degeneracy in the Calvinist United States); the presence of a child or children with no father and/or husband (moral deviance); and, finally, a charge on the collective U.S. treasury—a human debit. The cumulative totality, circulation, and effect of these meanings in a time of scarce resources among the working class and the lower middle class is devastatingly intense. The welfare queen represents moral aberration and an economic drain, but the figure's problematic status becomes all the more threatening once responsibility for the destruction of the American way of life is attributed to it. (Lubiano 1992, 337–38)

In contrast to the welfare mother who draws upon the moral capital attached to American motherhood, the welfare queen constitutes a highly materialistic, domineering, and manless working-class Black woman. Relying on the public dole, Black welfare queens are content to take the hard-earned money of tax-paying Americans and remain married to the state. Thus, the welfare queen image signals efforts to use the situation of working-class Black women as a sign of the deterioration of the state.

During this same period, the welfare queen was joined by another similar yet class-specific image, that of the "Black lady" (Lubiano 1992). Because the Black lady refers to middle-class professional Black women who represent a modern version of the politics of respectability advanced by the club women (Shaw 1996), this image may not appear to be a controlling image, merely a benign one. These are the women who stayed in school, worked hard, and have achieved much. Yet the image of the Black lady builds upon prior images of Black womanhood in many ways. For one thing, this image seems to be yet another version of the modern mammy, namely, the hard-working Black woman professional who works twice as hard as everyone else. The image of the Black lady also resembles aspects of the matriarchy thesis—Black ladies have jobs that are so all-consuming that they have no *time* for men or have forgotten how to treat them. Because they so routinely compete with men and are successful at it, they become less feminine. Highly educated Black ladies are deemed to be *too* assertive—that's why they cannot get men to marry them.

Upon first glance, Black ladies also seem far removed from charges of unearned dependency on the state that are so often leveled at working-class U.S. Black women via the welfare queen image. Yet here, too, parallels abound. Via affirmative action, Black ladies allegedly take jobs that should go to more worthy Whites, especially U.S. White men. Given a political climate in the 1980s and 1990s that reinterpreted antidiscrimination and affirmative action programs as examples of an unfair "reverse racism," no matter how highly educated or demonstrably competent Black ladies may be, their accomplishments remain questionable. Moreover, many Black men erroneously believe that Black ladies are taking jobs reserved for them. In their eyes, being Black, female, and seemingly less threatening to Whites advantages Black ladies. Wahneema Lubiano points out how images of the welfare queen and the Black lady evolved in tandem with persistent efforts to cut social welfare spending for working-class Blacks and limit affirmative action opportunities for middle-class Blacks: "Whether by virtue of not achieving and thus passing on bad culture as welfare mothers, or by virtue of managing to achieve middle-class success...black women are responsi-ble for the disadvantaged status of African Americans" (Lubiano 1992, 335). Thus, when taken together, the welfare queen and the Black lady constitute class-specific versions of a matriarchy thesis whose fundamental purpose is to discredit Black women's full exercise of citizenship rights. These intercon-nected images leave U.S. Black women between a rock and a hard place.

A final controlling image—the jezebel, whore, or "hoochie"—is central in this nexus of controlling images of Black womanhood. Because efforts to control Black women's sexuality lie at the heart of Black women's oppres-sion, historical jezebels and contemporary "hoochies" represent a deviant Black female sexuality. The image of jezebel originated under slavery when Black women were portrayed as being, to use Jewelle Gomez's words, "sex-ually aggressive wet nurses" (Clarke et al. 1983, 99). Jezebel's function was to relegate all Black women to the category of sexually aggressive women, thus providing a powerful rationale for the widespread sexual assaults by White men typically reported by Black slave women (Davis 1981; D. White 1985). Jezebel served yet another function. If Black slave women could be portrayed as having excessive sexual appetites, then increased fertility should be the expected outcome. By suppressing the nurturing that African-American women might give their own children which would strengthen Black family networks, and by forcing Black women to work in the field, "wet nurse" White children, and emotionally nurture their White owners, slave owners effectively tied the controlling images of jezebel and mammy to the economic exploitation inherent in the institution of slavery.

Rooted in the historical legacy of jezebel, the contemporary "hoochie" seems to be cut from an entirely different cloth. For one, whereas images of Black women as sexually aggressive certainly pervade popular culture overall, the image of the hoochie seems to have permeated everyday Black culture in entirely new ways. For example, 2 Live Crew's song "Hoochie Mama" takes Black women bashing to new heights. In this song, the group opens with the rallying cry "big booty hoes hop wit it!" and proceeds to list characteristics of the "hoodrat hoochie mama." The singers are quite clear about the use of such women: "I don't need no confrontation," they sing. "All I want is an ejaculation cos I like them ghetto hoochies." The misogyny in "Hoochie Mama" makes prior portrayals of jezebel seem tame. For exam-ple, 2 Live Crew's remedy for "lyin" shows their disdain for women: "Keep runnin ya mouth and I'ma stick my dick in it," they threaten. And for those listeners who remain confused about the difference between good and bad women, 2 Live Crew is willing to help out:

Mama just don't understand
why I love your hoochie ass
Sex is what I need you for
I gotta good girl but I need a whore

In the United States, guarantees of free speech allow 2 Live Crew and sim-ilar groups to speak their minds about "hoochies" and anything else that will make them money. The issue here lies in African-American acceptance of such images. African-American men and women alike routinely do not challenge these and other portrayals of Black women as "hoochies" within Black popular culture. For example, despite the offensive nature of much of 2 Live Crew's music, some Blacks argued that such views, while unfortunate, had long been expressed in Black culture (Crenshaw 1993). Not only does such acceptance mask how such images provide financial benefits to both 2 Live Crew and White-controlled media, such tacit acceptance validates this image. The more it circulates among U.S. Blacks, the more credence it is given. The "hoochie" image certainly seems to have taken on a life of its own. For example, an informal poll of my friends, students, and colleagues revealed a complex taxonomy of "hoochies." Most agreed that one category consisted of "plain hoochies" or sexually assertive women who can be found across social classes. Women who wear sleazy clothes to clubs and dance in a "slutty" fashion constitute "club hoochies." These women aim to attract men with money for a one-night stand. In contrast, the ambition of "gold-digging hoochies" lies in establishing a long-term relationship with a man with money. These gold-digging hoochies often aim to snare a highly paid athlete and can do so by becoming pregnant. Finally, there is the "hoochie-mama" popularized by 2 Live Crew, an image that links the hoochie image to poverty. As 2 Live Crew points out, the "hoochie mama" is a "hoodrat," a "ghetto hoochie" whose main purpose is to provide them sexual favors. The fact that she is also a "mama" speaks to the numbers of Black women in poverty who are single parents whose exchange of sexual favors for money is motivated by their children's economic needs.

Within assumptions that normalize heterosexuality, the historical jezebel and her modern "hoochie" counterpart mark a series of boundaries. Heterosexuality itself is constructed via binary thinking that juxtaposes male and female sexuality, with male and female gender roles pivoting on perceptions of appropriate male and female sexual expression. Men are active, and women should be passive. In the context of U.S. society, these become racialized—White men are active, and White women should be passive. Black people and other racialized groups simultaneously stand outside these definitions of normality and mark their boundaries. In this context of a gender-specific, White, heterosexual normality, the jezebel or hoochie becomes a racialized, gendered symbol of deviant female sexuality. Normal female heterosexuality is expressed via the cult of true White womanhood, whereas deviant female heterosexuality is typified by the "hot mommas" of Black womanhood.

Within intersecting oppressions, Black women's allegedly deviant sexuality becomes constructed around jezebel's sexual desires. Jezebel may be a "pretty baby," but her actions as a "hot momma" indicate that she just can't get enough. Because jezebel or the hoochie is constructed as a woman whose sexual appetites are at best inappropriate and, at worst, insatiable, it becomes a short step to imagine her as a "freak." And if she is a freak, her sexual partners become similarly stigmatized. For example, the hyper-masculinity often attributed to Black men reflects beliefs about Black men's excessive sexual appetite. Ironically, jezebel's excessive sexual appetite masculinizes her because she desires sex just as a man does. Moreover, jezebel can also be masculinized and once again deemed "freaky" if she desires sex with other women. 2 Live Crew had little difficulty making this conceptual leap when they sing: "Freaky shit is what I like and I love to see two bitches dyke." In a context where feminine women are those who remain submissive yet appropriately flirtatious toward men, women whose sexual aggression resembles that of men become stigmatized.

When it comes to women's sexuality, the controlling image of jezebel and her hoochie counterpart constitute one side of the normal/deviant binary. But broadening this binary thinking that underpins intersecting oppressions of race, class, gender, and sexuality reveals that heterosexuality is juxtaposed to homosexuality as its oppositional, different, and inferior "other." Within this wider oppositional difference, jezebel becomes the freak on the border demarking heterosexuality from homosexuality. Her insatiable sexual desire helps define the boundaries of normal sexuality. Just across the border stand lesbian, bisexual, and transgendered women who are deemed deviant in large part because of their choices of sexual partners. As a sexual freak, jezebel has one foot over the line. On this border, the hoochie participates in a cluster of "deviant female sexualities," some associated with the materialistic ambitions where she sells sex for money, others associated with so-called deviant sexual practices such as sleeping with other women, and still others attached to "freaky" sexual practices such as engaging in oral and anal sex.

Images of sexuality associated with jezebel and the hoochie not only mark the boundaries of deviant sexualities, they weave throughout prevailing conceptualizations of the mammy, matriarch, and the Janus-faced welfare queen/Black lady. Connecting all is the common theme of Black women's sexuality. Each image transmits distinctive messages about the proper links among female sexuality, desired levels of fertility for working-class and middle-class Black women, and U.S. Black women's placement in social class and citizenship hierarchies. For example, the mammy, one of two somewhat positive figures, is a desexed individual. The mammy is typically portrayed as overweight, dark, and with characteristically African features—in brief, as an unsuitable sexual partner for White men. She is asexual and therefore is free to become a surrogate mother to the children she acquired not through her own sexuality. The mammy represents the clearest example of the split between sexuality and motherhood present in Eurocentric masculinist thought. In contrast, both the matriarch and the welfare mother are sexual beings. But their sexuality is linked to their fertility, and this link forms one fundamental reason they are negative images. The matriarch represents the sexually aggressive woman, one who emasculates Black men because she will not permit them to assume roles as Black patriarchs. She refuses to be passive and thus is stigmatized. Similarly, the welfare mother represents a woman of low morals and uncontrolled sexuality, factors identified as the cause of her impoverished state. In both cases Black female control over sexuality and fertility is conceptualized as antithetical to elite White male interests. The Black lady completes the circle. Like mammy, her hard-earned, middle-class respectability is grounded in her seeming asexuality. Yet fertility is an issue here as well. Despite the fact that the middle-class Black lady is the woman deemed best suited to have children, in actuality, she remains the least likely to do so. She is told that she can reproduce, but no one except her is especially disturbed if she does not.

Taken together, these prevailing images of Black womanhood represent elite White male interests in defining Black women's sexuality and fertility. Moreover, by meshing smoothly with intersecting oppressions of race, class, gender, and sexuality, they help justify the social practices that characterize the matrix of domination in the United States.

CONTROLLING IMAGES AND SOCIAL INSTITUTIONS

Schools, the news media, and government agencies constitute important sites for reproducing these controlling images. Whereas schools and the scholarship produced and disseminated by their faculty historically have played an important part in generating these controlling images (Morton 1991), their current significance in reproducing these images is less often noted. Take, for example, how social science research on Black women's sexuality has been influenced by assumptions of the jezebel. Two topics, both deemed as social problems, take the lion's share—Black women's sexuality appears within AIDS research and within scholarship on adolescent pregnancy. Both reference two types of allegedly deviant sexuality with an eye toward altering Black women's behavior. In AIDS research, the focus is on risky sexual practices that might expose women, their unborn children, and their partners to HIV infection. Prostitutes and other sex workers are of special concern. The underlying reason for studying Black adolescent sexuality may lie in helping the girls, but an equally plausible stimulus lies in desires to get these girls off the public dole. Their sexuality is not that of risky sexual practices, but sexuality outside the confines of marriage. Embedding research on Black women's sexuality within social problems frameworks thus fosters its portrayal as a social problem.

The growing influence of television, radio, movies, videos, CDs, and the Internet constitute new ways of circulating controlling images. Popular culture has become increasingly important in promoting these images, especially with new global technologies that allow U.S. popular culture to be exported throughout the world. Within this new corporate structure, the misogyny in some strands of Black hip-hop music becomes especially troubling. Much of this music is produced by a Black culture industry in which African-American artists have little say in production. On the one hand,

Black rap music can be seen as a creative response to racism by Black urban youth who have been written off by U.S. society (Rose 1994; Kelley 1997, 43–77). On the other hand, images of Black women as sexually available hoochies persist in Black music videos. As "freaks," U.S. Black women can now be seen "poppin' that coochie"—yet another term by 2 Live Crew that describes butt shaking—in global context.

Government agencies also play a part in legitimating these controlling images. Because legislative bodies and, in the case of 2 Live Crew's obscenity trial (see, e.g., Crenshaw 1993), courts determine which narratives are legitimated and which remain censured, government agencies decide which official interpretations of social reality prevail (Van Dijk 1993). The inordinate attention paid to Black adolescent pregnancy and parenting in scholarly research and the kinds of public policy initiatives that target Black girls illustrate the significance of government support for controlling images. Because assumptions of sexual hedonism are routinely applied to Black urban girls, they are more likely to be offered coercive birth control measures, such as Norplant and Depo Provera than their White, suburban, middle-class counterparts (Roberts 1997).

Confronting the controlling images forwarded by institutions external to African-American communities remains essential. But such efforts should not obscure the equally important issue of examining how African-American institutions also perpetuate these same controlling images. Although it may be painful to examine—especially in the context of a racially charged society always vigilant for signs of Black disunity—the question of how the organizations of Black civil society reproduce controlling images of Black womanhood and fail to take a stand against images developed elsewhere is equally important.

Since 1970, U.S. Black women have become increasingly vocal in criticizing sexism in Black civil society (Wallace 1978; E.F. White 1984; Cleage 1993; Crenshaw 1993). For example, Black feminist Pauline Terrelonge confronts the issue of the Black community's role in the subordination of African-American women by asking, "If there is much in the objective condition of black women that warrants the development of a black feminist consciousness, why have so many black women failed to recognize the patterns of sexism that directly impinge on their everyday lives?" (1984, 562). To answer this question, Terrelonge contends that a common view is that African-Americans have withstood the long line of abuses perpetuated against us mainly because of Black women's "fortitude, inner wisdom, and sheer ability to survive." Connected to this emphasis on the strength of Black women is the related argument that African-American women play critical roles in keeping Black families together and in supporting Black men. These activities have been important in preventing the potential annihilation of African-Americans as a "race." As a result, "many blacks regard the role of uniting all blacks to be the primary duty of the black woman, one that should supersede all other roles that she might want to perform, and certainly one that is essentially incompatible with her own individual liberation" (p. 557).

This analysis shifts our understanding of Black community organizations. Rather than seeing family, church, and Black civic organizations through a race-only lens of resisting racism, such institutions may be better understood as complex sites where dominant ideologies are simultaneously resisted and reproduced. Black community organizations can oppose racial oppression yet perpetuate gender oppression, can challenge class exploitation yet foster heterosexism. One might ask where within Black civil society African-American women can openly challenge the hoochie image and other equally controlling images. Institutions controlled by African-Americans can be seen as contradictory sites where Black women learn skills of independence and self-reliance that enable African-American families, churches, and civic organizations to endure. But these same institutions may also be places where Black women learn to subordinate our interests as women to the allegedly greater good of the larger African-American community.

Take, for example, historically Black colleges and universities. In their goal of dispelling the myths about African-American women and making Black women acceptable to wider society, some historically Black colleges may also foster Black women's subordination. In *Meridian* Alice Walker describes an elite college for Black women where "most of the students—timid, imitative, bright enough but never daring—were being ushered nearer to Ladyhood every day" (1976, 39). Confined to campus, Meridian, the heroine, had to leave to find the ordinary Black people who exhibited all of the qualities that her elite institution wished to eliminate. Walker's description of the fence surrounding the campus symbolizes how stultifying the cult of true womanhood was for Black students. But it also describes the problems that African-American institutions create for Black women when they embrace externally defined controlling images:

> The fence that surrounded the campus was hardly noticeable from the street and appeared, from the outside, to be more of an attempt at ornamentation than an effort to contain or exclude. Only the students who lived on campus learned, often painfully, that the beauty of a fence is no guarantee that it will not keep one penned in as securely as one that is ugly. (Walker 1976, 41)

Jacquelyn Grant (1982) identifies the church as one key institution whose centrality to Black community development may have come at the expense of many of the African-American women who constitute the bulk of its membership. Grant asserts, "it is often said that women are the 'backbone' of the church. On the surface, this may appear to be a compliment.... It has become apparent to me that most of the ministers who use this term are referring to location rather than function. What they really mean is that women are in the 'background' and should be kept there" (1982, 141). At the same time, Black churches have clearly been highly significant in Black political struggle, with U.S. Black women central to those efforts. Historically, Black women's participation in Black Baptist and other Black churches suggests that Black women have been the backbone yet have resisted staying totally in the "background" (Gilkes 1985; Higginbotham 1993). One wonders, however, if contemporary Black churches are equipped to grapple with the new questions raised by the global circulation of the hoochie and comparable images. Denouncing "hoochies" and all they represent from the pulpit with a cautionary warning "don't be one" simply is not enough.

African-American families form another contradictory location where the controlling images of Black womanhood become negotiated. Middle-class White feminists seemingly have had few qualms in criticizing how their families perpetuate women's subordination (see, for example, Chodorow 1978). Until recently, however, because Black families have been so pathologized by the traditional family ideal, Black women have been reluctant to analyze in public the potential culpability of families in Black women's oppression. Black women thinkers have been more uniformly positive when describing Black families, and much more reluctant to criticize Black family organization than their White counterparts. As a result, Black studies emphasizes material that, although it quite rightly demonstrates the strengths of U.S. Black families in a context of intersecting oppressions, skims over problems (see, e.g., Billingsley 1992). But this emphasis on strengths has often come at a cost, and that cost has far too often been paid by African-American women. Thus, within Black feminist scholarship, we are finally hearing not only the long-hidden stories of those strong Black women (Joseph 1981; Collins 1987), but those of women whose gendered family responsibilities cause them trouble (Richie 1996; Kaplan 1997).

Some Black feminist activists claim that relegating Black women to more submissive, supporting roles in African-American organizations has been an obstacle to Black political empowerment. Black nationalist philosophies, in particular, have come under attack for their ideas about Black women's place in political struggle (White 1990; Lubiano 1997; Williams 1997; Collins 1998, 155–86). In describing the 1960s nationalist movement, Pauli Murray contends that many Black men misinterpreted Black women's qualities of self-reliance and independence by tacitly accepting the matriarchy thesis. Such a stance was and is highly problematic for Black women. Murray observes, "The black militant's cry for the retrieval of black manhood suggests an acceptance of this stereotype, an association of masculinity with male dominance and a tendency to treat the values of self-reliance and independence as purely masculine traits" (1970, 89). Echoing Murray, Sheila Radford-Hill (1986) sees Black women's subordination in African-American institutions as a continuing concern. For Radford-Hill the erosion of Black women's traditional power bases in African-American communities which followed nationalist movements is problematic in that "Black macho constituted a betrayal by black men; a psychosexual rejection of black women experienced as the capstone to our fall from cultural power.... Without the power to influence the purpose and direction of our collective experience, without the power to influence our culture from within, we are increasingly immobilized" (p. 168).

NOTES

1. Dona Richards (1980) offers an insightful analysis of the relationship between Christianity's contributions to an ideology of domination and the culture/nature binary. She notes that European Christianity is predicated on a worldview that sustains the exploitation of nature: "Christian thought provides a view of man, nature, and the universe which supports not only the ascendancy of science, but of the technical order, individualism, and relentless progress. Emphasis within this worldview is placed on humanity's dominance over *all* other beings, which become 'objects' in an 'objectified' universe. There is no emphasis on an awe-inspiring God or cosmos. Being 'made in God's image,' given the European ethos, translates into 'acting *as* God,' recreating the universe. Humanity is separated from nature" (p. 69). For works exploring the connections among Western thought, colonialism, and capitalism, see works by Marianna Torgovnick (1990), Rey Chow (1993), Edward Said (1993), and Anne McClintock (1995).

2. Brittan and Maynard (1984) note that ideology (1) is common sense and obvious; (2) appears natural, inevitable, and universal; (3) shapes lived experience and behavior; (4) is sedimented in people's consciousness; and (5) consists of a system of ideas embedded in the social system as a whole. This example captures all dimensions of how racism and sexism function ideologically. The status of Black woman as servant is so "common sense" that even a child knows it. That the child saw a Black female child as a baby maid speaks to the naturalization dimension and to the persistence of controlling images in individual consciousness and the social system overall.

REFERENCES

Amott, Teresa L. 1990. "Black Women and AFDC: Making Entitlement Out of Necessity." In *Women, the State, and Welfare*, ed. Linda Gordon, 280–98. Madison; University of Wisconsin Press.

Bannerji, Himani. 1995. *Thinking Through: Essays on Feminism, Marxism, and Anti-Racism*. Toronto: Women's Press.

Billingsley, Andrew. 1992. *Black Families in White America*. Englewood Cliffs, NJ: Prentice Hall.

Brewer, Rose. 1988. "Black Women in Poverty: Some Comments on Female-Headed Families." *Signs* 13(2):331–39.

———. 1993. "Theorizing Race, Class and Gender: The New Scholarship of Black Feminist Intellectuals and Black Women's Labor." In *Theorizing Black Feminisms: The Visionary Pragmatism of Black Women*, ed. Stanlie M. James and Abena P.A. Busia, 13–30. New York: Routledge.

Brittan, Arthur, and Mary Maynard. 1984. *Sexism, Racism and Oppression*. New York: Basil Blackwell.

Byerly, Victoria. 1986. *Hard Times Cotton Mills Girls*. Ithaca, NY: Cornell University Press.

Carby, Hazel. 1987. *Reconstructing Womanhood: The Emergence of the Afro-American Woman Novelist*. New York: Oxford University Press.

Chodorow, Nancy. 1978. *The Reproduction of Mothering*. Berkeley: University of California Press.

Chow, Rey. 1993. *Writing Diaspora: Tactics of Intervention in Contemporary Cultural Studies*. Bloomington: Indiana University Press.

Christian, Barbara. 1985. *Black Feminist Criticism, Perspectives on Black Women Writers*. New York: Pergamon.

Clarke, Cheryl. 1983. "The Failure to Transform: Homophobia in the Black Community." In *Home Girls: A Black Feminist Anthology*, ed. Barbara Smith, 197–208. New York: Kitchen Table Press.

Cleage, Pearl. 1993. *Deals With the Devil and Other Reasons to Riot*. New York: Ballantine.

Collins, Patricia Hill. 1989. "A Comparison of Two Works on Black Family Life." *Signs* 14(4):875–84.

———. 1998. *Fighting Words: Black Women and the Search for Justice*. Minneapolis: University of Minnesota Press.

Crenshaw, Kimberle Williams. 1993. "Beyond Racism and Misogyny: Black Feminism and 2 Live Crew." In *Words that Wound: Critical Race Theory, Assaultive Speech, and the First Amendment*, ed. Mari J. Matsudea, Charles R. Lawrence III, Richard Delgado, and Kimberle Crenshaw, 111–32. Boulder: Westview.

Davis, Angela Y. 1981. *Women, Race and Class*. New York: Random House.

———. 1997. "Race and Criminalization: Black Americans and the Punishment Industry." In *The House That Race Built*, ed. Wahneema Lubiano, 264–79. New York: Pantheon.

Dickerson, Bette J., ed. 1995. *African American Single Mothers: Understanding Their Lives and Families*. Thousand Oaks, CA: Sage.

Dill, Bonnie Thornton. 1980. " 'The Means to Put My Children Through': Child-Rearing Goals and Strategies among Black Female Domestic Servants." In *The Black Woman*, ed. La Frances Rodgers-Rose, 107–23. Beverly Hills, CA: Sage.

———. 1988. "Our Mothers' Grief: Racial Ethnic Women and the Maintenance of Families." *Journal of Family History* 13(4):415–31.

Du Bois, William E. B. 1969. *The Negro American Family*. New York: Negro Universities Press.

Dumas, Rhetaugh Graves. 1980. "Dilemmas of Black Females in Leadership." In *The Black Woman*, ed. La Frances Rodgers-Rose, 203–15. Beverly Hills, CA: Sage.

Frazier, E. Franklin. 1948. *The Negro Family in the United States*. New York: Dryden.

Gilkes, Cheryl. 1983. "From Slavery to Social Welfare: Racism and the Control of Black Women." In *Class, Race, and Sex: The Dynamics of Control*, ed. Amy Swerdlow and Hanna Lessinger, 288–300. Boston: G. K. Hall.

———. 1985. " 'Together and in Harness': Women's Traditions in the Sanctified Church." *Signs* 10(4):678–99.

Grant, Jacquelyn. 1982. "Black Women and the Church." In *But Some of Us Are Brave*, ed. Gloria T. Hull, Patricia Bell Scott, and Barbara Smith, 141–52. Old Westbury, NY: Feminist Press.

Gwaltney, John Langston. 1980. *Drylongso, A Self-Portrait of Black America*. New York: Vintage.

Halpin, Zuleyma Tang. 1989. "Scientific Objectivity and the Concept of 'The Other.' " *Women's Studies International Forum* 12(3):285–94.

Hansberry, Lorraine. 1959. *A Raisin in the Sun*. New York: Signet.

Harris, Trudier. 1982. *From Mammies to Militants: Domestics in Black American Literature*. Philadelphia: Temple University Press.

Higginbotham, Evelyn Brooks. 1993. *Righteous Discontent: The Women's Movement in the Black Baptist Church, 1880–1920*. Cambridge, MA: Harvard University Press.

hooks, bell. 1989. *Talking Back: Thinking Feminist, Thinking Black*. Boston: South End Press.

Jarrett, Robin. 1994. "Living Poor: Family Life Among Single Parent, African American Women." *Social Problems* 41(February):30–49.

Joseph, Gloria. 1981. "Black Mothers and Daughters: Their Roles and Functions in American Society." In *Common Differences*, ed. Gloria Joseph and Jill Lewis, 75–126. Garden City, NY: Anchor.

Kaplan, Elaine Bell. 1997. *Not Our Kind of Girl: Unraveling the Myths of Black Teenage Motherhood*. Berkeley, CA: University of California Press.

Keller, Evelyn Fox. 1985. *Reflections on Gender and Science*. New Haven, CT: Yale University Press.

Kelley, Robin D. G. 1997. *Yo' Mama's Disfunktional!: Fighting the Culture Wars in Urban America*. Boston: Beacon Press.

King, Mae. 1973. "The Politics of Sexual Stereotypes." *Black Scholar* 4(6–7):12–23.

Ladner, Joyce. 1972. *Tomorrow's Tomorrow*. Garden City, NY: Doubleday.

Lorde, Audre. 1982. Zami, *A New Spelling of My Name*. Trumansberg, NY: Crossing Press.

Lubiano, Wahneema. 1992. "Black Ladies, Welfare Queens, and State Minstrels: Ideological War by Narrative Means." In *Race-ing Justice, En-Gendering Power*, ed. Toni Morrison, 323–63. New York: Pantheon.

———. 1997. "Black Nationalism and Black Common Sense: Policing Ourselves." In *The House That Race Built: Black Americans, U.S. Terrain*, ed. Wahneema Lubiano, 232–52. New York: Pantheon.

Marshall, Paule. 1959. *Brown Girl, Brownstones*. New York: Avon.

McClintock, Anne. 1995. *Imperial Leather: Race, Gender and Sexuality in the Colonial Conquest*. New York: Routledge.

Morton, Patricia. 1991. *Disfigured Images: The Historical Assault on Afro–American Women*. New York: Praeger.

Moynihan, Daniel Patrick. 1965. *The Negro Family: The Case for National Action*. Washington, D.C.: Government Printing Office.

Mullings, Leith. 1997. *On Our Own Terms: Race, Class, and Gender in the Lives of African American Women*. New York: Routledge.

Murray, Pauli. 1970. "The Liberation of Black Women." In *Voices of the New Feminism*, ed. Mary Lou Thompson, 87–102. Boston: Beacon.

Myers, Lena Wright. 1980. *Black Women: Do They Cope Better?* Englewood Cliffs, NJ: Prentice-Hall.

Nash, June, and Maria Patricia Fernandez-Kelly, eds. 1983. *Women, Men and the International Division of Labor*. Albany: State University of New York.

Omi, Michael, and Howard Winant. 1994. *Racial Formation in the United States: From the 1960s to the 1990s, Second Edition*. New York: Routledge.

Omolade, Barbara. 1994. *The Rising Song of African American Women*. New York: Routledge.

Quadagno, Jill. 1994. *The Color of Welfare: How Racism Undermined the War on Poverty*. New York: Oxford University Press.

Radford-Hill, Sheila. 1986. "Considering Feminism as a Model for Social Change." In *Feminist Studies/Critical Studies*, ed. Teresa de Lauretis, 157–72. Bloomington: Indiana University Press.

Richards, Dona. 1980. "European Mythology: The Ideology of 'Progress.' " In *Contemporary Black Thought*, ed. Molefi Kete Asante and Abdulai S. Vandi, 59–79. Beverly Hills, CA: Sage.

Richie, Beth E. 1996. *Compelled to Crime: The Gender Entrapment of Battered Black Women*. New York: Routledge.

Roberts, Dorothy. 1997. *Killing the Black Body: Race, Reproduction, and the Meaning of Liberty*. New York: Pantheon.

Rollins, Judith. 1985. *Between Women, Domestics and Their Employers*. Philadelphia: Temple University Press.

Rose, Tricia. 1994. *Black Noise: Rap Music and Black Culture in Contemporary America*. Hanover, NH: Wesleyan University Press.

Said, Edward W. 1993. *Culture and Imperialism*. New York: Knopf.

Shaw, Stephanie J. 1996. *What a Woman Ought to Be and to Do: Black Professional Women Workers During the Jim Crow Era*. Chicago: University of Chicago.

Shockley, Ann Allen. 1974. *Loving Her*. Tallahassee, FL: Naiad Press.

Squires, Gregory D. 1994. *Capital and Communities in Black and White: The Intersections of Race, Class, and Uneven Development*. Albany: State University of New York Press.

Sudarkasa, Niara. 1981. "Interpreting the African Heritage in Afro-American Family Organization." In *Black Families*, ed. Harriette Pipes McAdoo, 37–53. Beverly Hills, CA: Sage.

Terrelonge, Pauline. 1984. "Feminist Consciousness and Black Women." In *Women: A Feminist Perspective*, 3d ed., ed. Jo Freeman, 557–67. Palo Alto, CA: Mayfield.

Torgovnick, Marianna. 1990. *Gone Primitive: Savage Intellects, Modern Lives*. Chicago: University of Chicago Press.

2 Live Crew. 1995. "Hoochie Mama." Friday Original Soundtrack: Priority Records.

Van Dijk, Teun A. 1993. *Elite Discourse and Racism*. Newbury Park, CA: Sage.

Walker, Alice. 1976. *Meridian*. New York: Pocket Books.

Wallace, Michele. 1978. *Black Macho and the Myth of the Superwoman*. New York: Dial Press.

White, Deborah Gray. 1985. *Ar'n't I a Woman? Female Slaves in the Plantation South*. New York: W. W. Norton.

White, E. Frances. 1984. "Listening to the Voices of Black Feminism." *Radical America* 18(2–3):7–25.

———. 1990. "Africa on My Mind: Gender, Counter Discourse and African-American Nationalism." *Journal of Women's History* 2(Spring):73–97.

White, Evelyn. ed. 1994. *The Black Women's Health Book: Speaking for Ourselves*. Seattle: Seal Press.

Williams, Patricia J. 1995. *The Rooster's Egg: On the Persistence of Prejudice*. Cambridge, MA: Harvard University Press.

Williams, Rhonda. 1997. "Living at the Crossroads: Explorations in Race, Nationality, Sexuality, and Gender." In *The House That Race Built: Black Americans, U.S. Terrain*, ed. Wahneema Lubiano, 136–56. New York: Pantheon.

Excerpt from *Families that Work: Policies for Reconciling Parenthood and Employment*

JANET C. GORNICK AND MARCIA K. MEYERS

American families are struggling. In the United States, fragmented contemporary discourses about the family cast these struggles alternately as the failure of parents to provide adequately for their children, as the difficulties women encounter in finding a balance between the demands of the workplace and the home, or as the failure of society to achieve the ideal of gender equality envisioned by many feminists. Each of these fragments captures an important dimension of the struggle. Yet they fail to suggest satisfactory solutions because they fail to situate families' dilemmas in a broader context.

The ongoing struggle of many families to find a manageable and equitable balance between work life and family life is rooted in a long history of gendered divisions of labor and in the United States' resolutely private conception of caregiving work. The contemporary social and economic organization of the American family has been shaped by two hundred years of dramatic change in the nature and location of economic activity and in gender roles. As first men and later women moved into waged work, families have had to create new arrangements for the unpaid domestic and caregiving work that has traditionally been performed by women. Although society as a whole has continued to reap the benefits of women's care work, we have done little, collectively, to help defray its costs. Families, and particularly women, have been left to craft private solutions that have exacerbated gender inequality and created new social problems.

The contemporary family model—highly gendered partial specialization between men and women—has created new demands in the form of a time crunch for families and a disproportionate caregiving burden for women.

The limited provisions of the American welfare state, combined with the widespread view that caregiving is a private concern, have left families to devise their own resolutions to these tensions. These private solutions have had serious consequences for gender equality and for family and child well-being.

The growth in married mothers' employment and the rise of single parenthood have fundamentally altered the profile of American families. Women's employment has reduced their presence in the home, in much the same way that the presence of men had been reduced a hundred years earlier (Goldscheider 2002). In 1930 only a minority of children lived in families in which both parents worked for pay; 55 percent lived in a two-parent family with a breadwinner father and homemaker mother. By the end of the century, a two-parent, single-earner family was the exception rather than the rule: 70 percent of children lived in a family in which both parents or the single parent were in the workforce (Hernandez 1994).

The social and economic organization of the American family changed dramatically during the latter half of the twentieth century. In terms of gender equality, however, the transformation was incomplete. The male-breadwinner–female-homemaker model rested on a nearly complete specialization of economic roles within those families that could afford to have a full-time homemaker. It has been replaced by a new arrangement in which most men invest their time primarily in earning while many women split their time between earning and caregiving. In economic terms, total specialization has been replaced by partial specialization. Partial specialization has created new opportunities for women to join men in the "public sphere" of commercial and civic activity, but it has not been accompanied by a corresponding shift of men's time from the labor market to the "private sphere" of caregiving in the home.

To understand the implications for American families, it is necessary to review another chapter of American history. The demise of the traditional family, the competing demands on parents, and continued gender inequality are problems not unique to the United States. The economic and social transformations of the past two centuries have created unprecedented opportunities and expectations for women and new challenges for families in all of the industrialized countries. In many countries that industrialized at about the same time as the United States, however, particularly the countries of western and northern Europe, these transformations have been accompanied by the development of welfare state programs and collective-bargaining arrangements that shift a portion of the cost of caregiving from the family to the larger society. The United States has lagged behind its European counterparts in welfare state development and industrial relations for more than a century, creating a legacy that defines caregiving in exceptionally private terms.

Between 1880 and 1930, the first large-scale welfare state programs were enacted in Europe, largely in response to new and heightened forms of economic insecurity resulting from industrialization and urbanization. By the early 1930s, when an economic downturn swept through Europe, nearly all countries had enacted most of the four broad programs that would become the core of the European welfare state: old-age, disability, and survivors' pensions; workers' compensation; unemployment compensation; and health, sickness, and maternity benefits. In the 1930s and 1940s, the later-developing European welfare states established the rest of these programs, and nearly all countries added a fifth—family allowances. By 1960, the last of the major European welfare states had enacted a family allowance program (Hicks 1999).

In comparison with most of the European countries, the United States has been characterized as having a reluctant, residual, or only partial welfare state (Katz 1986, 1989; Patterson 1986; Trattner 1994). While most European countries were developing universal social protections for their citizens, the United States continued its colonial tradition of localized, charity-based assistance for the "deserving poor" and forced work—or destitution—for those considered able-bodied and undeserving of charity. During the first two decades of the twentieth century, several of the American states established public income supports, including workers' compensation and mothers' pensions, but the national government took no substantial responsibility for protecting Americans from economic hardship. In 1935, largely as a response to the Depression, the United States became one of the last Western countries to establish national programs of old-age pensions and unemployment insurance; survivors' and disability were added later. When the architects of the New Deal initiated the American welfare state, however, they opted out of crucial elements of the European policy package—including national health insurance, sickness pay, and maternity benefits. In subsequent years, when family allowances were established across Europe, policy makers in the United States once again chose not to follow suit.

The American state has taken a much more confined role in supporting families, especially families with children below school age. Outside of public education, the public sector in the United States has largely resisted redistributing the costs of child rearing. While the European countries were adding universal family allowances, the United States pieced together means-tested (and now time-limited) cash assistance for poor families, supplemented by modest child credits for families with tax liabilities and (later) a refundable Earned Income Tax Credit (EITC) for low-income employed parents. While many of the countries of Europe were establishing child- or parent-based entitlements to public child care, the United States developed a child care market for parents who could afford to purchase substitute care and limited public programs for poor families. While our European counterparts were enacting paid family leave schemes, the United States left the vast majority of workers to negotiate with their employers for wage replacement following childbirth.

The extent to which the United States lags behind the social-welfare states of Europe in using the power of government to socialize some of the costs of caregiving is neatly summarized in a comparison of expenditures

TABLE 21–1 Cash Benefits for Families, 1998

Country	Expenditures as Share of GDP (Percentage)	Expenditures per Child Under the Age of Eighteen
Nordic Countries		
Denmark	1.5	$1,822
Finland	1.9	$1,883
Norway	2.2	$2,249
Sweden	1.6	$1,417
Continental Countries		
Belgium	2.1	$2,265
France	1.5	$1,390
Germany	2.0	$2,247
Luxembourg	2.4	$4,270
Netherlands	0.8	$884
English-Speaking Countries		
Canada	0.8	$793
United Kingdom	1.7	$1,557
United States	0.5	$650

Sources: Expenditures data from OECD (2001); population data from U.S. Bureau of the Census (2002).

Note: Expenditures include cash benefits for families, that is, programs targeted on families (family allowances for children, family support benefits, and lone-parent cash benefits) as well as paid family leave and refundable tax credits for families. Approximately 60 percent of the expenditures in the United States is accounted for by the EITC. Expenditures are in 2000 $U.S., PPP-adjusted.

on family-related benefits, including family allowances, family-support benefits, lone-parent allowances, paid family leave, and refundable tax credits for families (see Table 21–1). Most of the European welfare states spend in the range of 1.5 to 2.2 percent of gross domestic product (GDP) on these family cash programs; that translates to about $1,400 to $2,300 for each child under the age of 18. The United States, in contrast, spends only 0.5 percent of GDP (including the EITC), and average spending for each child is just $650.

THE RESPONSE OF FAMILIES: PRIVATE SOLUTIONS

The reluctant American welfare state, combined with the weak collective-bargaining strength of American workers, does little to redistribute the costs of caring for children or to support families who are combining employment and caregiving. In the United States, far more than in most European countries, families have been left to their own devices to craft solutions to the demands of balancing work in the home and in the labor market. More parents work for pay than a generation ago, and many are at work for more hours, yet their responsibilities in the home remain largely unchanged. Parents (mostly mothers) are expected to provide care for children and other family members without compensation and generally without adjustments in employment schedules. They are expected to find alternative care and supervision for children while they themselves are at work, largely without assistance from government. Families are left to craft private solutions when paid work and child rearing create competing demands on their resources.

Gender Inequalities in the Labor Market

One of the most significant problems associated with private solutions to work-family dilemmas is that women's withdrawal from employment to care for children (and to perform other domestic work) reinforces deep and costly gender inequalities in employment. Table 21–2 compares the average employment hours of American mothers and fathers as of 2000. (These averages include parents employed for zero hours—that is, they conflate gender differences in both employment rates and hours.) What is perhaps most striking is the constancy of fathers' hours with respect to the ages of their children. Fathers in two-parent families work for pay an average of forty-four hours a week, regardless of the ages of their children. In sharp contrast, partnered mothers' hours fall steadily with their children's ages and, presumably, the children's needs for care and supervision. As a result, fathers' weekly hours in the labor market exceed those of mothers across all children's age groups—and by as much as twenty hours a week for those with the youngest children.

Anecdotal evidence often attributes gender gaps in employment only to the most advantaged families (because women can afford to opt out of employment) or to those who are less advantaged (because women have fewer incentives to enter employment). A disaggregation of the data suggests otherwise. Gender gaps are similar when we compare women and men in families at different income levels (Table 21–2). In every income group, fathers' hours are largely invariant across the stages of childhood, whereas mothers adjust their labor force attachments to the demands of parenthood. Similar patterns emerge when the data are disaggregated by education (Table 21–3); fathers at every educational level spend substantially more time in the labor market than do their female partners.[1]

These care-related reductions in employment have far-reaching consequences for women. When women weaken their labor force ties to provide care work at home, they incur penalties in wages and opportunities for advancement that last well beyond the early child-rearing years. These employment reductions are the primary factor underlying gender inequality in both employment and earnings. Ann Crittenden (2001) has labeled the reduction in earnings owing to women's disproportionate caregiving responsibilities the "mommy tax" (Crittenden 2001). A number of researchers have estimated the magnitude of this tax. One approach examines the hourly wage penalty associated with motherhood. Jane Waldfogel (1998),

TABLE 21-2 Average Weekly Hours Spent in Market Work by Mothers and Fathers in Two-Parent Families, by Income Quartile, 2000

Age of Youngest Child (Years)	Mothers (A)	Fathers (B)	Total (A + B)	Difference (B − A)
All two-parent families				
Birth to two	24	44	68	20
Three to five	24	44	68	20
Six to twelve	28	44	72	16
Thirteen to seventeen	31	44	75	13
Low-income families				
(bottom quartile)				
Birth to two	16	40	56	24
Three to five	19	39	58	20
Six to twelve	21	38	59	17
Thirteen to seventeen	22	35	57	13
Middle-income families				
(middle two quartiles)				
Birth to two	26	45	71	19
Three to five	26	44	70	18
Six to twelve	30	44	74	14
Thirteen to seventeen	32	43	75	11
High-income families				
(top quartile)				
Birth to two	27	47	74	20
Three to five	27	47	74	20
Six to twelve	30	47	77	17
Thirteen to seventeen	34	48	82	14

Source: Authors' calculations, based on data from CPS.

Note: Data refer to parents aged twenty-five to fifty. Hours refer to "usual hours worked per week," exclusive of commuting time and lunch breaks. Average hours include persons spending zero hours in market work.

for example, finds that after controlling for various individual characteristics, young childless women earned 90 percent as much as men, but mothers earned only 70 percent as much as men. Using longitudinal data and a research design that rules out capturing spurious effects, Michelle Budig and Paula England (2001) estimate that mothers pay a wage penalty of about 5 percent an hour for each child.

Other researchers have estimated the mommy tax as the total reduction in earnings over a woman's entire working life. Crittenden (2001) estimates that the total lost earnings over the working life of a college-educated woman can easily top $1,000,000. In a middle-income family—for example, one in which a father earns $30,000 a year in full-time work and a mother $15,000 in part-time work—the mommy tax will still exceed $600,000. Although the mommy tax is highest for highly educated women, who can command high

TABLE 21–3 Average Weekly Hours Spent in Market Work, Mothers and Fathers in Two-Parent Families, by Educational Level, 2000

	Mothers (A)	Fathers (B)	Total (A + B)	Difference (B – A)
Less than high school	21	39	60	18
High school graduate	27	42	69	15
Some college	28	43	71	15
College graduate	27	45	72	18
Postgraduate degree	30	47	77	17

Source: Authors' calculations, based on data from CPS.

Note: Data refer to parents aged twenty-five to fifty. Hours refer to "usual hours worked per week," exclusive of commuting time and lunch breaks. Average hours include persons spending zero hours in market work.

market wages, it exacerbates gender inequality in the labor market at all levels of income. For families at the bottom of the skills and earnings distributions, particularly single-mother families, it greatly heightens the risk of economic instability and poverty. As Crittenden suggests, "There is increasing evidence in the United States and worldwide that mothers' differential responsibility for children, rather than classic sex discrimination, is the most important factor disposing women to poverty" (Crittenden 2001, 88).

In sharp contrast, men's lesser engagement in care work advantages them in the labor market. A recent study by Hyunbae Chun and Injae Lee (2001), for example, finds that having a wife raises a married man's hourly wage by about 12 percent on average and by more than 30 percent if the wife is a stay-at-home partner. They conclude that wage gains for men are explained by the degree of specialization within marriage. In other words, it is not the selection of high-ability (and potentially high-earning) men into marriage that explains the marriage wage premium; rather, it is the likelihood that wives shoulder a significant share of household tasks.

The resulting differences in mothers' and fathers' earnings are immense. Among working-age adults with no children, American women take home 41 percent of all labor market earnings each year; among married parents with children, however, women command only 28 percent of total labor market earnings (authors' calculations, based on CPS 2000). This means that among families with children, fathers earn almost three dollars for every one earned by mothers. In families headed by couples, this inequality translates into wives' economic dependency and unequal power in the home.[2] In single-parent families, which are overwhelmingly headed by women, it translates into lower incomes and higher poverty rates. For older women, who have contributed less to public and private retirement pensions during their working years, it heightens the risk of economic insecurity.[3]

The concentration of women's work in the home has other, noneconomic consequences as well. Men's lesser engagement in the home not only

advantages them in the labor market; it also invests them with disproportionate power in the family and positions them to engage more fully in
civic and political activities. As the British sociologist Ruth Lister observes,
"Women's caring and domestic responsibilities in the private sphere make
it very difficult for many of them to participate as citizens in the public
sphere" (Lister 1990, 457). Women without strong ties to paid work are
less likely to participate in civic activities such as arts and cultural groups,
neighborhood or civic groups, and volunteer work (Caiazza and Hartmann
2001). Robert Putnam (2000) finds, similarly, that working inside the home
reduces women's participation in public forms of civic engagement.

Gender Inequalities in the Home

Private solutions to work-family demands that rest on women's disproportionate assumption of household and caregiving work have other problematic consequences. Although women's hours of unpaid work have declined
with rising employment, their hours in domestic work and caregiving at
home continue to exceed men's by a large margin. This leaves many mothers with more total work time and less leisure time than either childless
women or men. Moreover, though the cost of gender specialization in the
home appears to be steepest for women, men also pay a price, in the form
of absences from their children's lives.

Women's disproportionate assumption of caregiving work leaves
them little time for other activities when they have dependent children.
As described earlier in this chapter, many mothers adjust to the presence
of children by reducing their hours in market work. Mothers who are
employed also appear to manage the time demands of the workplace and
their children by reducing hours devoted to everything else (Robinson and
Godbey 1997; Bianchi 2000). Employed mothers spend more than seven
fewer hours each week on housework than their nonemployed counterparts. Employed mothers also spend less time sleeping (fifty-five compared
to sixty-one hours a week), less time on personal care (sixty-nine compared
to seventy-four hours), and much less time in leisure activities (twenty-nine
compared to forty-one hours) (Bianchi 2000).

Women spend more time on housework and family caregiving than their
male counterparts; and the quality of this time also differs. As of the mid-
1990s, women spent about twice as many hours on housework as men.
Among married women, 81 to 89 percent of these hours (depending on the
data source) were spent on core housework tasks such as cooking, cleaning, and laundry. Among married men, in contrast, 50 to 64 percent of the
hours were spent on discretionary tasks such as repairs, paying bills, and
car maintenance (Bianchi et al. 2000). Men and women also differ in how
they spend their time with children—and when. Mothers, for example,
devote an average of nearly thirty-five hours a week to direct child care,
in contrast to less than twenty hours a week for men. Of the hours spent in
direct care, married mothers are one-and-a-half times as likely as fathers to

spend those hours during weekdays, when conflicts with employment are most intense. During those weekdays, one-third of the time women spend in direct care are devoted to children's personal-care activities (for example, bathing, dressing, changing diapers, or feeding) or having meals with children—twice the share of men's hours devoted to these tasks (Fuligni and Brooks-Gunn 2001).

Gender gaps are also evident with respect to "free time"—the time that remains after paid work, housework, child care, and self-care are all completed. Time-diary data suggest that American men and women do not differ greatly in their total hours of free time each day. In their study of the gender gap in free time, Marybeth Mattingly and Suzanne Bianchi (2003) report that men have an average of about five and a half hours' free time each day, while women have about a half hour less—a small but significant difference. On the other hand, though this difference is minimal on a daily basis, Mattingly and Bianchi point out that, if extended throughout the year, men's additional free time adds up to 164 hours a year—the equivalent of more than four weeks of vacation (at forty hours a week). In addition to having somewhat less total free time, women have significantly fewer hours of both "pure" free time (time that is not contaminated by nonleisure secondary activities) and "adult" free time (time with no children present).

Women appear to pay the steepest economic and personal costs when families solve work-family dilemmas by allocating a disproportionate share of the care work to women. However, gender inequalities, particularly in the care of children, may have costs for men as well. Most important, the gendered divisions of labor in unpaid work have marginalized men's engagement in the home, including the care and nurturing of their children. The "absent father" problem is most extreme in the growing number of families headed by a divorced, separated, or never married mother. Yet in a substantial number of two-parent homes, resident fathers are nearly as absent from their children's lives as fathers who live elsewhere.

CONCLUSION

American families are struggling to resolve tensions arising from new economic and social arrangements in the family and the labor market. Women expect, and are expected, to participate with men in the labor market; they are also expected to provide most care work in the home. Most parents are employed, but workplaces and social policies are still designed for workers with minimal family responsibilities. Families have increased their labor supply, but many have experienced little real economic progress or have even fallen further behind. Many parents are working nonstandard hours as a child care strategy. Others are purchasing child care in the market and, despite spending an appreciable share of their earnings, are leaving their children in care of mediocre or poor quality. Families are being forced to make compromises, and these compromises have a distinctly gendered cast: women continue to pay steep wage penalties for motherhood, to experience high rates of poverty, and to care for children for either no or for miserably low wages. These compromises may be imposing still other penalties on children, who get too little of their parents' time when they are very young and care of uncertain quality when their parents are at work.

Although families are facing the challenges of work-family balance in all industrialized countries, families in the United States are doing so in a context of limited public responsibility for the private costs of rearing children. Problems of income and time poverty, gender inequality, questionable child care arrangements, and poor outcomes for children may not be inevitable, however.

NOTES

1. Note that the results in Tables 21–2 and 21–3 are consistent with findings that we reported earlier in this chapter—that long hours spent in paid work are not simply the province of highly educated workers or workers in high-income families. Average joint labor market time in the middle two quartiles (about seventy-three hours a week) is similar to that reported in the top income quartile (about seventy-seven hours a week, on average). Time spent in paid work clearly lags at the bottom (the lowest quartile), consistent with Mishel, Bernstein, and Schmitt's (2001) finding that married males' hours lagged only in the bottom quintile. It is also important to note that the comparisons presented in Tables 21–2 and 21–3 use a different indicator. For the purpose of this comparison—about gender inequality—average hours include adults with zero hours. That conflates variation in employment rates with variation in hours, rendering this comparison across income and education groups somewhat different from those presented by Jacobs and Gerson (2004) and Mishel, Bernstein, and Schmitt (2001).

2. This is especially true in families in which women have left the labor market altogether (or never entered it). As Nancy Folbre observes, homemaker wives remain dependent on their husband's largess. Folbre argues that married women who divorce gain rights to joint property, but in most of the American states, "within marriage a person who specializes in nonmarket work has no legal right to any more than the partner earning a wage or salary chooses to give them" (Folbre 2001, 92).

3. Gender inequalities in paid work are mirrored in the structure of many public social-welfare provisions. The primary forms of government income replacement in the United States—old-age, disability, and unemployment insurance—are largely predicated on formal labor force attachment. In general, a woman's unpaid work history, in caregiving and other domestic work at home, entitles her to no compensation or social insurance of her own. At the same time, many women caregivers are eligible for public benefits, not specifically as caregivers but as the wives of breadwinners who are unable to support them owing to death, disability, or work-related injury. Eligible widows, married for at least ten years, can receive survivors' benefits if their breadwinning spouses die; benefits are paid to elderly widows and to those of any age raising dependent children.

In addition, some social-insurance programs—including the national Old-Age and Disability Insurance programs and, in some states, Workers' Compensation— add a "dependents' supplement" to the recipients' benefits, on behalf of an eligible spouse. Yet for the most part, women's uncompensated work does not grant them their own benefits; the entitlements they do have are not based on the value of their work.

REFERENCES

Bianchi, Suzanne M. 2000. "Maternal Employment and Time with Children: Dramatic Change or Surprising Continuity?" *Demography* 37(4):401–14.

Bianchi, Suzanne M., Melissa A. Milkie, Liana C. Sayer, and John P. Robinson. 2000. "Is Anyone Doing the Housework? Trends in the Gender Division of Household Labor." *Social Forces* 79(1):191–228.

Budig, Michelle J., and Paula England. 2001. "The Wage Penalty for Motherhood." *American Sociological Review* 66(2):204–25.

Caiazza, Amy B., and Heidi I. Hartmann. 2001. "Gender and Civic Participation." Paper presented at the Work, Family, and Democracy Conference. Racine, Wisconsin (June 11–13).

Chun, Hyunbae, and Injae Lee. 2001. "Why Do Married Men Earn More: Productivity or Marriage Selection?" *Economic Inquiry* 39(2):307–19.

Crittenden, Ann. 2001. *The Price of Motherhood: Why the Most Important Job in the World Is Still the Least Valued.* New York: Metropolitan Books.

Folbre, Nancy. 2001. *The Invisible Heart: Economics and Family Values.* New York: New Press.

Fuligni, Allison Sidle, and Jeanne Brooks-Gunn. 2001. "What is Shared in Caring for Young Children? Parental Perceptions and Time Use in Two-Parent Families." Paper presented at the Biennial Meetings of the Society for Research in Child Development, Minneapolis, Minn. (April 9).

Goldscheider, Frances. 2002. "Non-Domestic Employment and Women's Lives: Revisiting the Roles of Supply and Demand." Paper presented at the 2002 annual meeting of the Population Association of America. Atlanta, Georgia (May 9–11).

Hernandez, Donald. 1994. "Children's Changing Access to Resources: A Historical Perspective," *Social Policy Report, Society for Research in Child Development* VIII(1):1–23.

Hicks, Alexander. 1999. *Social Democracy and Welfare Capitalism: A Century of Income Security Politics.* Ithaca, New York: Cornell University Press.

Jacobs, Jerry A., and Kathleen Gerson. 2004. *The Time Divide: Work, Family, and Social Policy in the 21st Century.* Cambridge, Mass.: Harvard University Press.

Katz, Michael B. 1986. *In the Shadow of the Poorhouse: A Social History of Welfare in America.* New York: Basic Books.

———. 1989. *The Undeserving Poor: From the War on Poverty to the War on Welfare.* New York: Pantheon Books.

Lister, Ruth. 1990. "Women, Economic Dependency, and Citizenship." *Journal of Social Policy* 19(4):445–67.

Mattingly, Marybeth J., and Suzanne M. Bianchi. 2003. "Gender Differences in the Quantity and Quality of Free Time: The U.S. Experience." *Social Forces* 81(3).

Mishel, Lawrence, Jared Bernstein, and John Schmitt. 2001. *The State of Working America: 2000–2001*. Ithaca, New York: Cornell University Press, ILR Press.

Organisation for Economic Co-operation and Development. 2001. *Social Expenditure Database 1980–1998*, 3d ed. Paris: OECD.

Patterson, James T. 1986. *America's Struggle Against Poverty: 1900–1985*. Cambridge: Harvard University Press.

Putnam, Robert D. 2000. *Bowling Alone: The Collapse and Revival of American Community*. New York: Simon & Schuster.

Robinson, John P., and Geoffrey Godbey. 1997. *Time for Life: The Surprising Ways Americans Use Their Time*. University Park: Pennsylvania State University Press.

Trattner, Walter I. 1994. *From Poor Law To Welfare State: A History of Social Welfare in America*. New York: The Free Press.

U.S. Bureau of the Census. 2002. "International Database Summary Demographic Data." Accessed January 9, 2003, at: *www.census.gov/ipc/www/adbsum.html*.

Waldfogel, Jane. 1998. "Understanding the 'Family Gap' in Pay for Women with Children." *Journal of Economic Perspectives* 12(1):137–56.

PART 4

HOW DO SOCIETIES CHANGE?

Forces of Social Change

INTRODUCTION

The readings in this section focus on the question "How do societies change?" within a U.S. context. This inevitably leads to some lessons in American history. When we teach our classes about social change, we begin by telling students that the history of American society is essentially a history of social movements. Concerted actors, working together, create social change in society. You can trace American history from the American Revolution, through the Civil War, the Labor Movement, the Women's Suffrage Movement, the Civil Rights Movement, the Feminist Movement, the Environmental Movement, the Anti-War Movement, the Tea Party Movement, the Occupy Movement, and the many movements in between. The demands of each movement reflected major social concerns. The difference between how historians and how sociologists study these movements is that sociologists look at trends across movements and try to generalize about what causes movements' emergence, their decline, and other theoretical questions. Historians are more interested in the details of the stories of each particular movement. The first piece in the section lays out some big questions about our political system and the process of change, and the second and third pieces focus on two movements: the unemployed workers movement of the 1930s and the Civil Rights movement, with a focus on the early 1960s.

The first reading is an excerpt from William Gamson's classic book, *The Strategy of Social Protest*. In the book, Gamson assesses the outcomes of a representative sample of 53 protest organizations ("challenging groups") in the United States, covering the period from 1880 to 1945. He asks, Why do some succeed and others fail? Are there patterns? Which strategies are most successful? What organizational characteristics lead to success? You'll need to read the whole book or take a course in social movements to answer all of these questions. But a key finding is that there are patterns to the outcomes. For example, groups with narrowly focused goals are more likely to achieve their goals than groups with broad goals. This make sense. Part of the reason there are regularities has to do with the common context in which these struggles take place. The excerpt lays the foundation for analyzing the cases by laying out the system in which the protests play out: the U.S. democratic system. Gamson asks, Do we all have access to democracy? Can any group make a difference? His short answer is that while, in theory, we have a pluralistic system that is designed to provide access for all, some have more access than others.

(As I write, we are in the midst of an election season and the news reports regularly remind us that candidates need financial contributions to succeed.) Our democratic system is designed to prevent tyranny by a minority group and to provide responsiveness to citizen groups; however, when "challengers" (protest groups) try to change the status quo, they are not always successful.

The second reading details how unemployed workers and their allies engaged their sociological imaginations to change both (a) how people perceived the unemployed and (b) the benefits that unemployed workers received from the state. This is an excerpt from another classic, Francis Fox Piven and Richard Cloward's book *Poor People's Movements: Why They Succeed, How They Fail*. In the 1930s, there were masses of unemployed people in the United States. These people were ashamed by their "personal problem" of unemployment. They individualized their issue rather than seeing it as a systemic problem, which the Depression was. Exacerbating this was that fact that taking "relief" or being on the "dole" was deemed un-American. Americans were a hard-working lot and should not need handouts. Over time, unemployed workers began to recognize unemployment as a systemic problem that was shared by many and resulted in widespread hardship. They protested in cities, and city governments responded by providing "relief." However, cities were also facing their own financial problems (remember, it was the Depression). Cities and business leaders rallied around unemployed workers and lobbied the Federal government. In time, President Roosevelt was elected, a jobs program (the Civilian Conservation Corp) was enacted, and a Federal Emergency Relief Act was passed. This movement succeeded in shifting Americans' thinking about the "dole" and the increased material benefits that unemployed workers received during that tough economic period and continue to receive as a safety net today. This case study is qualitative; it uses historical materials, newspaper articles and other accounts from New York City, Chicago, and Philadelphia to explain the effects that persistent citizen protest had on the state in a time of fiscal crisis. Taken with the other cases in the book, it is used to build the argument that even movements that lack significant resources and organizational structure can make a difference.

The final selection also uses newspaper accounts of protest as sources of data, but in a much different way. The selection from Doug McAdam's book, *Political Process and the Development of Black Insurgency, 1930–1970*, looks at articles printed in the *New York Times* to show trends in the development of the Civil Rights movement. McAdam is less interested in the exact details of each news report than in what the collection of news events over time are able to tell us about what was happening with civil rights organizations, where they were focused geographically, and what issues were most important to them. This passage contains tables with quantitative data. Read the tables, don't skip over them! Think about what they mean and how McAdam integrates the quantitative data from the tables with his qualitative narrative. McAdam develops a theoretical model known as the political process model. There are three essential parts to the model, which seeks to explain the development of social movements. First, there are social movement organizations and the resources and decisions that they control. These include their goals, strategies, and the issues they choose to address. The second important area to understand is the political context—the aspects external to the movement organizations, in other words the trends going on in society. In the period that McAdam is writing about in this section, 1960 to 1965, he notes that the rising importance of the black vote is a trend that helps contribute to the impact of organizations' work for civil rights. The third key factor in understanding movements' development is the response that they receive from their targets. In this case, the federal government was a "neutral" ally to the movement, which sought to "keep the peace." Since the state did not directly repress the movement, it was able to gather strength. In sum, McAdam shows that black insurgency was able to persist because of elements within the movement and due to elements beyond the groups' control (notably political changes and neutral responses by the government). If you go on in sociology and study social movements, you will learn more about the political process model and apply it to other movements. You will also learn other theories that explain the rise, demise, and outcomes of social movements.

Taken together, these pieces show how challengers in the U.S. political process create social change. Change occurs because of concerted efforts by social actors. It is often resisted by those in power. Change is sometimes a slow, adaptive, and evolving process; but often, it is a messy, violent, contested affair. Social change agents possess the sociological imagination. They see their place in the larger social structure. They also see that if they want society to change, they must join forces with others in their predicament and must act.

READING 22

Excerpt from *The Strategy of Social Protest*

WILLIAM GAMSON

In May, 1937, shortly before Memorial Day, 78,000 steelworkers began a strike against the "Little Steel" companies of Bethlehem Steel, Republic Steel, Inland Steel, and Youngstown Sheet and Tube. The CIO-backed Steel

Gamson, William. 1990. "The Permeability of the Political Arena" from *Strategies of Social Protest*. Belmont, CA: Wadsworth Publishing Company.

Workers Organizing Committee (SWOC) was less than a year old at the time but had already enjoyed some notable success. A few months earlier, it had signed collective bargaining agreements with the five largest U.S. Steel subsidiaries, and, by early May, SWOC had signed contracts with 110 firms.

The Little Steel companies, however, were prepared to resist. Under the leadership of Tom M. Girdler, president of Republic Steel, they refused to sign an agreement which they felt, in Girdler's words, "was a bad thing for our companies, for our employees; indeed for the United States of America" (Galenson 1960, p. 96).

The decision to resist was made more ominous by the common practice of large employers of the time to stock arsenals of weapons and tear gas in anticipation of labor disputes. Much of our information comes from the report of the LaFollette Committee of the United States Senate,[1] which investigated the events surrounding the Little Steel strike. The committee report noted, for example, that during the years 1933 to 1937, over a million dollars' worth of tear gas and sickening gas was purchased by employers and law-enforcement agencies but that "all of the largest individual purchasers are corporations and that their totals far surpass those of large law-enforcement purchasers" (quoted in Sweeney 1956, p. 20). The largest purchaser of gas equipment in the country was none other than the Republic Steel Corporation, which "bought four times as much as the largest law-enforcement purchaser." The Republic Steel arsenal included 552 revolvers, 61 rifles with 1325 rounds of ammunition, and 245 shotguns in addition to gas grenades (Sweeney, p. 33).

The Little Steel strike began on May 26, 1937, and for a few days prior to May 30, picketing and arrests occurred near Republic Steel's mill in south Chicago. On Memorial Day, after a mass meeting at strike headquarters, the strikers decided to march to the plant to establish a mass picket line. A crowd of about 1,000 persons, "headed by two bearers of American Flags, ... started across the prairie toward the street which fronts on the mill. There was a holiday spirit over the crowd" (Sweeney, p. 33).

Chicago police were there in force and the paraders were commanded to disperse. Within a few minutes, seven strikers were dead, three lay fatally wounded, scores of others were seriously wounded, and 35 policemen were injured. The LaFollette Committee concluded on the basis of testimony from many eyewitnesses and photographs that "the first shots came from the police; that these were unprovoked, except perhaps by a tree branch thrown by the strikers, and that the second volley of police shots was simultaneous with the missiles thrown by the strikers." The strikers fled after the first volley but were pursued by the police. Of the ten marchers who were fatally shot, "... seven received the fatal wound in the back, three in the side, none in front. ... The medical testimony of the nature of the marchers' wounds indicates that they were shot in flight. ... The police were free with their use of clubs as well as guns. ... Suffice it to say that the evidence, photographic and oral, is replete with instances of the use of clubs upon marchers doing their utmost to retreat, as well as upon those who were on the ground and in a position to offer no show of resistance," the LaFollette Committee Report concluded (quoted in Galenson, 1960).

The "Memorial Day Massacre" at the Republic Steel Plant in Chicago was the most notorious but by no means the only violent clash in the Little Steel strike. The strike was effectively broken by these tactics. Within two weeks of the Memorial Day clash, the Republic Steel plant had resumed normal operation. Within another few weeks, other struck plants reopened as well and the strike was essentially over.

The victory of the companies was, as it turned out, only a temporary one. By the fall of 1941, all four Little Steel companies had agreed to recognize the SWOC, and in May, 1942, the Steel Workers Organizing Committee became the United Steelworkers of America. Today, the leaders of the union dine with Presidents and serve as labor spokesmen on a variety of governmental bodies. By any measure of membership of the polity, they are full-fledged and certified. In reading the bitter history of the Little Steel strike from the consciousness of today, it is difficult to credit the fact that these events occurred a mere 50 years ago, in the living memory of some readers or, at the very least, of their parents.

This particular challenger has, for better or worse, moved inside the salon. But the anterooms and corridors contain the battered hulks of less successful challengers. Their abortive careers also promise to tell us important things about the permeability of the American political system.

Take the Brotherhood of the Cooperative Commonwealth, for example. Born in the ferment of the 1890s, it was the brainchild of an obscure Maine reformer, Norman Wallace Lermond. "Its immediate and most important objective was to colonize *en masse* a sparsely inhabited Western state with persons desiring to live in socialist communities. Once established, the colonists would be in a position to capture control of the state's government and lay the foundation for a socialist commonwealth" (Quint 1964).

Not much happened for the first year of its existence but Lermond was "a letter writing dynamo and he bombarded reformers throughout the country with appeals for assistance." He began to get some results. Imogene C. Fales, a New York reformer, "who was a charter member of innumerable humanitarian and socialist movements in the 1880s and 1890s, agreed to serve with Lermond as co-organizer" (Quint).

But the big catch for the fledgling challenging group was Eugene V. Debs. Debs had been recently released from his prison term for defying the injunction against the American Railway Union which broke the Pullman strike. He was a genuine hero of the left, who was now, for the first time, espousing socialism. Debs was a thoroughly decent person who lacked the vituperative personal style so characteristic of many leftists. Furthermore, he was an extraordinarily effective platform speaker where, as Quint describes him, "the shining sincerity of his speeches and the flowing honesty of his personality more than compensated for the lack of knowledge of the more delicate points of Marxist theory. His soul was filled with a longing for social justice and he communicated this feeling to the audiences who gathered to hear him extol the new Social Democracy."

Debs became attracted to the colonization scheme. "Give me 10,000 men," Debs told a socialist convention, "aye, 10,000 in a western state with access to the sources of production, and we will change the economic conditions, and we will convince the people of that state, win their hearts and their intelligence. We will lay hold upon the reins of government and plant the flag of Socialism upon the State House" (quoted in Quint).

Many other socialists were appalled at what they considered a diversion of energy into a thoroughly impractical scheme. However, they were gentle with Debs personally, hoping to woo him back to the true path. Even the normally vitriolic socialist leader, Daniel DeLeon, was unaccustomedly polite. "With warm esteem for the good intentions of Mr. Debs, but fully appreciative of the harm that more failures will do," he wrote, "we earnestly warn the proletariat of America once more not to embark on this chimera; not to yield out of love for the good intentions of Mr. Debs, greater respect for his judgment than it deserves" (Quint).

Gradually, Debs began relegating the colonization scheme to be one of several strategies rather than to be *the* strategy of the socialist movement. The Brotherhood of the Cooperative Commonwealth did not particularly prosper. They did establish a colony, "Equality" in Edison, Washington, and later another at Burley, Washington, but these did not thrive. "By 1902, Equality contained 105 people, living on a very plain diet in two apartment houses, four log cabins, and fourteen frame houses, earning a bare subsistence by the sale of lumber and grain" (Quint). By 1914, there wasn't anything left of the colonization plans of the Brotherhood of the Cooperative Commonwealth.

How can we account for the different experiences of a representative collection of American challenging groups? What is the characteristic response to groups of different types and what determines this response? What strategies work under what circumstances? What organizational characteristics influence the success of the challenge?

The careers of challenging groups tell us about the permeability and openness of the American political system. To know who gets in and how is to understand the central issue in competing images of the American political experience.

THE PLURALIST IMAGE OF AMERICAN POLITICS

Until the turbulence of the 1960s caused many to rethink the issue, a particular interpretation of American politics dominated the thinking of most professional observers. It remains highly influential today if perhaps not as dominant as it once was in the face of a developing body of criticism. This interpretation presents an image of a highly open system with free access for would-be competitors. Furthermore, the image has behind it a well-

developed and elegant body of theoretical ideas usually presented under
the label "pluralist democracy" or simply "pluralism."

A democratic political system must be able to handle two great problems if it is to continue successfully: the danger of tyranny or domination
by a minority, and responsiveness to unmet or changing needs among
its citizens. Pluralist theory has the virtue of explaining how a political
system can handle both of these problems simultaneously. To the extent
that the American political system approximates the pluralist model, it is
argued, it will produce regular and orderly change with the consent of the
governed.

Those who support this interpretation are not unaware of urban riots and
the considerable history of violent conflict in the United States. However,
they tend to view such events as abnormalities or pathologies arising from
the gap between an always imperfect reality and an ideal, abstract model.
In other words, the occasional, admitted failures of American democracy to
produce orderly change are caused by departures from the ideal conditions
of pluralism. Furthermore, even a well-functioning thermostat sometimes
produces temperatures that are momentarily too hot or too cold as it goes
about giving us the proper temperature.

There is a vast literature on pluralism and the American political system,
and the discussion here will not attempt to do it full justice. A particularly
coherent and convincing statement of the case is made in Dahl's *Pluralist
Democracy in the United States* (1967). Now Dahl is no mindless celebrator of
the genius of American politics; he paints his subject with all its warts and
blemishes. But the important point is that this darker side of American politics is viewed as blemish and not as the essence of his subject.

Dahl suggests (p. 24) that the "fundamental axiom in the theory and
practice of American pluralism is...this: Instead of a single center of sovereign power there must be multiple centers of power, none of which is or can
be wholly sovereign." Why is this so important? Because the "existence of
multiple centers of power...will help to tame power, to secure the consent
of all, and to settle conflicts peacefully."

The brilliance of pluralist thinking is illustrated by its ability to handle
multiple problems simultaneously—the prevention of dominance by a single group or individual, responsiveness to the needs of its citizens, and the
prevention of extreme or violent conflict. It deals with two very different
threats to the political system. The first threat is that the delicate balance of
competition will be destroyed by a temporarily ascendant group that will
use its ascendancy to crush its competitors. The second threat is that in the
stalemate of veto groups and countervailing power there will be ineffective
government, leading to an accumulation of discontent that will destroy the
legitimacy and threaten the stability of the existing system.

We can examine the pluralist answer by addressing the question of how
an ideal pluralist system functions. To operate properly, pluralist political
institutions require an underlying pluralist social structure and values as
well. More specifically, the following conditions should prevail:

Procedural Consensus

There is acceptance of the "culture" of constitutional democracy. One operates within the rules, the rules are considered generally fair, and defeats are accepted because of the strong legitimacy attached to the manner of resolving conflicts. Dahl goes even further than procedural consensus and argues for a good deal of substantive consensus as well. "In the United States, there is a massive convergence of attitudes on a number of key issues that divide citizens in other countries. As one result, ways of life are not seriously threatened by the policies of opponents" (Dahl, p. 326).

Cross-Cutting Solidarities

Individuals have strong identifications and affiliations with solidarity groups at different levels below the total society—primary group, community, formal organization, religious group, ethnic group, social class, and so forth. Furthermore, these solidarities overlap and cut across each other in a complex web which creates multiple memberships linking individuals with different sets of others.

Open Access to the Political Arena

There are no barriers to a group getting a hearing. Dissatisfied groups are encouraged to translate their dissatisfaction into political demands, to find coalition partners among other powerful groups, and to create political reforms which remedy the unsatisfactory conditions. As Dahl argues (p. 24): "Because even minorities are provided with opportunities to veto solutions they strongly object to, the consent of all will be won in the long run." The political institutions offer multiple points at which to pursue one's demands. "The institutions... offer organized minorities innumerable sites in which to fight, perhaps to defeat, at any rate to damage an opposing coalition" (Dahl, p. 329).

Balance of Power or Countervailing Power Operation

There is a sufficiently large number of groups that no one group can dominate. Coalitions are fluid and impermanent, being formed more or less *de novo* for each issue or, at least, for each class of issues. Furthermore, issues partition groups in different ways so that many groups not in a present coalition are potential coalition partners on subsequent issues. "Because one center of power is set against another," Dahl writes (p. 24), "power itself will be tamed, civilized, controlled, and limited to decent human purposes, while coercion, the most evil form of power, will be reduced to a minimum."

When a political system meets these assumptions, it is argued, neither tyranny nor rigidity will result. No group will become dominant for several reasons. First, it will exercise self-restraint in exploiting any temporary ascendancy for normative reasons. The institutions will "generate politicians who learn how to deal gently with opponents, who struggle endlessly in building and holding coalitions together, who doubt the possibilities of great change, who seek compromises" (Dahl, p. 329). Thus, the political process encourages a normative commitment to a set of rules which would be violated by dealing too ruthlessly with an opponent.

Second, self-restraint is encouraged by long-run self-interest. In a world of constantly shifting coalitions, it is feckless to antagonize groups which may be tomorrow's allies on some other set of issues. Third, self-restraint is encouraged by short-run self-interest. Because of the nature of cross-cutting solidarities, any temporarily ascendant group is likely to include many members who *also* belong to those groups who might be the victims of the abuse of power. In such a situation, any efforts to use power to injure or to destroy the power of opponents are automatically threats to the *internal stability* of the groups that would attempt such action. Such efforts stimulate factionalism and costly division within the ranks.

Finally, if self-restraint is not sufficient, efforts to achieve domination will encourage neutral and uninvolved groups to join an opposing coalition which controls greater resources than the temporarily ascendant group or coalition. Power which threatens to get out of hand stimulates countervailing power.

Many of the same pluralist conditions help to produce responsiveness as well. The critical element in this argument is that in the normal operation of the political system dissatisfied groups are encouraged to organize and translate their dissatisfaction into concrete political demands. Several elements in the political system lead to such encouragement. First, competitive elections assure that political parties will woo dissatisfied groups that have achieved some degree of strength, either to broaden their base of support or to prevent the allegiance of such groups to their competitors. Second, existing interest groups with similar or overlapping interests will facilitate organizations of such dissatisfied groups, seeing in them new allies. Third, multiple points of access to the political system will encourage participation by making available many sites for possible influence. Fourth, such organization and participation will be encouraged by the normative commitment of existing competitors to open access.

Thus, no group will long remain unrepresented, and it will find its entry into the political arena smoothed and facilitated by powerful allies who find it useful to do so for their own purposes. There will be no need for such groups to violate the existing rules of democratic politics to bring about the remedy of legitimate grievances.

The American political system, in this argument, approximates the underlying pluralist social structure and values quite closely. The result is an image of American politics as a contest carried out under well-defined rules. The rules prohibit the use of violence or any efforts aimed at permanently removing other contestants from the game. The essence of the competition is bargaining for relative advantage with the attendant tactics of influence trading, coalition formation, logrolling and the like.

It is a game that any number can play. The only rule of entry is that the contesting group must agree to behave itself. More specifically, this means that it must honor the rights of the existing participants by not striving to destroy them or to render them permanently impotent, and it must not be too unruly in its means. Contestants who misbehave are excluded from the contest by general agreement. Subject only to this broadest of restrictions, all are welcome to come in and try their luck.

This, then, is the essence of the pluralist image. It is the product of a subtle and persuasive argument with roots going back to James Madison and extending through an array of subsequent political theorists. In suggesting its inadequacies and in exploring an alternative image, I intend no denial of the great intellectual insights into the workings of political systems in general, and of American politics in particular, that we owe to this body of thought.

FLAWS IN THE PLURALIST HEAVEN

"The flaw in the pluralist heaven," writes Schattschneider (1960, p. 35), "is that the heavenly chorus sings with a strong upper-class accent. Probably about 90 percent of the people cannot get into the pressure system." In one form or another, this theme is present in most writing that is critical of pluralist theory.

One line of criticism of the pluralist image of American politics challenges its argument about the lack of dominance by a single center of power. This theme is given classical expression in Mills' *The Power Elite* (1956). Mills argues for the existence of a level of power operation not touched by pluralist assumptions. The pluralist model, Mills grants, is applicable to a middle level of power, but a series of really major decisions are dominated by a small group which is not subject to the constraints operating at the middle level.

The pluralist interpretation seems more vulnerable and in need of modification on the issue of permeability and openness to efforts at change. "Groups provide a great deal of necessary social efficiency," Lowi writes (1971, p. 5). "They are effective means of articulating and representing interests and providing low-level social controls that reduce the need for governmental coercion. But the very success of established groups is a mortgage against a future of new needs that are not yet organized or are not readily accommodated by established groups."

From time to time, previously unorganized groups begin to find a political voice. Vague dissatisfactions begin to crystallize over some more specific claim or demand for change, be it incremental or revolutionary. These challenging groups vary in the responses they experience. Some collapse quickly without leaving a visible mark, some are destroyed by attack, some have their programs preempted by competitors, some are given the formal trappings of influence without its substance, some die and rise again from the ashes, some shove their way, yelling and screaming, into the political arena and become permanent fixtures, some walk in on the arm of well-placed sponsors, and some wander in unnoticed and remain in by fait accompli.

It is one task of any interpretation of American politics to explain the varied experience of these challenging groups.

NOTE

1. Hearings before a Subcommittee of the Committee on Education and Labor, United States Senate, 75th Congress, (LaFollette Committee). U.S. Government Printing Office, Washington, D.C., 1939.

REFERENCES

Dahl, Robert. 1967. *Pluralist Democracy in the United States: Conflict and Consent.* Chicago: Rand-McNally.

Galenson, Walter. 1960. *The CIO Challenge to the AFL.* Cambridge, Mass.: Harvard University Press.

Lowi, Theodore J. 1971. *The Politics of Disorder.* New York: Basic Books.

Mills, C. Wright. 1956. *The Power Elite.* New York: Oxford University Press.

Quint, Howard H. 1964. *The Forging of American Socialism: Origins of the Modern Movement.* Indianapolis, Ind.: Bobbs-Merrill.

Schattschneider, E. E. 1960. *The Semi-Sovereign People.* New York: Holt, Rinehart & Winston.

Sweeney, Vincent D. 1956. *The United Steelworkers of America: Twenty Years Later, 1936–1956.* Pittsburgh: The United Steelworkers of America.

READING 23

Excerpt from *Poor People's Movements: Why They Succeed, How They Fail*

FRANCES FOX PIVEN AND RICHARD A. CLOWARD

The depression movements of the unemployed and of industrial workers followed a period of economic breakdown that produced distress and confusion in the daily lives of millions of people, and produced

Piven, Frances Fox, and Richard A. Cloward. 1979. "The Unemployed Workers' Movement" from *Poor People's Movements: Why They Succeed, How They Fail.* New York: Vintage Books, a Division of Random House.

contradiction and confusion in the posture of elites. For those still working, the discontents released by economic collapse during the 1930s were expressed in struggles within the factory system. But the men and women for whom life had changed most drastically and immediately were no longer in the factories. They were among the masses of the unemployed, and their struggle had to take another form, in another institutional context. The depression saw the rise and fall of the largest movement of the unemployed this country has known, and the institution against which the movement was inevitably pitted was the relief system.

At the time of the Great Depression, formal arrangements for relief of the indigent were sparse and fragmented. In many places, including New York City and Philadelphia, there simply was no "outdoor" relief (the term used to describe aid given to people who were not institutionalized). Even where public relief agencies existed, what little was actually given was usually provided by private charities. But niggardly aid and fragmented adminstration did not signify an underdeveloped institution. To the contrary, a national relief system did exist. Despite the diversity of administrative auspices, the norms that guided the giving of relief were everywhere quite similar. The dole was anathema to the American spirit of work and self-sufficiency. Therefore, it should be dispensed to as few as possible and made as harsh as possible to discourage reliance upon it. Accordingly, very little was given, and then only to a handful of the aged and crippled, widowed and orphaned—to "deserving" people who clearly were not able to work.

These practices were not only a reflection of harshly individualistic American attitudes. They were also a reflection of American economic realities. Work and self-reliance meant grueling toil at low wages for many people. So long as that was so, the dole could not be dispensed permissively for fear some would choose it over work. Thus, most of the poor were simply excluded from aid, ensuring that they had no alternative but to search for whatever work they could find at whatever wage was offered. And if they found no work, then they would have to survive by whatever means they could.

The wonder of this relief system, however, was that it generated such shame and fear as to lead the poor to acquiesce in its harsh and restrictive practices. In part the poor acquiesced simply because they shared American beliefs in the virtue of work and self-sufficiency, and in the possibility of work and self-sufficiency for those who were ambitious and deserving.

Occasionally, however, unemployment reached calamitous levels and the jobless rebelled. At the depths of each of the recurrent depressions of the nineteenth and early twentieth centuries, people joined together and demanded some form of aid to ease their distress. In the slump of 1837 some 20,000 unemployed in Philadelphia assembled to demand, among other things, that the national government relieve distress among the unemployed by a public works program (Foner 1947, 162), and in New York City, a crowd of thousands in City Hall Park protested against the "monopolies" and the high cost of food and rent. The crowd then paraded to the wholesale flour depot, and dumped flour and wheat in the streets (Gutman 1976, 60–61). In the panic of 1857 protests of the unemployed emerged in several big cities. Ten thousand Philadelphians rallied "to stimulate their representatives in the State House to an appreciation of their troubles," and a system of ward associations was set up to issue food to the needy (Feder 1936, 32). In New York a meeting of 15,000 in Tompkins Square to demand work culminated in the destruction of fences and benches and the seizure of food wagons, although in this instance the workers got neither jobs nor relief, and federal troops were called in (Feder 1936, 35). The depression of 1873 stimulated new demonstrations. In New York City, rallies drew 10,000 to 15,000 people who were dispersed by mounted police, and in Chicago, mass meetings of the unemployed, organized by anarchists under the slogan "Bread or Blood," culminated in a march of 20,000 on the City Council (Feder 1936, 52; Boyer and Morais 1972, 86). Subsequently, unemployed workers stormed the offices of the Chicago Relief and Aid Society, swamping the Society with applications for aid. The Society surrendered, and about 10,000 were given relief over the next year (Feder 1936, 52; Seymour 1937, 8).[1] In the depression of 1884 the unemployed in Chicago marched again, this time into better-off neighborhoods (Montgomery and Schatz 1976, 20), and in 1893 a new and bitter depression led to a series of marches on Washington by the unemployed, the best known of which was of course "Coxey's army." Coxey's marchers got nothing, but mass demonstrations in the big industrial cities did succeed at least in getting soup kitchens and, in some places, local public works projects as well.

These experiences suggest that when unemployment is severe and widespread, at least a partial transvaluation may occur among the poor. The prohibition against the dole may weaken, if only because the extent of distress belies the customary conviction that one's economic fortunes and misfortunes are a matter of personal responsibility, of individual failure. At such times large numbers of the poor demand relief, the relief of work or the relief of food and money. This transvaluation occurred again in the Great Depression, and just as the scale of the calamity in the 1930s was unparalleled, so too was the protest movement that arose among the unemployed.

THE GREAT DEPRESSION: PRECONDITIONS FOR INSURGENCY

The depression came suddenly, at a time when the American belief in unprecedented and unbroken prosperity had never been so fervent, earlier depressions notwithstanding. People were taken by surprise, the rulers as much as the ruled, and it took time for the political forces set in motion by the calamity to emerge. Then, as the depression continued and worsened, the harshening and disordering of a way of life began to take form in rising popular discontent. The actions of elites added momentum to this process, for they too were shaken and divided, and their cacaphonic accusations and proposals heightened the sense of indignation that was spreading. In the period of general political uncertainty that ensued, protest movements emerged among different groups, focusing on different institutional grievances. The earliest uprisings occurred among the unemployed.

THE RISE OF PROTEST

Most of the people who were thrown out of work suffered quietly, especially at the start of the depression, when official denials helped to confuse the unemployed and to make them ashamed of their plight. Men and women haunted the employment offices, walked the streets, lined up for every job opening, and doubted themselves for not finding work. Families exhausted their savings, borrowed from relatives, sold their belongings, blaming themselves and each other for losing the struggle to remain self-reliant. But as the depression worsened, as the work forces of entire factories were laid off, as whole neighborhoods in industrial towns were devastated, and as at least some political leaders began to acknowledge that a disaster had occurred, attitudes toward what had happened and why, and who was to blame, began to change among some of the unemployed. They began to define their personal hardship not just as their own individual misfortune but as misfortune they shared with many of their own kind. And if so many people were in the same trouble, then maybe it wasn't they who were to blame, but "the system."[2]

Mob Looting, Marches, and Demonstrations

One of the earliest expressions of unrest among the unemployed was the rise of mob looting. As had happened so often before in history during periods of economic crisis, people banded together to demand food. By and large, the press refrained from reporting these events for fear of creating a contagion effect. In New York bands of thirty or forty men regularly descended upon markets, but the chain stores refused to call the police, in order to keep the events out of the papers. In March 1,100 men waiting on a Salvation Army bread line in New York City mobbed two trucks delivering baked goods to a nearby hotel. In Henryetta, Oklahoma, 300 jobless marched on storekeepers to demand food, insisting they were not begging and threatening to use force if necessary (Bernstein 1970, 422; Brecher 1974, 144). Indeed, Bernstein concludes that in the early years of the depression "organized looting of food was a nation-wide phenomenon" (1970, 421–423).

More consciously political demonstrations began as well. By early 1930, unemployed men and women in New York, Detroit, Cleveland, Philadelphia, Los Angeles, Chicago, Seattle, Boston, and Milwaukee were marching under such Communist banners as "Work or Wages" and "Fight—Don't Starve" (Karsh and Garman 1957, 87; Leab 1967, 300).

In March the demonstrations became a national event. The Communists declared March 6, 1930, International Unemployment Day, and rallies and marches took place in most major cities. Many of the demonstrations were orderly, as in San Francisco where the chief of police joined the 2,000 marchers and the mayor addressed them, or in Chicago where some 4,000 people marched down Halsted and Lake Streets, and then dispatched a committee to petition the mayor (Lasswell and Blumenstock 1939, 196). But in other places, including Washington, D.C., and Seattle, local officials grew alarmed and ordered the police to disperse the crowds with tear gas. In Detroit, Cleveland, Milwaukee, and Boston, the crowds resisted, and fierce battles broke out between the demonstrators and the police (Keeran 1974, 72–73; Leab 1967, 306–307).[3] The worst clash occurred in New York City.

The demonstration was sufficiently threatening to prod the mayor to agree to form a committee to collect funds to be distributed to the unemployed.[4] In October 1930 the unemployed gathered again in a mass rally at City Hall plaza to demand that the Board of Estimate appropriate twenty-five dollars a week for each unemployed person. The police again attacked the demonstrators, and two of the organizers were injured, but the Board of Estimate appropriated one million dollars for relief (Naison 1975, 72–73).

LOCAL FISCAL BREAKDOWN

The number of jobless continued to rise. In the big industrial cities, where unemployment was especially severe, the unemployed sometimes comprised voting majorities. Faced with mounting protests, local officials could not remain indifferent. Clearly the private agencies which had in many places handled whatever relief was given could not meet the surging demand, and various *ad hoc* arrangements were quickly invented, often with the cooperation of local businessmen and philanthropists. Committees were set up, local citizens were exhorted to contribute to charity drives, and in some places city employees found their wages reduced for contributions to the relief fund. By these methods, expenditures for relief rose from $71 million in 1929 to $171 million in 1931 (Chandler 1970, 192).

But this amount of relief in cities like New York, Chicago, Detroit, and Philadelphia barely scratched the surface of the need.

In New York City, where the charter of 1898 prohibited "outdoor" relief as distinct from relief in workhouses or poor houses, disruptions by the unemployed had led to the creation of an arrangement whereby the police precincts distributed direct relief to the most destitute from funds contributed by city employees. In 1931, on Governor Roosevelt's initiative, New York State established an emergency program which supplemented local relief funds with an initial outlay of $20 million. Even so, by 1932, the lucky among the unemployed in New York City were receiving an average grant of $2.39 per week, and only one-quarter were getting that (Schlesinger 1957, 253). Testimony before the Senate Committee on Manufactures in the summer of 1932 reported that 20,000 children in New York had been placed in institutions because parents could not provide for them.

Unable to resist the political pressures of the unemployed, local elites had brought their cities to the brink of fiscal collapse. But even so, city budgets could not handle the demand for relief, and so the pressure was not abated, but worsened as unemployment rose. Driven by the protests of the masses of unemployed and the threat of financial ruin, mayors of the biggest cities of the United States, joined by business and banking leaders, had become lobbyists for the poor.

It was the presidential election of 1932 that produced one of the most sweeping political realignments in American history, and it was the election of 1936 that confirmed it.

The man who rose to power through these dislocations was, of course, Franklin Delano Roosevelt; he won the Democratic nomination from a divided and uncertain Democratic Party on the fourth ballot, and then went on to campaign by making promises to everyone who would listen.[5] What working people listened to were the promises to "build from the bottom up and not from the top down, that put their faith once more in the forgotten man at the bottom of the economic pyramid" (Roosevelt 1938, 159–206, 625). Roosevelt won with a plurality of almost seven million votes, capturing the largest electoral majority since 1864, and sweeping in an overwhelmingly Democratic Congress. And much of Roosevelt's majority was concentrated in the big cities of the country, where unemployment and hardship were also concentrated. Economic catastrophe had resulted in a mass rejection of the party in power.

In a message to Congress three weeks after the inauguration, Franklin Delano Roosevelt called for a Civilian Conservation Corps, a public works program, and a massive program of federal emergency relief. The Civilian Conservation Corps provided jobs at subsistence wages for a mere 250,000 men. The Public Works Administration was slow in getting started, and in any case it was designed not so much to provide jobs for the unemployed as to stimulate the economy, so that most of the jobs went to skilled workers. By contrast the Federal Emergency Relief Act, drawn up by Senators Edward P. Costigan, Robert F. Wagner, and Robert N. La Follette, Jr., allocated $500 million for immediate grants to the states for relief of the unemployed, half of which was to be spent on a matching basis. The act was signed on May 12, Harry Hopkins was sworn in as administrator on May 22, and by the evening of that day, he made the first grants to the states. By early June, forty-five states had received federal grants for relief, and total expenditures on relief rose to $794 million in 1933, to $1,489 million in 1934, and to $1,834 million in 1935 (Brown 1940, 204). When the program was terminated in June 1936 the federal government had spent $3 billion as its share of relief expenditures.[6]

It had taken protest and the ensuing fiscal and electoral disturbances to produce federal relief legislation and it took continued protest to get the legislation implemented.

By the winter of 1934, 20 million people were on the dole, and monthly grant levels had risen from an average of $15.15 per family in May 1933 to an average of $24.53 in May 1934, and to $29.33 in May 1935. Harry Hopkins explained the new government posture toward the unemployed:

> For a long time those who did not require relief entertained the illusion that those being aided were in need through some fault of their own. It is now pretty clear in the national mind that the unemployed are a cross-section of the workers, the finest people in the land (Kurzman 1974, 85).

NOTES

1. Gutman (1965) describes these 1873 protests and the organizations that led them in a number of industrial cities.
2. Bakke (1934) provides vivid accounts of the demoralization and shame experienced by both unemployed American and English workers during this period. It was the sense of being *different*, if one was unemployed, that was so shameful: "And if you can't find any work to do, you have the feeling you're not human. You're out of place. You're so different from all the rest of the people around that you think something is wrong with you" (1934, 63). But clearly once people realized that by being out of work they were just the same as people around them, demoralization could more easily turn to indignation.
3. "In Detroit, despite police warnings to avoid the area, between 50,000 and 100,000 people gathered in the streets and on the sidewalks of the downtown district. Police Commissioner Harold Emmons mobilized the entire Detroit police force of 3,600.... For two hours the fighting raged, until in desperation the police ordered city buses and street cars to drive through the protesters in order to clear the streets....A riot comparable to Detroit's disturbance took place in Cleveland after the mayor informed 10,000 to 25,000 demonstrators that he was powerless to adjust their grievances. A three-hour riot in Milwaukee led to forty-seven arrests and four injuries" (Keeran 1974, 72–73).
4. The Communist organizers of the demonstration, however, were charged with "unlawful assembly" and "creating a public nuisance" and served six months on Blackwell's Island (Leab 1967, 310). The demonstrations on March 6 also sparked enough concern in the Congress to justify the creation of what was to become the House Un-American Activities Committee (Bernstein 1970, 427–428).
5. Raymond Moley (1972) writes of the campaign as follows: "I was charged in 1932 with mobilizing personnel and ideas to promote the presidential ambitions of Governor Roosevelt. I welcomed all points of view, planners, trustbusters, and money wizards. I expanded the so-called Brain Trust very considerably and maintained contact with a great variety of people from Bernard Baruch to Huey Long. The task was to win an election in an electorate comprising many ideologies, and mostly no ideology. The issue was recovery, and the therapy used was a combination of many prescriptions" (1972, 559–560).
6. On May 23, the day after he took office, Hopkins notified the states that the federal government would make grants-in-aid equal to one-third of the relief expenditure in the state during the first quarter of the year. But this ratio was disregarded as time went on, and the proportion of relief paid by the federal government increased until it was as much as three-quarters of the relief expenditure in some states (White and White 1937, 82).

REFERENCES

Bakke, E. Wight. 1934. *The Unemployed Man: A Social Study*. New York: E. P. Dutton and Co.

Bernstein, Irving. 1970. *The Lean Years: A History of the American Worker, 1920–1933*. Baltimore: Penguin Books.

Boyer, Richard O., and Morais, Herbert M. 1972. *Labor's Untold Story*. New York: United Electrical Radio and Machine Workers of America.

Brecher, Jeremy. 1974. *Strike!* Greenwich, Connecticut: Fawcett Publication.

Brown, Josephine C. 1940. *Public Relief, 1929–1939*. New York: Henry Holt and Co.

Chandler, Lester V. 1970. *America's Greatest Depression, 1929–1941*. New York: Harper and Row.

Feder, Leah H. 1936. *Unemployment Relief in Periods of Depression*. New York: Russell Sage Foundation.

Foner, Philip. 1947. *History of the Labor Movement in the United States*. New York: International Publishers.

Gutman, Herbert G. 1965. "The Failure of the Movement by the Unemployed for Public Works in 1873." *Political Science Quarterly* 80 (June).

———. 1976. *Work, Culture and Society in Industrializing America*. New York: Alfred A. Knopf.

Karsh, Bernard, and Garman, Phillip L. 1957. "The Impact of the Political Left." In *Labor and the New Deal*, edited by Milton Derber and Edwin Young. Madison: University of Wisconsin Press.

Keeran, Roger Roy. 1974. "Communists and Auto Workers: The Struggle for a Union, 1919–1941." Unpublished Ph. D. dissertation, University of Wisconsin.

Kurzman, Paul. 1974. *Harry Hopkins and the New Deal*. Fairlawn, New Jersey: R. E. Burdick Publishers.

Lasswell, Harold D., and Blumenstock, Dorothy. 1939. *World Revolutionary Propaganda*. Reprint. Plainview, N.Y.: Books for Libraries Press, 1970.

Leab, Daniel. 1967. "'United We Eat': The Creation and Organization of the Unemployed Councils in 1930." *Labor History* 8 (Fall).

Moley, Raymond. 1972. "Comment." *Political Science Quarterly* 87 (December).

Montgomery, David, and Schatz, Ronald. 1976. "Facing Layoffs." *Radical America* 10 (March–April).

Naison, Mark. 1975. "The Communist Party in Harlem, 1928–1936." Unpublished Ph. D. dissertation, Columbia University.

Roosevelt, Franklin D. 1938. *The Public Papers and Addresses of Franklin D. Roosevelt*, Vol. 1, compiled by Samuel I. Roseman. New York: Random House.

Schlesinger, Arthur M., Jr. 1957. *The Age of Roosevelt*, Vol. 1: *The Crisis of the Old Order, 1919–1933*. Boston: Houghton Mifflin Co.

Seymour, Helen. 1937. "The Organized Unemployed." Unpublished Ph.D. dissertation, University of Chicago, August.

White, Clyde R., and White, Mary K. 1937. *Relief Policies in the Depression*. Social Science Research Council Bulletin No. 38.

Excerpt from *Political Process and the Development of Black Insurgency, 1930–1970*

DOUG McADAM

One of the key tenets of the political process model is that social movements occur during periods marked by a significant increase in the vulnerability of the political establishment to pressure from insurgent groups. At such times, the power disparity between members and challengers is reduced, thus rendering insurgent action more likely, less risky, and potentially more successful. Consistent with this argument, the ongoing development of insurgency is expected to reflect fluctuations in the degree of political leverage exercised by the movement. Should the power disparity between insurgents and members return to premovement levels, the prospects for successful insurgency will necessarily decline. If, on the other hand, the political leverage exercised by insurgents remains high, the movement is likely to survive—perhaps even expand—over time.

ORGANIZATIONAL STRENGTH, 1961–65

In stressing the importance of existing institutions in the process of movement emergence, I made no claim that their dominance over the movement would last beyond the initial period of protest activity. In fact, the argument is quite the opposite. To survive over time, insurgent groups must be able to parlay their initial successes into the increased resource support needed to place the movement on a more permanent footing. The ad hoc groups and informal committees that typically coordinate the movement at its outset are ill-equipped to direct an ongoing campaign of social protest. To effect the transformation from a short-lived insurgent episode to a sustained political challenge, the movement must be able to mobilize the resources required to support the creation or expansion of a structure of formal movement organizations. If this effort proves successful, we can expect these organizations gradually to replace indigenous institutions as the dominant organizational force within the movement. That this transformation did occur in the case of the black movement is apparent from the data presented in Table 24–1.

McAdam, Doug. 1982. "The Heyday of Black Insurgency 1961–65" from *Political Process and the Development of Black Insurgency, 1930–1970*. Chicago: University of Chicago Press.

Table 24–1 Distribution of Movement-Initiated Events by Year, 1955–65

	1955–60	1961	1962	1963	1964	1965	1961–65
	% (N)	% (N)	% (N)	% (N)	% (N)	% (N)	% (N)
Campus/church-based groups or individuals	46 (342)	33 (90)	22 (43)	14 (70)	9 (53)	6 (39)	13 (295)
Formal movement organizations	29 (218)	42 (115)	57 (110)	53 (264)	53 (305)	47 (313)	50 (1107)
Black or mixed aggregate	22 (165)	24 (64)	19 (36)	30 (148)	31 (179)	44 (293)	33 (720)
Unaffiliated individuals	2 (18)	1 (3)	2 (4)	3 (17)	6 (34)	3 (19)	4 (77)
Total	99 (743)	100 (272)	100 (193)	100 (499)	99 (571)	100 (664)	100 (2199)

Source: Annual *New York Times Index*, 1955–1965.

Table 24–1 clearly shows the dominance of indigenous institutions in the movement during the 1955–60 period. Equally clear, however, is the dramatic transformation of the movement's organizational structure that occurred between 1961 and 1965. While only 29 percent of all movement-generated events between 1955 and 1960 were attributed to formal movement organizations, the comparable figure for the succeeding five-year period was 50 percent. Simultaneously, the proportion of all movement-generated events initiated by church or campus-based groups dropped from 46 to 13 percent.

The Concentration of Movement Forces

If support for the movement was both broad-based and substantial in the early 1960s, another factor contributed to the organizational strength of the movement during this period. In any conflict situation the strength of a particular group is determined as much by the deployment of its resources as by their absolute quantity. On both counts, movement forces were in good shape in the early 1960s. By confining their attack to targets that were narrowly defined, both substantively and geographically, movement groups were able to concentrate their forces so as to offset the basic resource discrepancy between themselves and their opponents. The result was a narrowly circumscribed, highly focused, effective insurgent campaign.

Geographic Concentration

One form this concentration of movement forces took was geographic. With the outbreak of the indigenous campaigns of the mid-1950s, the movement took on a decidedly southern cast, an emphasis it was to retain throughout the period under analysis here. Table 24–2 provides a breakdown of all movement-initiated actions, by geographic region, for the years 1955–65. As can be seen, the overwhelming majority of those actions occurred in the seventeen southern and border states. Though the later trend toward insurgency in the northern and western regions of the country is clearly foreshadowed in the data, as late as 1965 nearly 70 percent of all movement actions still took place in the South.[1] Even within the region, insurgent campaigns were usually centered in a particular area or town, thus serving to further concentrate the strength of movement forces. For example, the initial wave of activism in 1955–57 was almost exclusively centered in those half-dozen Deep South towns that experienced bus boycotts.[2] The 1960 sit-in campaigns, by contrast, were disproportionately centered in such upper South states as North Carolina, Tennessee, and Virginia. In 1961, the focus of movement activity again shifted to the Deep South with the initiation of CORE-sponsored Freedom Rides in Mississippi. In 1962, another Deep South state, Georgia, and in particular the town of Albany, was the focal point for considerable activity growing out of a campaign variously credited to SNCC, SCLC, or the local Albany movement. Finally, in 1965, the last concentrated mobilization of movement forces took place in Alabama, with the Selma campaign serving as the focal point. By marshalling their forces in this fashion, insurgents were able, throughout the period, to effect a concentration

Table 24–2 Location of All Movement Initiated Actions, 1955–65

Geographic Region	1955–60 % (N)	1961 % (N)	1962 % (N)	1963 % (N)	1964 % (N)	1965 % (N)	1961–65 % (N)
Deep South	37 (184)	54 (99)	60 (71)	36 (138)	25 (85)	59 (267)	47 (688)
Middle South	42 (207)	22 (40)	3 (15)	22 (82)	23 (76)	5 (23)	14 (208)
Border States	10 (47)	12 (23)	15 (18)	9 (36)	13 (45)	5 (23)	10 (144)
Total South	89 (438)	88 (162)	88 (104)	67 (256)	61 (206)	69 (313)	71 (1040)
New England	1 (7)	1 (2)	1 (1)	2 (7)	2 (7)	3 (14)	2 (32)
Middle Atlantic	6 (29)	4 (7)	7 (8)	18 (70)	26 (89)	13 (60)	16 (234)
East North Central	2 (12)	5 (9)	3 (4)	8 (30)	6 (19)	11 (51)	8 (113)
West North Central	0 (1)	1 (2)	0 (0)	2 (8)	0 (1)	0 (0)	1 (11)
Mountain	0 (1)	0 (1)	0 (0)	1 (2)	1 (4)	0 (2)	1 (9)
Pacific	1 (3)	1 (2)	1 (1)	2 (9)	3 (11)	3 (12)	2 (35)
Total	99 (491)	100 (185)	100 (118)	100 (382)	99 (337)	99 (452)	101 (1474)

Source: Annual *New York Times Index*, 1955–65.

Note: Except for geographic divisions within the South, the system of classification employed in this table derives from standard census categories. As regards the southern states, the following categories were used: *Deep South,* Alabama, Georgia, Louisiana, Mississippi, South Carolina; *Middle South,* Arkansas, Florida, North Carolina, Tennessee, Texas, Virginia; *Border states,* Kentucky, Maryland, Missouri, Oklahoma, West Virginia, District of Columbia.

of forces that offset the numerous tactical and resource disadvantages they would later face as a result of the geographic diffusion of protest activity.

Issue Concentration

More important than this geographic concentration was the broad-based issue consensus that prevailed within the movement during this period.[3] Table 24–3 provides evidence of just how strong this consensus was during the early 1960s.

Broadly defined, it was racial integration, in a variety of settings, that served as the fundamental goal of the movement until the mid-1960s. Whatever its limitations as a solution to America's racial problems, this substantive consensus nonetheless contributed to the organizational strength of the movement in two ways. First, it encouraged the regional concentration of movement forces discussed above, by suggesting that the fundamental problem confronting black Americans was their exclusion on racial grounds

Table 24–3 Issues Addressed in Movement-Initiated Events, 1955–65

Issue	1955–60 % (N)	1961 % (N)	1962 % (N)	1963 % (N)	1964 % (N)	1965 % (N)	1961–65 % (N)
Integration	84 (625)	78 (214)	65 (125)	76 (379)	48 (272)	34 (226)	55 (1216)
Public accommodation	38 (284)	42 (115)	37 (72)	49 (243)	35 (201)	15 (102)	33 (733)
Public transportation	15 (112)	16 (44)	8 (16)	2 (10)	0 (0)	0 (0)	3 (70)
Housing	1 (5)	1 (2)	1 (2)	0 (2)	0 (2)	2 (10)	1 (18)
Education	28 (212)	16 (43)	16 (31)	20 (99)	10 (55)	13 (88)	14 (316)
Other	2 (12)	4 (10)	2 (4)	5 (25)	2 (14)	4 (26)	4 (79)
Black political power	0 (2)	2 (4)	5 (10)	2 (8)	8 (46)	20 (132)	9 (200)
Black economic status/power	1 (9)	1 (3)	3 (5)	1 (3)	0 (3)	12 (78)	4 (92)
Black culture	0 (3)	0 (1)	1 (1)	0 (1)	0 (0)	1 (9)	1 (12)
Legal equality	5 (35)	6 (17)	5 (10)	2 (10)	4 (24)	5 (30)	4 (91)
White racism	1 (7)	2 (5)	2 (3)	2 (9)	3 (17)	1 (7)	2 (41)
Police brutality	0 (0)	1 (2)	1 (1)	2 (10)	6 (32)	4 (29)	3 (74)
General plight of black America	4 (31)	2 (6)	4 (8)	0 (1)	2 (12)	3 (18)	2 (45)
Others	3 (19)	3 (7)	11 (22)	13 (64)	20 (115)	19 (124)	15 (332)
Too vague to categorize	2 (14)	5 (13)	4 (8)	3 (14)	9 (50)	2 (11)	4 (96)
Total	100 (745)	101 (272)	100 (193)	101 (499)	100 (571)	101 (664)	99 (2199)

Source: Annual *New York Times Index*, 1955–65.

from the American mainstream. Obviously nowhere were such exclusion-ary practices so visible or oppressive as in the South.

Second, this substantive consensus provided movement leaders with a highly salient issue around which diverse factions within the movement could be mobilized in the effective mass action campaigns characteristic of the period. However, as this consensus began, under myriad pressures, to deteriorate, it became increasingly difficult to mount or sustain such united efforts, and the organizational strength of the movement declined accord-ingly. The beginnings of this deterioration are clearly visible in the decline in the salience of the issue during 1964–65.

STRUCTURE OF POLITICAL OPPORTUNITIES, 1961–65

During the early 1960s movement expansion was also facilitated by a vari-ety of external political pressures that functioned to sustain the supportive political context that had emerged as a result of the broad socioeconomic processes. Indeed, several of those earlier processes remain crucial to an understanding of the political conditions under which black insurgency flourished in the early 1960s.

Growing Importance of the Black Vote

Developments in the 1950s and early 1960s increased the significance of the black vote and, in turn, the pressure on national politicians to appear respon-sive to that constituency. Three factors contributed to this trend. The first was the continuing high rate of black out-migration from the South. Between 1950 and 1965 more than 2 million blacks left the region. And, as had been true in the 1930–50 period, it was the large industrial states of the North and West that continued to attract the majority of these migrants. Seven states in par-ticular—New York, Pennsylvania, New Jersey, Ohio, Michigan, Illinois, and California—controlling 212, or 79 percent, of all the electoral votes required to win the presidency, received 86 percent of the southern black migrants during the 1950s and approximately 80 percent between 1960 and 1965. The political significance of these numbers should be apparent on their face.

A second factor contributing to the growing importance of the black vote during this period was the increase in the size of the southern black electorate. Though continuing to lag well behind the comparable propor-tion of whites, the absolute number of southern blacks registered to vote rose sharply between 1950 and 1965 (see Figure 24–1). From approximately 900,000 registered black voters in the South in 1950, the number rose to more than 2,250,000 over the next fifteen years. Thus, by 1965, the black vote had become a significant factor in southern as well as national politics.

Finally, besides the absolute increase in black voters stemming from these trends, the outcome of the presidential contests during this period further enhanced the political significance of the black electorate. In both of the Stevenson–Eisenhower contests the Republican candidate was able to

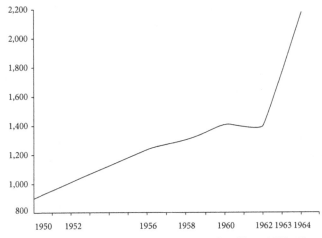

Figure 24–1 Number of Southern Blacks Registered to Vote, 1950–65.

Sources: For 1950, Bullock (1971:227); for 1952, 1956 and 1960, Ploski and Marr (1976); for 1958, Oppenheimer (1963:35); for 1962 and 1963, Muse (1968:58, 152); for 1964, Brooks (1974:242).

reverse the trend toward ever larger black Democratic majorities that had begun with Roosevelt's election in 1936. Republican gains were especially pronounced in 1956 with Eisenhower capturing an estimated 40 percent of the black vote (Lomax 1962:228). The practical result of this reversal was to render the black vote a more volatile political commodity than it had heretofore been, prompting both parties to intensify their efforts to appeal to black voters. Writing prior to the 1960 election, Glantz (1960) comments on the heightened party competition triggered by the surprisingly strong Republican showing four years earlier: "[n]either party can afford to ignore the numerical weight of the Negro vote. In the next campaign the Democratic candidate will have the responsibility of reversing the changing image of the Democratic party, while the Republican candidate will have the responsibility of enlarging... the appeal of the Republican party" (1960:1010).

Continuing Importance of Cold War Political Pressures

Another factor strengthening the political position of blacks in the early 1960s was the continuing importance of the cold war political pressures generated by the United States' ongoing battle with the Soviet Union for influence among the emerging third world nations of the world. These pressures stemmed from the obvious conflict between this country's professed democratic values and the reality of white racism at home.

Growing Salience, Support for the Issue

From 1961 to 1965, the salience of the "Negro question" reached such proportions that it consistently came to be identified in public opinion surveys as the most important problem confronting the country. In six of eleven national opinion polls conducted between 1961 and 1965, "civil rights" was identified as the most important problem facing the country. In three other polls it ranked second. Only twice did it rank as low as fourth.[4]

COLLECTIVE ASSESSMENT OF THE PROSPECTS FOR INSURGENCY, 1961–65

If there existed a favorable confluence of external political conditions and internal movement characteristics in the early 1960s it nonetheless was the sense of optimism prevalent among blacks regarding the prospects for insurgency that furnished the motive force for heightened movement activity. Evidence of this optimistic "state of mind" is again sketchy, but is so consistent as to leave little doubt that it was shared by large numbers of blacks in the early 1960s.

A *Newsweek*, Brink–Harris survey also conducted in 1963 yielded considerable evidence consistent with that reported by Cantril. Table 24–4 summarizes the responses of blacks to a series of questions asking them to assess how they expected their situation five years from now to compare

Table 24–4 Personal Assessment of Blacks in 1963 Concerning the Prospects for Future Gains

Issue Area	PERCENTAGE OF NONLEADERS				PERCENTAGE OF LEADERS			
	Better-off	Worse-off	About Same	Not Sure	Better-off	Worse-off	About Same	Not Sure
Pay	67	2	14	17	81	7	11	1
Work situation	64	3	15	18	76	5	10	9
Housing accommodations	62	2	24	12	52	4	44	0
Being able to get children educated with white children	58	1	21	20	66	2	30	2
Being able to eat in any restaurant	55	1	31	13	56	2	39	3
Being able to register and vote	42	1	48	9	15	2	81	2
White attitudes[a]	73	2	11	14	93	0	4	3

Source: Adapted from Brink and Harris (1963: 234, 238).

[a]The data reporting black estimates of white attitudes were taken from a question separate from the others.

with their present status on a number of dimensions. The level of optimism revealed in these responses is striking. Only in regard to voting did a majority of blacks fail to respond optimistically. And even here, those expecting an improvement in voting rights outnumbered those anticipating a deterioration, 42 percent to 1 percent. Similarly, by a margin of 73 percent to 2 percent, blacks expected white attitudes to improve "over the next five years" (Brink and Harris 1963:136). Reflecting even greater optimism were the comparable responses of 100 black "leaders" interviewed as a separate part of the survey. Fully 93 percent of the leaders questioned felt white attitudes would improve in the future, while none felt they would get worse. Given that these leaders were initiating much of the protest activity occurring at the time, their overwhelming optimism regarding the prospects for favorable change is significant indeed.

THE RESPONSE TO INSURGENCY, 1961–65

Finally, the responses of other organized parties to the movement also contributed to the dramatic expansion in movement activity during the early 1960s. Indeed, perhaps more than any of the aforementioned three factors it was these responses that were to shape the fortunes of the movement by determining the balance of supporting and opposing forces confronting insurgents.

One view of the federal government's relationship to the black movement has the government assuming the role of a committed ally aggressively working for the realization of movement goals. This view underlies many traditional liberal accounts of the movement. Representative of this perspective is the following statement by Benjamin Muse:

> The Supreme Court was a mighty bulwark of the revolution; the national administration a towering ally.... The Administration's drive for civil rights was centered in the Department of Justice.... These men and their assistants had drafted the President's omnibus civil rights bill, and were working intensively to secure its enactment. They were carrying on a volume of litigation related to school desegregation and voting rights that strained the capacity of the Civil Rights Division's forty overworked lawyers (Muse 1968:40–42).

Muse's statement conveys the image of a federal government wholly supportive of the movement, even to the point of taxing its available manpower in an effort to advance the cause.

In contrast to this view, the argument advanced here is that the federal government attempted to maintain a stance of tactical neutrality vis-à-vis the South's unfolding racial conflict throughout the 1955–65 period. In the face of the growing electoral strength of blacks and the continued strategic importance of the South, the national political elite sought to refrain from antagonizing either side through forthright support of the other. Their interest lay, instead, in curbing the disruptive excesses of both sides so as to avoid a dangerous confrontation that would force their involvement in the conflict. Only by avoiding such involvement could federal officials hope to continue to court the political favors of both groups. Thus, the watchword of every administration during this period was "the preservation of public order" rather than the realization of black equality.

The 1962–64 Voter Education Project (VEP) offers perhaps the best and most significant example of the government's efforts to direct movement activity into channels it viewed as less threatening. Though ostensibly sponsored by the Taconic Foundation, the real driving force behind VEP were officials in the Kennedy administration who viewed voter registration as a way of curbing the disruptive tendencies of the movement while, at the same time, systematically swelling the ranks of likely Democratic supporters.

SUMMARY

The period from 1961 to 1965 proved to be one of heightened activity and significant accomplishment for the movement. Consistent with a political process interpretation, the expansion of insurgency during these years would appear to have been the product of four broad sets of factors. First, throughout the period, insurgents were able to maintain organizational strength sufficient to mount and sustain an organized campaign of social protest. This strength stemmed in part from the profitable linkages movement groups were able to establish with external support groups. In addition, the narrow geographic and substantive focus of insurgency in the early 1960s contributed to the strength of the movement by enabling insurgents to concentrate their forces for an effective attack on limited targets.

Second, a series of external factors facilitated movement growth during this period by sustaining the supportive political context that had begun to develop in the 1930s. These factors had the effect of enhancing the political significance of the black population, thus granting organized elements within that population increased leverage with which to press their claims. Among the factors contributing to this favorable "structure of political opportunities" was the accelerated pace of northward migration among blacks, the growing public salience of the civil rights issue, and the continuing significance of certain international political pressures.

A third factor facilitating the growth of the movement during this time was the sense of optimism and political efficacy prevalent among blacks. In effect, these shared attributions provided insurgents with the will to act, while the confluence of external opportunity and internal organization afforded them the structural capacity to do so.

Finally, the responses of other groups to the burgeoning movement also contributed to a rapid expansion in insurgency. External groups were forthcoming with vital resource support, even if such support was neither as aggressive nor nonproblematic as some resource mobilization theorists have suggested. For its part, the federal government, though wary of the movement, could ill afford to oppose openly what were widely regarded as legitimate demands. Thus, it chose a stance of tactical neutrality that allowed it to court both insurgents and supremacists. However, through their successful orchestration of the "politics of protest," movement groups were able to pressure the government into supportive action by provoking white supremacists into violent disruptions of public order. Thus, even the characteristic response of the supremacists to the movement played a facilitative role in the unfolding conflict dynamic.

NOTES

1. However, even the outbreak of protest activity in the North, on many occasions, reflected the movement's essential southern basis. In fact, most of the early northern protest activity took the form of sympathy demonstrations or aggressive picketing in support of southern campaigns. For an example, see Meier and Rudwick's discussion of the effect that the outbreak of the sit-ins had on the revitalization of CORE activity in the North (1973:101–2, 121).
2. Of the eight towns in which boycotts are known to have occurred, only two, Chattanooga, Tennessee, and Tallahassee, Florida, are not in the Deep South. Of the other six towns, two are in Alabama (Birmingham and Montgomery), two in Louisiana (New Orleans and Baton Rouge), and one each in Georgia (Atlanta) and South Carolina (Rock Hill).
3. The question of how this consensus developed is an interesting topic in its own right. While integration had long constituted a powerful ideology in black sociopolitical thought, so had a well-developed separatist philosophy. What makes the period from 1930 to 1965 so unusual is the nearly exclusive dominance of the former over the latter. To account for the causes of this ideological dominance is beyond the scope of this book. No doubt part of the answer lies in the success of the campaign to discredit Marcus Garvey, the last significant proponent of separatism prior to this period. The myth, championed by elements within both the black and white communities, made Garvey out to be part charlatan, part buffoon. In truth, he was neither, but the strength of his following in the 1920s made him a threat to vested interests in both communities and resulted in the campaign of public vilification that reduced support for separatism within the black population.
4. This analysis was based exclusively on comparable Gallup polls conducted between 1961 and 1965. Smith (1980) has assembled a richer data set consisting of all such surveys conducted by the major polling organizations between 1946 and 1976. In all, he reports the results of nineteen such polls between 1961 and 1965. His findings, however, are consistent with those reported here. While he does not report the rank order of "civil rights" among all problems identified in each survey, the percentage of respondents listing that as the "most important" problem remained high throughout the period. In ten of the nineteen surveys, at least 20 percent of the respondents identified civil rights as the country's most important problem, while in another three the figure was between ten and 20 percent (Smith 1980:170–71).

REFERENCES

Brink, William, and Louis Harris. 1963. *The Negro Revolution in America*. New York: Simon and Schuster.

Brooks, Thomas R. 1974. *Walls Come Tumbling Down: A History of the Civil Rights Movement, 1940–1970*. Englewood Cliffs, N.J.: Prentice-Hall.

Bullock, Henry Allen. 1971. "Urbanism and race relations." In Rupert B. Vance and Nicholas J. Demerath, eds., *The Urban South*. Freeport, N.Y.: Books for Libraries Press, 207–29.

Glantz, Oscar. 1960. "The Negro Voter in Northern Industrial Cities." *Western Political Quarterly* 13(December):999–1010.

Lomax, Louis E. 1962. *The Negro Revolt*. New York: Harper and Row.

Meier, August, and Elliott Rudwick. 1973. *CORE, A Study in the Civil Rights Movement, 1942–1968*. New York: Oxford University Press.

Muse, Benjamin. 1968. *The American Negro Revolution*. Bloomington: Indiana University Press.

Oppenheimer, Martin. 1963. "The Genesis of the Southern Negro Student Movement (Sit-In Movement): A Study in Contemporary Negro Protest." Ph.D. dissertation, University of Pennsylvania.

Ploski, Harry A., and Warren Marr II, eds. 1976. *The Afro American*. New York: The Bellwether Company.

Smith, Tom W. 1980. "America's Most Important Problem—A Trend Analysis, 1946–1976." *Public Opinion Quarterly* 44(no. 2):164–80.

Global Dynamics

INTRODUCTION

The late twentieth and early twenty-first centuries are often referred to as an era of globalization. What is globalization? What makes this particular era more global than others? After all, people have been traveling great distances, exchanging ideas, goods, and cultures, making war, and forging alliances for thousands of years. What makes a social system and social structures "global"? How did the form and structures of globalization emerge? Much of what we think of as globalization was made possible by developments in communication and information technologies. Satellite and computer networks allow for instantaneous point-to-point communication, which means that production can be more easily organized across great distances, and capital can be moved with a keystroke. Changes in transportation, especially the construction of huge cargo ships and the containerization of shipping allow for vast amounts of goods to move around the world relatively cheaply. Goods, services, cultural products, and conversations can now be organized, produced, and distributed on a truly global scale with relative ease. Such sweeping change in what is technically possible is bound to lead to sweeping changes in social arrangements worldwide, and such sweeping change is the stuff for which the field of sociology initially emerged. The dynamics of global social systems in the twenty-first century is therefore likely to be a central focus for sociologists for some time. As you will see, these global changes, as well as the sociological lens through which we can make sense of them, have deep roots in the centuries that precede our own.

In *The Modern World System*, Immanuel Wallerstein presents a theoretical framework for understanding where globalization came from and how it is organized. He looks back to the sixteenth century to identify the elements that led to the emergence of a capitalist world economy. He argues that, at that time, economic factors began to operate on a scale larger than political units like countries. That is, the institution of economy began to be organized on a level beyond the organizational level of the institution of politics. In the sixteenth century, European ships began to travel the world on a scale and in a volume that facilitated a new geographic division of labor in production. Strong states, in which capital was accumulated and invested in technology (ships and production), became able to exploit land and labor in weaker states lacking capital accumulation. Dominant states became "core" countries in the world economy, while weaker states became "peripheral" countries in the world economy. Peripheral countries provided natural resources and agricultural products as raw materials, and core countries increasingly used those materials to produce higher value goods for an international market. In this way, land and labor in the periphery came to serve capital accumulation in the core in a colonial system of global production. Over the centuries, core states come and go, as the relative power of specific countries (Spain, Portugal, England, France, the United States) rise and fall. What remains in place, according to Wallerstein, is (a) the international division of labor in global production and (b) the unequal and exploitative relationship between core and periphery in a world economy. He sees the core's exploitation of the periphery, along with the periphery's refusal to accept exploitation, as neither inevitable nor just, but as a primary tension inherent in this world system. This tension is evident in world trade negotiations, climate change treaty discussions, and international military conflicts. For Wallerstein, the era of globalization, based on a capitalist world system, is both fluid and wrought with conflict.

We can see the specific dynamics of Wallerstein's world system played out as Deborah Barndt describes the origin and life course of the global tomato in *Tangled Routes: Women, Work, and Globalization on the Tomato Trail*. Her qualitative analysis also begins in the sixteenth century, with the Spanish conquest of Mexico and the "discovery" of the tomato at the start of the world economy. Barndt poses the sociological question, Where does your food come from? If the tomato on your sandwich could talk, what might it tell you about the social forces of globalization? Barndt answers that question by tracing the tomato commodity chain from corporate produced seed, through classed, raced, and gendered divisions of labor, across trade regulated borders, and into the local branch of your favorite grocery chain. Understanding the complex race, class, and gender relations, institutional arrangements, and global economic forces at work in determining where our food comes from, who produces it, who consumes it, and who profits from it, requires a keen sociological imagination. In the journey of the corporate tomato, Wallerstein's geographic division of labor is graphically illustrated by the roles played by Mexican workers and U.S.-based corporations. Mexican land and labor are fused with U.S. capital in the form of a "technological package" of engineered seeds, chemical fertilizers, and chemical pesticides, to bring uniform, ripe produce to consumers in the core year-round.

Why would populations in a wide range of very different countries around the world erupt in protest? What could cause a global pattern of protest? In the excerpt from *Free Markets and Food Riots: The Politics of Global Adjustment*, Mridula Udayagiri (and John Walton and John Seddon) trace the answers to global integration in a world economy. Being interdependent and interrelated in a world economic system causes populations in very different locations, with different cultures, races, ethnicities, and languages, to experience similar social pressures and policies. In a world economy, when one country sneezes, the rest can easily catch cold. In Udayagiri's analysis, the world economy reached a high level of integration in the late twentieth century, resulting in greater "simultaneity of events" or synchronicity. Due to their positions and integration in the world economy, the countries of Latin America, Africa, and Asia experienced similar economic conditions, including high levels of international debt. The prescription for dealing with debt from global institutional actors such as the World Bank, and International Monetary Fund, was taking new loans, but with certain conditions. Those conditions included, cutting government subsidies (for food, fuel and other necessities), selling public enterprises (like power utilities) to private corporations, and making poor populations pay for government provided basic medical services (like rural clinics). People throughout the global south experienced similar debt crises, and similar austerity policies, with similar impacts on inequality. One result was the emergence of a pattern of anti-austerity protests or "food riots" in widely disparate parts of the world. Udayagiri looks at the most stable of the three continents in question, Asia, to illustrate that global economic crisis, austerity measures, and subsequent protests were near universal phenomena. We more recently see this pattern in Europe as well. The global economy now functions as a single integrated social system, and so social experiences are becoming more similar across the planet.

The expansion of the institution of economy on a global scale has been a central focus of sociologists from the early foundation of the discipline. In the twenty-first century, this focus has taken on new significance, as technological change has facilitated global coordination of institutions, organizations, and social movements. Populations, nation-states, and corporations are now more closely integrated and interdependent. Coordination of complex organizations across time and space has never been easier, and the results are shifting norms, roles, and meanings across a wide range of social production. Every day, a greater portion of the global population is linked together through the expansion of the Internet, facilitating the rapid exchange of ideas, culture, services, and commercial products. What this means for the future of social relations, from the micro-level of interpersonal relationships, through the macro-level of transnational trade and conflict, remains to be seen, studied, analyzed, and theorized by sociologists.

READING 25

Excerpt from *The Modern World System*

IMMANUEL WALLERSTEIN

In order to describe the origins and initial workings of a world system, I have had to argue a certain conception of a world-system. A world-system is a social system, one that has boundaries, structures, member groups, rules of legitimation, and coherence. Its life is made up of the conflicting forces which hold it together by tension and tear it apart as each group seeks eternally to remold it to its advantage. It has the characteristics of an organism, in that it has a life-span over which its characteristics change in some respects and remain stable in others. One can define its structures as being at different times strong or weak in terms of the internal logic of its functioning.

What characterizes a social system in my view is the fact that life within it is largely self-contained, and that the dynamics of its development are largely internal. The reader may feel that the use of the term "largely" is a case of academic weaseling. I admit I cannot quantify it. Probably no one ever will be able to do so, as the definition is based on a counterfactual hypothesis: If the system, for any reason, were to be cut off from all external forces (which virtually never happens), the definition implies that the system would continue to function substantially in the same manner. Again, of course, substantially is difficult to convert into hard operational criteria. Nonetheless the point is an important one and key to many parts of the empirical analyses. Perhaps we should think of self-containment as a theoretical absolute, a sort of social vacuum, rarely visible and even more implausible to create artificially, but still and all a socially-real asymptote, the distance from which is somehow measurable.

Using such a criterion, it is contended here that most entities usually described as social systems—"tribes," communities, nation-states—are not in fact total systems. Indeed, on the contrary, we are arguing that the only real social systems are, on the one hand, those relatively small, highly autonomous subsistence economies not part of some regular tribute-demanding system and, on the other hand, world-systems. These latter are to be sure distinguished from the former because they are relatively large; that is, they are in common parlance "worlds." More precisely, however, they

Wallerstein, Immanuel. 1974. *The Modern World System I: Capitalist Agriculture and the Origins of the European World-Economy in the Sixteenth Century*, pp. 229–233. Reprinted with permission of Elsevier.

are defined by the fact that their self-containment as an economic-material entity is based on extensive division of labor and that they contain within them a multiplicity of cultures.

It is further argued that thus far there have only existed two varieties of such world-systems: world-empires, in which there is a single political system over most of the area, however attenuated the degree of its effective control; and those systems in which such a single political system does not exist over all, or virtually all, of the space. For convenience and for want of a better term, we are using the term "world-economy" to describe the latter.

Finally, we have argued that prior to the modern era, world-economies were highly unstable structures which tended either to be converted into empires or to disintegrate. It is the peculiarity of the modern world-system that a world-economy has survived for 500 years and yet has not come to be transformed into a world-empire—a peculiarity that is the secret of its strength.

This peculiarity is the political side of the form of economic organization called capitalism. Capitalism has been able to flourish precisely because the world-economy has had within its bounds not one but a multiplicity of political systems.

I am not here arguing the classic case of capitalist ideology that capitalism is a system based on the noninterference of the state in economic affairs. Quite the contrary! Capitalism is based on the constant absorption of economic loss by political entities, while economic gain is distributed to "private" hands. What I am arguing rather is that capitalism as an economic mode is based on the fact that the economic factors operate within an arena larger than that which any political entity can totally control. This gives capitalists a freedom of maneuver that is structurally based. It has made possible the constant economic expansion of the world-system, albeit a very skewed distribution of its rewards. The only alternative world-system that could maintain a high level of productivity and change the system of distribution would involve the reintegration of the levels of political and economic decision-making. This would constitute a third possible form of world-system, a socialist world government. This is not a form that presently exists, and it was not even remotely conceivable in the sixteenth century.

The historical reasons why the European world-economy came into existence in the sixteenth century and resisted attempts to transform it into an empire have been expounded at length. We shall not review them here. It should however be noted that the size of a world-economy is a function of the state of technology, and in particular of the possibilities of transport and communication within its bounds. Since this is a constantly changing phenomenon, not always for the better, the boundaries of a world-economy are ever fluid.

We have defined a world-system as one in which there is extensive division of labor. This division is not merely functional—that is, occupational—

but geographical. That is to say, the range of economic tasks is not evenly distributed throughout the world-system. In part this is the consequence of ecological considerations, to be sure. But for the most part, it is a function of the social organization of work, one which magnifies and legitimizes the ability of some groups within the system to exploit the labor of others—that is, to receive a larger share of the surplus.

While, in an empire, the political structure tends to link culture with occupation, in a world-economy the political structure tends to link culture with spatial location. The reason is that in a world-economy the first point of political pressure available to groups is the local (national) state structure. Cultural homogenization tends to serve the interests of key groups and the pressures build up to create cultural-national identities.

This is particularly the case in the advantaged areas of the world-economy—what we have called the core-states. In such states, the creation of a strong state machinery coupled with a national culture, a phenomenon often referred to as integration, serves both as a mechanism to protect disparities that have arisen within the world-system, and as an ideological mask and justification for the maintenance of these disparities.

World-economies then are divided into core-states and peripheral areas. I do not say peripheral *states* because one characteristic of a peripheral area is that the indigenous state is weak, ranging from its nonexistence (that is, a colonial situation) to one with a low degree of autonomy (that is, a neo-colonial situation).

There are also semiperipheral areas which are in between the core and the periphery on a series of dimensions, such as the complexity of economic activities, strength of the state machinery, cultural integrity, etc. Some of these areas had been core-areas of earlier versions of a given world-economy. Some had been peripheral areas that were later promoted, so to speak, as a result of the changing geopolitics of an expanding world-economy.

The semiperiphery, however, is not an artifice of statistical cutting points, nor is it a residual category. The semiperiphery is a necessary structural element in a world-economy. These areas play a role parallel to that played, *mutatis mutandis*, by middle trading groups in an empire. They are collection points of vital skills that are often politically unpopular. These middle areas (like middle groups in an empire) partially deflect the political pressures which groups primarily located in peripheral areas might otherwise direct against core-states and the groups which operate within and through their state machineries. On the other hand, the interests primarily located in the semiperiphery are located outside the political arena of the core-states, and find it difficult to pursue the ends in political coalitions that might be open to them were they in the same political arena.

The division of a world-economy involves a hierarchy of occupational tasks, in which tasks requiring higher levels of skill and greater capitalization are reserved for higher-ranking areas. Since a capitalist world-economy essentially rewards accumulated capital, including human capital, at a higher rate than "raw" labor power, the geographical maldistribution of these occupational skills involves a strong trend toward self-maintenance. The forces of the marketplace reinforce them rather than undermine them. And the absence of a central political mechanism for the world-economy makes it very difficult to intrude counteracting forces to the maldistribution of rewards.

Hence, the ongoing process of a world-economy tends to expand the economic and social gaps among its varying areas in the very process of its development. One factor that tends to mask this fact is that the process of development of a world-economy brings about technological advances which make it possible to expand the boundaries of a world-economy. In this case, particular regions of the world may change their structural role in the world-economy, to their advantage, even though the disparity of reward between different sectors of the world-economy as a whole may be simultaneously widening. It is in order to observe this crucial phenomenon clearly that we have insisted on the distinction between a peripheral area of a given world-economy and the external arena of the world-economy. The external arena of one century often becomes the periphery of the next—or its semiperiphery. But then too core-states can become semiperipheral and semiperipheral ones peripheral.

While the advantages of the core-states have not ceased to expand throughout the history of the modern world-system, the ability of a particular state to remain in the core sector is not beyond challenge. The hounds are ever to the hares for the position of top dog. Indeed, it may well be that in this kind of system it is not structurally possible to avoid, over a long period of historical time, a circulation of the elites in the sense that the particular country that is dominant at a given time tends to be replaced in this role sooner or later by another country.

We have insisted that the modern world-economy is, and only can be, a capitalist world-economy. It is for this reason that we have rejected the appellation of "feudalism" for the various forms of capitalist agriculture based on coerced labor which grow up in a world-economy. Furthermore, although this has not been discussed in this volume, it is for this same reason that we will, in future volumes, regard with great circumspection and prudence the claim that there exist in the twentieth century socialist national economies within the framework of the world-economy (as opposed to socialist movements controlling certain state-machineries within the world-economy).

If world-systems are the only real social systems (other than truly isolated subsistence economies), then it must follow that the emergence, consolidation, and political roles of classes and status groups must be appreciated as elements of this world system. And in turn it follows that one of the key elements in analyzing a class or a status-group is not only the state of its self-consciousness but the geographical scope of its self-definition.

Classes always exist potentially (*an sich*). The issue is under what conditions they become class-conscious (*für sich*), that is, operate as a group in the politico-economic arenas and even to some extent as a cultural entity. Such self-consciousness is a function of conflict situations. But for upper strata open conflict—and hence overt consciousness—is always *faute de mieux*. To the extent that class boundaries are not made explicit, to that extent it is more likely that privileges be maintained.

Since in conflict situations, multiple factions tend to reduce to two by virtue of the forging of alliances, it is by definition not possible to have three or more (conscious) classes. There obviously can be a multitude of occupational interest groups which may organize themselves to operate within the social structure. But such groups are really one variety of status-groups, and indeed often overlap heavily with other kinds of status-groups such as those defined by ethnic, linguistic, or religious criteria.

To say that there cannot be three or more classes is not however to say that there are always two. There may be none, though this is rare and transitional. There may be one, and this is most common. There may be two, and this is most explosive.

We say there may be only one class, although we have also said that classes only actually exist in conflict situations, and conflicts presume two sides. There is no contradiction here. For a conflict may be defined as being between one class, which conceives of itself as the universal class, and all the other strata. This has in fact been the usual situation in the modern world-system. The capitalist class (the bourgeoisie) has claimed to be the universal class and sought to organize political life to pursue its objectives against two opponents. On the one hand, there were those who spoke for the maintenance of traditional rank distinctions despite the fact that these ranks might have lost their original correlation with economic function. Such elements preferred to define the social structure as a non-class structure. It was to counter this ideology that the bourgeoisie came to operate as a class conscious of itself.

The European world-economy of the sixteenth century tended overall to be a one-class system. It was the dynamic forces profiting from economic expansion and the capitalist system, especially those in the core-areas, who tended to be class-conscious—that is to operate within the political arena as a group defined primarily by their common role in the economy. This common role was in fact defined somewhat broadly from a twentieth-century perspective. It included persons who were farmers, merchants, and industrialists. Individual entrepreneurs often moved back and forth between these activities in any case, or combined them. The crucial distinction was between these men, whatever their occupation, principally oriented to obtaining profit in the world market, and the others not so oriented.

The "others" fought back in terms of their status privileges—those of the traditional aristocracy, those which small farmers had derived from the feudal system, those resulting from guild monopolies that were outmoded. Under the cover of cultural similarities, one can often weld strange alliances. Those strange alliances can take a very activist form and force the political centers to take account of them. We pointed to such instances in our discussion of France. Or they can take a politically passive form that serves well the needs of the dominant forces in the world-system. The triumph of Polish Catholicism as a cultural force was a case in point.

The details of the canvas are filled in with the panoply of multiple forms of status-groups, their particular strengths and accents. But the grand sweep is in terms of the process of class formation. And in this regard, the sixteenth century was indecisive. The capitalist strata formed a class that survived and gained *droit de cité*, but did not yet triumph in the political arena.

The evolution of the state machineries reflected precisely this uncertainty. Strong states serve the interests of some groups and hurt those of others. From however the standpoint of the world-system as a whole, if there is to be a multitude of political entities (that is, if the system is not a world-empire), then it cannot be the case that all these entities be equally strong. For if they were, they would be in the position of blocking the effective operation of transnational economic entities whose locus was in another state. And obviously certain combinations of these groups control the state. It would then follow that the world division of labor would be impeded, the world-economy decline, and eventually the world-system fall apart.

It also cannot be that no state machinery is strong. For in such a case, the capitalist strata would have no mechanisms to protect their interests, guaranteeing their property rights, assuring various monopolies, spreading losses among the larger population, etc.

It follows then that the world-economy develops a pattern where state structures are relatively strong in the core areas and relatively weak in the periphery. Which areas play which roles is in many ways accidental. What is necessary is that in some areas the state machinery be far stronger than in others.

What do we mean by a strong state-machinery? We mean strength vis-à-vis other states within the world-economy including other core-states, and strong vis-à-vis local political units within the boundries of the state. In effect, we mean a sovereignty that is *de facto* as well as *de jure*. We also mean a state that is strong vis-à-vis any particular social group within the state. Obviously, such groups vary in the amount of pressure they can bring to bear upon the state. And obviously certain combinations of these groups control the state. It is not that the state is a neutral arbiter. But the state is more than a simple vector of given forces, if only because many of these forces are situated in more than one state or are defined in terms that have little correlation with state boundaries.

A strong state then is a partially autonomous entity in the sense that it has a margin of action available to it wherein it reflects the compromises of multiple interests, even if the bounds of these margins are set by the existence of some groups of primordial strength. To be a partially autonomous entity, there must be a group of people whose direct interests are served by such an entity: state managers and a state bureaucracy.

Such groups emerge within the framework of a capitalist world-economy because a strong state is the best choice between difficult alternatives for the two groups that are strongest in political, economic, and military terms: the emergent capitalist strata, and the old aristocratic hierarchies.

For the former, the strong state in the form of the "absolute monarchies" was a prime customer, a guardian against local and international brigandage, a mode of social legitimation, a preemptive protection against the creation of strong state barriers elsewhere. For the latter, the strong state represented a brake on these same capitalist strata, an upholder of status conventions, a maintainer of order, a promoter of luxury.

No doubt both nobles and bourgeoisie found the state machineries to be a burdensome drain of funds, and a meddlesome unproductive bureaucracy. But what options did they have? Nonetheless they were always restive and the immediate politics of the world-system was made up of the pushes and pulls resulting from the efforts of both groups to insulate themselves from what seemed to them the negative effects of the state machinery.

A state machinery involves a tipping mechanism. There is a point where strength creates more strength. The tax revenue enables the state to have a larger and more efficient civil bureaucracy and army which in turn leads to greater tax revenue—a process that continues in spiral form. The tipping mechanism works in other directions too—weakness leading to greater weakness. In between these two tipping points lies the politics of state-creation. It is in this arena that the skills of particular managerial groups make a difference. And it is because of the two tipping mechanisms that at certain points a small gap in the world-system can very rapidly become a larger one.

In those states in which the state machinery is weak, the state managers do not play the role of coordinating a complex industrial-commercial-agricultural mechanism. Rather they simply become one set of landlords amidst others, with little claim to legitimate authority over the whole.

These tend to be called traditional rulers. The political struggle is often phrased in terms of tradition versus change. This is of course a grossly misleading and ideological terminology. It may in fact be taken as a general sociological principle that, at any given point of time, what is thought to be traditional is of more recent origin than people generally imagine it to be, and represents primarily the conservative instincts of some group threatened with declining social status. Indeed, there seems to be nothing which emerges and evolves as quickly as a "tradition" when the need presents itself.

In a one-class system, the "traditional" is that in the name of which the "others" fight the class-conscious group. If they can encrust their values by legitimating them widely, even better by enacting them into legislative barriers, they thereby change the system in a way favorable to them.

The traditionalists may win in some states, but if a world-economy is to survive, they must lose more or less in the others. Furthermore, the gain in one region is the counterpart of the loss in another.

This is not quite a zero-sum game, but it is also inconceivable that all elements in a capitalist world-economy shift their values in a given direction simultaneously. The social system is built on having a multiplicity of value systems within it, reflecting the specific functions groups and areas play in the world division of labor.

We have not exhausted here the theoretical problems relevant to the functioning of a world-economy. We have tried only to speak to those illustrated by the early period of the world-economy in creation—to wit, sixteenth-century Europe. Many other problems emerged at later stages.

In the sixteenth century, Europe was like a bucking bronco. The attempt of some groups to establish a world-economy based on a particular division of labor, to create national states in the core areas as politico-economic guarantors of this system, and to get the workers to pay not only the profits but the costs of maintaining the system was not easy. It was to Europe's credit that it was done, since without the thrust of the sixteenth century the modern world would not have been born and, for all its cruelties, it is better that it was born than that it had not been.

It is also to Europe's credit that it was not easy, and particularly that it was not easy because the people who paid the short-run costs screamed lustily at the unfairness of it all. The peasants and workers in Poland and England and Brazil and Mexico were all rambunctious in their various ways. As R. H. Tawney says of the agrarian disturbances of sixteenth-century England: "Such movements are a proof of blood and sinew and of a high and gallant spirit....Happy the nation whose people has not forgotten how to rebel."

The mark of the modern world is the imagination of its profiteers and the counter-assertiveness of the oppressed. Exploitation and the refusal to accept exploitation as either inevitable or just constitute the continuing antinomy of the modern era, joined together in a dialectic which far from reached its climax in the twentieth century.

READING 26

Excerpt from *Tangled Routes: Women, Work, and Globalization on the Tomato Trail*

DEBORAH BARNDT

Step 1: Colonial Conquest of the "Love Apple"

In the sixteenth century, the Spanish conquistadores received tomatoes as part of tributes from Indigenous peoples in the Americas and eventually took the plant back to Europe along with other natural riches they had "discovered." There it was initially feared as poisonous and primarily considered decorative as a "love apple," until Italians began to embrace it in their cuisine. French settlers carried tomatoes to Quebec and Louisiana in the eighteenth century, and it was soon proclaimed medicinal and promoted by agricultural innovators such as Thomas Jefferson. Since then the tomato has been central to diets in the Americas and considered rich in vitamins (A and C) and minerals (calcium and potassium), especially when ripe. It has been bred into hundreds of hybrid forms; the most common big round red version, *Solanum lycopersicon* in Latin, is known in Mexico as *jitomate*.[1] The tomato is now the most widely grown fruit in the Americas as well as the most heavily traded.

Step 2: The Struggle for Land (Campo)

In recent decades, many Mexican *campesinos* (which means literally "of the land," or *campo*) have lost access to lands for cultivating the plant, either individually or collectively in peasant communities. Indigenous peoples have struggled for land for centuries, especially after the Spaniards arrived and sent them to work as peons in the mines and plantations. Mestizo and Indigenous campesinos gained greater access to land through the Mexican Revolution (whose battle cry was "Land and liberty!") and through agrarian reforms under President Lázaro Cardenas in the 1930s. In the 1980s, Mexican neoliberal policies privatized *ejidos* (communal lands) and encouraged foreign investment, and in the 1990s and 2000s, North American Free Trade Agreement (NAFTA) increased agroexports. Since then, more and more campesinos from the southern states of Mexico have migrated to richer northern states to work

Barndt, Deborah. 2008. "The Journey of the Corporate Tomato" from *Tangled Routes: Women, Work, and Globalization on the Tomato Trail*. Lanham, MD: Rowman & Littlefield.

as salaried labor for large agribusinesses. If they still own plots in their home regions, much of the land has been degraded through endless cycles of fertilizer and pesticide use.

Land, or the *campo*, is thus central to the story of the corporate tomato, particularly as it has become viewed as a natural resource and as private property by Western science and industrial capitalist interests, both national and global.

Step 3: Monocultures Led by U.S. Industrial Agriculture

Tomatoes were the first fruit produced for export in Mexico, beginning in the late 1880s, but their production intensified with the development of capitalist production in Sinaloa in the 1920s. Often financed by U.S. capital and inputs, Mexican companies adopted American industrial practices such as Taylorization, the assembly line production and standardization developed after World War I. The work was divided into small manageable units, and technology was introduced that didn't depend on physical force, opening up jobs for women. In the late 1920s, U.S. surplus and protectionist policies forced Mexican producers to standardize packing tomatoes in wooden crates[2] to compete with U.S. producers. In the 1950s, two technologies revolutionized tomato cultivation: the use of plastic covering "mulch" that kept the plants from direct contact with the earth[3] and the growth of seedlings in greenhouses.[4] By 2004, tomatoes accounted for 11.98 percent of the fruit and vegetable production in Mexico, even though they took up only 0.5 percent of the arable land.[5]

Monocultural and cash crop production is a central feature of the global food system today. It has, however, eliminated many types of tomatoes; 80 percent of the varieties have been lost in this century alone.[6] Now Indigenous and mestizo campesinos tend tomatoes as salaried workers in agribusinesses built on a Western scientific logic and rationalism. Each worker is relegated to a specific routinized task, in large monocrop fields or more recently in greenhouses (called "factories in the fields"), where the goal is to harvest thousands of tomatoes at the same time and in identical form primarily destined for export.

The industrialization of agriculture has, in fact, been accompanied by a feminization of agricultural labor, particularly in greenhouses and packing plants.

COMBINING SALARIED WORK WITH SUBSISTENCE AGRICULTURE

While large monocultural agribusinesses dominate tomato production in Mexico, the campesinos who work seasonally for them cannot survive without also cultivating their own staple crops. As the case study of Empaque Santa Rosa, the Mexican agribusiness, shows, the low wages of industrial agriculture are based on the assumption that workers will combine salaried work with subsistence agriculture. For the poorer Indigenous migrant farmworkers, this is becoming less possible as they must migrate to more and more harvests to survive and as they lose access to arable land in their home states. But many peasants maintain their subsistence knowledge and more environmentally sustainable practices by growing basic foods in plots on hillsides outside their village, working in their *milpa* (cornfield) after returning from picking tomatoes in large plantations. This double day not only assures their survival but keeps traditional knowledges alive alongside more industrialized practices. The interplanting of corn, squash, and beans (called the "three sisters" by North American Aboriginal people) uses the advantages of each crop to improve the growth of the others while maintaining the fertility of the soil.[7]

Step 4: Multinationals Control the Technological Package

Even though many tomato seeds originated in Mexico, they have now become the "intellectual property" of multinational companies, which claim patents on genetically modified forms of the seeds. They have been re-created in thousands of varieties, hybridized, and more recently genetically engineered by multinational agribusinesses such as Monsanto and its counterparts such as Western Seed of Mexico. In 1996, Western Seed produced, for example, a seed that is immune to the whitefly that destroyed thousands of tons of tomato production in Autlán, Jalisco, in the early 1990s.[8] These seeds sell for $20,000 a kilogram and are geared entirely to the export market.

For many Indigenous peoples and campesinos, this has meant not only a loss of ownership and control of the seeds but also a loss of their own knowledge about how to grow tomatoes in endless varieties. Ironically, Mexican producers such as Empaque Santa Rosa must now buy tomato seeds from foreign companies in the United States, Israel, and France; they also hire French and Israeli engineers who bring a whole technological package that must be used with the seeds, as well as an entire production process adopting European and North American management and work practices.[9]

Agrochemicals are central components of the "technological package," and their origins in the Green Revolution are examined later in this chapter. Long before tomato seedlings are planted in the ground, for example, the soil has been treated with fertilizers to enrich the soil for growth. As the tomatoes grow, there is a constant barrage of a variety of agrochemicals—pesticides, herbicides, and fungicides—aimed at killing pests, bacteria, and fungi. Under the mantra of efficiency and productivity, they are heralded as making the plants grow faster, stronger, more uniform, and in greater quantity; they are also critical to the production of the blemish-free tomatoes demanded by the export market.[10] The agrochemicals themselves are primarily imported from U.S. multinationals: Bayer, DuPont, Monsanto, and Cargill. There is neither training in their use, however, nor protective gear provided for workers in fields where pesticides are sprayed by hand, combine, or small plane. Every year an estimated three million people are poisoned by pesticides.[11]

ZAPATISTAS, NAFTA, AND FOOD

It is no coincidence that the poorest field-workers are Indigenous families from the south, forced away from their land for the myriad of reasons named earlier. Nor was it an accident that the Zapatistas chose 1 January 1994, the inaugural day of the North American Free Trade Agreement, as the moment for an uprising of Indigenous communities who had lost their land and livelihoods through colonial practices and neoliberal policies. The Zapatista struggle, for bread and dignity, has been transformed into an international movement that is reclaiming Indigenous rights and knowledges as critical not only for the survival of poor campesino communities but also for the survival of the planet. Food is a political centerpiece of this initiative, reflecting the continuing struggle for the land (campo) as well as for cultural identity of campesinos and Indigenous peoples.

Step 5: Gendered Fields: Women Workers Plant and Pick

Primarily young women plant the seeds in Empaque Santa Rosa's large greenhouses in Sinaloa and nurture them into seedlings, ready to be distributed to production sites in other parts of the country. Once shipped to Sirena, they are transplanted in the surrounding fields by the few full-time workers hired by Santa Rosa from neighboring villages. The young plants are watched carefully over the first few weeks, pruned by campesino women who pluck off the shoots so the stems will grow thicker, faster, and straighter. If tomatoes grow from a main stalk, they take up less space, are less vulnerable to pests on the ground, and are easier to pick. When the plants reach a certain height, women workers tie the vines to strings that hold them up, so they can grow without being crushed on the ground.[12]

As one of the most labor-intensive crops, tomato picking requires many more person hours and careful work than does picking bananas, for example. While most agribusinesses in the United States now have mechanical harvesters that pick tomatoes very fast and in massive amounts, in most Mexican monocultural plantations, tomatoes are still handpicked by campesinos. Hired by the companies, many of them are Indigenous families who have been brought on a one- to two-day journey from the poorer southern states for the harvest season, and they live precariously in migrant labor camps near the fields.

At Empaque Santa Rosa, the tomato workers usually start picking tomatoes at 7:30 A.M., stop for a lunch at 10:30 A.M., and are finished by 2:30 P.M., by which time the sun has become unbearably hot. They pluck them fast, too, so that they can fill the quota of forty pails a day to earn their twenty-eight pesos (approximately U.S. $5 in 1997).[13] Both men and women (as well as children) pick tomatoes, but women pickers are considered more gentle, so there is less damage to the crop. Men, on the other hand, are the ones who stack crates on flatbed trailers that they pull by tractor from the field to the packing plant. This gender dynamic needs to be understood in the context of a *machista* culture perpetuated by an international sexual division of labor.

Step 6: Selecting and Packing the Perfect Tomato

Men unload the tomatoes in crates from the trucks and dump them into chutes that send them sailing into an agitated sea of 90 percent chlorinated water, a bath to remove the dirt, bacteria, and pesticide residue from their oversprayed skins. They are dried by blasts of warm air, then moved along on conveyor belts through another chute that coats them with wax. It keeps the moisture in and the bacteria out, protecting the tomatoes from further breakdown during their long journey, but it also gives them a special shine that makes them more attractive to wholesalers and shoppers in the north.[14]

Not all tomatoes will make the longer trip north, as only the "best" are selected for export. To be chosen, they must be large, well shaped, firm, and free of any cracks, scars, or blemishes. The "nimble fingers" that decide which tomato goes where belong to young women, many of them brought by Santa Rosa from its larger production site in Sinaloa to handle this delicate task. They sort the fruit according to grades and destinations but also by size (determined by how many fit into a box—e.g., 5 × 5s or 6 × 7s) and by color (from shades of green to red), because this is how the importers order them.[15] In Santa Rosa's packing plants, tomatoes are sorted by hand, while in the greenhouses, they are sorted partially by a computerized system that weighs and scans them by laser, then sends them down specific chutes for packing by size and color.

As the tomatoes move along the conveyor belt, primarily women sorters determine their destiny. If they are perfect by international standards, they are deemed "export quality" and divided into second and first grades.[16] If they are regular sized, they go to belts for national consumption and are again categorized as second and first grade. The domestic tomatoes are sent to the big food terminals in Guadalajara and Mexico City, where they may be sold at one-third the price that they will draw internationally.

Women packers have even more responsibility with the tomatoes. They pick them up from depositories that have divided them by color but often have to resort them, checking on the sorters' work. Then they put them gently but quickly into boxes. It's a contradictory tension for these women because they are paid by the box and not by the day (as the sorters are); so they try to put several tomatoes into boxes at the same time, while also being careful not to damage the fruit. The contents are inspected before being closed. In the past few years, as Empaque Santa Rosa has more fully entered the global export market, little round stickers are pasted on the skin of the tomatoes before they are packed up and sent off. Also delicately applied by women, these stickers indicate the particular variety of tomato, according to an international numbering system (e.g., Roma tomatoes are #4064, while cherry tomatoes are #4796).[17]

Step 7: Tomatoes, Trade, and Agroexports

It is easy to tell the difference between those destined for local or export markets: If they're going north, they're packed in cardboard boxes with "Mexican tomatoes" written in English on the outside, often with Styrofoam or plastic dividers that hold each tomato in place; those chosen for domestic consumption are packed, without separators, in wooden crates marked with the company's Mexican label, Empaque Santa Rosa. The real rejects are dropped unceremoniously through a big chute into a truck outside the packing plant and sold to local farmers as animal feed.

Once packed and stickered, the boxes that will carry the tomatoes north are sealed, stacked, wrapped, and moved by men working in the packing plant. They are stacked into skids of 108 boxes and wrapped with a plastic netting that keeps them intact en route. Bar codes are also stuck on the skids by ticketers (usually men); when scanned, the lines on the bar code identify the company, tomato variety, the field they were grown in, the day they were packed, and so forth, allowing inventory to be recorded and problems to be traced.[18] An additional sticker bears a number identifying the worker who packed and inspected the boxes at the point of origin. Men driving motorized forklifts deposit most skids directly onto big trailer trucks, while leaving others in temporary storage.

Structural adjustment programs and neoliberal policies in Mexico in the 1980s encouraged agroexports, and NAFTA in the 1990s opened the doors for competition with northern producers. Tomatoes are one of the few Mexican crops to really "win" with NAFTA, because Mexico maintains the comparative advantage with more intense and consistent sun, easier access to land, and cheaper labor than the United States and Canada. Empaque Santa Rosa, for example, used to produce tomatoes as much for domestic production as for export, but by 2000, it sent 85 percent of its harvest north across the border; an ever-increasing number of greenhouse operations produce cherry tomatoes entirely for export. Mexico ships almost nine hundred thousand tons of tomatoes annually to the United States and Canada.[19] Prices are better in the north, and with the asymmetry of currencies and wages, companies like Santa Rosa can make much more money in the export market.

Tomatoes are ordered by international brokers who request them not only in specific sizes, but also in different shades, from green to red (1 = green, 6 = red).[20] Their journey north may be delayed while the company owners wait for the prices in the United States to rise so they can be sold for more profit. Thus, they might be stored away in refrigerated rooms at the packing plants or near the food terminals, at a temperature that keeps them from ripening too fast, remaining there for a few days up to a week, until the market is more favorable. When the producers decide to fill an order, then, depending on the color requested as well as the destination, the tomatoes may be gassed with ethylene, the same substance that naturally causes ripening, so that the ripening process, temporarily slowed down, is now speeded up. The doors of the storage rooms are closed for twenty-four hours, while the tomatoes are gassed, as the ethylene is dangerous for humans to inhale.

Step 8: Erratic Weathers: El Niño or Climate Change?

Besides being sprayed incessantly with chemicals, tomatoes have been sub-jected recently to intense rains and even freak snowstorms. If a premature freeze occurs in the fields, the juice and pulp of the tomato freeze like ice, as though they had been put in a refrigerator. The journey for some tomatoes dead-ends here, causing the company economic losses and ending the work season prematurely for thousands of poor campesinos.

These erratic weather conditions are often blamed on El Niño, which originates in Peru and is caused by the clashing of hot and cold currents off the Pacific coast. But many contend that human intervention is also affecting global weather patterns, and crops have suffered from their erratic nature in recent years. Global warming is particularly accelerated by the emission of greenhouse gases into the atmosphere, slowly depleting the ozone layer. Among the greatest culprits of this process are the large trucks that trans-port food over long distances, the focus of step 10.

Step 9: Detour to Del Monte Processing Adds "Value"

Second-rate tomatoes are sent in wooden crates to the major food termi-nals (in Guadalajara, Mexico City, and Monterrey), to local markets, and sometimes to food-processing plants. Santa Rosa, for example, supplies Del Monte with tomatoes for processing into canned tomatoes, ketchup, or salsa at its plant in Irapuato, Guanajuato. Tomatoes received at Del Monte are dumped into an assembly production line that moves them along to be weighed and washed, sorted and mashed, then processed through cooking tanks, evaporating tanks, and pasteurizing tanks. Again, primarily women workers fill the bottles through tubes, and the bottles are capped, cooled, labeled, and packed into boxes.[21]

While one might think Del Monte would prefer overripe tomatoes for pro-cessing, they actually prefer firmer varieties, so that the tomatoes won't get caught in the automated conveyor systems and mess up the technology for transporting them into the plant.[22] More and more, however, ketchup producers like Del Monte are buying tomato paste rather than whole tomatoes, because the paste-making business draws on cheap labor and facilitates the process for the manufacturer. In bottled form, tomatoes join many other processed and frozen foods that are increasingly replacing fresh food in North America; known as "value-added" products, they increase the price more than the quality.

Step 10: Trucking: A Nonstop Dash North with Perishable Goods

Empaque Santa Rosa owns a few of its own trailer trucks to transport tomatoes to both domestic and northern markets; they guzzle fossil fuel and also contribute to the depletion of the ozone layer. More often, however, Santa Rosa contracts independent truckers to deliver tomatoes to the Mexico–U.S. border at Nogales. It often hires UTTSA, for example, a trucking company whose refrigerated units can carry fifty thousand–pound shipments of fresh produce. The tomatoes are sometimes precooled in a hydrocooling machine that brings their core temperature from 75 degrees down to 34 degrees, because if the temperature drops from 75 to 34 during the two-day journey north, the fruit might deteriorate.

Trucking is a male job. Truckers often work in pairs, so that one can sleep in the back of the cab while the other takes over the driving. The trip to Nogales from Sirena may take thirty to forty hours, depending how many drivers there are; time is of the essence, because tomatoes are highly perishable and preferred at a certain ripeness, but not overripe. Their average life span, in fact, is 4.7 days, so the faster the drive, the quicker they arrive, and the more market days remain for the critical activity of selling them.

We now enter the second phase of the journey of the corporate tomato from Mexico to Canada, highlighting issues of trade and transport, inspection and distribution. While it involves processes in all three NAFTA countries, this phase is clearly controlled by U.S. regulatory agencies, political interests, and multinational corporate needs. Contending political, economic, and legal interests converge in activities around the borders, especially the highly charged U.S.–Mexico line.

Step 11: Controlling the Gates: Dumping, Drugs, and Deportees

To better control and facilitate the border inspection process, the U.S. Department of Agriculture (USDA) has installed its own inspectors within many Mexican agroexport plants to check the tomatoes before they're even loaded onto the trailer trucks. Mexican environmental laws are not as strict as those in the United States and Canada, though NAFTA has provided some pressure to "harmonize." U.S.-based companies, however, sometimes "dump" pesticides in Mexico after they have been banned in their own country. The problem comes back to haunt them when tomatoes are exported back to the United States, carrying higher concentrations of agrochemicals and threatening the health of U.S. consumers.

The USDA hopes to eventually complete all inspections at the point of origin, in the Mexican plants where the tomatoes are packed. Nonetheless, loads of tomatoes are inspected again and again along the route to the border, and the trucks carrying them are stopped regularly by inspectors at four checkpoints. Usually it is not the tomatoes that interest them as much as other possible cargo that could be smuggled within the trucks, such as narcotics or Mexicans seeking illegal entry into the United States. Narcotraffic is actually a much more lucrative (and volatile) enterprise than tomato production, and a lot of the border activity centers on attempts to control or eradicate it.

The border patrol complex in Nogales is located in a sandy ravine with desert brush competing with enormous spotlights and police cruisers on the hillside, a veritable militarized zone.[23] U.S. Customs officials, guns bulging at their hips, check for truck fraud and narcotics; the work of sniffing dogs has recently been complemented by high-tech X-ray equipment that can scan entire truckloads for suspicious objects. The increasing drug trade is just one more sign of deepening despair and uncontrollable violence in both countries, but particularly Mexico.[24] The U.S. government and the Mexican government have joined forces to address this matter.

Second to drugs is concern for the growing number of desperate Mexicans who try to escape poverty and unemployment by illegally crossing the border, securing jobs in the United States where they earn in one hour what they would make in a day at home. Horror stories abound about the ways they try to smuggle themselves in, under truck cabs, amid produce, or across rivers at night, and about how they are often captured, mistreated, and sent back to Mexico. Surveillance of the border area has intensified since September 11, 2001, and in 2006, U.S. President George W. Bush mandated the construction of a 1,125-kilometer wall along the notorious border, further inhibiting the movement of Mexicans seeking work in the north.

Tomatoes account for 56 percent of the cargo of the nine hundred to thirteen hundred big trailer trucks that cross the Nogales border daily. Truck traffic has been increasing at such a dramatic pace since NAFTA (in peak season in 1998, over twenty-seven thousand trucks crossed here in one month) that new lanes are being added to the highway to ease the congestion.

Step 12: Checking for Quality: Appearance Matters

Most food inspection actually takes place on the Mexican side of the border. At the complex of the Confederation of Agricultural Associations (CAADES), in Nogales, Sonora, six kilometers south of the U.S. border,[25] tomatoes are run through a series of checks by the USDA officials. First they weigh the trucks, to be sure they don't surpass the total limit of eighty-eight thousand pounds; if the loaded trucks are overweight, they must unload and reload the tomatoes in smaller trucks. Then a USDA inspector goes through a truckload and randomly stamps boxes of tomatoes at the top, middle, and bottom of a skid. Ten boxes are opened and inspected at a time.

Some tomatoes get their temperature taken to be sure that the refrigeration of the truck has not failed; if they were packed pink and register higher than 50 degrees, they may be deteriorating too fast and are turned back. Of the long list of potential "quality defects" and "condition defects" used to check the tomatoes, most (such as "smoothness" and "color") relate primarily to the appearance of the fruit.[26] To be deemed suitable as a U.S. No. 1 grade, no more than 10 percent of a load can have either quality defects or condition defects.

Step 13: The Line Is Drawn: Border of Inequalities

There is a stark contrast at the border between the huts dotting the hillsides on the Mexican side and the more elegant homes on the U.S. side; just as the price of tomatoes rises the minute they cross the line, the wages and standard of living also rise. The way business is organized on both sides of the border area also reflects this asymmetry between nations. A growing number of maquiladora plants, set up since the 1960s on the northern Mexican border by multinational companies, employ thousands of young women in assembling electronics, in piecing together garments, and, in lesser quantity, in food processing. On the U.S. side, on the other hand, an immense infrastructure of administrative offices and warehouses has been established to facilitate the speedy movement of tomatoes beyond the border to northern consumers. The border thus also separates the workers in the south (Mexico) from the managers in the north (the United States).

Step 14: Keeping Pests and Pesticides at Bay

Truckers who have passed the inspection in Nogales, Sonora, on the Mexican side, and are transporting tomatoes from a reputable agribusiness, can pass through the rapid transit lane, merely handing in the paperwork and moving quickly north. Others, however, may be directed into the U.S. Customs complex on the Arizona side of the border, for further inspections by the FDA and USDA. The Food and Drug Administration officials randomly select a box from a truck and cut a chunk out of a sample tomato to send to an FDA lab in Phoenix, Arizona. About 1 percent of the produce is tested for pesticide residues. This is one way officials can check to see whether Mexican tomato producers are following the standards regarding the acceptable levels of pesticide residue permitted in the United States. The lab testing may take a few weeks, by which time the chemically suspect tomatoes may have already been unwittingly digested by U.S. or Canadian consumers. Growers whose produce is proven to have certain chemicals[27] above the legal limit are warned that enforcement action might be taken if the problem continues.

What can be detected more immediately, however, are the pests or plant life that may be carried inadvertently in the trucks or boxes in which the tomatoes are packed. USDA botanists don rubber gloves and check the fruit for microbes or markings (a hard scar may be evidence of a pest). If found defective, they may be sent back to Mexico for domestic consumption, sent on to Canada "in bond" (quarantined and wrapped with unbreakable metal straps), or sprayed by a Nogales fumigation company, with USDA officials monitoring the process.[28]

Step 15: Exporting/Importing: Brokers and Wholesalers

When a Mexican trucker is not certified to cross the border, he will pay an American trucker $20 to drive the truck through customs and to a warehouse a few miles north of the border. The warehouses are owned by exporters as well as brokers; Empaque Santa Rosa, for example, has its own office on the U.S. side to manage international sales and distribution within the United States and into Canada. The skids are unloaded in thirty to sixty minutes and stored temporarily in the warehouse. Throughout the day, brokers arrange sales by phone, fax, and e-mail. This is clearly a man's world, and tomatoes are constantly repacked and reloaded on the trucks of brokers or distributors for U.S. and Canadian wholesalers and retailers.

The Blue Book lists hundreds of wholesalers and retailers in the United States and Canada who purchase tomatoes, especially during peak season. Loblaws supermarkets in Ontario, for example, brings up three truckloads of tomatoes daily from the Nogales border. Like other wholesalers and retailers in Canada, they deal with brokers or shippers in Nogales who receive their orders and seek out the best deal from warehouses in the area.

It takes about three days in refrigerated trucks (kept at 48 degrees Fahrenheit) for the tomatoes to reach Ontario from the Mexican border; if coming from Florida, it's only two days, while from California it may be four. Three National Grocers trucks leave Nogales daily filled with three key varieties of tomatoes: the extra large Romas, vine ripes, and Gas Greens. Loblaws has its own warehouse, National Grocers, near the Toronto airport, open seven days a week, twenty-four hours a day, and employing one thousand people (mainly men). Supplying Loblaws, Zehrs, Valu-Mart, No Frills, and some Atlantic chains, National Grocers also brings tomatoes in by air daily from around the world (France, Morocco, the Canary Islands, and Israel), especially between December and February when local hothouse production is closed down because of cold weather.

NOTES

1. The historical information on the tomato is drawn from several sources: Sophie D. Coe, *America's First Cuisines* (Austin: University of Texas Press, 1994), 46–50; Jennifer Bennett, ed., *The Harrowsmith Tomato Handbook* (Camden East, Ontario: Camden House, n.d.), 6–13; Philip Hardgrave, *Growing Tomatoes* (New York: Avon, 1992), 7–9; World Resources Institute, "Food Crops and Biodiversity" (Washington, D.C.: World Resources Institute, 1989), also on its Web site: http://www.wri.og/wri/biodiv/foodcrop.html.

2. The production of wooden crates, in fact, upset the ecosystem balance in rural Mexico and contributed to a plague of *la roña* (a whitefly), which destroyed tomato harvests in Autlán in the early 1990s. The forests surrounding the planta-tions were cut down to make crates, and the whitefly that had lived from the leaves of the trees was forced into the tomato fields for sustenance. Personal com-munication with Antonieta Barrón, Miami, Florida, 17 March 2000.

3. The plastic sheets have several functions: They keep the moisture in and the weeds out, they maintain uniformity among the plants, and the shine on their surface repels pests.

4. Sara Lara, "Feminización de los procesos de trabajo del sector fruti-horticola en el estado de Sinaloa," *Cuicuilco* 21(April–June 1988):29–36.

5. FAOSTAT, http://faostat.fao.org/site/340/DesktopDefault.aspx?PageID=340.

6. A study by the Rural Advancement Foundation International (RAFI) of seventy-five types of vegetables found that 97 percent of the varieties on the old USDA lists are now extinct. Of the 408 varieties of the common tomato, *Lycopersicon exculentum*, existing in 1903, only 79 varieties are now held by the U.S. National Seed Storage Laboratory, perhaps the major seed bank in the world. Cary Fowler and Pat Mooney, *Shattering: Food, Politics, and the Loss of Genetic Diversity* (Tucson: University of Arizona Press, 1996), 51, 62–63, 67.

7. Sometimes called *polycropping*, this approach has multiple advantages. "The beans 'fix' organic nitrogen, thereby enhancing soil fertility and improving corn growth. The corn in turn provides a trellis for the bean vines, and the squash plants, with their wide shady leaves, help keep the weeds down." Scientists have proven that total yields of these three crops grown together are higher than if the same area were sown in monocultures. John Tuxill, "The Biodiversity That People Made," *World Watch* (May/June 2000): 27.

8. "Jalisco produce un jitomate libre del virus de la mosca blanca," *Economía*, 5 December 1996, and "Western Seed colocará 400 kilos de semilla de jitomate híbrido," 6 December 1996.

9. Interview by author and Sara San Martin with Yves Gomes, San Isidro Mazatepec, Jalisco, 24 July 1996.

10. The cosmetic standards that Mexican agroexport companies feel pressured to adhere to have been written under pressure from U.S. growers as one tactic to keep the competition down. Mexican agronomists admit that much higher amounts of pesticides are used to avoid blemishes and irregularities caused by pests. Entomologist Mayra Aviles Gonzales suggests that anxious growers who use an irrationally high quantity of pesticides could get the same production and cosmetic results with 50 percent the amount used. Angus Wright, *The Death of Ramón González: The Modern Agricultural Dilemma* (Austin: University of Texas Press, 1990), 33–35.

11. Tuxill, "The Biodiversity That People Made," 32.

12. Interview by Maria de Jesus Aguilar with Milagros Baltazar, Santa Rosa field-worker, Sayula, Jalisco, 23 August 1997.

13. Interview by author and Sara San Martin with Santa Rosa field-worker Gomez Farias, Jalisco, 26 April 1997.

14. Interview by author and Lauren Baker with Cesar Gil, plant manager, Santa Rosa packing plant, 7 December 1996. See also Wright, *The Death of Ramón González*, 34.

15. Interview by author with Angelo Vento, Ontario Food Terminal, Toronto, January 1999.

16. Lara, "Feminización de los procesos de trabajo," 29–36.

17. Produce list used by Loblaws supermarkets, for the week of 28 July–3 August 1996. It identifies almost five hundred items by name and PLU number.

18. Interview by author and Lauren Baker with Enrique Padilla, greenhouse worker, San Isidro Mazatepec, Jalisco, 10 December 1996.

19. FAOSTAT, http://faostat.fao.org/site/343/DesktopDefault.aspx?PageID=343. Less than 1 percent comes to Canada, over 99 percent to the United States.

20. The Blue Book used by exporters and importers of tomatoes uses the following categories to classify the range of colors: Green—completely green, Breakers—not more than 10 percent turning, Turning—10 to 30 percent turning, Pink—30 to 60 percent pink or red, Light red—60 to 90 percent pink or red, and Red—more than 90 percent red. Tomatoes may be ordered in any of these categories. Those harvested for distant transport are often picked in the mature green state, are gassed, and ripen during transport if kept at temperatures between 55 and 70 degrees Fahrenheit.

21. Interview by author and Maria Dolores Villagomez with Alfredo Badajoz Navarro, Irapuato, Guanajuato, 28 April 1997. See also Lara, *Cuicuilco*, 35.

22. According to California producers, juicy and tasty tomatoes are not ideal for processing; rather, they prefer those that are "bred for thick walls and lots of 'meat' per tomato." While dry and flavorless when raw, such tomatoes apparently "provide just the right color and texture for prepared sauces, salsas, and paste." The major concern, however, seems to be for the transport, not the taste: "The thick walls are what allows a pretty red tomato to survive at the bottom of one of those big truck bins." Carlos Alcalá, "California Really Is the Big Tomato," *Sacramento Bee*, 10 August 1997, B6.

23. Somewhat naively, I crossed this border by foot with three graduate students, armed with video cameras and tape recorders. It wasn't until we had passed by several checkpoints that one of the customs officials stopped us. "Do you realize you are in a highly sensitive area?" he queried and then admonished us: "You really shouldn't be here; we would be liable if there was a shootout or if something happened to you."

24. In 1999, mass graves were discovered in what is being called a "narcocemetery" ten kilometers south of the border city Ciudad Juárez, where the city's ruthless drug cartel (topping tourism and sweatshops as the leading industry) allegedly killed more than one hundred people—mostly Mexicans but also Americans—since 1990. John Stackhouse, *Globe and Mail*, 1 December 1999, 1A.

25. By February 1999, a new CAADES complex had opened at a location thirteen kilometers south of the border and equipped so that all of the inspections could be done on the Mexican side of the border, facilitating quick passage through customs and easing the growing bottlenecks.

26. The "Quality Defects" listed in the Blue Book include maturity, cleanness, shape, smoothness, development, bacterial spot, bacterial speck, catfaces, puffiness, growth cracks, field scars, hail injury, insect injury, cuts or broken skins, and sun scald, while "Condition Defects" include color, sunken and discolored, sunburn, internal discoloration, freezing injury, chilling injury, alternaria rot, gray mold rot, and bacterial soft rot.

27. One problem with the FDA testing procedure is that it only tests for a limited number of chemicals and for single chemicals, while the impact of pesticides on humans comes from a cumulative or synergistic effect that results from being exposed to a variety of pesticides. Wright, *The Death of Ramón González*, 196.

28. Personal interview with Jonathon Barnes, USDA inspector, Customs Complex, Nogales, Arizona, 17 February 1999.

Excerpts from *Free Markets and Food Riots: The Politics of Global Adjustment*

JOHN WALTON, JOHN SEDDON, AND MRIDULA UDAYAGIRI

INTRODUCTION

The roots of the current crisis lie back in the 1960s, when the industrial capitalist economies began to experience a profits squeeze reflecting a crisis of overaccumulation (Armstrong, Glyn, and Harrison 1984). Measures adopted by western governments to help resolve the crisis included austerity measures directed primarily at reducing real wages, particularly in the public sector. According to this analysis, it was the induced recession and austerity measures of the mid-1960s, designed to restructure and rationalize working processes, which established the conditions for the subsequent crisis (Armstrong, Glyn, and Harrison 1984: 276). The austerity measures introduced as part of the process of restructuring provoked unprecedented popular protest and a wave of strikes swept across Europe between 1968 and 1970, resulting in a rapid increase in money wages. Broadly similar developments took place in north America around the same time (cf. Armstrong, Glyn, and Harrison 1984: 271–90). The clampdown which followed was associated with a "mini-recession" in 1970–1 and succeeded by a "mini-boom" in 1972–3, which proved to be the final phase of the long postwar boom.

The mini-boom effectively marked the end of an era. The U.S. dollar devaluation of 1971, the "oil crisis" of winter 1973–4, and an international "crash" in the summer of 1974 brought the golden years to an abrupt and painful halt. The remainder of the decade fell into two phases: a fragile recovery, followed by a renewed and more serious recession in the wake of the second major oil-price rise of 1979 what some referred to as "the second slump" (Mandel 1980). The two deep recessions (of the mid-1970s and of the early 1980s) experienced by the advanced capitalist countries were followed by a period of uneven recovery (1983–9), but it would appear clear now that another recession, starting around 1989, has begun to affect them

Walton, John and John Seddon. 1994. "Introduction" From *Free Markets and Food Riots: The Politics of Global Adjustment*. Cambridge, MA: Blackwell.
Udayagiri, Mridula. 1994. "The Asian Debt Crisis: Structural Adjustment Programs and Popular Protest in India" from *Free Markets and Food Riots: The Politics of Global Adjustment*. Cambridge, MA: Blackwell.

once again. Despite periods of recovery, it is possible to see the entire period from the late 1960s to the present as one marked essentially by recession and crisis.

Frank, for example, has written of "a deep and widespread economic, social, and political crisis in the world, which seems to be centered on a new crisis of overaccumulation of capital in the capitalist West and on the consequent transformation of its relations with the socialist East and the underdeveloped South" (Frank 1981:ix). Others concur with this view of the last two decades as a period of significant transformation on a world scale, and emphasize that the crisis is associated with a long recession. Thus Fröbel remarks that "in the two decades following the Second World War, the capitalist world economy experienced the greatest boom in its history. This boom came to an end toward the close of the 1960s. Since then the world economy has been in a phase of decelerated growth, intensified structural change, and heightened political instability" (Fröbel 1982: 507). Even the World Bank, with its very different perspective, recognized towards the end of the 1980s that "in some developing countries the severity of this prolonged economic slump already surpasses that of the Great Depression in the industrial countries, and in many countries poverty is on the rise" (World Bank 1988: 3).

But while some emphasize the similarities between this "contemporary crisis" and previous capitalist crises (in the 1930s and 1870s, for example), others draw attention to the novel features of this latest crisis:

> The post-war period, at least up to 1973, saw the greatest boom in economic history. Since then there has been slower growth, marked by two recessions which, some have argued, make this later period rather more like the condition of capitalism prior to 1939. However, in this more recent period, there are signs that a new stage in the development of the political economy has emerged, with conditions which differ considerably from those which prevailed in the 1930s. (*Gill and Law 1988: 127*)

The distinctive character of the last two decades is associated with the increasing integration of capitalism on a world scale, its "internationalization."

This has ensured that a crisis of capitalism is, increasingly, and unavoidably, a crisis on a world scale, even if that crisis is experienced unevenly and differently at different moments and in different places. For Gill and Law,

> the global political economy has reached an unprecedented stage of development. The present is not like the past. Today, the security, trade, money, direct investment, communications, and cultural dimensions of global interdependence, are such that there is now an integrated global political economy, whereas in the past, there was a less complex international political economy (and before 1500 a series of regional political economies). (*Gill and Law 1988: 378*)

One of the major consequences of this deepening integration is a greater "synchronicity" or "simultaneity" of events in different parts of the world and in different countries. Evidence suggests that, from the late 1960s onwards, the advanced capitalist countries of the West in particular have become both more closely integrated and mutually interdependent. Consequently, they demonstrate, in recession and in recovery, an increasingly high degree of synchronicity in economic rhythms relative to earlier periods; only Japan stands somewhat apart. By the early 1980s the same was becoming more generally the case for the developing world as a whole, although the unevenness of capitalist development in the Third World and the continuing survival of state socialism in the Second World until the late 1980s ensured that global synchronicity was still not achieved at the beginning of the 1990s. Increasingly, however, the successive booms and recessions of the advanced capitalist West have been "passed on" to the rest of the world in a variety of ways and as a consequence a major process of restructuring on a world scale has taken place.

THE ASIAN DEBT CRISIS: STRUCTURAL ADJUSTMENT AND POPULAR PROTEST IN INDIA

While Latin America has been at the forefront of austerity protests that have accompanied Third World debt crisis, Asia has been characterized by democratic struggles and economic miracles. By the 1970s Newly Industrializing Countries such as South Korea, Taiwan, and Hong Kong were considered exemplars of industrialization for other Third World nations according to purveyors of international development, the World Bank and the International Monetary Fund (IMF) (Garnaut 1980; Robison, Higgott, and Hewison 1987). However, the mid-eighties have seen an economic downturn which resulted in pressure from international sources to undertake major structural adjustments of Asian economies (*Far Eastern Economic Review*, 26 September, 1984). Thus it can be argued that far from being exempted from this Third World adversity, debt crisis in Asia came later in comparison with Africa and Latin America, and was more selective in its incidence.

The task of this chapter is to examine Asia's seeming immunity from the debt crisis, and to show how this crisis is somewhat delayed in comparison to Latin America and Africa. The debt problem has already manifested itself in some nations and austerity protests are gathering force in some of the heavily indebted nations such as India, the Philippines, and Nepal. This chapter will provide a brief discussion of the probable explanations for the variation in intensity and timing of Asia's pattern of austerity protest and in particular, analyze India's experience of the structural adjustment programs that were instituted in July 1991. Although austerity protests have been common in countries such as Bangladesh, Nepal, and the Philippines. India's new economic program marks Asia's introduction into the wave of large-scale international austerity protests. The arguments presented here will be based on consideration of only those nations in Asia which are loosely referred to as Third World, that is, nations categorized by international organizations as developing and so thereby excluding Japan. China as a centrally planned economy is also excluded from the analysis.

India is a significant case for comparative study of international austerity protests as a modern democracy is at stake: it is acknowledged that never before has such a large and diverse and desperately poor population been held together in a commonly accepted, basic framework of democratic rights for as long as four decades (Bardhan 1984). A great aspiration of the founders of the Indian republic was to relieve the crushing, burden of poverty that India had inherited at the end of British rule and this has been the ongoing litany of various Five Year Plan documents, electioneering slogans, and political speeches. Although the state is committed to structural adjustment reforms, socialist and nationalist objectives are deeply embedded in the Indian polity not only on the basis of purely altruistic motives but because they constitute the single largest source of power and patronage for its own legitimacy. Indeed, the large-scale protest articulates questions of moral economy, which in turn may deflect hard economic choices before the government and blunt the effect of austerity reforms. Explanations of an apparent lack of a debt crisis in Asia need closer consideration in view of changes already under way in the world's largest democracy and of what those portend for the rest of Asia.

Scale of Asia's Debt

Although many poor nations are located in Asia, they have escaped the scale of debt adversity of some Latin America and African nations. The geography of debt crisis reveals that the major debtor nations are located in Latin America although countries of Africa and Eastern Europe are also included in this crisis. In the 1970s, southern African nations showed a tremendous increase in debt compared to Latin America (Altvater and Hubner 1991:9). It was estimated that at the end of 1985 low-income countries of this region had average debt ratios (i.e., total external debt to exports) of around 400 percent, ranging from less than 50 percent (Gabon, Botswana, and Lesotho) to more than 1,000 percent (Sudan, Mozambique, and Guinea-Bissau). The following section provides a brief overview of the impact of the debt crisis in Asia, mainly to establish that several nations in the region have experienced both debt and austerity programs.

Debt Crisis in Asia

The 1960s and 1970s did not show any major variation in economic growth in different regions in the Third World. In the 1980s however, the differences manifested themselves. They are reflected in the intensity of economic crises that affected Latin America and Africa even as economic growth in Asia remained somewhat steady in comparison to the other regions. Comparative data from Africa, Asia, and Latin America, presented in Table 27–1, are instructive as to the level [of] economic growth in the three regions. Decline in growth rates was most dramatic in Latin America in the 1980–90 period.

Table 27–1 Annual Gross Domestic Product (GDP) Growth Rate for Selected Countries in Africa, Asia, and Latin America, 1960–1990

Country	1960–70	1970–81	1980–90
Asia			
India	3.4	3.6	5.3
Indonesia	3.8	7.8	5.5
Korea, South	8.6	9.5	9.7
Philippines	5.1	6.2	0.9
Sri Lanka	4.6	4.3	4.0
Taiwan	—	—	—
Thailand	8.4	7.2	7.6
Median	5.1	6.7	4.6
Latin America			
Argentina	4.3	1.9	−0.4
Brazil	5.4	8.4	2.7
Chile	4.5	2.1	3.2
Ecuador	—	8.6	2.0
Mexico	7.2	6.5	1.0
Peru	4.9	3.0	−0.3
Venezuela	6.0	4.5	1.0
Median	5.1	5.0	1.1
Africa			
Algeria	4.3	6.9	3.1
Côte d'Ivoire	8.0	6.2	0.5
Egypt	4.3	8.1[a]	5.0
Kenya	5.9	5.8	4.2
Morocco	4.4	5.2	4.0
Nigeria	3.1	4.5	1.4
Tunisia	4.7[b]	7.3	3.6
Median	4.4	6.2	3.6

[a] 1970–80 figures
[b] 1961–70 figures

Source: World Bank 1983, 1992

Although some of the aggregate values of growth rates are positive in Table 27–1, the low values reflect negative growth rates in the 1980–4 period, especially for countries in Africa and Latin America. The countries with negative growth rates include Benin, Burkina Faso, Morocco, Nigeria, Tunisia, Zambia, and Zimbabwe in Africa; and Argentina, Bolivia, Brazil, Mexico, and Venezuela in Latin America (International Monetary Fund 1992).

A superficial look at regional economic performance excludes Asia from the crippling burden of the international debt crisis. Aggregate figures, given

Table 27-2 Regional Debt Indicators and Debt-Service Payments, 1981–1991

	1981	1985	1986	1987	1988	1989	1990	1991
Debt % of GNP								
Africa	44.4	59.9	74.9	92.4	96.1	99.8	98.2	99.6
Asia	21.3	29.2	30.6	32.1	27.5	25.3	26.1	26.5
Latin America	37.3	60.9	62.9	64.0	53.9	47.4	40.7	37.3
Debt % of export								
Africa	146.2	224.0	303.1	325.3	320.1	308.2	263.1	260.3
Asia	121.3	172.9	182.6	169.1	143.6	133.0	128.2	124.4
Latin America	233.1	331.7	399.3	388.8	333.1	290.5	266.7	280.6
% Debt service to export								
Africa	18.7	26.4	30.0	24.9	28.4	27.3	24.0	25.6
Asia	11.6	16.1	15.8	15.5	12.1	10.5	10.0	9.3
Latin America	0.4	37.6	43.3	37.5	39.5	29.2	25.2	29.4

Source: United Nations 1992

in Table 27–2, for the debt-service burdens of Africa, Asia, and Latin America, show that the debt crisis in Asia has not shown the same alarming proportions as that of Latin America and Africa. For Asia, the debt problem peaked from 1985 to 1987. But regional aggregate figures obscure national realities, and we may tend to assume an optimistic picture based on the Newly Industrialized Country (NIC) experience.

Comparing national figures for individual debt–service burden or debt–service ratio in Table 27–3 yields a disaggregated picture of the debt crisis in Asia. Walton and Ragin (1990) argue that debt service as a percentage of export earnings is a better measure than absolute debt. The measure of debt burden used in this table includes workers, remittances under exports, which is useful as many Asian nations export labor in significantly large numbers, especially to the Middle East.

At the beginning of the eighties, the countries in the Latin American region had the heaviest debt burden, followed closely by African nations. A careful analysis of Table 27–3 reveals first, that fiscal crises are creeping into nations once considered invulnerable to international economic shocks; and second, that the debt crisis is geographically more diffused. Several Asian nations such as India and Indonesia, and Algeria in Africa have seen a significant escalation of the debt burden compared to Latin American nations. Peru shows the lowest debt burden, falling from 30.2 percent in 1985 to 6.8 percent in 1989.

Studies show that the variations in the timing and intensity of economic crisis in Africa, Asia, and Latin America stem from Asia's dependence on "self-reliance" and import substitution industrialization (ISI) (Maddison 1985; Singh 1985; Hughes and Singh 1991).

Table 27-3 Debt Indicators for Selected Countries in Africa, Asia and Latin America, Total Debt Service to Export of Goods and Services, 1980–1989

Country	1980	1985	1989
Africa			
Algeria	27.2	35.8	68.9
Côte D'Ivoire	28.3	44.7	40.9
Egypt	20.8	23.6	21.8
Kenya	22.3	41.9	33.3
Latin America			
Argentina	37.3	58.9	36.1
Brazil	63.1	38.6	31.3
Mexico	49.5	51.5	39.5
Peru	46.5	30.2	6.8
Asia			
Bangladesh	23.2	21.6	19.9
India	9.1	22.3	26.3
Indonesia	13.9	29.5	35.2
Korea, South	19.7	27.3	11.4
Nepal	2.9	7.2	17.2
Philippines	26.5	32.0	26.3
Sri Lanka	12.0	16.5	17.8
Taiwan	—	—	—
Thailand	18.7	31.9	15.5

Source: World Bank 1992

The choices suggest that ideological motives underpin economic strategies. More generally, the delayed debt crisis in Asia is attributed to nationalist and socialist principles. Nationalist and socialist claims constitute Asia's moral economy and legitimize patriotically driven development strategies. The fundamental goal for newly independent Asian nations was to become politically autonomous, free-standing actors in the international economy and this imparted a powerful influence on development strategies. State involvement in the economy contributed to socialist goals in addition to providing the impetus to nationalist sentiments. The state had a legitimate role to play in promoting social objectives to temper the effects of colonial policies. Legitimacy for the interventionist state was also provided by a strident promotion of domestic investment, which could be made possible only by controls over foreign companies and investment. This dual trend, of national capitalism with socialist goals, was and is evident in countries with politically diverse systems such as Indonesia, India, Malaysia, and Thailand. Although the goals have been subverted over time through international and domestic pressures, the ideological construction of an autonomous nation has been a powerful force in directing development strategies.

The broad pattern of economic policy that dominated in Asian nations therefore derived from nationalist ideology and was an attempt to wrest autonomy from colonial relations. Anderson (1991) proposes that contemporary nationalism is a conscious *policy* and that as an *official* policy it always emanates from the state. Indeed, state intervention for economic growth turns on nationalist assumptions and in the case of Asia is legitimated on grounds of socialist objectives. Economic policies that stress self-reliance and self-sufficiency are as much cultural outcomes of nationalism as are poetry, prose, fiction, and music. Economic nationalism as a powerful ideology which emerged within the context of anti-colonial struggles provided a fertile ground for strategies such as import substitution industrialization in the first developmental decade. It restrained multinational investment and openness to the world economy, but it also demonstrated that nationalist economic strategies were limited by the structural constraints of an international economy.

Nowhere is this more sharply illustrated than in the experience of countries such as Brazil and Mexico which left them more vulnerable to international economic downturns. Similarly, import substitution industrialization seemed feasible in Asia as a strategy for growth that relied on tariffs, quotas and import licensing. Some nations moved into import substitution production of intermediate and capital goods, but the limitations of this strategy became apparent when it reached saturation point (Portes and Walton 1981). The failure of ISI was predictable as it relied on a narrow base of consumer goods production that was not sustained by sufficient domestic consumer demand. Waning arguments for the ISI strategy resulted in a push towards export-oriented production primarily advocated by international finance institutions in East Asian nations such as Malaysia, the Philippines, and Thailand. ISI could not be abandoned easily as elite patronage was vested in this strategy. Besides there was a ready availability of finance capital in the international markets which was selectively handed out to those countries which were well integrated into the world economy (Robison, Higgott, and Hewison 1987). There was no immediate urgency to meet the expenses of high-cost industries with increase in exports or foreign-debt payments and the 1970s proved to be economically stable for Asia on the whole. By the end of the decade however fiscal crisis overtook some nations as international recession was more intensely felt in some of these impoverished Asian nations.

The fiscal crisis brought political turmoil to the fore and led to conflicts over policy and development strategies. In particular, the fiscal crisis expressed the tensions of an international aid regime (Wood 1986). The strain was between the power of international financial institutions on one hand and domestic concern for nationalist and socialist obligations on the other. One way that multilateral aid agencies sought to alleviate the economic crisis in Asia in the early 1980s, particularly in countries like the Philippines, Thailand, and Malaysia, was to push for export-oriented industrialization (EOI) again. But structural constraints limited EOI solutions for the Asian economic crisis. The "look East" policy could work in the presence of certain geopolitical conditions such as in South Korea, Taiwan and Hong Kong, and Thailand but could not be expanded to other countries. In addition, there were protectionist pressures from advanced capitalist nations along with a decline in demand associated with the recession in the early eighties (Cho 1985; *Far Eastern Economic Review* September 26, 1985). Thus EOI provided only partial amelioration from burgeoning deficits.

In addition to the limitations of the ISI and EOI strategies, Asian nations had to weather global recession and falling commodity prices in the late seventies and the early eighties that affected traditional agricultural, mineral, and energy exports, and economic shocks such as the oil-price crash. A conjunction of factors was responsible for the differential impact of global recession in Asia.

Reliance on an ISI strategy based on oil exports in Indonesia staved off an intense debt crisis, although the oil-price collapse of the early seventies and early eighties led to an escalating debt burden and a restructuring of the economy. Robison (1987) argues that state control over the economy since 1949 has emphasized nationalist objectives, allowing power and patronage to accrue to local elites. In the aftermath of a failed communist coup and the fall of the Sukarno regime in 1964, there was a reversal in economic nationalism as a result of a fiscal crisis that led to increasing dependence on foreign investment. But, a reassertion of economic nationalist policies began in the mid-seventies and reached well into the eighties. However, the oil-price collapse in the beginning of the eighties created an adverse balance-of-payments situation that was met with fiscal intervention from international finance institutions such as the World Bank. The package of reforms suggested removal of fuel and food subsidies, and reduction in state investment in resource and industrial projects (World Bank 1981; *Far Eastern Economic Review*, May 16, 1985). Although cutbacks in food subsidies were first imposed in the 1982–3 budget, they have been reinstated over subsequent years (Dick 1982). State-owned and managed industrialization and growth is now moving towards deregulation and privatization in what is called a "quiet revolution" (*New York Times*, October 11, 1989). Austerity has resulted in reduced social spending for health, education, and industrial projects (*New York Times*, January 7, 1987). Radical austerity programs have been instituted as conditionalities for debt, which grew from $27 billion to $51 billion in 1989 (*Economist*, November 17, 1990).

Indonesia's attachments to nationalist and socialist objectives are gradually unraveling. Tariffs have been lowered, financial services have been deregulated, and foreign firms allowed easier entry into Indonesia than into South Korea and Taiwan. The government has eased restrictions on foreign direct investment portending a dramatic increase in domestic private investment. Sweeping changes have been instituted with no threat to political stability which can be explained by the absolute state control that military rule has imposed over Indonesia.

While Indonesia's debt crisis emerged from an overreliance on oil exports, the Philippines' earlier introduction to the debt crisis no doubt stemmed from political factors such as crony capitalism, rampant corruption, and profligate election spending which saddled the nation with a deep fiscal crisis. By 1979 this was compounded by the falling prices of agricultural commodities which constituted the core of its exports (Bello 1982; Boyce 1990; Broad 1988). The Philippines obtained formal political independence in 1946, but its economic and political policies are still influenced by Americans. Although ISI was advocated as a strategy of economic nationalism, Jayasuriya (1987:83) finds that the Philippines had the least nationalistic stance among Asian nations owing to its clientele status with the United States. The first fiscal crisis was predictably brought about by the Marcos government's heavy spending in the 1969 election year. An emergency mission from IMF in January 1970 resulted in an economic package that included a drastic currency devaluation. Consequently, national consumption was also reduced, but austerity measures provoked mass protest by youth and students. The militancy forced the government to temper the intensity of austerity measures.

Discontent with austerity measures and rampant government corruption accumulated in the late seventies and early eighties. The austerity protests induced Benigno Aquino's return from political exile in mid-1983, initiated the democratic movement after his assassination, and helped the overthrow of the Marcos government. In the 1983–4 period public displeasure could no longer be contained; there were several protests in Manila against unpopular economic measures. Although these protests are not singularly defined as "austerity protests" as they mounted demands for democratic reforms, economic issues became precipitating factors for protests in 1983–4. One such protest that articulated both economic discontent and demands for democratic reform took place on October 5, 1983 in the financial district of Manila. A peaceful protest by 3,000 people, mostly office workers and students, against the Marcos government came several hours after the second devaluation of the peso in less than 6 months (*New York Times*, October 6, 1983). Protesters called for an end to the Marcos regime amidst the growing fiscal crisis that necessitated IMF intervention and austerity measures.

By the late eighties external debt had accumulated to alarming proportions. It was left to the Aquino government to confront the debt burden with the help of the IMF. The Philippines government committed to redress the debt crisis and secured a loan of $1.3 billion of which $1.1 billion was used to repay old loans, mostly a legacy of the corrupt Marcos government (Pineda-Offreneo 1991). The debt conditionalities that directly affected the public were increased taxes, the transfer of debt from private corporations to the national government, the removal of government subsidies for rice, increased charges for public utilities, and the limitation of government personnel expenditure.

Some economic policies have been particularly harsh, especially those affecting the lives of the poor. Opposition to austerity measures has been expressed in protests in urban areas to force the attention of the government. One of the most protracted protests emerged from teachers who have resisted the deteriorating standard of living, falling wages, and crowded school rooms. The Philippines Constitution (1987) guarantees that the state will accord the highest priority to education as a means to acquiring jobs and employment. In 1990 it was estimated that debt service accounted for 37 percent of the budget whereas education received only 14 percent. For teachers, this translates into low salaries and increasing teaching loads. In September 1990 teachers went on a strike for four weeks which resulted in the dismissal of 844 teachers and the suspension of 2,000 more. Punitive actions did not deter the teachers from protesting. Several more went on a hunger strike the same year. In the case of the Philippines, resistance to austerity measures may force the government to temper their intensity, but in the absence of a long-term solution for a self-sustained economy, political and financial instability remain a reality.

Although the impact of global economic shocks were not as widely and deeply felt as in African and Latin American nations, they did expose Asian economies to reform pressures from international finance institutions. The delayed and modified debt crisis in some countries can be explained by three economic factors. Oil exports, export-oriented development (in the Asian NICs such as South Korea, Taiwan and Singapore, and Thailand), and import substitution have worked either singly or in combination to protect Asia from the severity of the global debt problem. In conclusion, a disaggregated analysis of Asia reveals that several nations are already in the throes of a debt crisis. The intensity may not be on the same scale as that of other severely indebted African and Latin American nations, but the situation is serious enough to warrant loans to alleviate the debt crises by structural reforms. By the end of the eighties, at least two Asian nations, Indonesia and the Philippines, had to grapple with sizable debt burdens and austerity programs. Meanwhile, India quietly became the second-largest borrower from the IMF in 1991, having run up a $70 billion external debt in the late 1980s.

Several conclusions can be drawn from the Asian experience with international financial restructuring. First, invincible as it may seem in comparison to Africa and Latin America, Asia's economic growth has been far from stable. While economic nationalism and socialist principles have exerted powerful ideological influences on industrial and growth strategies, they have not been adequate in protecting Asian economies from international financial downturns. Even invincible Asian NICs have proved to be vulnerable to global economic restructuring. In disaggregating national experiences, we find that austerity protests and opposition to market reforms have been largely prevalent in Asia and occurred as early as 1972 in India. Despite repressive, authoritarian rule, South Korea, often exemplified as a stable NIC, experienced protests in late 1979 and early 1980 that culminated in popular democratic struggles.

Second, introduction of market reforms is not accomplished smoothly since this entails a retreat from nationalist and socialist principles that often provokes fierce populist opposition. The resistance has often compelled Asian governments to scale back these reforms, in effect, promoting a diluted version of privatization. The realization of a full-scale market economy is often incomplete, the result is most often a weaker version of an IMF/World Bank ideal type. Growth and industrialization often rest on contradictory canons. These are shaped by legitimacy needs to retain national sovereignty within the constraints imposed by international finance capital. The varied experiences of countries such as Indonesia and the Philippines demonstrate this, and in particular, India which institutionalized its own variant of socialism.

REFERENCES

Altvater, E., and K. Hubner. 1991. "The Causes and Course of International Debt." In E. Altvater, K. Hubner, J. Lorentzen, and R. Rojas (eds.), *The Poverty of Nations: A Guide to the Debt Crisis—from Argentine to Zaire*, trans. Terry Bond. London. Zed Books, 3–15.

Anderson, B. 1991. *Imagined Communities: Reflections on the Origin and Spread of Nationalism*. London: Verso.

Armstrong, P., Glyn, A., and Harrison, J. 1984. *Capitalism since World War II: The Making and Breakup of the Great Boom*. London: Fontana Books.

Bardhan, Pranab. 1984. *The Political Economy of Development in India*. Oxford: Basil Blackwell.

Bello, W. 1982. *Development Debacle: the World Bank in the Philippines*. San Francisco: Institute for Food And Development Policy.

Boyce, J. 1990. *The Political Economy of External Indebtedness: A Case Study of the Philippines*. Manila: Philippine Institute for Development Studies.

Broad, Robin. 1988. *Unequal Alliance, 1979–1986: the World Bank, the International Monetary Fund, and the Philippines*. Quezon City: Ateneo de Manila University Press, and Berkeley: University of California Press.

Cho, S. K. 1985. The Dilemmas of Export-Led Industrialization: South Korea and the World Economy." *Berkeley Journal of Sociology* 30:65–94.

Dick, H. 1982. "Survey of Recent Developments." *Bulletin of Indonesian Economic Studies* xviii(1).

Frank, A. G. 1981. *Crisis in the Third World*. London: Heinemann.

Fröbel, F. 1982. "The Current Development of the World Economy Reproduction of Labor and Accumulation of Capital on a World Scale." *Review* 5(4):507–55.

Garnaut, R. (ed.) 1980. *ASEAN in a Changing Pacific and World-Economy*. Canberra: Australian National University Press.

Gill, S., and Law, D. 1988. *The Global Political Economy: Perspectives, Problems and Policies*. London and New York: Harvester Wheatsheaf.

Hughes, A., and Singh, A. 1991. "The World Economic Slowdown and the Asian and Latin American Economies: A Comparative Analysis of Economic Structure, Policy, and Performance." In Tariq Banuri (ed.), *Economic Liberalization: No Panacea: The Experiences of Latin America and Asia*. Oxford: Clarendon Press, 57–97.

International Monetary Fund. 1992. *International Financial Statistics Yearbook*, Washington, DC.

Jayasuriya, S. K. 1987. "The Politics of Economic Policy in the Philippines during the Marcos era." In R. Robison, K. Hewison, and R. Higgott (eds.), *South East Asia in the 1980s: The Politics of Economic Crisis.* London: Allen and Unwin, 80–113.

Maddison, A. 1985. *Two Crises: Latin America and Asia, 1929–1938 and 1973–1983.* Paris: OECD Development Center.

Mandel, E. 1980. *The Second Slump: A Marxist Analysis of Recession in the Seventies.* London: Verso Books.

Pineda-Ofreneo, R. 1991. *The Philippines: Debt and Poverty.* Oxford: Oxfam.

Portes, Alejandro, and Walton, John. 1981. *Labor, Class, and the International System.* New York: Academic Press.

Robison, R. 1987. "After the Gold Rush: The Politics of Economic Restructuring in Indonesia in the 1980s." In R. Robison, K. Hewison, and R. Higgott (eds.), *South East Asia in the 1980s: The Politics of Economic Crisis.* London: Allen and Unwin.

Robison, R., Higgott, R., and Hewison, K. 1987. "Crisis in Economic Strategy in the 1980s: The Factors at Work." In R. Robison, K. Hewison, and R. Higgott (eds.), *South East Asia in the 1980s: The Politics of Economic Crisis."* London: Allen and Unwin, 16–51.

Singh, A. 1985. *The World Economy and the Comparative Economic Performance of Large Semi-Industrial Countries.* Bangkok International Labor Organization, Asian Regional Team for Employment Promotion (mimeo).

Walton, John, and Ragin, C. 1990. "Global and National Sources of Political Protest: Third World Responses to the Debt Crisis." *American Sociological Review* 55(December):876–90.

Wood, Robert E. 1986. *From Marshall Plan to Debt Crisis: Foreign Aid and Development Choices in the World Economy.* Berkeley: University of California Press.

World Bank 1981. *Annual Report.* Washington, DC: World Bank.

World Bank 1983: *World Development Report, 1983.* New York and Oxford: Oxford University Press.

World Bank 1988: *World Development Report, 1988.* Washington, DC: World Bank.

Public Sociology

INTRODUCTION

What does it mean to "do" sociology? In the course of reading this book, you have seen the work of many sociologists whose research and writing spans more than a dozen decades. You have seen that they use a variety of research methods, qualitative and quantitative, to describe the social world and have developed many theoretical frameworks to make sense of what their research has revealed. But what is it like to be a professional sociologist? What social roles do sociologists themselves play? Does sociology as an enterprise, a profession, and an academic discipline have a mission? Do we do sociology just to understand how the social world works? Should sociologists promote the application of sociological knowledge in the world that we study? How could we do that? Is there more to it than teaching sociology and writing or editing sociology textbooks? The sociologists featured in this concluding section argue that sociologists have an important role to play in identifying and solving social problems, and that they fulfill this role in a variety of ways, as teachers and scholars, as policy-makers and organizational leaders, and as advocates and activists.

In 2004, the President of the American Sociological Association (ASA), Michael Burawoy, addressed the annual meeting of the ASA and called upon American sociologists to actively engage in what he calls "public sociology." For sociologists, many of whom saw themselves as primarily dispassionate academic observers of society, rather than active participants with a role to play in advocating for social improvement, his remarks were challenging. In "A Public Sociology for Human Rights," Burawoy calls for a public sociology that directly speaks with, for, and to the public rather than to states (or they to each other). He identifies three waves of market expansion that correspond to three periods of sociology. The first period focused on labor rights, responding to social changes wrought by the industrial revolution in the nineteenth century. The second period focused on social rights as states came to regulate markets in the twentieth century. The third period, he argues, should focus on human rights to respond to social changes wrought by the emergence of neoliberal globalization in the twenty-first century. It is this third period in sociology's development that he understands as the period of "public sociology." Drawing lessons from hurricane Katrina in New Orleans and the genocide in Darfur, he proposes that sociologists should develop an integrated approach to the study of human rights and make public the analyses that result. For Burawoy, the goal, role, mission, purpose, and use of sociology in the twenty-first century is in asking the questions that are important to people (especially those who are disempowered) and applying sociological analysis to them.

In *The Next Upsurge: Labor and New Social Movements*, Dan Clawson turns the sociological lens to popular struggles involving college student activism, aimed at improving the conditions for workers in the global south who make college-logo apparel. His qualitative analysis of social movement actions raises important questions about the appropriate and most effective means of making improvements in the social world. Do the well-intentioned efforts of the students he examines empower or disempower the workers whose lives they seek to improve? Do their efforts ultimately improve working conditions? Clawson analyzes how college students focused their efforts to improve workers' lives on universities, as the institutional organizations in which they have economic and political leverage. He looks at the ways in which they employed a combination of public disclosure of information and consumer pressure to call for the establishment and enforcement of minimum standards for garment worker wages and working conditions. In doing so, he notes that the United Students Against Sweatshops may have bypassed the empowerment of the working class they sought to help, as the movement's goals, tactics, and strategies were largely determined by relatively affluent and well-educated consumers. Clawson, in essence, gives us a class analysis of a movement rooted in another class' struggle. Clawson's focus is on the balance of power between workers and capital, with an explicit concern for the empowerment of low-wage workers and their human rights in a global economy. Clawson's analysis is just the type of "public sociology" that Burawoy prescribed for the discipline in the twenty-first century.

Gene Shackman, Xun Wang, Ya-Lin Liu, and Jammie Price state explicitly that their goal as sociologists is to improve society's conditions and people's lives. In "Doing Sociology Worldwide," they identify three roles or activities for sociologists. One is to conduct research on social conditions. The second is to develop theoretical frameworks or models that explain the causes of social conditions and that suggest solutions. The third activity is as policy-makers or activists to facilitate improvement in the social conditions they have studied. They begin by identifying and describing global social trends using quantitative data. Based on those data, they develop a sociological question: Why are some countries' social conditions declining while most are improving? Most importantly from a public sociology standpoint, they don't stop at that question, but continue by asking the follow-up question: What can be done about it? In answering that last question, they look at the activities that professional sociologists are engaged in in Cypress, Nigeria, South Africa, Ghana, and India to apply their sociological imaginations to making people's lives better. Shackman and his colleagues argue that doing sociology at the institutional level includes direct intervention, by identifying social problems and their causes, identifying possible solutions, and facilitating the implementation of those solutions in a wide variety of ways. If you decide to be a professional sociologist, you can be involved in this as an academic in universities, as an employee of an international governmental agency or organization (like the World Health Organization or the United Nations), or as part of a non-governmental organization (like Human Rights Watch or Friends of the Earth). The authors further note the need to publicize what sociology is and what sociologists do in all of these (and other) organizational roles.

Public sociology is about bringing the insights gained from sociological analysis into the public conversation about social issues and problems. It is about tempering hotly debated opinion and ideology with the results of rigorous social scientific analysis so that accurate causes and effective solutions can be identified. It is about promoting social policies based on reliable data and facilitating reliable assessment of policy outcomes. And it is about making the tools of sociology available to those who have least access to the levers of power, so that their issues can be addressed and their voices can be heard in discussions of our collective social future. Public sociology is about helping everyone to develop their sociological imaginations, to understand how our social history impacts their individual biographies and how to use those insights to make our society better.

READING 28

Excerpt from *Public Sociologies Reader*

MICHAEL BURAWOY

What could more exemplify the devastation of society at the hands of market and state than Hurricane Katrina? To be sure this was no tsunami. As I write, two months after the storm, the death toll is at 1,055 but still climbing as more bodies are continually being recovered. Yet in neighboring Cuba it is a national tragedy if a single person dies in a hurricane, even one so fierce as Katrina. And so it should be; hurricanes are predictable in their effects and give ample warning of their arrival. But warnings were ignored by a state bent on war abroad and repression at home, sacrificing levees for arms, and social relief for "homeland" security. When the water flooded out, markets flooded in—corporate America would gorge itself on the disaster, on lucrative contracts to rebuild New Orleans for a

Burawoy, Michael. 2006. "Introduction: A Public Sociology for Human Rights" from *Public Sociologies Reader*. Eds. Blau, Judith and Keri E. Lyall Smith. Lanham, MD: Rowman & Littlefield.

new privileged class, a New Orleans rebuilt on the backs of cheap imported labor, suspended labor codes, and the expulsion of indigenous poor and blacks. When the state fuels corporate America with outsourcing, suspending labor rights and withdrawing social rights, then "the other America," the underside of urban apartheid, whose livelihood depends upon those hard-won rights, must resort to the most basic human rights as the only rights they have left to defend.

One can indict this individual or that, President Bush or Mayor Nagin; this agency or that, the Federal Emergency Management Agency (FEMA) or the National Guard; this organization or that, the media or the churches; but such a politics of blame misses the bigger picture: The levees of society came crashing down in the storm of a rapacious capitalism—a rapacious capitalism that destroys everything in its path, from wetlands sacrificed to real estate and the leisure industry, to oil extraction from the Gulf, leading to the subsidence of its coastlands, to global warming that intensifies the hurricanes that sweep through the region. To grapple with the destruction of human community, we need a new public sociology that brings together state, economy, and society; that draws on different disciplines; and that is not bound by the nation-state. It will be a sociology, as Eric Klinenberg (2002) shows in *Heat Wave*, of everyday immiseration and isolation that stand revealed in human catastrophe.

The race and class wars of the United States are, so far, silent if nonetheless palpable in their effects. Another area for a public sociology of human rights is the not-so-silent civil wars of the post–Cold War period, with their untold human suffering. Ahead of Rwanda, Afghanistan, Bosnia, and Herzegovina, the civil war in Sudan tops the list of the ten deadliest armed conflicts in the world between 1986 and 2000, with nearly 1.3 million people killed (Ron, Ramos, and Rodgers 2005:569). This figure does not include the latest round of atrocities in Darfur—an all-too-little understood war in the west of Sudan, which has so far left over four hundred thousand dead and two million displaced: The majority were killed at the hands of the Sudanese state and its marauding Arab militia, known locally as the Janjaweed, the devil on horseback.

It was no accident that the hostilities in Darfur began in February 2003 just as Sudan's twenty-one-year Second Civil War between the so-called Arab north and the so-called African south was coming to an end. The rebel groups in Darfur—the Sudanese Liberation Movement (Army) and the Justice and Equality Movement—wanted to be included in the spoils of the peace agreement that would divide up the Sudanese oil revenues between the elites of north and south. There were festering local antagonisms too with nomadic Arab herders encroaching on the shrinking lands of African farmers. The military cabal running the government in Khartoum sided with the Arab population, colluding with the Janjaweed, on the pretext of quelling the rebel movements. The Sudanese government turned Darfur into a zone of ethnic cleansing, and so it became a maelstrom of international forces as concerned to protect the rich oil deposits of south Sudan as to protect the population of Darfur from murder, rape, and pillage.

The United States has been deeply involved here, as in other epicenters of human devastation. In this case it used social science to justify an opportunistic reversal of policy, which would turn a blind eye to the genocide in Darfur. In the summer of 2004 both houses of Congress unanimously passed resolutions condemning genocide in Darfur. It was left to the State Department to produce compelling evidence for genocide, that is, the deliberate, premeditated attempt to destroy a population in whole or in part. Based on a survey conducted in the refugee camps of Chad, Colin Powell, then secretary of state, did indeed conclude that there had been genocide, perpetrated by the Sudanese government. That was September 2004. Less than a year later in April 2005, with Powell gone, Assistant Secretary of State Robert B. Zoellick refused to repeat or confirm the claim of genocide. This coincided with his mission to Sudan to seek, so it was reported, the cooperation of the Sudanese government in the war on terrorism. The Sudanese government had been host to Osama Bin Laden and a center of Al Qaeda operations in the 1990s, but now was supposedly developing a strong partnership with the CIA.

Along with the renewed ties between the Sudanese government and U.S. intelligence forces came revised figures of the death toll. The State Department claimed that between 60,000 and 160,000 people had died in Darfur since the hostilities began, much lower than the previously cited figures. At this point, sociologist John Hagan and his collaborators entered the war of numbers to lay bare the war of atrocities. The State Department's lower figure, Hagan, Rymond-Richmond, and Parker (2005) argue, came from a misleading review of surveys conducted by various international health organizations and the Sudanese Ministry of Health in the summer of 2004. This survey was based only on deaths within the refugee camps, that is, deaths from disease and starvation, since the Sudanese government obstructed surveys of death through violence. The latter were calculated by Hagan et al. from a survey also conducted in 2004 by the Coalition for International Justice, sponsored by the U.S. State Department in support of Powell's earlier testimony concerning the Darfur genocide. It was administered in the refugee camps in Chad where a large sample was interviewed about deaths in the villages from which they had fled. Hagan et al. came up with a total death toll of 390,000—a figure close to other calculations—which, together with the descriptions of hostilities given in the interviews, led them to conclude that this was indeed a case of genocide. This claim based on the larger mortality figures was given some play in the national media, in opinion columns in the *New York Times* and the *Washington Post*. Nonetheless, the U.S. government stuck to its lower figures, but with little attempt at justification.

In a paper he wrote with Heather Schoenfeld and Alberto Palloni, John Hagan (2006) reflects on his frustrated advocacy of public sociology around human rights. First, criminology has been in a state of denial when it comes to crimes against humanity, genocide, and ethnic cleansing. Just as criminology made a great leap forward when Sutherland recognized corporate crimes so now it must also be prepared to take on states. Criminology must step into the field of human rights, but it must do so together with demographers who study mortality from "natural" causes. By accepting the separation of the investigation of public health from violence, the U.S. state has been complicit in covering up the crimes of its intermittent ally, the Sudanese government. The U.S. government, as well as the United Nations (UN) and other major world powers, was unwilling to consistently declare genocide in Darfur not only because they did not wish to offend their collaborator in the war against terrorism or disturb the exploration of the rich oil deposits in southern Sudan, but because they did not want to have to deploy troops in Darfur. Whatever the reason, the United States colluded in a defense of the indefensible. It might be more difficult for governments to hide genocide, Hagan and his colleagues concluded, if social scientists were to develop an integrated approach to human rights that would, for example, connect the analysis of state crimes and public health. This would be just a small piece of the revamping of sociology to meet the urgent need for an effective public sociology of human rights.

THREE WAVES OF MARKETIZATION, THREE ERAS OF SOCIOLOGY

The framework that presents society as an endangered species in the face of state and market aggression derives from Karl Polanyi's (1944) *The Great Transformation*—the classic analysis of the devastation wrought by the market. If the state initially sponsored the rise of the market in eighteenth-century England, once established the market generated a momentum of its own, attempting to reduce everything to a creature of itself. There were no limits to commodification, even entities that were never intended to be commodities, what Polanyi calls fictitious commodities. Paramount among these were labor, land, and money. If labor is commodified, bought and sold at will, then it will lose its human form and thus its character as labor, capable of creatively and spontaneously transforming nature. If land—and we could substitute the environment—becomes a commodity, defiled in the interests of profit, then it will no longer serve to nourish the human species. Finally, if money itself is freely bought and sold, businesses themselves will be threatened by the uncertainty of fluctuating exchange rates. When it becomes subject to arbitrary changes in value, money can no longer function effectively as a medium of exchange.

In short, markets tend to destroy the very conditions of their own existence and generate a countermovement by society for its self-protection. Here Polanyi focuses on how the commodification of labor in England in the first half of the nineteenth century led to a counterrebellion by society. The rise of labor organizations, cooperatives, and Chartism conspired to impose restrictions on the commodification of labor, imposing minimal conditions on employment such as the length of the working day, constraining the whim of the employer. The landed classes sought to protect agriculture from competition through tariffs as well as erect legal limits on the use of land, while the business classes forged the control of national currencies through the creation of a central bank. Similar defenses against the market came somewhat later in Europe and the United States, defenses that involved political parties and the state in the former and more laissez-faire social self-protection in the latter.

This was the first period of sociology, responding to the rawness of markets with a strong moral and reformist bent. You might call this the period of *utopian sociology*. In England it was represented by the critical thinking of practitioners such as Robert Owen, while in the United States utopianism was rife in the postbellum period. Many of these schemes were rooted in the *rights of labor*, the defense against its commodification, against the tyranny of the unforgiving market in labor. In the era of the Gilded Age, sociology took up the cause of the working class, especially when economics, within which sociology had hitherto developed, distanced itself from the critique of capitalism and adopted the professional mantle of neoclassical theory, of marginalism.

The countermovement to the first epoch of market expansion was impelled by the self-organization of society in the nineteenth century, starting out at the local level and finally rising to the level of the state. In Polanyi's scheme the next century saw the renewed expansion of the market at the international level. The movement for free trade was temporary halted by World War I but then redoubled its momentum in the 1920s with the advance of the gold standard. In the 1930s, however, nation-states recoiled against the menacing uncertainty of the global market, leading to extreme reactions—Fascism, Communism (Stalinist collectivization and planning), New Deal, and Social Democracy—all aiming at insulation from international markets and at the same time subjugating national markets to state control. In Polanyi's view, these new forms of state—destroying society or reconstructing it in the image of the state— owed their origins to the overextension of the market. In some countries—Nazi Germany and Stalin's Soviet Union—this meant the end of sociology, while in other countries, such as the United States, sociology turned toward policy science. Funded by foundations such as Rockefeller or Carnegie, and then by the state itself during the Depression and World War II, and most extensively after the war, academic sociology engaged social issues defined by various clients. This was the era of *policy sociology* concerned with *social rights*. It was the era in which sociology, as we now know it, was established with its distinctive concerns, namely, social inequality, status attainment, stability of liberal democracy, participation in organizations, and the conditions for modernization. State and civil society were viewed as allies in the containment of the excesses of the market economy.

With the experience of the nineteenth and twentieth centuries, Polanyi assumed that the lesson of the market had been learned, namely it had to be carefully regulated if it was to serve humanity. Writing *The Great Transformation* in 1944, he imagined a socialist world in which market and state would be subordinated to the self-organization of society. He was overly optimistic. The twentieth century ended just as it began with a renewed commitment to the market—the neoliberal messianism that surpasses, both in ideology and in practice, the previous two rounds of market idolatry. It began with the economic crisis of the 1970s and was consolidated by the collapse of hold-outs against market supremacy, the disintegration of the Soviet Union, the market transition guided by the Chinese party state, and the slow erosion of social democracy in Europe. This third wave of marketization, the era of neoliberalism, has a global dimension never before achieved, promoted this time by supranational agencies such as the International Monetary Fund (IMF), World Trade Organization (WTO), and World Bank, as well as by nation-states themselves, often organized into regional consortia.

The countermovement by society has therefore had to grope forward from local and national to a global scale, something never anticipated by Polanyi. Insofar as it speaks for this countermovement, sociology has to keep its distance from states and even supranational regulatory agencies since these are now no longer opposing or containing the market but promoting its expansion. Neoliberalism and militarism become partners in the destruction of community. The collusion takes different forms: In Darfur, neoliberalism turns its back on genocide, while in New Orleans the neoliberal state casts militarism in the form of limited social support. Whether distant or proximate, the connection of neoliberalism and militarism calls for a countermovement that appeals to multiple publics knitted together across the world, often sustained by nongovernmental organizations (NGOs) and social movements. This is the period of a *public sociology* concerned to protect distinctively *human rights* of local communities—freedom from the depredations of markets and states, freedoms to survive and collectively self-organize.

If labor rights were won on the terrain of the economy and social rights on the terrain of the state, then human rights will be won on the terrain of self-organizing society. This succession of rights is an ascendant movement toward ever greater universality—just as social rights include labor rights, so human rights include social rights as well as labor rights. The universality of rights is the reaction or countermovement to the universality of markets. Human rights are a last ditch defense against (a) the headlong retreat of labor rights before capital's property rights and (b) the retreat of social rights before the state's regulatory rights.

REENVISIONING SOCIOLOGY

Public sociology may start at home but we cannot stay there—not in today's world. Living in the third wave of market expansion presents a specific set of challenges and opportunities. In the first wave the destructive power of markets was countered by local communities that hung on to labor rights enshrined in custom and practice rather than in a system of law. As the second wave of marketization eroded labor rights, it generated a countermovement. This time it was states that would regulate commodification, restoring labor rights but also promoting welfare or what I call social rights.

Today, we face a very different situation. Nation-states no longer contain markets; instead they unleash them through deregulation of industry, privatization of public services, and the reversal of both labor rights and social rights. Once again society has to spring to its own defense, drawing on its own resources. This time the scope of societal self-protection is not confined to the local or national but extends to the global. Accordingly, the language of its defense has to be universal—the language of human rights, of self-determination that includes both labor and social rights. The era of human rights opens up the era of public sociology—that is, a sociology that first engages with publics and only secondly with states.

As we saw in the case of Darfur, where we began, this involves understanding the local in terms of state and global forces. Sociology of the second wave of marketization took the nation-state as its unit of analysis, which continues to be an abiding framework for theorizing. We have to absorb it, however, into a global context, which means not only seeing things through an international perspective but also in terms of transnational connections, supranational agencies, and postnational consciousness—all three being terms of a human rights framework. It is not only a matter of increasing the scale of the sociological investigation, it is also a matter of reconfiguring the internal relations among subfields—criminology must join hands with public health, environmental studies must insinuate themselves into the study of social inequality, and so forth. Finally, sociology will have to join forces with other disciplines as it tackles environmental catastrophes, civil wars, famines, militarization, and so forth. It will have to forge alliances with human geographers and cultural anthropologists, with dissident groups in political science and economics—in other words, with those who recognize society as a value worth preserving.

I am not, however, proposing a single social science. Far from it. We have to maintain the integrity of sociology's critical standpoint, namely civil society, in the face of challenges from economists and political scientists who are largely responsible for ideologies justifying the collusion of market tyranny and state despotism and, thus, the abrogation of labor rights and social rights. If we don't follow the methods and models of conventional economics and political science, we have still much to learn from them, in particular the way their power derives from constituting a distinct object of investigation. The success of the economists in the policy world, but also in the public world, lies in their creation of a distinct object, the market economy, about which they have a monopoly of knowledge—a monopoly of knowledge that then furthers the autonomy of the economy with its untrammeled rights of property and free exchange. A successful public sociology will depend upon and encourage sociology to constitute its own object—society—and the project would be to subjugate state and markets to societal self-organization and the defense of human rights, including the initiation or restoration of labor rights and social rights.

REFERENCES

Hagan, John, Wenona Rymond-Richmond, and Patricia Parker. 2005. "The Criminology of Genocide: The Death and Rape of Darfur." *Criminology* 43(3):525–61.

Hagan, John, Heather Schoenfeld, and Alberto Palloni. 2006. "The Science of Human Rights, War Crimes and Humanitarian Emergencies." *Annual Review of Sociology* 32:329–349.

Klinenberg, Eric. 2002. *Heat Wave: A Social Autopsy of Disaster in Chicago.* Chicago: University of Chicago Press.

Polanyi, Karl. 1944. *The Great Transformation.* New York: Farrar and Rinehart.

Ron, James, Howard Ramos, and Kathleen Rodgers. 2005. "Transnational Information Politics: NGO Human Rights Reporting, 1986–2000." *International Studies Quarterly* 49:557–87.

Excerpt from *The Next Upsurge: Labor and New Social Movements*

DAN CLAWSON

On campuses everywhere, students have demanded that their colleges or universities adopt Codes of Conduct pledging that T-shirts, sweatshirts, and caps bearing the university logo not be made in sweatshops. Under pressure, some colleges have agreed to accept independent monitoring to ensure that the workers producing college-logo goods are adults, not children, are paid a decent wage, are working reasonable hours, and have a right to organize to protect their own interests.

Cities and towns across the country have adopted living wage ordinances, promising that city employees, and the employees working for contractors doing city business, will be paid not just the minimum wage, but a living wage. "Living wage" definitions vary from place to place, but the

Clawson, Dan. 2003. "Code of Conduct and Living Wage Campaigns" from *The Next Upsurge: Labor and New Social Movements.* Ithaca, NY: Cornell University Press.

basic principle is: enough so that a full-time year-round worker can support a family at the poverty line. A modest demand and immediately comprehensible benchmark, but also a substantial advance: in 2002, the federal minimum wage was $5.15 an hour, but a living wage would need to be at least $8.63 an hour.

These campaigns are among the most exciting harbingers of what might be a new direction for labor and a component of a new labor upsurge. Although the campaigns differ in many ways, significant similarities tie them together. These campaigns share three strengths that indicate their potential, but the campaigns also are united by their vulnerability to a significant peril.

The first strength of these campaigns is that they benefit low-wage workers who have generally been beyond the reach of the labor movement. Unions have not been able to organize sweatshop workers, in this country or abroad, and have trouble organizing most minimum wage workers. If the labor movement is to fight for social justice, it needs to involve and represent the bottom of the workforce as well as more privileged workers.

Second, these campaigns are often *movements*, generating an energy, excitement, and sense of mission that are all too rare in today's unions. As a result, participants develop innovative tactics and adopt militant approaches, often capturing the public imagination.

Third, more than almost anything else, these campaigns create a fusion between labor and other groups and social movements. The antisweatshop movement focuses on labor issues, but the participants are overwhelmingly students. Living wage campaigns focus on raising workers' wages, but not through a traditional union strategy; the coalitions that promote these ordinances meld labor, community, and religious groups. More than simply alliances, the groups' issues and activities interpenetrate so thoroughly that it would be difficult to categorize them as one rather than another.

These three strengths create the potential for a radically different labor movement, one whose organizational basis would differ from that of today's unions. The struggles discussed here show the potential, as yet unrealized, for the construction of entirely new organizational forms.

The labor movement can be understood in at least two fundamentally different ways. In one conception, the labor movement is about raising wages and winning benefits for workers. If the goal is to raise workers' wages and benefits, then other organizations and individuals can do it for workers. Union staff, living wage coalitions, student antisweatshop activists, or perhaps even employers can bring benefits to workers. If workers' conditions improve, it can be argued, what difference does it make how this happens?

In the other conception, the labor movement is about empowering workers—giving them a voice, a capacity to influence the circumstances of their own lives. Democracy is extended from the polling place to the workplace, from occasional days in November to the routine of everyday life. Instead of organizations and activities being run by professionals and managers, workers demonstrate and develop their own ability to democratically decide what they want, make tough choices, and carry out creative actions to exercise power or influence, all through organizations that workers create and control.[1]

In the first model, it's not a problem if workers are dependent on others; in the second, the key is that workers become subjects, the agents deciding what matters to them and controlling their own fate. If we consistently and one-sidedly do things for others it is because they are seen as not fully capable beings. (Or, alternatively and in very different circumstances, because they have power over us.) Thus parents take care of their children. But if a healthy eighteen-year-old does not know how to tie his or her own shoes because their parent always does it for them, our reaction is not that this is a wonderful parent who will do anything for their child. Rather we feel that the parent has created an unfortunate dependency that will harm, rather than help, the son or daughter. If other people do things for workers, if workers don't develop the organizations and capacity to do things for themselves, then they remain forever dependent. Partly it's an issue of whether the outside groups want the same things for workers that workers would want for themselves. More fundamentally it's a question of whether organizing builds people's long-run capacity to take control of their lives and circumstances. Workers need not just a solution to today's problem, but also to develop the capacity to defend themselves and exercise power tomorrow and the day after. When Karl Marx drafted the rules for the First International, the first sentence was: "The emancipation of the working classes must be conquered by the working classes themselves."

THE PREHISTORY OF ANTISWEATSHOP ACTIONS

Sooner or later, living wage campaigns usually win, in part because they are in the public sector. It's been far harder to make advances in private sector sweatshops. One early victory was by a workers center, Asian Immigrant Women Advocates (AIWA), in a campaign to get back pay for twelve Chinese immigrant women cheated by a contractor who had been making dresses for Jessica McClintock. The campaign featured memorable full-page ads in the *New York Times* ("Jessica McClintock Says: 'Let Them Eat Lace' ") and a year-long campaign of rallies and public pressure.[2] Another campaign, which ultimately became of enormous importance, targeted Nike, again relying on clever ads and savvy media presence. Jeff Ballinger's two-page article in the August 1992 *Harper's* showed a photocopy of a worker's pay stub and Ballinger's commentary on it. The worker, Sadisah, earned fourteen cents an hour; during the pay period she had worked sixty-three hours of overtime, for which she received a two-cent-per-hour bonus. Ballinger calculated that "the labor cost for a pair of Nike shoes selling for eight dollars in the United States was about twelve cents." The anti-Nike campaign did not take off until 1996, when it was boosted by Bob Herbert columns in the *New York Times*, and even more so by the explosion of publicity over Kathie Lee Gifford.

The popular TV show host had lent her name to a line of Wal-Mart clothing. Charles Kernaghan of the National Labor Committee testified at a hearing of the Congressional Democratic Policy Committee that the clothing was made in terrible conditions, by workers as young as fourteen. With him was worker Wendy Diaz, fifteen years old, who had worked making Kathie Lee clothing since she was thirteen. She testified that she had to work from 8:00 A.M. to 9:00 P.M., and sometimes was forced to work all night.

> The supervisors insult us and yell at us to work faster. Sometimes they throw the garment in your face, or grab and shove at you. The plant is hot like an oven. The bathroom is locked and you need permission and can use it twice a day. Even the pregnant women they abuse. Sometimes the managers touch the girls, our legs or buttocks . . . We have no health care, sick days, or vacation.[3]

The testimony gained its media visibility not from the fact that *workers* were being exploited, but rather because Wendy Diaz was female, a person of color, and above all young; the media (and public) rarely are concerned by the exploitation of adult male workers. Kathie Lee at first claimed she was innocent, but broke down crying on her own TV show, soon vowed to clean up the situation and actually took steps to do so. Because of the publicity over this incident, both the media and the public were more interested in and sensitive to other stories about sweatshops, which increased Nike's vulnerability.

Global Exchange helped arrange a tour by an Indonesian Nike worker dismissed (with twenty-three co-workers) for "daring to demand that their employers pay the minimum wage" according to a Bob Herbert column in the *New York Times*. New reports exposed further Nike abuses and led to a string of hard-hitting Doonesbury cartoons. Nike claimed it was now paying minimum wage, but "a few weeks later more than ten thousand workers at a factory making Nike shoes in Indonesia burned cars and ransacked the factory's offices over the company's refusal to pay the new minimum wage."[4]

These sustained campaigns hurt Nike's image and its profits. In fiscal 1998 its profits were down 49 percent from the year before. "Nike stock fell 39 percent in 1997 while the market as a whole rose more than 20 percent."[5] The campaigns may have had only modest success in improving conditions for Nike's workers, but the blow to its profits did not go unnoticed by other corporations. A new verb has entered the advertising and corporate public relations worlds: "to be Nike-ed" is to have your labor practices questioned and your good name attacked, with consequences for the bottom line. Today's shoe or garment manufacturers make money not through production, but rather via advertising and a brand name. The companies with identifiable logos prefer to do all of their production through subcontractors in a framework controlled by the brand-name company and with the lion's share of the profits flowing to it. The problem for corporations, however, is that the more identifiable their brand name, the more vulnerable they are to exposure. Now that the precedent has been set and the public is on the watch, if the word gets out on e-mail networks or articles are run in the media, the better-known the company the more likely word is to spread. This makes the employer side vulnerable and gives the worker side leverage, but so far it has not resulted in significant and sustained gains for workers.

The campaigns targeting Jessica McClintock, Nike, and Kathie Lee Gifford dramatically raised public awareness of sweatshops and the exploitation of workers. All these campaigns were driven almost exclusively by media exposés. There was much less organizing on the ground and few efforts to win a systematic change in labor practices except through an employer's voluntary adoption of higher standards in order to avoid future embarrassment. The student antisweatshop movement, by contrast, took the issue to a higher level through on-the-ground mass mobilization to force the adoption of codes determined by (or at least negotiated with) the demonstrators, rather than those adopted at the discretion of the manufacturer.

UNITED STUDENTS AGAINST SWEATSHOPS

Sweatshops were in the popular consciousness in 1996 at the inception of Union Summer, and some student groups were beginning to make an issue out of their universities' relationships with Nike.[6] The next step came in the summer of 1997, when "interns at UNITE! [the garment workers union] designed the first organizing manual for [what became the student antisweatshop] campaign and brought the idea to Union Summer participants and campus labor activists around the country."[7] Over the next two years this seed developed into the biggest student movement since the South Africa divestment struggles of the 1980s.

The student antisweatshop movement is often portrayed as students using their leverage as consumers. In one sense that's absolutely correct, but it also misses a crucial aspect of the campaign: students did not focus on individual decision making, but rather used their collective power and their standing as members of their universities' communities, in effect asserting a democratic right to decide what sorts of goods would bear the university standard. Apparel with college and university logos is big business, $2.5 billion a year.[8] Students argued that their colleges or universities should not use sweatshop labor. How could anyone wear a university logo with pride if they feared the clothing had been made in sweatshop conditions? In order to uphold their own ideals, the universities needed to guarantee that their names were associated only with sweat-free goods.

For the United States, scholars typically define a modern sweatshop as a factory or homework operation that violates two or more significant labor laws. Typically that means it pays less than minimum wage, or fails to pay the overtime wages required by law, or skips town without paying wages at all, or seriously violates health and safety laws. In a 1998. Department of Labor survey of garment firms in Los Angeles, 61 percent were violating wage and hour regulations. In a 1997 survey, 54 percent of the firms had health and safety violations that could lead to serious injury or death, and 96 percent were in violation of some regulation.[9]

Even the largest and best-known companies may use and benefit from the worst of sweatshop conditions, so universities that wanted to be sweat-free couldn't just buy caps and sweatshirts from well-known companies. Consider what is probably the most notorious example of sweatshop labor, the Thai slave workers in El Monte, California, a workshop exposed in an August 1995 raid by state and federal officials. The compound was surrounded by barbed wire; the workers, all undocumented immigrants from Thailand, lived eight to ten in a room and worked an average of eighty-four hours a week for $1.60 an hour. "The garments they sewed ended up in major retail chains, including Macy's, Filene's and Robinsons-May, and for brand-name labels like B.U.M., Tomato, and High Sierra." In fact, the El Monte compound was placing its goods through front shop D&R, and D&R was supposedly being monitored to ensure its compliance with the highest standards. The monitoring was not by some fly-by-night outfit, but rather by the largest monitoring firm in California—which failed to detect that a large quantity of work was being sent out.[10]

In the summer of 1998 student activists from thirty schools founded United Students Against Sweatshops (USAS) and a delegation went to Central America to talk to workers and meet with members of activist and human rights groups. In the spring of 1999 the antisweatshop movement took off, with sit-ins at Duke, Georgetown, Wisconsin, Michigan, North Carolina, and Arizona, all of them victorious, winning varying degrees of university commitment to avoid any future use of sweatshop labor for college-logo goods.

At the next USAS conference, in July 1999, some two hundred students gathered from more than a hundred campuses across the nation. The problem they faced was: What next? How could the movement go beyond raising consciousness and holding militant demonstrations in order that it could have an impact on the actual conditions of sweatshop workers? That is, if students were winning, what should they be demanding, and would their current demands accomplish their purposes?

The obvious solution was monitoring, but that was a demonstrated failure. The most extensive recent experience with garment industry monitoring came under what should have been unusually favorable conditions: a California program imposed by the government under the threat of severe sanctions. In the 1990s the Los Angeles office of the U.S. Department of Labor rediscovered, and began to enforce, the "hot goods" provisions of the 1938 Fair Labor Standards Act.[11] Under this New Deal–era law, the government may seize goods manufactured in violation of federal law if those goods enter into interstate commerce. Therefore, goods made in sweatshops that fail to pay minimum wage or overtime are subject to seizure. In order to avoid having their goods seized, manufacturers agreed to pay the back wages owed; recidivist corporations agreed to monitor their subcontractors in preference to the other penalties the Department of Labor could have imposed. Because these corporations "are presumably making a good-faith effort to monitor their contractors, they are exempted from lawsuits or the seizure of hot goods when violations do occur.[12] Note, however, how kindly corporations and their executives are treated: even repeat violators, implicated in stealing thousands of dollars from low-wage workers, do not face jail. Rather, they simply promise to be sure it doesn't happen again.

We have one careful study of what such monitoring has involved, that by Jill Esbenshade, and the results are extremely discouraging. Even a program imposed under government threat—and seizure of goods is a much more meaningful threat than filing a normal regulatory complaint—is only minimally effective. On the one hand, monitoring is a huge operation, involving hundreds of corporations (most of them cooperating "voluntarily," sixty as a result of signed agreements). "Monitoring has become a multimillion dollar industry. Private compliance firms conducted more than 10,000 audits in 1998 in Los Angeles alone. This is about ten times the combined number of investigations carried out by the state and federal enforcement agencies."[13]

Does monitoring eliminate abuses? Not even close. In a survey that looked only at registered contractors (the ones least likely to have serious abuses), of the monitored shops, in 1996 only 58 percent were in compliance with applicable laws, and in 1998 only 40 percent were in compliance.[14]

Companies choose their own monitors, and monitors are paid by the companies; monitoring, as Esbenshade argues, is a privatization of the government's regulatory function. Reports are sent to the manufacturer, although the manufacturer may force the contractor to pay for the cost of the monitoring. In order to stay in business monitors must be hired by manufacturers, and are therefore under pressure to compromise their strictness: "For instance, one monitoring firm had a policy of conducting all unannounced visits, but changed this when clients demanded announced visits." Since manufacturers are paying the costs, they pressure to hold down the number of audits. Although workers are sometimes interviewed, the employer knows which workers are being interviewed and the interviews are not effectively confidential. Many of the monitors are themselves anti-union and see monitoring as better than a union; one key proponent of monitoring told Esbenshade that now "workers don't need to organize, they don't need to pay dues," and that monitoring provides "stronger forces" than the union. (By this, however, he meant stronger forces to guarantee the payment of minimum wage and overtime, apparently the only benefits he could imagine garment workers wanting or getting.) Because the goal of monitoring is to prevent the company from being embarrassed, a monitor at the largest monitoring firm in Los Angeles "explained that he considered armed guards a plus in terms of a given factory's rating because guards prevented the entrance of muckrakers."[15]

Because of the demonstrated problems with industry-financed monitoring, students and labor advocates want to be sure that business does not control the process, that monitoring is truly independent. But more: USAS and labor advocates do not want the process exclusively controlled by any outside group, however well-meaning. USAS wants workers themselves to play a leading role, in part from a commitment to empowering workers and in part from a pragmatic recognition that workers are everywhere. Workers know the conditions firsthand and are vitally concerned day after day, but any monitoring system will be episodic and the monitors may lose their passion. Moreover, it will be much easier to deceive monitors than to deceive the workers, the people experiencing the conditions.

In July 1999 the students of USAS decided to create their own mechanism, the Workers Rights Consortium (WRC). Universities were pressured to join the WRC instead of (or in addition to) the Fair Labor Association, an industry-created association. While the Fair Labor Association board is dominated by garment manufacturers, the WRC board contains no manufacturers. David Unger, a sophomore at Cornell University, explained that "we don't want to have an antagonistic relationship with manufacturers. At the same time, we don't want them involved in running the organization that is supposed to be monitoring them."[16]

The WRC does not certify factories or companies, instead seeking full disclosure. "The WRC seeks to open up conditions in the apparel industry to public scrutiny and respond to the needs of the workers sewing licensed products for institutions of higher education."[17] USAS insists that companies producing college-logo goods must publicly disclose the names and addresses of the factories producing the goods so that non-governmental organizations (NGOs), human rights groups, and unions can check whether production is meeting the standards specified in the college's Code of Conduct. The WRC makes all reports of factory investigations public, but affiliated colleges and universities that are directly affected by a report receive the report in advance of its public release. The WRC also aims to conduct "trainings for workers at collegiate apparel factories to inform them of their rights under college and university Codes of Conduct. Our goal is to establish a mechanism for workers to bring complaints about violations to the attention of trusted NGOs and, through them, to the WRC."[18] That is, USAS and the WRC are self-consciously working to create a system that will empower workers, rather than a structure where others benevolently take care of workers.

Because our political system is business-dominated, the laws and the courts say that the brand-name manufacturer (the only entity that consumers can target) has no legal liability for the actions of its contractors. Manufacturers use contractors to produce the goods, although the "manufacturer" may own the material from beginning to end, and the contractor may be making the goods by prearrangement with every detail specified, including a price per garment that *requires* workers to be paid less than minimum wage. If workers attempt to unionize, the theoretical employer is the contractor, but organizing the contractor will accomplish nothing, since contracts are short-term. "Manufacturers have the ability to quickly move production from one plant or country to the next. Contractors have no reputation to protect, few assets, and are extremely mobile."[19] No matter how tightly manufacturers control contractors, no matter how little choice or autonomy contractors have, no matter if the manufacturer in practice demands the creation and use of sweatshops, legally this has nothing to do with the brand-name manufacturer. USAS and the WRC are trying to make an end run around the courts and Congress, where business hegemony remains strong, to reach out to the public, which hates sweatshops and does not want to be associated with them. If it becomes possible to identify the products produced in sweatshops, no college or university will want its symbol identified with a sweatshop; if this can be extended beyond college-logo gear to all clothing, consumers will boycott those products. Whatever the legal liability, the moral case will be compelling.

PATERNALISM OR EMPOWERMENT?

No campaigns do more than living wage and antisweatshop struggles to show the potential for a dramatic shift in the labor movement. The 1930s expanded the conception of "union" from just skilled workers to everyone at a workplace and from white to multiracial. Living wage and antisweatshop struggles hold the potential for a new paradigm, one that further expands the notion of "union," or perhaps replaces "union" with "labor movement." These struggles go beyond a single worksite or employer to make the issue of concern to the entire community, whether the community is a city or university. This further broadens who is included and the focus of solidarity, building coalitions that reach beyond all the usual bounds (of race, employer, skill), implicitly creating a class struggle of (almost the entire) community against employers. Moreover, these campaigns have often been social movements, involving mass demonstrations and a willingness to go beyond what the system defines as acceptable.

At the same time, however, these campaigns have the potential to remove responsibility and control from the people most concerned, the workers themselves. Typically living wage and antisweatshop struggles directly involve few if any of the workers to whom the new policies would apply. The course of the struggle depends on students or community activists; they decide what the priorities should be and they are the ones involved in a transformative process of struggle. The workers who will benefit may not even know a struggle is under way; they are not involved in decisions about priorities, and they do not learn and grow during the struggle. In practice this is sometimes true of ordinary union campaigns as well, but if union certification requires majority support, ultimately it must be the workers who decide. Even more than bureaucratic unions, therefore, living wage and antisweatshop struggles have the potential to become a form of benevolent charity:

other people doing things for workers who do not develop their own capacities or their ability to engage in future collective action. Gay Seidman notes that consumer boycotts are blunt instruments—hard to turn on, and even harder to turn off, thus potentially damaging workers even after an agreement has been reached. She also argues that boycotts typically leave control in the hands of affluent and well-educated activists in advanced industrial societies, who determine which struggles should be privileged and which issues selected; however much such activists may aim to empower workers, the workers themselves cannot make these decisions.[20]

If this new form of struggle were to become others doing things for workers, it would undercut the greatest, most democratic premise of the labor movement: that workers have both the right and the capacity to get together, organize, decide for themselves what is in their own interests, and then go out and fight to win. Employers may claim to be concerned about workers, may even think they are doing what is best for workers. Well-meaning allies, whether social workers, lawyers, nongovernmental organizations, or student movements, may intend to defend workers. Government regulators may enforce laws to protect workers. All of those are valuable, but none can substitute for workers getting together and deciding on their own priorities, for workers developing the power to stand up for themselves rather than having one or another external protector take care of them.

Any group, *any* group that argues that it acts *on behalf of* workers, and that therefore workers do not need to organize and select representatives of their own choosing, is not to be trusted. Whatever good it may do in the short run, in the long run it will undercut worker power and promote goals and strategies that differ significantly from those the workers themselves would choose. If men decide what is in women's interests, if whites decide what is in black people's interests, if employers—or human rights organizations— decide what is in workers' interests, the process is fundamentally undemocratic and cannot lead to the kind of society we are striving to create.

The mechanism by which workers get together, decide on their interests, select representatives to speak for the collectivity, and mobilize worker solidarity/power is a union. That's what unions are. Unions in practice often fall short of this ideal: the staff substitutes for the workers and acts (as it sees it) on behalf of workers, few workers participate, the union is ineffective. Labor needs to revitalize itself and create a social movement, but if the social movement is one that displaces and attempts to substitute for workers it will undercut the very premises for which it hopes to stand.

NOTES

1. See Mike Parker and Martha Gruelle, *Democracy Is Power* (Detroit: Labor Notes Books, 1999).
2. The most extensive treatment of this case is found in Randy Shaw, *Reclaiming America: Nike, Clean Air, and the New National Activism* (Berkeley: University of

California Press, 1999), pp. 99–113; Shaw's book is also the main source for the following account of Nike. See also Ruth Needleman, "Building Relationships for the Long Haul: Unions and Community-Based Groups Working Together to Organize Low-Wage Workers," in *Organizing to Win: New Research on Union Strategies*, ed. Kate Bronfenbrenner et al. (Ithaca, NY: ILR Press, 1998), pp. 71–86.

3. Quoted in Kitty Krupat, "From War Zone to Free Trade Zone: A History of the National Labor Committee," in *No Sweat: Fashion, Free Trade, and the Rights of Garment Workers*, ed. Andrew Ross (New York: Verso, 1997), p. 60.

4. Bob Herbert, *New York Times*, July 12, 1996; see Shaw, op. cit., pp. 38–39. Indonesia: ibid., p. 63.

5. Shaw, op. cit., p. 91.

6. Or, at the University of Wisconsin Madison, Reebok.

7. United Students Against Sweatshops web site, narrative history: www.usasnet. org.

8. The total "apparel retail market reached $180 billion in 1997" according to Edna Bonacich and Richard P. Appelbaum, *Behind the Label: Inequality in the Los Angeles Apparel Industry* (Berkeley: University of California Press, 2000), p. 322, n. 13.

9. Ibid., p. 3.

10. For El Monte see Richard Appelbaum and Peter Dreier, "The Campus Anti-Sweatshop Movement," *American Prospect*, September 1, 1999, pp. 71ff. See also Bonacich and Appelbaum, op. cit., p. 165. For monitoring see Jill Esbenshade, "The Social Accountability Contract: Private Monitoring from Los Angeles to the Global Apparel Industry," *Labor Studies Journal* 26 (2001): 98–120; El Monte is discussed on p. 104.

11. Note that this act had been rediscovered earlier during the southern California drywall tapers' strike.

12. Bonacich and Appelbaum, op. cit., p. 233.

13. Esbenshade, op. cit., p. 103.

14. Ibid., p. 106.

15. Ibid., pp. 108, 114.

16. See WRC web site, www.workersrights.org. Unger quoted in Martin Van Der Werf, "The Worker Rights Consortium Makes Strides Toward Legitimacy," *Chronicle of Higher Education*, April 21, 2000. Larry Carr, the director of the book-store at Brown University, insisted, "Sooner or later, there needs to be some corporate presence. It is going to take a while for it to sink in with the students how necessary that is." Another student said that definitely would not happen, that it is "basically a nonnegotiable issue."

17. USAS web site, www.usasnet.org.

18. WRC web site, www.workersrights.org.

19. Esbenshade, op. cit., p. 100.

20. Gay Seidman, "Deflated Citizenship: Labor Rights in a Global Era" (paper delivered at the meetings of the American Sociological Association, August 18, 2002, Chicago).

READING 30

Excerpt from *Doing Sociology:*
Case Studies in Sociological Practice

GENE SHACKMAN, XUN WANG, YA-LIN LIU, AND JAMMIE PRICE

As sociologists, we are interested in applying our sociological knowledge to improving society's conditions and people's lives. But how do sociologists do this? In general, we play three different roles in doing sociology. First, we conduct research to systematically analyze social conditions and possible solutions to problems in the conditions. Second, we develop models, theories, and perspectives to further help us understand how the social conditions might be changed for the better. Third, we facilitate improving the social conditions as policy makers and activists (see Table 30–1).

Probably our most common role is conducting research, searching for possible causes of problems, and evaluating possible solutions. For example, a review of a number of sociological associations indicates that their main focus is research, which we will discuss later in the paper. Similarly, in the United States, about 75% of sociologists are in academic institutions (National Science Foundation 2006). Less commonly, doing sociology might include direct intervention, including things like improving access to clean water or training people on how to advocate for their rights.

In this chapter, we focus primarily on this third role, direct interventions by sociologists around the world. We would like to explore how our efforts could collectively work together in helping to change the world for the better.

The chapter includes three parts. First, we briefly describe the current world social, political, and economic conditions. This is the context in which sociologists are working. A description of the world sets the stage for a description of the work of the sociologists described in this chapter. In the second section, we describe several sociological associations worldwide. How sociologists work is very much influenced by the general condition of sociology in the country. The more sociology and sociological methods are accepted, the more options the sociologists have in conducting their projects. In the third section, we introduce some sociologists who are currently involved with direct interventions aimed at changing people's lives. We start with describing the general sociological

Shackman Gene, Xun Wang, Ya-Lin Liu, and Jammie Price. 2009. "Doing Sociology Worldwide" from *Doing Sociology: Case Studies in Sociological Practice*. Eds. Jammie Price, Roger Straus, and Jeff Breese. Lanham, MD: Lexington Books.

Table 30–1 Roles of Sociologists

Areas	Specific Tasks
Describe social conditions	Conduct research
	Surveys
	Census
	Observations
	Use existing data
	Develop systematic interpretations to help people understand how to improve social conditions
Understand and improve social conditions	Models
	Theories
	Perspectives
Facilitate and improve social conditions	Develop intervention to change social conditions in people's lives
	Policies
	Training programs
	Activists

conditions of various countries, based on information from the sociologists, or from other sources. The above sociological conditions can serve as indicators of what kinds of sociological activities or practices are possible. Last, we describe what the sociologists are actually doing, as they apply sociology throughout the world; what kinds of activities they do and how they do it.

We hope that, by reading this chapter, people can develop a better understanding about what sociologists do, around the world. People can then see how and where sociology may be useful in understanding, explaining, and helping to change the world.

CURRENT GLOBAL CONDITIONS AND TRENDS: A SOCIOLOGICAL VIEW

There are a number of major trends in the world concerning population, health (represented by infant mortality rate [IMR]), economics, and politics (represented by freedom).

First, the population in the Less Developed Countries (LDCs) is becoming an increasingly large proportion of world population, growing from 70% in 1960 to 81% in 2001 (Table 30–2). However, population growth is declining, in both the LDCs and More Developed Countries (MDCs). Second, IMR declined significantly between 1960 and 2001, for the world,

Table 30–2 Population

	N	Mid-year Population, 1960 (millions)	Mid-year Population, 1980 (millions)	Mid-year Population, 2001 (millions)	Annual Average Growth Rate 60–80	Annual Average Growth Rate 80–01
All	223	3,039	4,456	6,157	2.33%	1.82%
Less Developed Countries	167	2,129	3,375	4,968	2.93%	2.25%
More Developed Countries	6	910	1,081	1,189	0.94%	0.48%
Ratio of LDC to MDC populations		2.3	3.1	4.2		

Source: U.S. Census Bureau, International Database, www.census.gov/ipc/www/idb/. Also presented at Shackman, Gene, Xun Wang, and Ya-Lin Liu (2002). Brief review of world demographic trends. Available at http://gsociology.lcaap.org/report/demsum.html.

Table 30–3 Infant Mortality Rates (Infant deaths per 1,000 births)

	1980	2001
More Developed Countries (N = 30)	13	6
Less Developed Countries (N = 83)	102	61
World	89	54

Source: U.S. Census Bureau. International Database. www.census.gov/ipc/www/idb/. Also presented at Shackman, Gene, Xun Wang, and Ya-Lin Liu (2002). Brief review of world demographic trends. Available at http://gsociology.lcaap.org/report/demsum.html.

and for both LDCs and for MDCs (Table 30–3). While both LDCs and MDCs, on average, made dramatic improvements, gains for LDCs were much slower than were gains among the MDCs. Third, in the last several decades, gross domestic product (GDP) per capita increased in both developing and developed countries (Table 30–4). GDP—the market value of all goods and services produced in a given year—is one of the measures used to describe a country's economy. In general, GDP per capita increased about the same in both developed and developing countries. Finally, in the last several decades, there has only been moderate growth in freedom, and in 2000, about 43% of people in LDCs still lived in countries that were not free (Table 30–5).

However, the general trends of improving living conditions described above don't apply to every country. For example, five countries (three in

Table 30–4 GDP Per Capita (in thousands of dollars)

	1980	2000
More Developed Countries	$18,491	$28,168
Less Developed Countries	$961	$1,491
World	$3,973	$5,229

Source: International Macroeconomic Data. www.ets.usda.gov/Data/Macroeconomics/. Also presented at Shackman, Gene, Ya-Lin Liu, and Xun Wang 2005. Brief review of world economic trends. Available at http://gsociology.icaap.org/report/econ/econsum.html.

Table 30–5 Percent of People Living in Countries That Are Free

	1980	2000
More Developed Countries	88%	99%
Less Developed Countries	27%	32%
Percent of People Living in Countries That Are Not Free		
More Developed Countries	7%	0%
Less Developed Countries	45%	43%

Source: Freedom House ratings available at www.freedomhouse.org/template.cfm?page=1. Combined with U.S. Census Bureau's population data from the International Data Base. Also presented at Shackman, Gene, Ya-Lin Liu, and Xun Wang (2004). Brief review of world political trends. Available at http://gsociology. icaap.org/report/polsum.html.

Africa) recently had increases of IMR greater than 10 percentage points (Shackman, Wang, and Liu 2002). Also, seven countries had GDP per capita declines of more than 40 percent, and four of these countries were in the Middle East (Shackman, Liu, and Wang 2005). Finally, twelve countries experienced a large decline in freedom, and seven of these were in Asia (Shackman, Liu, and Wang 2004).

In sum, there were large gains in many aspects of society. On the other hand, there were also many countries that did not share in these gains. It would seem reasonable to use sociology to understand why some of the countries did not improve, and what could be done about it. This is the rationale behind a project developed by the chapter authors called the Global Social Change Research Project (Shackman, Liu, and Wang 2008). The project provides a set of reports showing global social, political, economic, and demographic trends, hopefully in formats that are easy for everyone to read. The Global Social Change Research Project provides a sociological point of view of where the world is, where it is going, and how it might get there. The project facilitates others who may want to apply sociology to address various social problems, either globally or locally.

DOING SOCIOLOGY AT INSTITUTIONAL LEVELS

There are a number of international, regional, national, and topic specific sociological associations (see Table 30–6). In this section, we briefly review information from these organizations. We also briefly describe several sociologists working at major institutions. Through these reviews, we demonstrate what sociologists are doing worldwide at the institutional level, which, as mentioned above provides indicators of the varying conditions throughout the world in which sociology can be applied.

The major theme of most sociological associations is to promote sociology, sociological knowledge, and research, and also to develop networks for sociological researchers. For example, the International Sociological Association supports activities to: "(a) secure and develop institutional and personal contacts between sociologists and other social scientists throughout the world; (b) encourage the international dissemination and exchange of information on developments in sociological knowledge; and (c) facilitate and promote international research and training" (ISA 2008). Most other associations have similar statements.

A few associations specifically have goals of promoting sociological interventions in public affairs. For example, the Association for Applied and Clinical Sociology has a goal to "promote the use of applied and clinical sociology in local, regional, state, national, and international settings" (AACS 2008). A few other institutions have a similar statement. It seems possible that in those countries or regions where organizations can include these statements, sociologists may have more opportunity to practice sociology, or use more sociological methods.

Other ways that sociologists engage in international intervention include working directly with government agencies, or with government affiliated associations such as the World Health Organization (WHO), the World Bank, the International Monetary Fund, the World Trade Organization, or the United Nations (UN), or with any of the thousands of non-governmental organizations (NGOs). For example, one of the authors developed a training program for Chinese officials to deal with unemployment and reemployment problems in China (Wang and Statham 2004). A web search on "sociologist at the UN" returned a chair of a panel of Civil Society (UN 2008a), several members of a High-Level Panel about Gender Dimensions of International Migration (UN 2006), and a moderator of a Human Rights Workshop (UN 2008b). A brief search of WHO returned a sociologist working as a research director, and another as a program commissioner (WHO 2008).

Doing sociology at the institutional level includes direct intervention, including, as mentioned in the beginning of this chapter, things like improving access to clean water in one village or training people on how to advocate for their rights. In this section, we describe some of the direct interventions sociologists are doing, using examples primarily from the sociologists who volunteered descriptions of their work. The activities

Table 30–6 Sociological Associations

Name	Missions	Key Research/Practice Activity
The International Sociological Association http://www.isa-sociology.org/	Represent sociologists everywhere	Facilitate and promote international research and training
The Asia Pacific Sociological Association http://www.asiapacificsociology.org/	Link sociological associations,…and… sociologists	Promote and assist the publication of social research. Encourage co-operation between sociologists, planners, and policy makers
The Latin American Studies Association (LASA) http://lasa.international.pitt.edu/	Foster intellectual discussion, research, and teaching	Recognize scholarly achievement and represent Latin American interests and views before the U.S. government and at times to governments elsewhere
The Australian Sociological Association http://www.tasa.org.au/	Further applied sociology…provide a network for sociologists	Hold annual conference… publish the *Journal of Sociology*
The Association for Applied and Clinical Sociology http://www.aacsnet.org/wp/	Further applied sociology	Advance theory, research, methods, and training that promotes the use of sociological knowledge, and promote the use of applied and clinical sociology in local, regional, state, national, and international settings
The Association for Humanist Sociology http://www.altrue.net/site/humanist/	Share a commitment to using sociology to promote peace, equality, and social justice	Holding an annual meeting to build the community and to share ideas and experiences
The European Sociological Association http://www.europeansociology.org/	Facilitate sociological research, teaching, and communication …give sociology a voice in European affairs	Facilitate sociological research…and communication between…sociologists and other scientists…contribute to understanding and solving social problems improving the quality of life in Europe
African Sociological Association http://www.afsanet.org/	Provide professional home for sociologists working on or interested in African issues	Devoted to the advancement of the study of "sociational life" rooted in, and concerned with the African condition. It is devoted to valorising distinct African voices and insights into the global sociological enterprise

they describe include work in a variety of settings including using evaluations to train and build capacity, creating workshops on gender sensitivity, sexual harassment, sexual education, and abuse issues, empowering community development, and training in human rights education. These sociologists work in a variety of countries including Cyprus, Ghana, India, Nigeria, and Russia. These sociologists were contacted through various sociology related organizations and e-mail lists. These sociologists volunteered information about their activities in practicing sociology. We changed their names to maintain confidentiality.

Doing Sociology in Europe

Three sociologists from Cyprus described their work and situations. Cyprus lies in the Mediterranean Sea, just south of Turkey and just west of Syria. The population of Cyprus is almost 800,000. About 81% are Greek Cypriots, 11% are Turkish Cypriots and 8% are foreigners residing in Cyprus (Cyprus Government Portal 2008). The quality of life in Cyprus is not too different from that of the rest of the European Union (EU) countries. For example, Cyprus's IMR of 7 per 1,000 is nearly the same as the average IMR of all MDCs (U.S. Census Bureau 2008), the GDP per Capita was $15,000 compared to the EU's $20,000 (USDA 2008). People in Cyprus also enjoy freedom of religion, as do most people in the developed world (U.S. Department of State 2008a). Also, the most recent government was elected in free and fair elections, and generally respects the human rights of its citizens (U.S. Department of State 2008b).

The sociologists from Cyprus reported their experiences as sociologists in Cyprus. For the most part, their story is about difficulties in finding sociological work in Cyprus. The main point here is that there are limited opportunities for practicing sociology in Cyprus.

Kyrenia wrote "in Cyprus the percentage of young people who are tertiary educated is very high, it is one of the highest in Europe, and the result is that many young scientists cannot find a job that is compatible to their degrees. For instance we have members in the Cyprus Sociological Association that are cashiers, café owners, secretaries, etc." She also wrote that sociologists cannot work in social services because that is the role of social workers, and sociologists also cannot teach sociology in the schools. Kyrenia continued, "Therefore, many sociologists try to find other solutions. For instance they establish counseling companies; they go to the Police Academy and after their graduation they work as policemen/women." One study came to a similar conclusion, that, in Cyprus, students with degrees in social and political sciences were among the least likely to be hired (Economics Research Centre, University of Cyprus 2008).

The situation in Cyprus is improving, though. Loukia wrote "Only recently, the last 5–10 years television and radio producers had realized the contribution of sociologists presenting and explaining publicly some social problems. They tend to invite sociologists to their programs for some explanations when presenting a social problem."

Chloe wrote, "The most important change that has happened in Cyprus in the past few years is the accession of the island to the EU. This means that 3% of the GDP has to be allocated to research by 2010. This has given a boost to research and gave more possibility to sociology as an active component.... Cyprus is also involved in European projects. This has helped towards the direction of improving quantity and quality in research, especially academically."

Two other sociologists told us about working in other European countries: one in Russia and one in Kosovo. Andrei helps to empower community development in Russia: "we helped to create self-help groups among the poor populations" with the goal of eradicating poverty. There is little information about sociology in Russia. On the one hand, there is a Sociological Institute as part of the Russian Academy of Science (Russian Academy of Science 2008) and there are thousands of sociology academics (Novikova 2008). On the other hand, not many Russian faculty are published in peer reviewed journals outside of Russia, and a large number of sociologists leave the profession (Novikova 2008).

Naim, in Kosovo, has worked for a number of international NGOs. His current position is to "coordinate an inter-ministerial and stakeholder Working Group for compiling a strategy for" agricultural development.

Doing Sociology in Africa

Two of the other participating sociologists work in Nigeria, which is on the coast of West Africa. Nigeria has the largest population of any African country and is the 14th largest geographically (Embassy of the Federal Republic of Nigeria 2008). Nigeria has 250 ethnic groups but the "dominant ethnic group in the northern two-thirds of the country is the Hausa-Fulani, most of whom are Muslim.... The Yoruba people are predominant in the southwest. About half of the Yorubas are Christian and half Muslim" (U.S. Department of State 2008c). Despite the fact that the country is one of the world's top crude oil producers (and a leading supplier to the United States), the quality of life in Nigeria is much lower than that of other LDCs, for the most part. The IMR of Nigeria is 96 per 1,000, much higher than the average IMR of LDCs (typically 52 per 1,000), but on par with the IMR of sub-sub Saharan Africa, 89 per 1,000 (U.S. Census Bureau 2008). The GDP per capita of Nigeria is $466, rather lower than the average of $1,900 for developing countries (USDA 2008). Human rights conditions in Nigeria are poor, including absence of a freely and fairly elected government and, overall, a poor human rights record (U.S. Department of State 2008b). On the other hand, people enjoy relative freedom of religion (U.S. Department of State 2008a).

Abeke works for an NGO with the goal of empowering women and communities to improve economic, social, and political rights of women. Abeke is the project director, which involves designing organizational programs—identifying community needs and sourcing funds (writing proposals) to implement such programs; overseeing program/project implementation. She also oversees the daily operations of the organization.

Ehioze works at the research unit of a financial institution. "I assist in designing tools for appraisal of service providers, obtaining feedback on client services, designing training that is tailored to address skills gaps. The basic approach is that I work within a system and understanding its dynamics is important in designing risk management frameworks. In designing intervention strategies to address vulnerabilities, we try to understand underlying human behavioral patterns and address potentially predictable expectations, while at the same time building scenarios for proactive actions."

Two other sociologists provided information about working in Africa, one in South Africa and the other in Ghana. Alan in South Africa works on local government planning and community development. He is part of a group that "physically goes into a community with questionnaires, focus group meetings, fieldwork, photography, planning sessions to research and study every social aspect of that community. Our reports are then presented before mayoral committees, decision makers and give direction to their decision making processes." Jacob, in Ghana works with an NGO as a monitoring and evaluation specialist, "tracking what smallholder farmers think of the success or otherwise of the program and how best we can improve on our assistance to these farmers."

There appears to be some opportunity for the practice of sociology in Africa, working either in institutions or independently. Opportunities for sociologists might be a relatively new phenomenon, for example, it was only recently that the International Sociological Association held a world conference in Africa (International Sociological Association 2006). Similarly, until recently sociologists in South Africa had little interaction with sociologists outside of South Africa (Jubber 2007). Thus, while sociology is practiced in Africa, there may be limited but emerging opportunities and roles for either academics or practitioners.

Doing Sociology in Asia

Two of the sociologists reported working in India. India is the dominant nation of South Asia. The world's second-largest country in population, with 1.12 billion people, India is 80% Hindu, and 13% Muslim, with an estimated 2,000 ethnic groups (U.S. Department of State 2008d). The quality of life in India is somewhat mixed. India's IMR of 35 per 1,000 (U.S. Department of State 2008d) is much better than the average for developing countries, of 63 per 1,000 (see Table 30–2). India's social structure is characterized by dramatic class and regional disparities, as seen in the recent hit movie, *Slumdog Millionaire*. While, the GDP per capita of India is $909 (U.S. Department of State 2008d), somewhat lower than the average for developing countries (see Table 30–4), the country has a huge and growing middle class. Politically, the government of India had some degree of respect for citizen rights but there is also a good deal of corruption and abuse, including torture. Overall, there is inadequate enforcement of human rights laws, although there have been some investigations into individual abuse cases and punishment of perpetrators (U.S. Department of State 2008b). Presenting a consistent mixed picture, the national government displays general respect for religious freedom, but some state and local governments were rather more restrictive (U.S. Department of State 2008a).

On the one hand, academic sociology in India seems to be progressing, with a continuingly growing association, journals, and popular conferences (Indian Sociological Society 2008). On the other hand, academic growth does not seem to translate to sociological involvement with applied issues. For example, there seems to be only a limited number of sociologists working with or in the government of India. A search from the government of India's website (http://india.gov.in/) found no sociologists as such (although as in the United States, sociologists may be working under other job titles). A Google search for sociologists with URL's ending in "gov.in" found only two sociologists, in advisory capacities (Ministry of Culture 2005; National Water Development Agency 2004). In one recent book review (Vasavi 2003), the author criticizes Indian sociologists for not becoming involved with major societal issues. It is difficult to find any further information about the position of sociology in India.

One of the Indian practitioners we contacted, Dalaja, works on education and advocacy for an NGO. Recently Dalaja has been focusing on creating workshops on gender sensitivity, sexual harassment, sexual education, as well as abuse issues among teenage students and teachers in low income communities. These workshops are being developed for one specific organization. The administrators of the organization requested the workshops but based on conversations so far with people she will be working with, Dalaja feels that the workshops may not be well received by people working in that organization. The other sociologist, Aadesh is the lead researcher for a project on the coping strategies among the poorest in rural India. Aadesh, was involved in problem formulation, methodology development, conduct of actual research, analysis, and publication.

Dalaja writes that her sociological training was useful. "My sociological training actually is employed in critically analyzing the way in which I conduct research among already victimized groups. I find that while there are a lot of NGOs that work in the field, there is a surprising lack of ethical conduct or conversations about confidentiality in the field. I discovered this when I was collecting data for my dissertation. So, my future interest primarily lies in making sure that the participants of research study are treated ethically."

CONCLUSION

What are sociologists doing globally, and are they contributing? It is clear from this review that sociologists are active in a very wide variety of fields internationally. The position of sociologists in society seems somewhat mixed, at times fairly well accepted and involved in government or community projects as agents of change, and at other times, somewhat restricted to supporting the status quo. As indicated in the introduction, our participation seems largely in academics, but there are also many sociologists who take a direct role in applying sociology in the global community. In sum of where we are, there is still a good deal of room for growth among sociologists worldwide.

One of the issues that may be limiting sociologists in terms of direct intervention is lack of recognition. Pilar, from Argentina and now attending graduate school in Europe, wrote of this, "Usually when I am in other countries people don't know what sociology is or they mix it with psychology, so I am always obliged to say that I study society and that this is useful for teaching at University or for Public Policy (this is my short version for ordinary citizens of what sociology is)." Thus, one step that sociologists could take is to develop better information resources, easily available to the public, about sociology, describing what sociology is, and what sociologists do. The American Sociological Association began a project on public sociology (American Sociological Association 2008), but this has had little impact. As sociologists and sociological practitioners have long noted, there remains need to publicize what our discipline is all about and what we can do—both here in the United States and globally.

Another related step to furthering the ability of sociologists to work in direct intervention (whether clinical or applied sociology, or what is coming to be considered "public sociology") is expanding recognition of our abilities to use sociology beyond "pure research." At least in the United States, the sociology community is increasingly coming to recognize intervention in the tenure and promotion process (Jaschick 2007). Sociologists are expanding the use and understanding of sociology outside the academic community, at least in the United States. Hopefully this trend will continue, and will further develop throughout the rest of the world as well.

REFERENCES

American Sociological Association. 2008. Public Sociology Web Site. http://pubsoc.wisc.edu/news.php. Retrieved December 1, 2008.

Association of Applied and Clinical Sociology. 2008. www.aacsnet.org/wp/. Retrieved November 29, 2008. Mission statements.

Cyprus Government Portal. 2008. www.cyprus.gov.cy. Click on "About Cyprus" and then "Towns and Population."

Economics Research Centre. University of Cyprus. 2008. www.eurofound.europa. eu/ewco/2008/05/CY0805019I.htm. Retrieved February 3, 2009.

Embassy of the Federal Republic of Nigeria. 2008. www.nigeriaembassyusa. org/. Retrieved November 5, 2008. Pages about history, people, business, and economy.

Indian Sociological Society. 2008. "About Us." www.insoso.org/aboutus.htm. Retrieved November 15, 2008.

International Sociological Association. 2006. World Congress of Sociology, Durban, South Africa. www.ucm.es/info/isa/congress2006/index.htm. Retrieved December 18, 2008.

———. 2008. www.isa-sociology.org/. Retrieved November 29, 2008. See main page statement and statutes page.

Jaschick, S. 2007. "Tenure and the Public Sociologist." www.insidehighered.com/ news/2007/08/15/tenure. Retrieved December 1, 2008.

Jubber, K. 2007. "Sociology in South Africa. A Brief Historical Review of Research and Publishing." *International Sociology* 22(5):527–546. Abstract available at http://iss.sagepub.com/cgi/content/abstract/22/5/527. Retrieved December 18, 2008.

Ministry of Culture. 2005. "Anthropological Survey of India." www.ansi.gov.in/ policy_interventions.htm. Retrieved November 21, 2008. The National Advisory Committee for establishing a National Repository on Human Genetic Resource and Data includes Prof. E. Haribabu, a sociologist.

National Science Foundation, Division of Science Resources Statistics. 2006. "Table 13, Employed Doctoral Scientists and Engineers, by Field of Doctorate and Sector of Employment, 2003. Characteristics of Doctoral Scientists and Engineers in the United States, 2003." Arlington, VA (NSF06–320) (June 2006). Available at www. nsf.gov/statistics/nsf06320/tables.htm.

National Water Development Agency. 2004. http://nwda.gov.in/indexmainasp?li nkid=88&langid=1. Retreived November 21, 2008. A committee of environmentalists, social scientists and other experts on interlinking of rivers. Set up by the the Government of India. The Ministry of Water Resources had constituted a Task Force on Interlinking of Rivers, which includes "Shri Rajinder Singh, Noted Sociologist."

Novikova, Helen. 2008. "Uneasy Questions for Russian Sociology." State University, Higher School of Economics. www.hse.ru/lingua/en/news/4508743.html. Retrieved November 26, 2008.

Russian Academy of Science. 2008. "Branch of Philosophy, Psychology, Sociology and Law." www.ras.ru/win/db/show_org.asp?P=.oi-852.vi-.fi-.id-852.ln-en. oi-855. Retrieved December 18, 2008.

Shackman, Gene, Xun Wang, and Ya-Lin Liu. 2002. "Brief Review of World Demographic Trends. http://gsociology.icaap.org/report/demsum.html. Retrieved November 12, 2008.

Shackman, Gene, Ya-Lin Liu, and Xun Wang. 2004. "Brief Review of World Political Trends." http://gsociology.icaap.org/report/polsum.html. Retrieved November 12, 2008.

———. 2005. "Brief Review of World Economic Trends." http://gsociology.icaap. org/report/econ/econsum.html. Retrieved November 12, 2008.

Shackman, Gene, Y. Liu, and X. Wang. 2008. "Understanding the World Today." The Global Social Change Research Project. http://gsociology.icaap.org. Retrieved December 7, 2008.

United Nations. 2006. "Commission on the Status of Women. 50th Session. High-Level Panel." www.un.org/womenwatch/daw/csw/csw50/HighLevelPanel. html. Retrieved September 24, 2008.

———. 2008a. "Reform at the United Nations. Panel on Civil Society, Biographies." www.un.org/reform/civilsociety/bios.shtml. Retrieved September 24, 2008.

———. 2008b. "Reaffirming Human Rights for All 2008 Conference, the Importance of Education and Learning Human Rights as a Way of Peace and Communication among Peoples." www.un.org/dpi/ngosection/conference/workshthu11.shtml. Retrieved September 24, 2008.

U.S. Census Bureau. 2008. International Database, Population Division. www.census. gov/ipc/www/idb/. Retrieved September 19, 2008.

USDA. 2008. Real Historical Gross Domestic Product (GDP) Per Capita and Growth Rates of GDP Per Capita for Baseline Countries/Regions (in billions of $2,000), 1969–2007. www.ers.usda.gov/Data/Macroeconomics/. Retrieved September 19, 2008.

U.S. Department of State, 2008a. International Religious Freedom Report 2008. Released by the Bureau of Democracy, Human Rights, and Labor, 2008 report on International Religious Freedom. www.state.gov/g/drl/rls/. Retrieved September 19, 2008.

———. 2008b. Human Rights 2007. Released by the Bureau of Democracy, Human Rights, and Labor. March 11, 2008. www.state.gov/g/drl/rls/. Retrieved September 19, 2008.

———. 2008c. Background Note: Nigeria. July 2008. www.state.gov/r/pa/ei/ bgn/2836.htm. Retrieved November 8, 2008.

———. 2008d. Background Note: India. June 2008. www.state.gov/r/pa/ci/ bgn/3454. htm. Retrieved November 17, 2008.

Vasavi. V. A. 2003. Sociology in India. "Review of *Contemporary India*—A Sociological View, by Satish Deshpande." Review published in *The Hindu*, June 2003. www.hinduonnet.com/thehindu/br/2003/06/03/stories/2003060300100300. htm. Retrieved November 22, 2008.

Wang, Xun and Anne Statham. 2004. "Teaching About Social Welfare in United States: An International Education Program." *Education Global* 8:147–158.

World Health Organization. 2008. "Community-Based Care Can Improve Access." TB Community Involvement Publication. www.who.int/tb/people_and_ communities/involvement/community_who_story_sep08.pdf. Retrieved December 1, 2008.

CPSIA information can be obtained at www.ICGtesting.com
Printed in the USA
BVOW06s2249080116

432126BV00005B/9/P